KING DAVID'S
NAKED DANCE

KING DAVID'S DANCE

NAKED DANCE

THE DREAMS, DOCTRINES, — AND — DILEMMAS OF THE HEBREWS

ALLAN RUSSELL JURIANSZ

iUniverse LLC
Bloomington

KING DAVID'S NAKED DANCE
The Dreams, Doctrines, and Dilemmas of the Hebrews

iUniverse books may be ordered through booksellers or by contacting:

iUniverse LLC
1663 Liberty Drive
Bloomington, IN 47403
www.iuniverse.com
1-800-Authors (1-800-288-4677)

Because of the dynamic nature of the Internet, any web addresses or links contained in this book may have changed since publication and may no longer be valid. The views expressed in this work are solely those of the author and do not necessarily reflect the views of the publisher, and the publisher hereby disclaims any responsibility for them.

Any people depicted in stock imagery provided by Thinkstock are models, and such images are being used for illustrative purposes only.
Certain stock imagery © Thinkstock.

ISBN: 978-1-4759-9568-8 (sc)
ISBN: 978-1-4759-9570-1 (hc)
ISBN: 978-1-4759-9569-5 (ebk)

Library of Congress Control Number: 2013911581

Printed in the United States of America

iUniverse rev. date: 07/09/2013

Cover Credit: 'David Bringing the Ark of the Covenant to Jerusalem', watercolour by Balage Balogh, Archaeology Illustrated, Baltimore.

CONTENTS

The Sacrifice by Abraham,
painted by Rembrandt

Jacob's Dream,
painted by Raphael

The Ark of the Covenant,
Crossing the Jordan River, by Balage Balogh.

Jerusalem from the Mount of Olives,
(in Biblical times)
by Balage Balogh.

DEDICATION

This book is dedicated to my parents, Edith Ondatje and Benjamin John Juriansz, who acknowledged God and lived in the reality of redemptive religion. They unwittingly carried some genes from the line of Judah. They were enlightened by the primacy of the Tanak and lived their lives in the Messianic hope of primitive redemptive Judaism. I salute and thank them for this rich legacy.

PREFACE

This book is written with the specific purpose of defining the primitive theology of Tanakian Judaism. It is a sequel to my previous publication, The Fair Dinkum Jew—The Survival of Israel and the Abrahamic Covenant. In that book I am concerned for the security of Israel, and I point out the importance of the Abrahamic Covenant in maintaining Israel's safety. *King David's Naked Dance—The Dreams, Doctrines, and Dilemmas of the Hebrews* is motivated to secure Israel's return to primitive Tanakian Judaism. This return is the vehicle for fulfilment of the Covenant.

The name Judaism invokes the name Judah, one of the sons of Jacob. It also invokes the Tribe of Judah. Further, it invokes the Kingdom of Judah that came into being, when Solomon's glorious kingdom split into two kingdoms, the northern segment being named Israel. That kingdom of Israel, representing the larger segment of the descendants of Jacob (usually stated as the 10 tribes, the descendants of 10 of the sons of Jacob), was annihilated by the Assyrians and lost its identity. The mixed residuum of people who lived in the north in the time of the Romans was called Samaritan. The Samaritans, who considered themselves part of Israel, had their own brand of Judaism and made their religious capital Mount Gerizim. The Kingdom of Judah (including some descendants from the Tribes of Benjamin and Levi) remained in existence and has come down to modern times as the Jewish people. The Jews are therefore the genetic descendents of this kingdom, plus those non-Jews who have become Jews by adoption and conversion. The AD 70 diaspora scattered most of the remnants after the Roman devastation all over the world. The structure of this people is variously described as a race, a nation, and a religion, but it cannot be denied that from their inception as an identity, they primarily constituted a religion that persisted when their national status was in limbo. The term "religion," although appropriate, is too vague a word to embody the Jews. It is far better to describe them in terms of the Torah: a people in conversation with their God. For substantiation of this statement, I will discuss two wondrous topics:

1. God's request: "Let them make Me a sanctuary that I may live among them" (Exod. 25:8). The Shechinah was the fiery manifestation of His presence with them. It replaced the Pillar of Cloud by day and the Pillar of Fire by night once the Tent Tabernacle was built. It transferred to Solomon's Temple.

2. The evolution of the Torah, which took its final shape as the Tanak.

That conversation (or Torah) is what best identifies, defines, and describes the Jewish people. That conversation with God led to the Abrahamic Covenant and designated them to be a race (Seed of Abraham), which defined their ethnicity and nationhood (occupying the kingdom of Israel). It gave them land and a mission. They are therefore a race, a nation, and a religion, which legitimises them as a people in a contract with their God. The conversation that started in Eden with Adam and Eve was the Oral Torah. But when Moses wrote it down at Mount Sinai, it became the Written Torah, the Pentateuch; this document expanded into the Tanak. Since then, it is quite clear that the mighty literary and legal works, which evolved since the "closure" of the Tanak, constitute the Mishnah and Gemara, collectively called the Talmud.

In the 21st century, the religion called Judaism is a mosaic of thought and practice, a widely varying philosophical plurality. From the one extreme of secularism, where the only vestige of Judaism is the nominal claim to being Jewish, it travels the gamut of plurality to the other extreme, where factions specialise in the Talmudic minutiae of ultra-Orthodoxy. Some modern observers (see Tracey Rich in Judaism 101 on the Internet) want to see the beginning of Judaism with Adam and Eve and the Creation story.

This is legitimate. Although Moses the Patriarch started here, many observers and a great number of Jewish thinkers would start Judaism with Abraham and relegate the pre-Abraham Oral Torah to mysticism and metaphysics. Jewish ethnicity, then, correctly started with Abraham. But the Oral Torah as applied to humanity's practical existence started with Creation. In fact, some sages who contributed to the Mishnah and Gemara started it earlier, when the plan for the creation of the universe entered the mind of God. Abraham Cohen, (pp. 28-29) citing Prov. 8:22 f., where "The Torah said, I was the architectural instrument of the Holy One, blessed be He . . . looked into the Torah and created the Universe accordingly." (Gen. R. 1, 1). The Talmud starts the Torah with God's wisdom, which pre-existed from eternity. This claim is not farfetched.

Therefore the solid foundation for the claim of Jewish ethnicity is the call of Abraham by God and the Covenant God made with him. But at his call by God, Abraham did not concoct a belief system on which to base the call. He had inherited the Oral Torah that had come down to him through the Patriarchs from Adam. This firmly connects Abraham to Eden and the creation of the world. The Covenant contained a mission entrusted to Abraham, where land, Torah, and Messianic promise were bestowed as a redemptive instrument. *There was no other reason for the covenant.* Prosperity, multiplication of their numbers, and the blessedness of all nations through them were to be realised. Although the history of all nations must start with the creation of the planet and the beginning of life thereon, the interposition of the Jews as an instrument in God's hands to redeem the world logically starts with Abraham. Because of this special relationship between God and Abraham, certain qualities became characteristic of the Jews. They were rightly classified as the chosen people. The land bestowed to them rightly became called the Promised Land and became their God-given birthright. Their dialogue with God was named Torah, which owned a magnificent and sacred authority. And the expected Messiah was to bring them and all peoples Redemption. This new world order would result in the blessedness (happiness) of all nations. I challenge both Islam and Christianity, who connect themselves with Abraham, to contradict this layout planned by the Almighty.

The conversation with God was recorded in the books of the Pentateuch, Nevi'im, and Kethuvim, which became the Tanak. The Tanak became the eventual Closed Torah. The Tanak authenticates all this because it contains their original primitive Judaism and their initially glorious—but later turbulent, troubled, forlorn, persecuted, cruel, and tragically bloody—history. The turbulence continued further after the approximately 400 BC dating of the Book of Malachi, the last descriptive and prophetic document in the Tanak. Jewish history is clearly seen in the Tanak and in hindsight over the 2,500 years that have elapsed since the closure of the Tanak. Since AD 1948, a fresh chapter of history as a nation is being written, which can be considered troubled but glorious, with much promise for the future fulfilment of the Abrahamic Covenant and the promises of God for the whole world. The eschatology of the Tanak clearly states that the Messianic kingdom will eventually dominate the world not by the Jews, but through the Jews. The Messiah belongs to all humanity. Unfortunately, the Jews have not been proactive in deciphering this eschatology. Some Jews who perceive it are afraid of it; others relegate it to mysticism and metaphysics, and still others relegate it to fossilization and irrelevance. The majority of Jews are lost in secularism and ignore it.

There is a danger that the sight of the Abrahamic Covenant will again be lost, as it has been over and over again in the Tanakian history of the Jews. It is therefore of the utmost importance to orient the future of Israel and worldwide Jewry to the Abrahamic Covenant, which is the sole foundation of their conversation with God as a special people with a special mission. If they disown this mission, they are no longer relevant. For this reason, the closed Tanak must be regarded as Israel's only absolute guide and sacred Torah and canon, and the only document on which to base primitive Judaism. The loss of this basic, primitive Judaism and the Abrahamic Covenant is the greatest threat to their security; this loss could result in eventual assimilation. The eschatology of the Tanak does not allow this and demands fulfillment.

My life has changed since I have seen the significance of the return of the Jews to their home in Palestine, but it is a great distress that Jewry is so divided. My book *The Fair Dinkum Jew* significantly and stridently criticizes the Jews for the divisiveness in Judaism. I believe Judaism lies at the basis for the enduring story of the Jewish race, as well as the blessedness for all nations to be achieved through them. Their future stability lies in their allegiance to the Abrahamic Covenant, wherein lies the plan of Almighty God, blessed be He, to restore perfection and immortality to the human race. This is no idle dream or mystic longing; it is why God has sustained them through 2,500 years of national limbo. And now that they have some of their land back, they must identify their authentic Torah and embrace the Messianic vision. The Messianic vision must be centred on a rebuilt Temple and Jerusalem. Till the third Temple is rebuilt, the redemptive service administered by the Aaronic priesthood must determine their religious contemplation and dedication toward achieving unity. It is the basic primitive Tanakian Judaism that they have lost. This is not a call for the renewal of animal sacrifices, but a call for Messianic definition and identification.

It is very satisfying and exciting to discover many reformers of the past in the diasporic period. A great debt is owed to the modern Zionist visionaries who have made it possible to return to the Jewish homeland. But now it is important to accomplish the reformation needed in Judaism to fulfil its mission of the Abrahamic Covenant. Torah and the Messiah are the future of the Jews and their legitimacy and security.

At Sinai, Moses splendidly outlined two great and solidly linked bulwarks: the law of God and the Aaronic Priesthood. The law was magnified by Moses and had moral and ceremonial components. The Aaronic priesthood outlined the consequences of breaking the law, which required repentance, confession, restitution, and forgiveness, achieved through the sacrificial system, the symbol of Messianic atonement and redemption. This dualism of law and grace is basic to primitive Judaism. The Talmud clearly defines this dualism in redemptive and grace terminology (See Joma

69b, Tosifta Sot. IV. I, cited in *Everyman's Talmud* by Abraham Cohen, p. 17). The concepts of redemption and grace are not original, empirical Christian doctrinal concepts. Christianity has expropriated these vital ingredients from basic Tanakian theology. In this book I call on the writings of several Talmudic rabbis and Jewish reformers for the purpose of discussing law and grace. The Talmud vociferously declares that one of the great important questions that will be asked at the judgement bar of God is, "Did you hope for the salvation of the Messiah?" (Shab. 31a, quoted in Cohen, p. 375).

The law has an important place in Judaism without a doubt, because all of us need a standard by which to live. Whether we know it or not, we are all guilty before the law. The law does not cleanse us—the law accuses us. The law wants us dead. Keeping it perfectly is the standard required. But God "knows our frame and remembers that we are dust," and that we continually fall short. He has therefore provided a redeemer for us. The Talmud is of the opinion that God planned for the Messiah before He created the world. As the basis for the reformation I call for, I will point out that the nature of primitive Judaism is redemptive, and this is based on the Tanak. I do not seek to destroy the Talmud, but to elevate it to its correct lofty status and orientation in Judaism. I have had great pleasure in reading exhaustively in the redemptive theology of the Talmud. No Jew should see theological perfection in the document that is the Talmud. It is a document that records the discussion and differences of opinion amongst the great rabbinic sages; it magnifies halachah. The Talmud demands its own respect. There is no claim in the Talmud that it is the sacred word of God, but rather it is presented as and constitutes the discussions of various Jewish schools of thought. Much of the Talmud contains opposing opinions, the debate that occurred between sages and various schools. The Tanak is the only sacred canon. The perceived inconsistencies and blemishes in the Tanak are the human hallmarks of its imperfect writers who were inspired. There are no contradictions in the basic conceptual and contextual theology of the Tanak.

There will appear to be repetition in this book, and indeed there is. I found it necessary. It is because the history and future of the planet is bound up in three actions of God: Creation, redemption, and glorification. I repeat the evidentiary language appropriate to these great Tanakian events.

Allan Russell Juriansz

ACKNOWLEDGEMENTS

This book would never have been written if I had not met Desmond Ford in 1957. The acuity and clarity of his incisive mind made a great impact on me at our first transient meeting in Cooranbong, Australia. His vision of Ha-Mashiach captivated my thinking. He pursued his journey in biblical theology, which culminated in fourteen years of the chairmanship of the theology department of Avondale College, Seventh-day Adventists' prestigious university in Australia. I went on my journey as a urological surgeon in Canada, but wherever we were in the world, his influence affected me, and we kept in touch. He became a reformer in the Seventh-day Adventist Church, from which he was eventually ejected in 1980. In his continuing ministry of Good News Unlimited he has not given up that endeavour. His dedication to and exposition of the Ha-Mashiach in the primitive Judaism of the Tanak opened my eyes to this wondrous document, wherein lies the plan of redemption of the Jews and all humanity. It is the triumphant hope of the world.

A guru may not always agree with all his pupils' ideas, but that is his prerogative. This acknowledgement is the way this pupil pays tribute to his brilliant and magnificent guru, Desmond Ford. (See the biography *Desmond Ford—Reformist, Theologian, Gospel Revivalist* by Milton Hook, available online. See also the biographical note in this book on Desmond Ford).

I am also exceedingly grateful to my editors at iUniverse for their help, which was so meticulously, instructively, and graciously dispensed.

Introduction

Life on planet Earth requires—indeed, demands—explanation. It is a transitory phenomenon. From our observation, we have not found tangible scientific evidence of life outside this planet. But no rational scientist will deny that possibility. Scientists have previously thought of physical existence in terms of a universe, which was governed by one strict set of mathematical rules. That set of rules enabled our journey to the moon and back. But astrophysicists have recently posited as a logical consequence of current theories of physics the existence of the multiverse—that is, the necessity of other universes that exist alongside our universe, which are governed by different sets of precise mathematical rules. There is more that is unknown than that is known, although our frontiers are expanding. No rational person would deny this state of affairs. It never pays to be too arrogantly confident about the extent and completeness of our knowledge. Human knowledge is not static, perfectly understood at any given time, or complete.

In our state of existence on this planet, we observe qualities that exist in opposition to each other in human terms. In the physical sphere, infinity exists in opposition to finiteness. Space, which is intangible, also contains the opposite quality of physical tangibility. In the spiritual sphere, immortality was lost to mortality, and so life exists in opposition to death. Love exists in contrast to hate. And on this planet and outside of it, we see examples of chaos in opposition to perfect order. The presence of polarity is existential and undeniable, and it connects philosophy to reality. The logical explanation for this polarity was understood by Moses the Patriarch through inspiration from God, and it was laid down in the Torah. It constitutes the Creation story and an ethical system by which to live on the planet. This polarity excited and produced consternation in the Greek civilization of Socrates, Plato, Xenophon, Aristotle, and others (See Plato's *Timaeus*). On retrospective analysis, the Genesis account is noted to be the basis of their contemplation. Plato (who also speaks for Socrates, who never wrote anything) was alleged by Philo to be "Moses speaking Greek." Charles Freeman, in his book *A New History of Early Christianity* (p. 180) gives a good account of this connection. The musings of these Greek philosophers are challenging but attain clarity only in the light of Tanakian Judaism, which encompasses God's plan for our world.

The origin of all things needs explanation. Some astronomers have come up with the Big Bang theory but this idea is not a beginning because it assumes energy and matter pre-existed the Big Bang. The idea is not called a religion, but it is an equivalent. Like all religions, it is an attempt to provide an explanation for the state of our existence. Darwinism is similar. Both Darwinism and the Big Bang theory have some developmental plausibility and provide some reasonable ideas that appear to have some factual basis. To all human attempts at explanation of existence, there has to be the presumption of the pre-existence of matter and energy. Albert Einstein proved to us that matter and energy arc interchangeable. The God particle is misnamed: It does not put God in a crucible, but extols the Creator's ability. The crucible is in God's hands. Matter and energy are God's creation.

In my opinion, primitive Judaism is the earliest system of thought that comes up with the explanation of the concepts of divinity and humanity, which run the parallel ideas of immortality and mortality. The Eden story is its most plausible foundation. The concepts of primitive Judaism provide the best explanation available for life on the planet. Moses is the author of primitive Judaism. The book of Job and the Pentateuch belong to Moses, who deserves the credit for the systematization of basic, primitive Tanakian Judaism. As stated already, Moses received it by inspiration. There is evidence that the writings of Moses were edited and re-edited in their passage to the current level of literary expression. The word "primitive" is very important in defining the system implanted by Moses. For my purposes, it must be considered as the original and basic foundation of Judaism.

Present-day Judaism is no longer the Judaism of Moses. The Talmud (Mishnah and Gemara) has arisen out of Jewish history and religious discussion. Current Judaism has become a philosophy that no longer reflects the basic ideation of Moses, which is contained in the Tanak. It is no longer the Judaism that Abraham, Jacob, and Moses practiced. The Mishnah was conceived from the study of the Tanak. Out of the study of the Mishnah were born the Babylonian and Jerusalem Gemara. In this evolution of Jewish literature, there has arisen a system of extreme concentration on the minutiae of the ritual and legal discussion. This has caused a major dichotomy in Judaism. There is nothing intrinsically wrong about this evolution; the Mishnah and the Gemara are great documents and are not to be undervalued or despised. They are the natural production of the brains of a brilliant people. The Talmud is clearly an erudite record of this, but it should not be designated as canon. Slavish obeisance to it has created a tangle of philosophy, and the primitive Judaism of Moses is not clearly at the forefront. The plurality that has resulted is staggeringly divisive. The Judaism that is out there is confused and not the religion of Abraham, Jacob, and Moses. Their Judaism is a *redemptive* religion. The Mosaic law of the Torah is important and functions to define its redemptive theology. But instead, Halachah has totally obliterated redemption, which became relegated to an obscure mysticism. No one will deny that the modern "post-destruction of the Second Temple" Judaism constructed on the Talmud has magnified the law and thus placed redemption on the edge of oblivion. But the Talmud does significantly emphasize redemption, and this book intends to show it; these neglected features will be discussed in detail. The spectrum of modern Judaism prevailing today is a very far cry from the sacrificial system established at Eden, which was the system of worship used by the Patriarchs. The Aaronic priesthood and Temple services, which emphasize the redemptive nature of primitive Judaism, are the solid components instituted at Sinai. The loss of Solomon's Temple occurred because of Israel's idolatry and led to further eclipsing of primitive Judaism. God allowed the Babylonians to destroy it. The Second Temple was lost because of lustful money-making, blemished sacrificial animals, and mismanagement of the temple funds, as well as a host of other corrupt practices. These desecrated the worship of God and eclipsed the sacrificial system, and so God allowed the Romans to destroy it. The Temple must be rebuilt by modern Israel, with Judaism returned to the redemptive religion of the Patriarchs.

Moses was a complex man who should be considered the product of his time. A lot needs to be understood in his makeup and the sources of his ideas. The great concept of inspiration has to be described, defined, and explained before one can adequately understand Moses and his background, and before he can be believed. Basic to Moses are the most powerful words he ever wrote: "In the beginning God . . ." He was indeed the product of the universities of Egypt as well as the Oral Torah that had passed to him from the Patriarchs, from Adam to Abraham. These influences captivated his mind, motivated his life, and gave utterance to the book of Job and the five books of the Pentateuch. These books are the ideas emanating from his contemplation of his universe and his God. Primitive Judaism cannot be understood without a realisation of his background, education, and inspiration.

This book is an attempt to define the primitive Judaism of Moses using the Tanak as the only source of basic ideas. For my purposes, we shall have to define several basic foundation pillars that make primitive Judaism make sense. Deity and humanity are the ingredients in the equation, and they assume the great, divine act of Creation. Moses said, "In the beginning God created the heavens and the earth," and that is where the great confluence occurred, between God and humanity. There has now been another "recent" confluence between God and humanity during the 2,000 years of the wilderness existence of the Jewish people. That confluence has given the Jews time to rethink their covenant with God. This rethinking has been accomplished through their blood, sweat, and tears. Communion with God now has a new clarity in Israel's arrival back in their homeland. The great love relationship God had with humanity is back in focus. God's love has never been withdrawn, but the intensity of that love relationship, which existed from the beginning, can now be resumed and embraced.

The realisation of this relationship and its definition were the greatest achievements and contributions of Moses, and they encapsulate the foundation stone of primitive Judaism. The Tanak has no other reason to have been written or to exist, and because Moses accepted the responsibility of defining and making sense of Abraham's relationship with God, the Jews became the Chosen People. Moses did not decide this, but God did, and this places the burden squarely on Abraham's shoulders. Abraham must take half the responsibility (or blame) because he made the Covenant with God. And Moses takes the story back to Adam and Eve, because that is when the act of Creation occurred.

Moses was unique, and God waited for him. His definition and enunciation of primitive Judaism were influenced by inspiration (communion with God) and education (communion with his environment). Education came from his Egyptian university. Mediated by the Ruach Hakodesh, inspiration produced the Oral Torah, which had been passed down to him from the great Patriarchs, from Adam to Abraham to Jacob. In order for us to make sense of primitive Judaism, these two factors must be examined carefully, and the Pentateuch and the Book of Job, which are the initial and basic foundation parts of the Tanak, must be critically examined in this light. The great writers and religious figures of the Tanak were all made of the same two ingredients, inspiration and education. The entire Tanak will make better sense when we consider these two factors in trying to understand it. Because we live in a modern scientific world, it behoves us to bring the understanding of the Tanak, which was written in a different age, into our modern age. This can be done without damaging the great principles contained in the sacred book (see *The Year of Living Biblically* by A. J. Jacobs). These great principles are eternal and can only be ignored with dire consequences; they cannot be designated into irrelevance and oblivion. Faith, denied by some men of science, is an important ingredient of life and must be exercised carefully in this task. The motivation to understand the Tanak must also be approached with worship and love, because God is in the equation as the supreme lover of humans. Free will prevents humans from being puppets and bestows responsibility for all human acts on humans themselves. This reality cannot be sidestepped.

This book is intended to magnify the Tanak as the only foundation for primitive Judaism, which it is, and to emphasize the Abrahamic Covenant to be the only legitimate reason for the existence and future of the Jews as a minority people. The eschatology of the Tanak clearly defines the Jews as the channel through which redemption is to be funnelled to all nations. The Jews will never become an extinct people. The great aim of Jehovah is the restoration of the perfect status that existed in Eden. The loss of Eden is the beginning of all finiteness, imperfection, and mortality, and regaining Eden brings back perfection and immortality to humanity. Messianic atonement is God's instrument intended to bring this to pass, and the Jewish nation is the vehicle to clothe and propagate that end. That was the religion of Abraham, Moses, and Jacob, a redemptive religion. They had no Mishnah or Gemara. These works have the capacity to enrich primitive Judaism, but they must not be allowed to obscure and confuse it. They must not be given authority over the Tanak.

This book is an attempt to provide ordinary people with an account of what the Tanak is saying. As a person who is not a trained theologian, but whose life has been deeply immersed in the contemplation of theology and who is committed to the Tanak as God's conversation with humanity, I want to impart a message to ordinary people like me. Ordinary people need to embrace the great concept of our continued communion with God, which is basically the fulfilment of God's request to live amongst us now and in the hereafter. The main ingredient of the Tanak is a redemptive religion.

Today, the vast majority of worldwide Jewry is secular. This is a powerful form of assimilation, whether in Israel or the now self-imposed diaspora. The religious minority of worldwide Jewry is engaged in ritualistic and legalistic minutiae. There is no exciting

Judaism that thrills and enthrals and liberates the soul, as it should. It is because the brands being practiced are not salvific. Primitive, redemptive Judaism is what God intended and outlined in the Tanak. It can transform worldwide Jewry into an inspiring, joyous, and redeemed people that will transform the world. This would be the fulfilment of the Abrahamic Covenant.

CHAPTER 1

KING DAVID'S NAKED DANCE

The Ark of the Covenant was a box. God commissioned it be made of acacia wood, two and one half cubits long, one and one half cubits wide, and one and one half cubits high. It was overlain with pure gold and with a thick rim of pure gold. The four corners each had a ring of gold; these were to facilitate its carriage by poles of acacia wood overlain with gold, which were permanently placed on either side through the rings. Inside the Ark were placed the two tables of the Ten Commandments, which were tables of stone.

The Mercy Seat was also commissioned by God. It was a structure two and a half cubits long and a cubit and a half wide, a platform made of pure gold. Two cherubim of beaten gold were mounted one at each end of the Mercy Seat, facing each other. Their wings were to be outstretched covering the Mercy Seat.

> And thou shalt put the Mercy Seat above upon the Ark . . .
> And there I will meet with thee, and I will commune with
> thee from above the Mercy Seat between the two cherubim.
> (Exod. 25:21a, 22a, KJV)

The Ark and the Mercy Seat were placed in the mobile Tent Tabernacle Temple, in the Most Holy Compartment. It was here that the fiery presence of the Shechinah dwelt. This fulfilled the desire God had to "dwell among" the Israelites (Exod. 25:8).

The juxtaposition of Shechinah, law, and mercy in the Most Holy Place was no accident. God demanded perfect obedience to His law, but He knew that Israel was not capable of that perfect obedience, and therefore His mercy must be there as well. A fourth ingredient was then introduced into the Most Holy Place, once a year: the blood of the sacrificial animal without blemish. It was sprinkled on the Day of Atonement by the high priest on the Mercy Seat. Here was the symbolic Ha-Mashiach blood by which God activated His mercy. The blood cleansed *all* the sins of all the people. Shechinah, law, mercy, and blood were the composite substance and complete essence of the Almighty God's plan to restore humanity to immortality. This combination guaranteed the individual to pass the judgement. It is the cataclysmic power that will effect the resurrection to immortality. (See Exodus 30 and Leviticus 16[1]).

What other explanation for these emblems can make such perfect sense?

The Ark of the Covenant, coupled with the Mercy Seat stained with the blood of the Day of Atonement, became the great symbol of power in the camp of Israel. Joshua had used it to part the River Jordan so that they could walk across and possess the Promised Land (Josh. 3, Ps. 114). He also used it in the capture of the city of Jericho (Josh. 6). On Israel's arrival in the Promised Land, the Tent Tabernacle had been camped at Shiloh, a landmark established by Jacob in his travels to and from Padan-Aram. He had built an altar there (Josh. 18:9, Judg. 21:19, 1 Sam. 1:3).

Israel had slid into idolatry at the time of Eli's high priestly tenure. In a lost battle with the Philistines, 4,000 Israeli warriors were slain. Instead of putting away idolatry, they (Eli's sons, Hophni and Phineas, appear to have been the perpetrators) tried to use the Ark of the Covenant as a voodoo weapon of destruction to overcome the enemy. But God was not with them, and in the battle that followed, the Philistines captured the Ark and killed another 30,000 Israelite soldiers. Eli fainted at the shock of the news, breaking his neck and dying in the fall. The wife of Phineas went into premature labour with the shock and gave birth. As she was dying in the abrupt delivery, she named the infant Ichabod, which means "the glory is departed from Israel," meaning the Ark had been taken (1 Sam. 4).

But the Philistines were troubled with the presence of the Ark of the Covenant in their midst. After seven months they returned the Ark to Bethshemesh, where Levites took charge of it. But the Bethshemites did not revere the Ark, and 50,070 men died in Bethshemesh. They therefore sent it on to Kiriathjearim to the house of Abinadab, where it stayed for 20 years. This story tells you how decrepit Israel's spirituality had become.

> And all the House of Israel lamented after the Lord. And Samuel spoke . . . saying, If ye do return unto the Lord with all your hearts, then put away the foreign gods . . . and He will deliver you out of the hand of the Philistines. Then the children of Israel did put away Baalim and Ashtaroth, and served the Lord only. (1 Sam. 7:2-4, KJV).

Israel subsequently defeated the Philistines and regained the territory they had lost. But the Ark of the Covenant stayed with Abinadab at Kiriathjearim until after David was proclaimed king. The Most Holy Place in the Tent Tabernacle at Shiloh remained empty, a sad and tragic vacuum, all those 20 years.

David's significant act after becoming king was to smite the Philistines again and again, in an effort to destroy idolatry. In a massive rout, he gathered all their idols in the Valley of Rephaim and burned them (2 Sam. 5). Despite all his later lasciviousness, David was an absolute monotheist like Abraham, and he never wavered into Canaanite idolatry. How could anyone who had God in his conversation on a daily basis waver into idolatry? David turned his attention to the empty Most Holy Place in the Tent Tabernacle at Shiloh, and he vowed to bring back the Ark of the Covenant. He relocated the Tent Tabernacle to the city of David. He brought an army of 30,000 soldiers to emphasize the power of Israel. He formed an orchestra composed of all manner of instruments: woodwinds, harps, lyres, psalteries, timbrels, cornets, and cymbals. As an accomplished musician, he created glorious and victorious music in the worship of God. *The Jewish Study Bible* states that David danced to the music (2 Sam. 6:3-6). He placed the Ark on a new cart and proceeded towards the city of

David in Jerusalem. At Nacon's threshing floor, the oxen drawing the cart stumbled, and Uzzah, the son of Abinadab, who was not a priest, reached to steady the Ark and died instantly upon touching it. The music and the procession stopped abruptly, and there was a great silence; the fear of God was palpable in the throng. The Ark was hurriedly sequestered in the house of Obededom, the Gittite, and it remained there for three months (2 Sam. 6:9-11).

David was highly displeased and upset with God for smiting Uzzah the son of Abinadab (2 Samuel 6:8). After all Uzzah's father Abinadab had cared for the Ark for twenty years. Uzzah, he figured, had innocently reacted to prevent the Ark from crashing to the ground. David became greatly fearful of God. He cancelled the transfer. But after three months, on hearing of the prosperity of Obededom, he determined again with gladness to reunite the Tent Tabernacle and the Ark in the city of David:

> Thereupon David went and brought up the Ark of God . . . with great rejoicing. When the bearers of the Ark of the Lord moved forward six paces, he sacrificed an ox and a fatling. David *whirled* with all his might before the Lord; David was girt with a linen Ephod. Thus David and all the House of Israel brought up the Ark of the Lord with shouts and with blasts of the horn. As the Ark of the Lord entered the City of David, Michal, daughter of Saul looked out of the window and saw King David *leaping and whirling before the Lord* and she despised him for it . . . . When David finished sacrificing the burnt offerings and the offerings of well-being, he blessed the people in the name of the Lord of Hosts. And he distributed among all the people—the entire multitude of Israel, man and woman alike—to each a loaf of bread, a cake made in a pan, and a raisin cake. Then all the people left for their homes.

> David went home to greet his household. And Michal daughter of Saul came out to meet David and said, 'Didn't the King of Israel do himself honour today—exposing himself today in the sight of the slavegirls of his subjects;

as one of the riffraff might expose himself?'. David answered Michal, 'It was before the Lord who chose me instead of your father and all his family and appointed me ruler over the Lord's people Israel. I will *dance* before the Lord and *dishonour* myself even more, and *be low* in my own esteem; but among the slavegirls that you speak of I will be honoured. So to her dying day Michal daughter of Saul had no children. (2 Sam. 6, *The Jewish Study Bible*; emphasis added)

It was clearly a party atmosphere that pervaded the transfer of the Ark of the Covenant, although at every six paces a sacrifice was made. Perhaps only the king comprehended the deep spirituality of the event. The Shechinah was being restored to the Most Holy Place with the Ark of the Covenant and the Mercy Seat and the Blood Stains. God came back to His earthly abode in all His fiery glory. This event was of cosmic significance. David's behaviour conformed to God's will (or he would have been dispatched, just like Uzzah). Although his behaviour catered to a great party atmosphere, with the music, the dancing, and the goodies to eat, David realised the full Messianic scene he was acting out. When the guests went home, he also went home to face the great disapproval of his wife, Michal, daughter of King Saul and sister of his beloved best friend, Jonathan. Saul and Jonathan were both now dead. It was at home in the palace, facing his wife's searing criticism, that the cosmic significance of the naked dancing became apparent. Michal's criticism must be considered sensible and of great value, but it was a superficial assessment that cost her her fertility. God would not overlook her lack of spiritual insight. David had exposed himself in public, and she felt that his nakedness belonged solely to her. She was to discover that his naked dance was of the deepest spiritual significance. Modern social values would sympathize with her. Unfortunately she did not accept David's spiritual explanation. She rejected the great spiritual significance of the occasion, and that is why she was smitten with being barren her whole life.

And what was this great spiritual truth that was demonstrated by King David's naked dance?

David was not totally nude when he danced; he wore an ephod. The ephod was a special part of the dress of the high priest (Exod. 28).[2] Its description surpasses the richness and extravagance of royalty. The most important parts of it were the two large onyx stones, one for each shoulder of the Ephod. On each onyx stone, six of the names of the sons of Jacob were engraved in gold. The high priest was to carry the full responsibility for the 12 tribes of Israel on his shoulders when he wore the ephod. The high priest was dressed in his full regalia on only very important occasions, such as the crowning of a monarch. But the one great yearly event for which the high priest dressed in his full regalia and donned the ephod was the Day of Atonement. On that day, he entered the Most Holy Place to sprinkle the blood of the animal without blemish on the Mercy Seat; all the sins of all the people would be forgiven. It was the holiest day of the year. Law, mercy, and blood mingled in the presence of the Shechinah on that one most holy day when repentance and forgiveness and the expiation by the blood would render Israel of perfect standing before God, worthy of the promised return to immortality. And the high priest also personified the responsibility God was taking through His Ha-Mashiach power to effect this return to immortality.

So King David stripped to his nakedness and donned the ephod. He was not the high priest, or even a Levite. For wearing the high priest's regalia, he should have been struck dead. If he was doing this as an ordinary man or an ordinary king—like King Saul, the people's choice for king—he was being extremely presumptuous and deserved death. Like Uzzah, he should have been struck dead; God should have liquidated him instantly. Why did God not do it? *Because he was of the tribe of Judah.* So what? Because he was no ordinary king but was God's own anointing, a type of the Messiah, and through whose loins the Messiah would come.

Stupendously, David was recalling the three greatest redemptive ancestral events in Jewish history. And what were they? From the record of the Tanak, we have the knowledge that Jacob had the greatest understanding of the Messianic event—even greater than the comprehension of Moses. Jacob figured in all three events:

1. Jacob's Dream at Bethel

Here the Abrahamic Covenant was repeated by God to Jacob.

> And he [Jacob] dreamed, and behold a ladder set up on
> the earth, and the top of it reached to heaven; and behold
> the angels of God ascending and descending on it. And,
> behold the Lord stood above it, and said, I am the Lord
> God of Abraham, thy father, and the God of Isaac: the land
> whereon thou liest, to thee will I give it, and to thy seed . . .
> and in thy seed shall all the families of the earth be blessed.
> (Gen. 28:12-14, KJV)

David was as yet in the loins of his forefather Jacob. Looking back
to Jacob's dream, he knew that he was to be the ancestor of the
Messiah, for the Messiah would appear through the line of Judah.

2. Jacob's Wrestle with God at the Brook Jabbok (Peniel)

Here was the assurance that God would save him from death at the
hands of Esau. He had no army at his back to protect him from
his brother, but he had to be disabled further to rely completely on
the power of the Messiah, who would save him from eternal death.
This indicated that humanity would entirely rely on the Messiah for
salvation. He realised this as he limped helplessly up the banks of
the Brook Jabbok.

> And Jacob called the name of that place Peniel; for I have
> seen God face to face, and my life is preserved . . . . The
> sun rose upon him, and he limped upon his thigh. (Gen.
> 32:30, 31 KJV).

When he did not rely on his own self-accomplishments for
salvation, then the Messiah stepped in and delivered him from
eternal death. Esau's heart was softened, and he could not kill
his brother. David would later recall Jacob's limp dance and his

own naked dance when the paraplegic Mephibosheth, Jonathan's son, would be carried to his royal festal table. These were all manifestations of the sinful, mutilated, and helpless state of humanity, totally without merit, lame, paraplegic, and naked before God. The Messiah would bear this shame for all humanity; He would be "crushed" in a state of lameness, paraplegia, and nakedness. But the Messiah, in this His condescension, would rise to clothe in His righteousness and carry humanity in His divine arms to the royal festal table of the Almighty God (2 Sam. 2; 9).[3]

3. Jacob's Prophecy on His Death Bed

As Jacob lay dying, he predicted the future of his sons. He spoke in blessings and cursings. His Messianic prophecy poured out for his son, Judah.

> And Jacob called unto his sons, and said, Gather yourselves together, that I may tell you that which shall befall you in the last days . . . . The Sceptre shall not depart from Judah, nor a Lawgiver from between his feet, until Shiloh come; and unto Him shall the gathering of the people be. (Gen. 49:1, 10 KJV)

Kind David comprehended that he was not only the ancestor of the Messiah, but also a type of the Messiah. And as the Messiah was to come from his loins, as the Son of David, he presumed greatly and dared God to let him act the part. David immortalized it in Psalm 18. This is a direct explanation from the Talmud:

> Great deliverance giveth he to his king, and showeth loving kindness to His Anointed [Heb. Messiah], to David and to his seed, for evermore. (Psalm 18)[4]

Rabbinic literature calls the Messiah the Son of David.

Years after David, Isaiah would describe that part that the Messiah would carry out as "the leprous one," described so well by the very perceptive Rabbi Judah the Prince, redactor of the Mishnah.[5]

King David said to his wife, "I will dance before the Lord and dishonour myself even more, and be low in my own esteem." He was describing the sinbearer, the sacrificial lamb without blemish, who would be "crushed by the load of sins of all humanity" (Isa. 52-53, *The Jewish Study Bible*). Here is the Messiah, snuffing out His life to redeem humanity and restore them to immortality. And David felt he could bravely don the ephod without risking instant death. As a type of the Messiah, he took upon his shoulders the responsibility involved in bearing the two onyx stones engraved with the names of Jacob's sons, representative of all humanity. The redemption of humanity was heavy on David's mind. He saw down the corridors of time, when the responsibility for Israel and all humanity would be heavy on the Messiah's shoulders. He danced furiously, not caring that the exposure of his nakedness lowered him to the basest and vilest in existence, as he himself impersonated the Messianic sinbearer. He was the "riff raff" for all humanity in its degraded, sinful condition. But the slave girls would honour him. Figuratively, the slaves to sin would honour the Messiah for their deliverance, because their sins were forgiven, and they stood perfect before God because of Messianic redemption. The Jews enact this Messianic sacrifice on every yearly Day of Atonement. Do they do it unwittingly?

The ephod structurally in two parts, like aprons fore and aft, joined at the waist but barely reaching to the hips, could not conceal his nakedness. The flaps of the ephod were waving in the breeze of the furious dance, the "leaping and whirling before the Lord." His nakedness was certainly visible. The Queen saw him from the palace window. King David was ecstatic that the Messiah would come through his loins. The words spoken by Jacob, "The Sceptre shall not depart from Judah, nor a Lawgiver from between his feet, until Shiloh comes," were ringing loudly in excessive decibels in his ears as he jumped and whirled in the air. The entire universe watched in silence at the great depiction of the Messianic condescension and redemption of all humanity by the naked king. They could not understand the mixture of David's mirth and the depiction of Messianic crushing in His human nakedness, shame, and punishment. It was a strange spectacle of God's great love for the human race. The angels folded their wings in awful incomprehension, and all around David, the people viewed his nakedness. Did any of them understand the significance of David's shameful exposure? He sank to the depths as the leprous one in condescension. This is a picture of the Messiah that not many Hebrews have recognised, but Rabbi Judah the Prince saw it and embraced it.

> The Rabbis maintain that his name is "the leprous one of the School of R. Judah the Prince," as it is said, "Surely He hath borne our griefs, and carried our sorrows; yet we did esteem Him stricken, *smitten of God,* and afflicted." (Isa. 53:4; emphasis added)[6]

King David saw himself as he danced joyously, naked in his sinfulness outside the Gates of Eden, in the forlorn and doleful dying derelict bodies of his first ancestors, Adam and Eve. But he also danced joyously outside those gates in the wonderful realization that he was bringing together the Shechinah, law, mercy, and the blood of the Messiah, the Son of David, who would restore immortality to all humanity—and with it, restoration to Gan Eden. The King comprehended Messianic redemption and rejoiced in it. God loved David for it, as the Almighty Elohim wept tears of joy at this expression of His immortal love for Israel. David was relocating the Ark of the Covenant and the Mercy Seat to the Tent Tabernacle, reuniting it with Shechinah and the blood. What a thrilling and joyously salvific redemptive religion is here defined as primitive Judaism.

One wonders what David sang in his nakedness. Perhaps it was these Psalms.

> Why do the nations rage so furiously together, why do the people imagine a vain thing? The kings of the earth rise up

and the rulers take council together against the Lord and against His Anointed, Let us break their bands asunder, and cast away their yokes from us. He that dwelleth in heaven shall laugh them to scorn; the Lord shall have them in derision. (Ps. 2:1-4)

But Thou didst not leave His soul in hell; nor didst Thou suffer Thy Holy One to see corruption. (Ps. 16:10)

All they that see Him shall laugh Him to scorn, they shoot out their lips, and shake their heads saying: He trusted in God that He would deliver Him; Let Him deliver Him if He delight in Him. (Ps. 22:7-8)

Thy rebuke hath broken His heart: He is full of heaviness. He looked for some to have pity on Him, but there was no man, neither found He any to comfort Him. (Ps. 69:21)

The great rabbinic sages over the ages have agreed that these Tanakian passages, all songs of David, are references to the Messiah.

The Tanak views nakedness as both shame and purity. Shame and purity are Messianic pictures; their solid combination belongs only to Ha-Mashiach. Adam and Eve were naked in the Garden of Eden but did not know it because the glory of their immortality and face-to-face communion with God enveloped them. But as soon as disobedience overtook them, they found themselves naked with shame. Their purity had gone. Their first apparel was made from the animal skins that resulted from their sacrificial sin offerings of the animals without blemish, signifying Messianic redemption.

The prophets used nakedness when bearing Messianic messages. The nakedness of prophets is mentioned as a part of prophesying. There is no erotic component in the following depictions.

Samuel has recorded that King Saul was filled with the Holy Spirit and prophesied:

> The Spirit of God came upon him [Saul] too, and he walked on, speaking in ecstasy, until he reached Naioth in Ramah. Then he too stripped off his clothes and he too spoke in ecstasy before Samuel; and he lay naked all that day and all night. That is why people say, Is Saul too among the prophets? (1 Sam. 19:23-24, *The Jewish Study Bible*)

Micah prophesied about the idolatry of Samaria and Jerusalem:

> Because of this I will lament and wail; I will go stripped and naked. (Mic. 1:8, *The Jewish Study Bible*)

Isaiah records:

> It was the year that the Tartan came to Ashdod—being sent by King Sargon of Assyria—and attacked Ashdod and took it. Previously, the Lord had spoken to Isaiah son of Amoz, saying, Go untie the sackcloth from your loins and take your sandals off your feet, which he had done, going naked and barefoot. And now the Lord said, It is a sign and a portent for Egypt and Nubia. Just as My servant Isaiah has gone naked and barefoot for three years, so shall the King of Assyria drive off the captives of Egypt and the exiles of Nubia, young and old, naked and barefoot and with bared buttocks—to the shame of Egypt. (Isa. 20:1-4, *The Jewish Study Bible*)

Jeremiah records Messianic condescension thus:

> Behold and see if there be any sorrow like unto His sorrow. (Lam. 1:12)

Jacob had dreamed about the Messianic deliverance (See the chapter titled "Jacob's Dream"). King David's naked dance depicted the Messianic role, bearing the shame and condescension for all humanity. Modern Judaism has lost the recognition of this Messianic redemptive power since the second Temple was destroyed. There is no longer any blood in their Day of Atonement.

Ah, David, will you dance naked again before your people?

King David had seized the throne of Israel after Saul and Jonathan were killed in battle. God had willed that David should be king. King Saul was the son of Kish, of the tribe of Benjamin. But Jacob had blessed and named Judah as the ancestor of the Messiah. Saul had been the people's choice, but while Saul was still king, God had sent Samuel to anoint David, His own choice, to succeed Saul. David was of the tribe of Judah, and God had determined that this royal line would beget the promised Messiah.

When David seized the throne, the remnant of Saul's family took flight and went into hiding to save their lives. The nurse caring for Jonathan's baby son dropped him as she fled, but she gathered the young child to save him from being slaughtered and ran with him. He was badly injured in that fall and was left a paraplegic. After David secured the kingdom, he searched for survivors of his beloved friend Jonathan's family, and he found Mephibosheth, the paraplegic. He invited him to a royal feast at the palace. Mephibosheth, now a young man, was afraid that this was a plan to kill him, so that he could never challenge King David for the throne. As the chariot brought him to the palace gates, he shuddered in fear of death. As he was helped out of the chariot at the palace gate, David immediately saw his disability. He rushed to the road and carried Mephibosheth in his arms to the royal table. Ah, David! A Messianic figure was dramatizing the function of the Ha-Mashiach in carrying decrepit and paraplegic humanity into immortality!

When he wrote the lyrics for his song 'Carried to the Table' Leeland Dayton Mooring was a 16-year-old rock singer from Texas. He was totally imbued with the redemptive concept and poured out his soul in grateful adoration. He has immortalized the event in lyrical music. He has captured the broken state of humanity being carried in the Messiah's arms. I quote four lines from his heartfelt song:

Carried to the Table (Mephibosheth's Song)

. . . .

> Am I good enough to share this cup? This world has left me
>> lame
> Even in my weakness The Saviour called my name
> In His holy presence I'm healed and unashamed.
> I am carried to the table, The table of the Lord

. . . .

Would to God that Israel and all humanity will feast at Messiah ben David's royal festal table. Would to God that we all will dance with David, exposing the nakedness of our honesty. The admission of our breaking the law requires the mingling of the law with mercy and the blood in the presence of the Shechinah.

CHAPTER 2

THE ORIGIN OF GOD

God has no origin.

> Before the mountains were brought forth, or ever Thou
> hadst formed the earth, and the world, even from everlasting
> to everlasting, Thou art God. (Ps. 90:2)

He exists and has always existed and will always exist. There never was a time when He was not. He has been there and will always be there forever. And forever is a long, long time. Does anyone want to challenge this axiom? Those who do must contemplate space and infinity. There are no limits to space; it is limitless. The further we look, the further it extends. Infinity by definition has no beginning and no end. Both space and infinity are scientific axioms. Would it be impudent to ask an astronomer to show where space and infinity begin and end? To religious people like me who are also steeped in the wonders of science, there is no incongruence; we like to fill space and infinity with God, not as a pantheistic pervasion but as a personal God who not only lives forever but loves forever. God is life and love.

> Yea I have loved thee with an everlasting love, therefore,
> with loving kindness have I drawn thee. (Jer. 31:3)

> In His love and in His pity He redeemed them. (Isa. 63:9)

That is what existence is all about. Can science explain love? Can science explain the breath of life? We can describe both qualities extremely well. I can dare to speak as a scientist; I have been steeped in the miracles of the human body ever since

I entered medical school. My belief in God strengthened with every understanding of the miracle that is the human body. The intricate workings of the human cell, the physico-chemical structural component of existence, is governed by the strictest laws that cannot be broken without the deterioration and destruction of the breath of life that makes us "live and move and have our being."[7] (See the work of Nobel Prize winner Ada Yonath, who has opened up the complex machinery of the ribosomes.) The Psalmist declared that he was "fearfully and wonderfully made" (Ps. 139). His song has been the banner of my journey through medicine. I love the literary brilliance of the King James Bible as it spells this out.

> O Lord, Thou hast searched me and known me.
> Thou hast known my downsittings and uprising;
> Thou understandest my thoughts afar off.
> Thou compassest my path and my lying down
> And art acquainted with all my ways
> For there is not a word in my tongue
> But, lo, O lord, Thou knowest it altogether.
>
> Thou hast beset me behind and before,
> And laid Thine hand upon me.
> Such knowledge is too wonderful for me;
> It is high, I cannot attain unto it.
> Whither shall I go from Thy Spirit?
> Or whither shall I flee from Thy presence?
> If I ascend up into heaven Thou art there;
> If I make my bed in Sheol, behold, Thou art there.
> If I take the wings of the morning
> And dwell in the uttermost parts of the sea,
> Even there shall Thy hand lead me
> And Thy right hand shall hold me.
>
> If I say, Surely, the darkness shall cover me;
> Even the night shall be light about me.
> Yea, the darkness hideth not from Thee,
> But the night shineth as the day

The darkness and the light
Are both alike to Thee.
For Thou hast possessed my inward parts;
Thou hast covered me in my mother's womb.

I will praise Thee for I am fearfully and wonderfully made
Marvellous are Thy works, and that my soul knoweth right
    well.
My substance was not hidden from Thee,
When I was made in secret and intricately wrought
In the lowest part of the earth.
Thine eyes did see my substance, yet being unformed
And in Thy book all my members were written
Which in continuance were fashioned,
When as yet there was none of them.

How precious also are Thy thoughts unto me,
O God! How great is the sum of them. (Ps. 139:1-17 KJV).

In this Psalm of David, we are given knowledge of God's eternity, infinity, and creatorship. As a scientist I see the sperm and the ovum, made in secret, intricately wrought, uniting in the uterus. And the embryo, with all its genetic predeterminants, bursting forth into the life of a new creation—an individual who will breathe the breath of life, live, think, move, and love. There is a lot about God we do not know, but His creatorship thrills my soul. He made us of the dust of the ground and breathed into our nostrils the breath of life, and we became living souls.

I used to be doubtfully introspective about how the human body could have eternal life, but not after Elizabeth Blackburn discovered the action of telomerase on telomeres.[8] Blackburn was awarded the Nobel Prize for her work. She has added proof to my armamentarium on the existence of God. He built us to last. But our disobedience has damaged our telomeres and the efficiency of our telomerase enzyme in our DNA machinery.

The doctrine of God in the Tanak is wonderfully treated by the Talmud. The valuable comments in the Talmud are not original but are inspired by Moses the Patriarch. There are ideas in the Talmud that are not congruent with the Tanak. Sound, contextual use of the Tanak can differentiate what is valuable in the Talmud and what is not. We owe a debt to Abraham Cohen for his study of it, and his bringing us the cogent messages from it. The Talmud discusses God in terms of His existence, unity, incorporeality, omnipresence, omnipotence, omniscience, eternity, justice, mercy, fatherhood, holiness, perfection, and ineffable name. All these qualities are from the description of God in the Tanak. Without reproducing the Talmud or reproducing Abraham Cohen totally, it is of great value for my purposes to quote and comment from Abraham Cohen's discussion of the Mosaic doctrine of God.

His Pre-Existence

See 1 Kings 8:27; Psalm 139:7-12; Jeremiah 23:23-24; and Isaiah 66:1. Belief in the Tanakian pre-existence of God has already been discussed.

His Unity

The Tanak sets out the dogma that the Holy Spirit and Messiah are part and parcel of a monotheistic God. The Lord our God is one, blessed be He. The rabbis at the time of the emergence of Christianity misunderstood the Christian doctrine of the Trinity. Christians do not believe that there are three Gods. Mainstream Christians are monotheists, as strictly are the Jews. Christians see the power of the one God manifested in the Spirit, which is God's medium of communion with humanity, and the Messiah, which is God's demonstrated redemptive power. God is one and has provided companionship and redemption to us by what we understand as His power to reclaim a perfection we cannot obtain on our own (see Isa. 44:24).[9] The Tanak does not support a created

Messiah, as has already been pointed out. Isaiah 9:6 abundantly declares the Messiah to be the same as the mighty God, the everlasting Father. He is Elohim, whose powers are plural like His name.

His Incorporeality

Does God have a body? Since humans were made in God's image, is He built like us? The Tanak gives Him human-like features. God saw, so He has eyes. He breathes, so He has lungs; He spoke, so he has tongue and lips. He hears, so He has ears. He thinks, so He has a brain. He has hands because He holds us, and we rest in His everlasting arms. He has legs because He walked in Eden in the cool of the day. Our desire to understand Him and explain Him has been expressed in human terms.

The Tanak also gives Him other features. In Psalm 91 He is a fortress. He is a bird, because He covers us with His feathers, and under His wings we trust.

Neither the Tanak nor the Talmud define God empirically as having a human-like body; their adoration of God is couched in human terms. Being made in the image of God is being able to love. He will be understood better when we consider His fatherhood.

His Omnipresence

Nothing is hidden from Him. He is everywhere.

His Omnipotence

He is the strongest force in the universe.

His Omniscience

He knows the past, present, and future. He knows everything about everything.

His Eternity

This has already been discussed. Who can define the days of eternity? How far is the East from the West?

His Justice and Mercy

God has instituted law and order, but He gives His creatures the power of choice so that they serve and obey Him voluntarily. There are two problems we know about concerning created beings in the universe: there are bad angels and bad humans. Therefore two lots of His creatures have been derailed by disobedience. When God is disobeyed, His law is broken, and judgement and justice follow. The "soul that sinneth" will die. But God is a God of mercy, and He has ordained repentance, forgiveness, and absolution through the Holy Spirit and Messianic intervention. Creation of humans was followed by disobedience and death, but He made a provision for redemption, and glorification follows. The Messiah restores eternal life. The sacrificial system instituted at Eden and practiced by Adam and his son Abel, down to Abraham—and then the Aaronic priesthood, the Tabernacle sanctuary services, and the Temple glory—were all symbolic of Messianic redemption to come. (See the books of Exodus and Leviticus.) These were all about His justice and mercy.

The Talmud argues for the provision of justice and mercy as twins conceived by a compassionate God before the creation of humanity. Cohen makes a very strong statement on his own.

> If compassion was the deciding cause of Creation, its victory over stern justice is the reason of the world's

20

continuance in the face of wickedness . . . . The Bible relates that when God revealed His attributes to Moses, Moses "made haste and bowed his head toward the earth and worshipped" (Exod. 34:8).

To the question: What overwhelmed him so much? The answer is given, "The recognition of the Divine forbearance' (Sanh. 111a) . . . . God subdues His anger and shows longsuffering with the wicked; and it is likewise the manifestation of His terrible acts, without which how could a single nation be allowed to continue in existence? (Joma 69b) . . . . "The attribute of grace," it was taught, "exceeds that of punishment (i.e. justice) by five-hundredfold" . . . Even in the time of His anger He remembers mercy," declares the Talmud (Pes.87b).[10]

In the Talmud, R. Ishmael b. Elisha uttered a very Messianic doctrine. Having entered the most holy place in the Temple, he had a conversation with God, and strangely God requested a blessing from him. The rabbi replied:

May it be Thy will that Thy mercy may subdue Thy wrath; and may Thy mercy prevail over Thy attribute of justice, so that Thou mayest deal with Thy children in the quality of mercy and *enter on their behalf within the line of strict justice.*[11]

R. Ishmael b. Elisha was uttering the great Messianic entrance of Ha-Mashiach on behalf of fallen humanity condemned to die by the justice of the law. God declares, "I have no pleasure in the death of the wicked, but that the wicked turn from his way and live" (Ezek. 33:11).

While believing, therefore, that He is the Judge of the Universe, the rabbis delighted in calling God "Rachmana" (the Merciful), and taught that "the world is judged by grace."[12]

Grace is defined here in the quality of God's mercy and is His unmerited favour to humanity. This statement in the Talmud is colossal. It is Messianic. It is absolution from the sentence of death meted out by the law, which is the standard of God's judgement.

Kabbalah is in grave error when teaching: "You have to earn it" [entrance into the upper reaches of heaven]. Kabbalah nullifies Grace when it states:

> We cannot achieve fulfilment without doing the spiritual work of earning fulfilment. Our essence is of the Creator, whose nature is to give and to share, and for whom the whole concept of "'free gifts" is inadmissible. There is a Hebrew phrase in the Talmud that is pertinent to this idea—nahama dichisufa, which can be translated "bread of shame"
>
> . . . On a spiritual level . . . it's against our interests and against our nature to accept "something for nothing."[13]

Kabbalah is not implying here that the work to be done is repentance, but rather the achievement of the highest degree of piety (perfection, total obedience to the law) in order to be able to face God, qualify to be immortal, and be in His presence. *Kabbalah is in gross error here.* How can a "Creator whose nature is to give and to share" have the concept that "free gifting" is inadmissible? Where is the place in Kabbalah for repentance, mercy, and forgiveness, which come by the atonement procured by the sacrificial lamb without blemish on that holiest of days? Kabbalah is not in harmony with the Tanak, which provides grace, the unmerited favour, obtained and bestowed by the Messiah. The Talmud speaks for both sides of the issue: salvation by grace and salvation by works. God regards our righteousness to be as filthy rags when we stand before the law, but He values our good works when we demonstrate them in love to Him and our fellow humans. Good works are a form of praise to God, but our good works do not earn our salvation.

The personal nature of God has to be understood in His dealings with His created beings, particularly humanity because of our involvement with Him.

His Fatherhood

Moses declared in Deuteronomy 14:1, "Ye are the children of the Lord your God." As children reflect their father's genetic makeup, we reflect His likeness in the ability to love and when we love. "Like as a Father pities His child, so the Lord pities a sinner defiled," wrote Franklin Belden, who was inspired by the Psalmist who wrote, "As a father pitieth his children, so the Lord pitieth them that fear Him. For He knoweth our frame; He remembereth that we are dust"(Ps. 103:12-13, KJV). A father is also a disciplinarian, and the Lord chastens His wayward children. But He is eternally our father. We are separated only when we ourselves break the relationship—which remains anyway, pending the restoration of that relationship of love.

His Holiness and Perfection

God's holiness is extraordinary because it is perfect, and He is perfect because He is holy. Holiness is a state of blamelessness, a state of righteousness, a state of full sanctification. He exhorts us to be holy like Him: "You shall be holy, for I, the Lord your God, am holy" (Lev. 19:1-2, *The Jewish Study Bible*). He sets a very high standard, and He instructs us to emulate Him.

His Ineffable Name

God's name reflects His character, and therefore it commands utmost respect, both in the use of language and lifestyle. We profane His name when we use it glibly. We profane it when we are hypocritical and when we misrepresent Him by our behaviour. The third commandment states, "You shall not swear falsely by the name of the Lord your God; for the Lord will not clear one who swears falsely by His name" (Exod. 20:7, *The Jewish Study Bible*).

One of the most glorious pictures of our holy and ineffable God, compiled from the Tanak, is that of Claude G. Montefiore in his book *The Old Testament and After.* Here is an excerpt.

> The statement in Exodus 34:6, 7 says nothing about the divine unity or His omnipotence or His eternity or His immateriality or His wisdom or His omniscience or His ubiquity; it speaks solely about His moral qualities or attributes: His pity, His graciousness, His justice, His lovingkindness, and His truth. (*The Old Testament and Beyond,* p. 34)

Claude Montefiore extracts richness from the two Hebrew words "chesed" (loving-kindness) and "emet" (truth, fidelity), and he contrasts them with "zedakah" (justice, righteousness). He declares that chesed is dominant with God, who is everlasting love, His dominant attribute.

Despite all our knowledge of God, we know very little of the Almighty. When Solomon was at the peak of his wisdom and knowledge, the Queen of Sheba decided to investigate and paid him a visit. When she saw the extreme wealth and splendour of the kingdom and the Temple, she exclaimed, "Behold, the half was not told me: thy wisdom and prosperity exceedeth the fame which I heard . . . . Blessed be the Lord thy God, Who delighteth in thee, to set thee on the throne of Israel. *Because the Lord loved Israel forever,* therefore made He thee king, to execute justice and righteousness" (1 Kings 10:7, 9 KJV).[14] Similarly, when we have delved into the depths of the knowledge we have of God, behold the half has not been told "of love so full and free!"

CHAPTER 3

THE POPULATION OF HEAVEN
AND THE ORIGIN OF EVIL

The possibility of the existence of extraterrestrial life has always challenged the people on planet earth. Most religious people have always believed that life exists elsewhere. The religious Jew not only believes in the existence of extraterrestrial life but firmly attaches his existence to it. The Tanak bases its ideation on it. Moses assumed this belief, and his inheritance of the Oral Torah firmly entrenched and strongly imprinted itself on his mind. Nowhere in the Pentateuch or the Book of Job is there the slightest shadow of a doubt about it; it was part and parcel of the foundation and central continuing core in Moses's religion and entire life. The primacy of the existence of God is the central and most solid foundation in Judaism. All life emanates from God and likely fills the universe.

The existence of God is understood in terms of His transcendence and immanence. The Tanak establishes it and the Talmud affirms it. But apart from God's omnipresence and infinity, Moses recognised God had a site-specific residence called Heaven. It was a vast area commensurate with God's greatness but had an earth-like central dimensional core consisting of a throne, which recognised His kingship and majesty, and a heavenly temple, where a "tangible" presence of God resided for religious purposes. Religion exists for two basic reasons or purposes: the worship and adoration of God, and the upliftment or redemption of humanity. Moses duplicated that great concept of the divine in a symbol on earth. He was instructed by God to do this according to the Pentateuch. It was established upon earth as the Tent Tabernacle, later the Temple.

The Temple, specifically the Most Holy Compartment, duplicated God's abode in Heaven upon the earth. The Shechinah and the high priesthood manifested God's function for religious purposes. Both existed already in Heaven, for it is seen in the Zebul described by Moses; the word Zebul means habitation. God reigns and officiates in both spheres of His function; He is king and priest. He is king because He created and rules, and He is priest and sacrifice because He redeems. He is creator and redeemer; He is Shechinah, and He is Michael, the sacrifice in that stupendous, immortal scene in Zebul, which is one of the seven heavens of God's habitation, elaborated in the Talmud.

The Hebrew word for Heaven is Shamayim, which literally means "The place where there is water," or Esh and Mayim, literally "fire and water." There are seven different designations in Hebrew for Heaven in the Tanak. The Talmud reasonably gives structural definition to heaven in terms of seven layers. This can be recognised as an attempt to accommodate the ideas floating around. "There are seven heavens, named respectively Vilon, Rakia, Shechakim, Zebul, Maon, Machon, and Araboth."[15] Abraham Cohen deciphers the Talmud to base the existence of these layers on Tanakian quotes, and despite the nonscientific nature of these descriptions culled by the rabbinic sages, they do justice to the thought processes in the minds of Moses and the authors of the Tanak.

Vilon performs no other function in that it retires in the morning and issues forth in the evening, and renews the work of Creation daily, as it is said: "It is He who sitteth on the circle of the earth . . . That stretcheth out the heavens as a curtain and spreadeth them out as a tent to dwell in" (Isa. 40:22).

Rakia is that in which the sun, moon, stars, and planets are fixed, as it is said: "And God set them in the firmament (rakia) of the heaven'" (Gen. 1:17).

Shechakim is that in which the millstones are located and grind manna for the righteous, as it is said: "He commanded the skies

(Shechakim) above and opened the doors of heaven, and He rained down manna upon them to eat" (Ps. 78:23-[f25]).

Zebul is that place where the celestial Jerusalem is and the Temple in which the altar is erected, and Michael, the great prince, stands and offers a sacrifice upon it, as it is said: "I have surely built thee an house of habitation (Zebul), a place for thee to dwell in for ever" (1 Kings 8:13). Whence do we know that it is called Heaven? Because it is written, "Look down from heaven and behold from the habitation (Zebul) of Thy holiness and of Thy glory" (Isa. 64:15).

Maon is that in which are bands of ministering angels, who utter a song in the night but are silent during the day for the sake of the honour of Israel, as is said: "The Lord will command His lovingkindness in the daytime and in the night His song shall be with me" (Ps. 42:8). Whence do we know that it is called Heaven? Because it is written, "Look down from Thy holy habitation (Maon) from heaven" (Deut. 26:15).

Machon is that in which are the treasuries of snow and the treasuries of hail, the loft containing harmful dews, the lofts of the round drops (which injure plants), the chamber of the whirlwind and storm, and the cavern of noxious smoke, the doors of which are made of fire, as it is said: "The Lord shall open thee His good treasure" (Deut. 28:12). Whence do we know that it is called Heaven? Because it is written, "Hear Thou in heaven, the habitation (Machon) of Thy dwelling" (1 Kings 8:39).

Araboth is that in which are righteousness, judgement, and charity; the storehouses of life, of peace, and of blessing; the souls of the righteous; the spirits and souls that are still to be created; and the dew which with the Holy One, blessed be He, will hereafter revive the dead. These are the Ophannim, Seraphim, holy Chayyoth, the ministering angels, the Throne of Glory, and the King, the living God, high and exalted, abiding above them in the clouds, as it is said: "Cast up a highway for Him that rideth upon the clouds (Araboth); His name is Jah'" (Ps. 68:4).[16] It is therefore deduced that this group of ministering angels is situated just below the heavenly Temple.

Although in this scientific day and age we can see a great distance between these layers of heaven, we are able to understand the thought processes of the Tanakian writers and the interpreting rabbinic sages. They comprehended heaven in terms of what they understood and could explain in the milieu of the science of their time. In "scientific" terms Heaven appears more distant than ever. From our current perspective, Heaven seems to be a combination of Zebul, Maon, and Araboth, which are in close proximity. The heavenly Jerusalem, within which is the heavenly Temple (whatever their structure), wherein dwell God and His function of Michael, is surrounded by angels. Zebul, Maon, and Araboth might be logically called Grand Central Heaven. If it is assumed that the seven layers of heaven have been built over eternity, then at some point in that building process, and perhaps synchronous with it, God created this world.

The enumeration of the heavenly population must start with Genesis 1. Assuming God was in His particular layer of Heaven (Zebul), in which He shares space with Michael the great Prince, we see God on the throne in the Most Holy Place of the heavenly Temple, within the heavenly Jerusalem. Michael stands in the Temple by the altar, making sacrifice. This is an enormous and astounding statement in the Talmud introducing a concept of cosmic significance. The identity of Michael becomes extremely important and significant because he is alone in the heavenly Temple with Jehovah, performing a redemptive function. Questions arise: Does he reside there permanently with God? Or has he been invited there for the function that he is stated to be performing, that of offering sacrifice? Is he the heavenly high priest sacrificing on the heavenly Day of Atonement? If so, why has he been chosen? He is described in the Tanak as "Michael one of the chief princes" and "'a prince of the first rank" and "your prince" in Daniel 10:13, 21, and again in Daniel 12:1 as "Michael . . . the great prince who standeth for the children of thy people," or "who stands beside the sons of your people." The Tanak does not identify or label Michael as an angel. The Tanak does not call him a created being. Daniel calls him a prince three times. *The Jewish Study Bible* comments in the margin that the references to Michael are made in a discussion of the end of the world, which is correct: he stands up at the end of the world. What origin he has and what function he is to perform at the end of the world is fascinating and demands deciphering. The most significant characteristic of Michael is that he stands as the high priest of the heavenly Temple.

Strangely, Abraham Cohen calls Michael the Archangel[17] when debating the Talmud's disclaiming the possibility that Michael and Gabriel shared Creation of the universe with God (Isa. 44:24).[18] In the B'rit Hadasha, Jude and John the Revelator call Michael the Archangel (Jude 1:9; Revelation 12:7). Has Abraham Cohen borrowed from the B'rit Hadasha? This is surprising.

The Talmud refers again to Michael: "If trouble befall a man, let him not cry to Michael or Gabriel; but let him cry to Me and I will answer him at once."[19] This is not a quotation from the Tanak. The Tanak does not call Michael an angel, although the B'rit Hadasha does call him an archangel. But the Talmud goes on to name ranks of angels, and it selects Michael as being superior to Gabriel and standing at the right hand of the throne, and being the guardian angel of Israel. And here is an astounding statement: "and wherever he [Michael] appears the glory of the Shechinah is also bound to be found."[20] Here is an inference that Michael is deity, manifested by the Shechinah that He owns and that always surrounds Him. The Talmud assigns special events in the Tanak to have been performed by Michael.

1. Michael brought the news to Sarah that she would give birth to a son.[21] If so, he was in the company of two other heavenly beings when visiting Abraham and Sarah (Gen. 18:2). If Michael was the main heavenly being in that visit, Moses gives him the appellation of God ("The Lord").
2. Michael was the instructor of Moses.[22]
3. Michael smote the army of Sennacherib,[23] and 185,000 soldiers died. Later Sennacherib's two sons assassinated

Sennacherib while he sacrificed to Nisroch, his god (2
Kings 19:35-37).
4. Michael protected the Persian Jews from Haman through
Esther.[24]
5. Michael cured Abraham's wound after his circumcision got
infected.[25]

Michael is not specifically mentioned in the Tanak as being
involved in these events, but the Talmud takes the liberty to name
Michael as having initiated these events. He did them on his own
authority because the record does not say he was commissioned
to do them by God, so he appears to act on his own volition. In
the case of breaking the news to Sarah, Moses labels the divine
person as God. Here again is an indication that Michael is deity,
doing things on his own and acting like a deity. The word Michael
in Hebrew means "Who is like God." But since monotheism must
be adhered to, Michael cannot be a separate deity—he has to be
one with God Almighty. "Hear O Israel, the Lord our God is One,"
blessed be He. Michael is therefore a function of God in redeeming
humanity, and not a separate deity. He is the Messiah.

The news to Sarah that she would give birth to a son was spoken
by God. This is recorded in Genesis 18. The Tanak does not say
that Michael was involved here. It was God Himself with two
unidentified companions: "The Lord appeared To him [Abraham]
by the terebinths [oaks] of Mamre (Gen. 18:1). And again: "Then
the Lord said unto Abraham 'Why did Sarah laugh . . . Is anything
too hard for the Lord?'" (Gen. 18:13-14). If the Talmudic rabbinic
sages are right—and on the consensus opinion of the Tanak they
are—then Michael is deity, being interchangeable name-wise with
God. He is the promised Messiah in His prearrival splendour,
One with God, in the heavenly holy Temple, making sacrifice and
redeeming the world. The Talmud says the Messiah is a created
being, so the Talmud is clearly wrong in that respect. He cannot be
one with God and also be a created being. The Messiah appears as
the "Divine penetrance of humanity."

30

The angel Gabriel is mentioned twice in the Tanak, both times in the Book of Daniel. Gabriel is commissioned by God to help Daniel understand the vision (Dan. 8:16, 9:21). There is no Messianic function assigned by the Tanak to Gabriel.

The Talmud assigns angels to a certain level of Heaven (Maon), which must be in close proximity with the throne because they are constantly praising God. There are good and bad angels. The Tanak indicates that the bad angels reside on this earth and keep tempting humanity, as they did in the Garden of Eden. The Talmud names two good angels besides Gabriel, namely Uriel and Raphael. Uriel and Raphael are not mentioned in the Tanak. The Talmud also names some bad angels: Samael and Satan, the latter being mentioned in the Tanak.

The Talmud teaches that good impulses (Jetzer Tov) and bad impulses (Jetzer Hara) were inbuilt in Adam and Eve in their perfect state, built in by God.[26] This idea that God built into Adam and Eve a propensity for evil is preposterous—it taints God's perfection and blames Him for the origin of evil. The Jetzers are not free will, which is a different gift to humanity (Gen. 4:7).[27] The Jetzers will be discussed again fully elsewhere in this book, but it must be emphatically denied here that it accounts for the origin of evil. The Tanak does not support the Jetzer theory. An excerpt from Talmudic teaching is instructive because it admits to a source other than Jetzer Hara for the origin of evil. Abraham Cohen tries to have it both ways and makes excuses for the rabbinic utterances about evil angels with the statement, "In the writings of the Rabbinic period the evil angels are nothing more than an invention to express the divine wrath, and their function is to carry out the decree when God has to punish men for their wickedness."[28] This stance almost leads to the opinion that God is in collusion with evil angels. But then, in commenting on the event of the worship of the golden calf, the Talmud elaborates a group of bad angels. Moses was on Mount Sinai with God when the golden calf was worshipped. Commenting on the Talmudic account, Cohen states,

When the Holy One, Blessed be He, said to Moses, "Arise, get thee down quickly from hence" (Deuteronomy 9:12), five angels of destruction heard it and wished to do him harm. They are Aph, Chemah, Ketzeph, Mashchith (destroyer) and Mechalleh (consumer).[29]

The wicked angel Samael, the chief of all the Satans[30]—in this way is the army of the evil angels and their captain designated. "Satan" is the personification of wickedness. A significant remark is: Satan, the Jetzer Hara and the Angel of Death are all one.[31]

This statement confuses the issue by reverting back to Jetzer Hara as the prime source of evil. To make his argument more confusing, Cohen states,

One should always be alert to escape the power of Satan; and a Rabbi suggested as a suitable blessing for a guest to pronounce over his host: "May he prosper in all his possessions; may not Satan have power over the works of his hands nor over ours; and may there not leap before him or us any thought of sin, transgression or iniquity from now and forevermore" (Ber. 46a).

It is recommended: "Let not a man open his mouth to Satan" (Ber. 19a).[32]

Satan is described in the Tanak, but Samael is not. Some scholars use the identity of Samael, the Angel of Death, as synonymous with Satan. A "female demon-beast" named Lilith is mentioned by Isaiah (34:14). Lilith is a figure in Hebrew mythology, and I will not digress upon her here. Bad angels were thought to dwell in the underworld, synonymous with Sheol, Hades, and the grave.[33]. But Satan, a bad angel, appears to have had access to Heaven according to the Tanak (see Job). The questions arise: Who is Satan? What is his origin and role in the Tanak? Who are the bad angels and how did they become bad? The biggest and weightiest question has to be: How did badness originate in Satan and the bad angels?

They were not created bad. *The occurrence of their badness is the Tanakian origin of evil in the universe.*

The answers to these questions, which will explain the origin of evil, are found in the Tanak. The Talmudic explanation for the origin of evil is not Tanakian. Jetzer Tov and Jetzer Hara are not Tanakian teachings. The concept of the 'two impulses' is Talmudic and at great variance with the Tanak. The Tanak explicitly states that God is only good. He is goodness personified. God is pure and perfect in all His manifestations to the human race. He is not the author of evil. He did not place the Jetzer Hara propensity to evil in Adam and Eve. The story of the Garden of Eden will have to be expunged from the Tanak if it is interpreted that when God made humans (Adam and Eve), he put inside them propensities for evil. Torah commanded obedience. They had the free will to choose. Free will is not synonymous with the propensity to sin. Jetzer Tov and Jetzer Hara are "inclinations" or "propensities" to obey or disobey God.[34] A being with inbuilt propensity to sin is not a perfect being, so we cannot accuse a perfect God of having formed a imperfect being. There certainly is a difference between free will and an inbuilt inclination to disobey Torah, placed there by God. There is no free will if evil is already inside the human, built in there by a "perfect and good God." It is an absolute and total impossibility.

The sojourn in sin outside the Gates of Eden and the familiarity and enjoyment of evil actions made our natures weak and prone to disobedience. We thus fall very easily to temptation, and our free will is not exercised strongly to obey Torah. Adam and Eve could not have been invested with immortality when they were created, if they had evil inclinations to sinfulness. In Adam and Eve, we chose freely to believe the Serpent's lie: "You will not surely die but you will be as gods, knowing good and evil" (Gen. 3:4-5). Moses wrote the story very carefully. The first humans were perfect till they disobeyed the Torah. Disobedience was a voluntary act of free will, and disobedience tainted us. Moses did not teach Jetzer Tov and Jetzer Hara. God instituted Messianic sacrifice to reinstate perfection and immortality. That is the concept of Mosaic Judaism. That is the context of Messianic sacrifice.

That the Tanak teaches that the Serpent and Satan are synonymous is congruent with its whole context. But we must try to identify the origin of evil in fallen angels. The books of Job, Isaiah, Ezekiel, and Obadiah hold the answer. There is an antecedent parallel story to the Garden of Eden within the context of the Tanak. This provides the answer to the question of bad angels and the origin of evil.

Since astrophysicist—cosmologists Max Tegmark and Brian Greene (see online) assert there is a multiverse, it is highly likely that before God created our universe, He had previously created other universes. He had created angels, all perfect and all with the power of free will. They enjoyed a layer of Heaven, Maon, described as an area close to the throne. Perhaps it is an area like the Earth, but unlike humans, angels have greater access of travel all over their universe and elsewhere in God's creation. The obvious and reasonable conclusion is that there had been a previous, similar wrong use of the will among the angels, which had originated as pride and jealousy. The story is well documented in Job, the oldest book of the Tanak. Built on this information, the origin of evil is couched in three other stories, in Isaiah, Ezekiel, and Obadiah. Although interpretation of the Tanak must be true to the concepts and context, and must be in harmony with the entire Tanak, we find encapsulated within these stories the skeleton that hearkens back to the original happening. Coincidentally, Isaiah, Ezekiel, and Obadiah hearken back to the same core happening. In His creation of angels, God had created special offices for a select few angels (that we know about), who were pre-eminent. The Tanak names only two, Gabriel and Lucifer. The Talmud enlarges on the model and names others, such as Raphael and Uriel.

The Isaiah (Is. 14:12-22) and Ezekiel (Ezek. 28:12-19) stories are excellently treated within Tanakian concept and context by the Tekton Education and Apologetics Ministry, answering the question, "Do Ezekiel and Isaiah refer to Satan as Lucifer?" It is well worth reading. Obadiah 1 also deals with this subject. All three writers follow the same model. All three stories concern Israel's sins, their punishment, and their redemption. Although the documentation is solid in the Book of Job, the events in the cosmos leading to the origin of evil will be examined first in the accounts of Isaiah, Ezekiel, and Obadiah.

The Isaiah Story

This Scripture is written about the Babylonian devastation of the kingdom of Judah and Judah's return.

> But the Lord will pardon Jacob, and will again choose Israel, and will settle them on their own soil . . . . And when the Lord has given you rest from your sorrow and trouble, and from the hard service that you were made to serve, you shall recite this song of scorn over the king of Babylon. (Isa. 14:1-4, *The Jewish Study Bible*)

This agony of Israel is an epitome of the disobedience, which caused the entrance of sin into the universe, and it also completes the story of return and redemption. The "editorialised" Song of Scorn follows. The Babylonian king has claimed for himself god-like powers and exalted himself. He is brought down. The Babylonian king who devastated Israel will be crushed, and "I will sweep it with a broom of extermination—declares the Lord of Hosts" (Isa. 14:23). It portends what God will finally do with evil. Within the Song of Scorn are elements that hearken to an experience outside the realm of the earthly Babylonian king. This experience has commonly expressed similarity to Greek and Canaanite legends. But under "inspiration," Isaiah is equating it to the fall of the "Shining One, the Son of Dawn," who was felled to earth from heaven. What was the cause of the fall?

> Once you thought in your heart "I will climb to the sky, higher than the stars of God, I will set my throne . . . . I will match the Most High." Instead you are brought down to

35

Sheol, to the bottom of the pit. (Isa. 14:12-15, *The Jewish
Study Bible*)

There is significant doubt that the Babylonian king had any concept
of the magnificence of the Most High God of Israel. But he did lord
it over a sinful Israel. And then Isaiah continues on in another Song
of Scorn on Philistia, another vanquished enemy of Israel. Isaiah,
under inspiration, picks up another experience outside the realm of
the Philistines.

Rejoice not, all Philistia . . . For from the stock of a snake
there sprouts an asp, a flying seraph branches out from
it . . . I will kill your stock by famine and it shall slay the
very last of you . . . . For a stout one is coming from the
north, and there is no straggler in his ranks. And what will
he answer the messengers of any nation? *That Zion has
been established by the Lord.* (Isa. 14:29-32, *The Jewish
Study Bible*; emphasis added)

This recalls the experience that occurred outside the Garden of
Eden when the Gates were shut after their expulsion. The enmity
between the Serpent and the woman whose seed, the Messiah,
coming from "the sides of the north," synonym of God's throne,
will crush the Serpent's head. There is no doubt that the references
are to the fall of Lucifer from Heaven and his impending conquest
in his role of Satan.

How art thou fallen from Heaven, O Lucifer, son of the
morning! How art thou cut down to the ground, who didst
weaken the nations. For thou hast said in thine heart, I will
ascend into Heaven, I will exalt my throne above the stars
of God; I will sit also upon the mount of the congregation,
in the sides of the north. (Isa. 14:12-13, KJV)

These references are elegantly, inspirationally, and prophetically
couched in sublime language. Great is the God of Israel, and
mighty is His power. Neither Lucifer nor the king of Babylon can
challenge God and get away with it.

36

The Ezekiel Story

This story is again about the abject suffering plight of captive Israel. Tyre's royalty is depicted gloating, taking advantage, and finding security in the accumulation of immense riches. The story actually starts in Ezekiel 26:1.

> In the eleventh year, on the first of the month, the word of the Lord came to me [Ezekiel]: Oh mortal, because Tyre gloated over Jerusalem. "Aha! The gateway of the peoples is broken, it has become mine; I shall be filled now that it [Jerusalem] is laid in ruins"—assuredly, thus said the Lord God: I am going to deal with you, O Tyre! I will hurl many nations against you, as the sea hurls its waves. They shall destroy the walls of Tyre . . . I will scrape her soil off her and leave her a naked rock. (Ezek. 26:1-4, *The Jewish Study Bible*)

God does not take kindly to anyone who gloats over the destruction of Israel and Jerusalem. The vengeance He will exact from Tyre continues in the succeeding chapters, to the epic Dirge of Lamentation. The essence of the destructive dirge against Tyre is retribution for the pride in which Tyre shrouds itself.

> Because you have been so haughty and have said, "I am a god; I sit enthroned like a god . . . whereas you are not a god . . . you deemed your mind equal to a god's . . . They shall bring you down to the Pit . . . you shall die the death of the slain." (Ezek. 28:1-10, *The Jewish Study Bible*)

Here again is the allegorical recall of the entrance of sin into the universe. Here is the recall of the prophetic voice to the Creation of the world and the Garden of Eden. The rulers of Tyre have no connection with this next part of the story, except for the pride and self-exaltation to a god-like status. Instead there is a connection to celestial events and the status of the Garden of Eden.

> You were the seal of perfection, full of wisdom and flawless
> in beauty. You were in Eden, the Garden of God . . . I
> created you as a cherub with outstretched shielding wings;
> and you resided on God's holy mountain; you walked
> among stones of fire. You were blameless in your ways,
> from the day you were created *until wrongdoing was found
> in you* . . . . And you sinned, so I have struck you down
> from the mountain of God . . . . You grew haughty because
> of your beauty . . . [so] I have cast you to the ground."
> (Ezek. 28:11-17, *The Jewish Study Bible*; emphasis added)

It is quite obvious that the rulers of Tyre were not players in Eden,
and they were never in the mountain of God. The Scripture clearly
hearkens to the celestial event of the fall of Lucifer. Again, as in
Isaiah, the prophetic gift is uttering a double application, the
celestial events being more applicably implicated and applied in
this scripture to the fall of Lucifer.

The Obadiah Story

Here again there is a foreign power, Edom, who is deserving of
doom for persecuting Israel. Edom has exalted itself against God.

> Your arrogant heart has seduced you, you who dwell in the
> clefts of the rock, in your lofty abode. You think in your
> heart 'Who can pull me down to earth? (Obad. 1:1-4, *The
> Jewish Study Bible*)

Again, the rulers of Edom were not living in Heaven, and so from a
conceptual point of view of the whole Tanak, this is a reference to
the fall of the angel Lucifer. God uses the story of the entrapment
and misery of the human race by the evil Satan as being parallel to
the persecution and suffering that Israel endured under the powers
of Babylon, Tyre, and Edom.

In reinterpreting these scriptures to recognise in them the origin of
evil in the universe, I am invoking the "apotelesmatic principle."

38

This principle was first enunciated by Desmond Ford in his PhD thesis submitted to Manchester University, England, in 1972. He reaffirms this principle in his book *Commentary on Daniel*, published in 1978. Ford stated, "By apotelesmatic principle we mean dual fulfilment or more."[35] Though original with Ford in the modern era of Christian theology, the apotelesmatic principle is not a new concept. In reading the Talmud, there comes the realisation that the great rabbinic sages used the apotelesmatic principle very extensively, without having made such a rule for themselves. They sometimes carried it too far, so that there was no resemblance between their didacted interpretation and the original Tanakian excerpt of scripture, which was the subject of their study. Giving a scripture a dual meaning or connecting application that is sensible and true to the Tanakian concept is perfectly Kosher and must take precedence to other offered solutions. In this case, the Jetzer Tov and Jetzer Hara theory, which embarrasses God by accusing Him of creating evil propensities in Adam and Eve, must be discarded. Any proffered application of the apotelesmatic principle must stay true to and harmonious with the conceptual and contextual interpretation of the whole Tanak. If it does not, the principle is being misused and the application should be discarded.

The subject of the history, characteristics, and future of Satan is eminently explored in the Book of Job. Moses is quite explicit regarding the denouement of the origin of evil in this oldest book of the Tanak. In *The Jewish Study Bible*, the translators' comments in the introduction to the book concerning authorship and date of composition state that it was composed between the mid-sixth to the mid-fourth centuries BC, because of its allusions to Psalms 111:10 and Proverbs 1:7 and 9:10, and the post-exilic Zechariah 3. I totally disagree. I would rather conclude that David, Solomon, and Zechariah were expressing things in common with the book of Job, to which they had access. And I agree with the Talmud, which credits Moses with its authorship. The entire life of Job is found in summary in a conversation between God and Satan.

> Now there was a day when the sons of God came to present
> themselves before the Lord, and Satan came also among

them. And the Lord said unto Satan, From where comest
thou? Then Satan answered the Lord, and said, From going
to and fro in the earth, and from walking up and down in
it. And the Lord said unto Satan, Hast thou considered
my servant Job, that [there is] none like him in the earth,
a perfect and an upright man, one who feareth God, and
shunneth evil? Then Satan answered the Lord and said,
Doth Job fear God for nothing? Hast Thou not made a
hedge about him, and about his house, and about all that
he hath on every side? Thou hast blessed the work of his
hands, and his substance is increased in the land. But put
forth Thine hand now, and touch all that he hath, and he
will curse Thee to Thy face. And the Lord said unto Satan,
Behold all that he hath is in thy power; only upon himself
put not forth thine hand. So Satan went forth from the
presence of the Lord. (Job 1:6-12, KJV)

Several facts are learned here. Satan is located on the earth. His
probation is not over at this interaction about Job because he is
still allowed access to Heaven. He continues to taunt God, who
also taunts him. God allows Satan to prey on the inhabitants of
the earth. Generally, prosperity comes with uprightness. God does
allow Satan to have access to Heaven for reporting to Him. Job
was a "perfect and upright" man, but it did not provide him with
redemption. He still depended on Messianic redemption.

For I know that my Redeemer liveth and He shall stand at
the latter day the upon the earth; And though after my skin
worms destroy this body, yet in my flesh shall I see God,
Whom I shall see for myself, and my eyes shall behold, and
not another; though my heart be consumed within me. (Job
19:25-27, KJV)

Job and Moses believed in Messianic redemption and the
resurrection of the dead. This was the greatest thing in the life of
Job, and God saw it and was exultant about it. God was so happy
that He boasted to Satan about it.

The conclusion is that originally Lucifer occupied a very close and important proximity to God as a created being. But in his heart, he began to extol his own beauty and gifts above the Creator who made him, and that was his downfall. The record says that he was cast to the earth and lost his privileged position (Ezek. 28). His pride and jealousy destroyed him. The B'rit Hadasha describes a war in Heaven between Michael and Lucifer and the bad angels in sympathy with him. They were cast out of Heaven (Rev. 12).

The story of the angels is amply described in the Talmud and is worth discussing here. It is based on Job 1:6-12, 1 Kings 22:19, and Isaiah 6:1. In 1 Kings 22, the author has the events of that chapter pivot on a scene in Heaven where God, sitting on His throne, "holds court with all the host of Heaven standing in attendance" (1 Kings 22:19, *The Jewish Study Bible*). Isaiah 6 describes another glorious scene: "In the year that King Uzziah died, I beheld my Lord seated on a high and lofty throne; and the skirts of His robe filled the Temple. Seraphs stood in attendance on Him. Each of them had six wings" (Isa. 6:1, *The Jewish Study Bible*). The Talmud indulges in much non-Tanakian conjecture, which the rabbinic sages seem to have utterly enjoyed in their discussion and disagreements about the subject![36]

As He did in the Garden of Eden for fallen humanity, did God provide a plan of redemption for Lucifer and the fallen angels? Again the answer must be: deity has created, deity will redeem. The mercy of God is fathomless. Death is not God's desired end for any of His creatures.

This preamble provides an adequate elucidation of what has gone on in heaven. And thus we arrive at the population of Heaven mentioned in the Tanak:

1. The Deity: One God who manifests Himself in our context as creator, redeemer, and glorifier. The sum of His declared powers presents a totality which is self-evident. He creates with His totality, redeems with His totality, and will glorify with His totality. The Lord our God is one. Blessed be He. His redemptive power is manifest to humans as the synonymous Messiah and Michael. His sanctifying power is manifest in the Holy Spirit, and His glorifying power will be shown with the restoration of perfection and immortality, the great eschatological event for which humanity yearns with groanings that are often unutterable. There is so much suffering and death on the planet that the apocalyptic, Messianic intervention is long overdue. Glorification here is used as synonymous with the state, which Gershom Scholem describes as the apocalyptic utopia.

2. The Angelic Host: The angels are also created beings. The good angels are based in Heaven, from where they are on mission in the service of God. The presence of bad angels indicates a simmering war between good and evil in the universe. Satan is the leader of the bad angels, and they are constantly tempting humanity and causing misery. The bad angels are located to the planet earth because the eschatology of the Tanak has the final scenes involving bad angels down here. They have been disseminators of sin and misery, and they are active in trying to turn humans against their creator. The Tanak talks about the end time and the last days. The arrival of the Messiah is pivotal to these impending eschatological events. Gershom Scholem describes an impending catastrophic apocalypticism that inaugurates his utopia.

There are multiple references to angels in the Tanak.

(i)   II Samuel 14:20—Refers to the "wisdom of an angel."
(ii) I Kings 19:5—An angel came down to encourage Elijah.
(iii) Nehemiah 9:6—Talks about the "host" of heaven.
(iv) Job 25:3—The "armies" of heaven are mentioned.
      Job 38:7—"When the morning stars sang together, and all the sons of God shouted for joy".
(v)   Psalm 68:7—"The chariots of God are twenty thousand, even thousands of angels."
      Psalm 91:11—"For He shall give His angels charge over thee, to keep thee in all thy ways."

Psalm 103:20—"Bless the Lord, ye His angels, that excel in strength, that do His commandments, hearkening unto the voice of His word."
Psalm 104:4—"Who maketh His angels spirits, His ministers a flaming fire."
Psalm 148:2—"Praise ye Him, all His angels, praise ye Him, all His hosts."

(vi) Isaiah 6:2—"Above it stood the seraphim: each one had six wings."

(vii) Ezekiel 1—His first vision of the glory of the Lord.

(viii) Daniel 6:22—"My God hath sent His angel and hath shut the lions' mouths."

(ix) Hosea 12:4—"Yea, he had power over the angel, and prevailed."

3. The Living Saints: Enoch and Elijah were taken up to Heaven. These two patriarchs are up there with Messianic credit notes. They have been atoned for in advance and passed judgement ahead of time.

4. Sons Of God: Mentioned in Job (Job 1:6; 2:1), these are "unfallen," created beings similar to humans, but who are perfectly obedient to their Torah and live immortally in happiness, and perpetually praise God. Strictly speaking they are not part of the population of Heaven, but they live in their space with access to Paradise. The Tanak does not elaborate on or discuss these. The Tanak is a local phenomenon on planet earth, in a multi-universe creation.

Sons of God are also mentioned in Genesis 6:4. The Hebrew translation of all three texts (Job 1:6, 2:1; Gen. 6:4) is the same: be ne (the sons) ha-Elohim (of God). However the Sons of God in the Book of Job are heavenly beings, in a heavenly context. The Genesis Sons of God are terrestrial and not in a heavenly setting. They are linked with giantism, referred to also in Numbers 13:32-33.

The Sons of God of Genesis 6:1 are those who cohabited with the daughters of men. Genesis 6:1-2 links directly with Genesis 6:4, which describes the result of the cohabitation in terms of giantism and renown. Strangely, Genesis 6:3 and 6:5 deal with the fact that God had come to the end of His tether with the intermingling and corruption that had resulted from the cohabitation of the "righteous Sons of God" with the "wicked daughters of men." Intermarriage of Israel with the idolatrous has always been a great irritation to God and has facilitated their several sinful slides into idolatry. No doubt it was God's great chagrin and disgust with the antediluvian world that led him to destroy the earth with the flood (Gen. 6).

The above summarizes the Tanakian account of the population of Heaven and the origin of evil in the universe. It also gives insight into the Tanakian scope and activities of the population of heaven. The Talmudic idea of the origin of evil being the Jetzer Hara, which was built into Adam and Eve by God,[37] must be discarded as a variant idea that has no place in Tanakian theology. This will be further discussed elsewhere in this book.

CHAPTER 4

"In the Beginning God"

These are the first four English words of the Tanak, the very beginning of Moses's writings, the Pentateuch. They commence the account of the creation of the Heavens and the earth. Moses, who was finite, must start with a beginning, and the first recognition of existence is the recognition of God. God was already in eternal existence before He created the Heavens and the earth. The earth was without form, and it was void; darkness existed in space. The Spirit (Hebrew word "Ruach") of God moved upon the waters, and God said, "Let there be light," and there was light. The creation week followed, culminating in the formation of the primal couple, Adam and Eve.

In the Pentateuch, Moses gives us a wonderful description of God. He is infinite, immortal, invisible, incorporate, omnipresent, omniscient, omnipotent, and transcendent. His character is the standard of goodness, and His government is by law. Obedience to that law by the choice of free will was the requirement for the continued immortality of humanity. His relationship with humanity is a love relationship, for God is love. These characteristics of God are reinforced by all the authors of the Tanak.

God is one: "Hear, O Israel: The Lord our God is one Lord" (Deut. 6:4). He is one in existence: "I am the Lord, and there is none else, there is no God beside Me" (Isa. 43:11; 45:5, 21). He is one in creation: "Thus saith the Lord, thy Redeemer, and He who formed thee from the womb; I the Lord who maketh all, who stretcheth forth the heavens alone; who spreadeth abroad the earth by Myself" (Isa. 44:24). He is one in redemption. Here is the foundation definition and expression of monotheism.

But God's name in Hebrew, Elohim, is a plural form. He, who is infinite, blessed be He, expresses Himself in ways that He chooses. He is a spirit (in Hebrew, "Ruach Hakodesh"'), as stated in Genesis 1:2 and 6:3. Abraham Cohen, the great modern expositor of the Talmud, explains:

> There was general agreement that prophecy, in its special connotation, ceased with the overthrow of the first Temple . . . . When the latter prophets, Haggai, Zechariah, and Malachi, died, the Holy Spirit departed from Israel.[38]

But Cohen need not be downcast about the absence of more prophets. The Sanhedrin closed the Tanak with the last prophet. Malachi predicted the next awesome event was to be the Messianic event. There will be no need for prophets when Messiah comes, for He ushers in perfection. "The supreme message of Hebrew prophecy was the call to erring men and women to retrace their steps to God." Cohen again quotes the Talmud:

> Every prophet only prophesied for the days of the Messiah and the penitent.[39] In this sense must the rather strange dictum be understood: "The time will come, when the prophets and Hagiographa will be abolished, but not the Pentateuch."[40] When everybody is obedient to the commandments there will be no further need for the prophetic exhortations which were only intended for a sinful world and not the era of perfection to be inaugurated by the Messiah.[41]

Cohen was looking forward to the ushering in of Messiah, the redeemer and king of kings, the propitiation for sin, cleansing all who would be cleansed and providing sinless perfection to qualify all for immortality. Messiah will be perfect Himself, very God Himself, who comes to provide atonement and perfection to others. He is the Lamb without blemish sacrificed for the reimmortalization of His fallen ones. All humanity who trust in the Messiah will be able to claim His perfection as theirs, since no human born on earth has achieved perfection (perfect obedience to the law) in their lifetime. The Messiah is deity, inclusive in one God. Messianic redemption was laid down before the creation of the universe. The plurality of Elohim encompasses Ruach Hakodesh and Ha-Mashiach. The Lord our God is one. Blessed be He.

God expresses Himself in the Messiah: "For unto us a Child is born, unto us a Son is given, and the government shall be upon His shoulder. And His name shall be called Wonderful, Counsellor, The Mighty God, The Everlasting Father, The Prince of Peace" (Isa. 9:6 KJV). Also, "And the Lord whom ye seek shall suddenly come to His temple, even the Messenger of the Covenant, Whom ye delight in . . . . For He is like a refiner's fire" (Mal. 3:1-3 KJV). Contrary to what the Talmud would assert, the Messiah is not a created being—the Messiah is deity, He is very God, one with God, another expression of the Father, like the Holy Spirit, blessed be He. Again, contrary to the Talmudic assertion that Messiah is a created being, Isaiah declares He is the Mighty God, the Everlasting Father, the Prince of Peace. There is no declaration in the Tanak that Messiah was created. His penetration of humanity was not to be a creative event, but an *incarnation,* as Isaiah declares He would be born into humanity, born like a son.

The Talmud equates the spirit of God with the Comforter and the Shechinah.[42] The Hebrew word for Shechinah is not found in the Tanak; it was used in the Jewish Targums, the Aramaic translation of the Hebrew Bible. Answers in Torah Study Online quotes this as Mishnaic Hebrew "sakina," from the Hebrew "sakan," to dwell. It is held synonymous with the "glory of the Lord" that filled the Temple by which God dwelt with Israel (Exod. 25:8, 21-22; 29:45-46; 40:35; Lev. 16:2). He was the pillar of cloud by day and the pillar of fire by night, and He filled the Temple. What a glorious time to be living and to behold the physical presence of God, demonstrated as a very bright light in the Temple, living with Israel. Ruach Hakodesh is very God, an expression of the One God, and this is not denied in Talmudic writings. Blessed be He, the Lord our God is one.

The Talmud makes many references to the Messiah. The Messiah pre-existed before the creation of the world.[43] Cohen states that the rabbis were unanimous that the Messiah would come as a human being, and nowhere does the Talmud indicate that he would be a superhuman deliverer. This is incongruous with the Tanak. It is incongruous with the parallel Talmudic teaching that the Messiah existed before the creation of the universe. It is also incongruous with the other definitions applied to the Messiah. The rabbinic opinion in the Talmud is that the Messiah would come through the line of David, and that the Messiah is the anointed one; the Hebrew word is Ha-Mashiach (Ps. 18:50).[44] The Messiah is addressed by the Talmud as Saviour and Redeemer. It is incongruent to restrict Messiah to an ordinary but outstanding human being.

In a discussion of repentance and atonement, Cohen quotes Talmudic opinion.

> The Rabbis declared that repentance was one of the things which were designed by God even before the world itself was formed. "Seven things were created before the Universe came into being. They are: Torah, Repentance, Paradise, Gehinnom, The Throne of Glory, The Sanctuary, and the name of Messiah."[45]

The Talmud is very explicit in the belief that the Messiah provides redemption through repentance when God's law has been transgressed.

> Great is repentance, for it reaches to the Throne of Glory.
> Great is repentance, for it makes the redemption (by the Messiah) to come near.[46]

Repentance is a gift the sinner claims when the sinner makes a claim on Messianic redemption. One must conclude the Talmudic teaching: that the Messiah is born as a human, that it is an incarnation. He has eternal pre-existence, and therefore He will arrive as an incarnation. It could be interpreted that God, before the creation of the world, assigned Himself the work of redemption by the concept that He Himself would be the redeemer.

And again, in exalting charity, the Talmud exudes Messiah. "Great is charity, for it brings the Redemption (of the Messiah) near."[47] The Messiah figures in the final judgement of the world. The great and vital question He poses to the accused who broke God's law is, "Did you hope for the salvation of the Messiah?" So the Messiah is the saviour of the world.[48]

The conclusion is that God Himself manifests Himself as the plural Elohim, the one God, who expresses Himself in the roles of Ruach Hakodesh and Ha-Mashiach. This is not a departure from monotheism—it is an amplification of monotheism. God is omnipotent and manifests His power to restore humanity to immortality by His own deity. His law is obeyed through the perfect provision of Ha-Mashiach. There is nothing in the Tanak that contradicts this dictum. It is an axiom of fallen humanity that no human is perfect. "All we like sheep have gone astray; we have turned everyone to his own way, and the Lord hath laid on Him the iniquity of us all" (Isa. 53:6, KJV). *The Jewish Study Bible—Tanakh Translation* amplifies this statement.

> We all went astray like sheep, Each going his own way; And the Lord visited upon Him The guilt of us all. (Isa. 53:6)

> But we are *all* as an unclean thing, And *all* our righteousness are as filthy rags; And we *all* do fade as a leaf, And our iniquities, like the wind, Have taken us away. (Isa. 64:6, KJV; emphasis added)

Again, *The Jewish Study Bible* proclaims in Isa. 64:5-6 (emphasis added):

> It is because You are angry that we have sinned; We have been steeped in them from of old, And can we be saved? We have *all* become an unclean thing, And *all* our virtues

like a filthy rag. We are *all* withering like leaves, And our
iniquities, like a wind, carry us off.

The Tanak does not teach a final state of perfection having
been achieved by repeated trying and repeated reincarnations
(Kabbalah). The Book of Isaiah clearly declares that "all [are]
become an unclean thing," and the Messiah bears all our iniquities
and forgives us. That is what happens on the Tanakian Day of
Atonement. All Israel is cleansed of all her iniquities by the
propitiation of the sin offering, the blood in the Most Holy Place.
Forgiveness makes all perfect before God. The Messianic redeemer
provides that perfection.

Isaiah further declares the oneness of the Messiah with God:

> Surely You are Our Father: Though Abraham regard us not
> And Jacob recognize us not You, O Lord, are our Father;
> From of old, Your name is "Our Redeemer." (Isa. 63:16,
> *The Jewish Study Bible*)

In the beginning God was creator, companion, and redeemer. His
Ruach Hakodesh power gives the gift of repentance and nourishes
and sanctifies us. God's Ha-Mashiach power redeems us and
restores us to immortality. "Hear O Israel, the Lord our God is
One." In the beginning Elohim.

CHAPTER 5

LOVE AND INSPIRATION

The word "'inspiration" indicates a relationship between two constructs. For our purposes in this setting, it is the relationship between God and a human being to whom a message is imparted. Originally there was a face-to-face communion in which an intermediary was not necessary, but that was lost when Eden was lost.

God is always on the lookout for people through whom He can work. That human being becomes inspired because he is in a special relationship with God and receives the message from God. The message is perceived by that human through his brain, which orients it in a setting containing all the past experiences, thoughts, and personality of that individual. That individual understands the message, coloured by who he is and what he knows. But there is a certain divine guidance implied, which is governed and measured by the influence of that individual's relationship with God. The human factors can be overwhelmed by the message. But these pre-existent human factors in the brain do not disappear, and neither are they necessarily excluded. The message is couched in human terms; it is clothed in the garb of that person's complex neural makeup, the language of contemplation and understanding, and the ability of expression. That person does not absorb deity. The message is divine in source, expressed and coloured by the blemishes of his make-up, but its source is divine. It cannot be claimed to be absolutely within the bounds of what existed in the divine intention. The message can be flawed, but it will be delivered from that human in harmony with the great principles of life and love, apparent in God's government. The messenger has his life in tune with God. The message conforms to the divine attributes that he perceives and to which he is loyal.

Inspiration implies closeness to God. God has chosen that person for that purpose, and that is what gives the message authority. Why is authority a necessary quality? It is necessary to be able to command attention, acceptance, and obedience to the message. Deity is the key factor in that authority. The message accrues authority to the degree that it can show and prove the closeness of the message to the mind of God. Are there degrees of closeness? Are there degrees of authority, which are imbued by the estimates of closeness? Should not the conviction that the message comes from God be sufficient to command all or complete authority? Does the quality of closeness to God take away the ability of the person to whom the message is given, and to question the logic and import of the message? Does the authenticity of the message imply that it should be obeyed? Does the human mind's ability to understand the message play a part in determining the obedience it should command? The answers to these questions are difficult, and deep pondering is necessary to fathom the depths of the human understanding of God's desired affinity to the human race. These questions imply the closeness to God that He is using to communicate with humans, and they fathom the core meaning of devekut.

There are human characteristics that theoretically make it difficult for God (or the messenger of God) to penetrate. Therefore it behoves the recipient and the people for whom the message is intended to realise that human frailties and misunderstandings can cloud the message, its intent and content, and the human understanding where it is received. Does this make the message flawed so that it should be disregarded? The message should always be in harmony with God's original intention and blueprint, given in the primitive situation. The Eden story becomes the great foundation and governing statement, which establishes the redemptive nature of God's plan. Therefore, Judaism cannot and should not forsake the nature of the redemptive plan of God as its cornerstone. Primitive Judaism is totally congruent with the Eden story. When it forsakes that redemptive plan, it becomes garbled and philosophic, and it loses its practicality and usefulness in the lives of its adherents. It is by inspiration that the Tanak was produced over a thousand years. If the principles already laid down by God in the Torah are contravened, then any message should be doubted and checked for conceptual and contextual compatibility; if it does not measure up, it should be discarded. If messages from other writings such as the Mishnah and Gemara are not in harmony with the Tanak, then they should be discarded. As Israel's only canon, the Tanak cannot be set aside; it is supreme.

Inspiration is God's necessary vehicle to communicate. The Tanak attests to the fact that God used it to enhance His redemptive nature. This was already laid down in the eternal Torah of the mind of God, and the Talmud wholeheartedly agrees. God's interference with humanity is for the sole purpose of reclaiming humanity as His work of Creation, with which He was "well pleased." The Tanak is inspired, has stood the test of time, and has influenced the whole world in all ages. It continues to do so. Therefore it is the definitive Torah of Jewish and all human existence.

How did inspiration come to exist? It is a gift from God. The Ruach Hakodesh or Holy Spirit is the divine agent effecting inspiration. The nature and work of the Ruach Hakodesh is discussed fully in the chapter titled "The Eschatology of the Tanak." Suffice it to say for now that the Ruach Hakodesh is God Himself. The Talmud does not deny this. The Lord our God is one, blessed be He. The conviction that the human messenger is inspired is based on God's acceptance of that human messenger. He is fertile ground for the Holy Spirit to inspire. The access available and the communion with the Ruach Hakodesh are important factors. Confidence is established in the messenger by the demonstration of the harmony of the lifestyle with Torah. Every author of the Tanak can be evaluated; every one of them passes the test, and every one of them believed in the Eden story. It was the yardstick the Sanhedrin used to choose the books for inclusion in the Tanak, and the firebrand that made them close it. The Holy Spirit was the instrument that created the Tanak through the intermediaries chosen.

No inspiration is available apart from the Holy Spirit. The work of the Holy Spirit on the heart of the hearer of the message is also necessary. The interpretation, belief, and action that follow the hearing of the message is again the work of the Holy Spirit. Does that mean that the messenger must be infallible? Certainly not, because the Eden story clearly states that fallibility and mortality became the lot of all humanity after disobedience to Torah. So humanity must labour on with the essential guidance of the Holy Spirit. Possession of the Tanak gives post-Tanakian humanity a huge advantage. They live with hindsight, and this brings a clarity of the divine plan to human understanding. Civilization thus has a great blueprint already outlined for what God wants for us. Thank you, Moses and the authors of the Tanak.

The Holy Spirit constantly speaks to the mind of every human born on the planet. Unfortunately, some people, by their place and culture of birth, are not as readily accessed. But there exists in every human a sense of justice, fairness, and need for love (even though in some very evil humans, there seems to be hardly any traces of these), and this is the work of the Holy Spirit. Inspiration resulted from God's continuing desire to talk to His children, and the Holy Spirit is the vehicle, or God in the act of wooing us. It is God Himself persevering in this universal effort to win us back. The message is a conversation with God. God's longing for a companionship with humanity has only intensified over the thousands of years since Eden. There is a happy progression in this effort as the Tanak outlines a very glorious future, an eschatology to achieve His goal. The Messianic consummation is coming; it is restorative, apocalyptic, and utopian. All the Tanakian prophets wrote of it. Gershom Scholem argued for this and believed it with all his heart.

The story of Eden is enchanting. The work of the Holy Spirit immediately took over when the face-to-face communion with God ceased. From where did Moses get the story? It came from God by inspiration. It came down orally, through the Patriarchs: Adam, Abel, Seth, Enosh, Cainan, Mahalalel, Jared, Enoch, Methuselah, Lamech, Noah, Abraham, and Jacob. There likely were others (1

Chron. 1:1). This story that had been orally transmitted benefited from being written down by Moses in the Hebrew language. Moses had the capability of writing the story down. because he was educated in the universities of Egypt. Did the original story get coloured by his education? We must assume so, because he was human. Did it decrease his authority or clarity or degree of inspiration? The original story is so simple that we are hard put to make it more complicated, unless we place it in the straightjacket of what we have qualified as science, having set up the rules for that straightjacket. The original story is scientific in certain respects, but not in every respect. We must allow for how things that were created came into being, composed of matter and energy. The record tells us that "God spake and it was done"—energy. "He commanded and it stood fast"—matter (Ps. 33:9). There is a lot to fathom here. Moses did not have all the modern knowledge of science when he wrote down the story; it came garbed in the understanding of his time.

The Creation story, the simple Eden story, is the source of the whole meaning of the Tanak. It became defined by the inspired Moses and went on to include the early history of the Hebrews. It introduces the next great theme of the Torah: the Abrahamic Covenant. The Hebrew race was chosen by God as a special vehicle in His great redemptive plan, which would eventuate in the Messiah.

Why should humanity pay any special attention to the Hebrews? It is because God chose to be strongly present in their existence. His desires are vital; He demands attention from the humans he created. The Hebrews are His choice as the vehicle for his machinations. The Hebrews embraced this calling of God, so it all stems from the Eden story and the Abrahamic Covenant. They connect God and humanity, the Creator and the created. Why did God create? The only answer we have is that He did it for His pleasure (Prov. 16:4). If you do not believe in God, the Eden story is meaningless. But the Eden story is carried in the abstract setting, which is what scientists who do not believe in God are wont to do, because they cannot understand infinity in terms of God. There is no satisfactory explanation of the cosmos, of the existence of matter and energy, other than in terms of God. People ask the question, "And what, pray you, existed before God?" The answer is, "Nothing, because God is infinite; He always existed." The scientist who does not believe in God must also ask the question, "And what existed before infinity?" He answers his own question: "Nothing, stupid, because infinity has no beginning or ending." Moses was governed by his humanity. He had to have a "beginning," and he did splendidly by the initial powerful words of his narrative: "In the beginning God . . ." Does infinity have a beginning? It cannot by simple definition, because the quality of infinity is defined as there being no beginning and no ending. Moses understood it within the scope of his Egyptian education and within the scope of the primitive Torah passed down to him. This education shaped the expression and provided the background context. He was talking to humans, who are born and die, and so he started with a beginning for humans, which in his understanding was God, because God was there at humanity's beginning. Moses believed that God by definition has no beginning and no ending. The Hebrew story of Eden is unsurpassed and is the foundation stone of the story of Judaism. Full marks to Moses for preserving it!

The story of Eden is the foundation setting of inspiration. It continued as a necessity for the beginning of human life, the beginning of the relationship (a love relationship) between God and humanity. Do not scoff, because no one truly understands love, either human love or divine love. Love in the human setting started its existence in Eden: love between God and humanity, and love between humans. love is the dominant quality in the universe, because as soon as existence takes place, there is love. Scientific thought has not as yet fathomed love. Life exists for love. Love is essential for fullness of life. And so there was in humanity's existence divine love, reaching out to Adam and Eve. They were in a love relationship with God, and there was also love between them, so they were able to understand God's emotion of love for them. As soon as life starts, it is bathed in the pervading perfume of God's love. There is nothing more perfect than God as life and love; it is the story of Eden and the foundation of the world. The love relationship between God and humanity is the beginning of human Torah. Torah is the love, communion, and communication between the two partners, the divine and the human. The Hebrews call it devekut. "And the Lord God walked in the Garden in the cool of the day and called out: Adam, where art thou? God was motivated to express His love and went searching for them" (Gen. 3:8-9). When God said, "Let us make man in our own image" (Gen. 1:26), He was talking of love. The capability of loving is the greatest and most complete likeness between God and humans, not hands and feet. The brain is the organ of love in humans, and it develops to capture every expression of love that all the senses provide. The brain rules the rest of the body in the expression of love. That love relationship between God and humans was necessarily endowed with free will in order to prevent the creature from being the puppet of the Creator. In true love, there can be no puppets.

Love cannot exist in the absence of free will. Forced love without consent is not love, but rape and slavery. There is no such thing as forced love. Love must be voluntary and be aroused from inner magnetism and intense desire. When expressed, it inspires a response and solicits reciprocity. This quality has no scientific explanation. Sexual love may have the impetus and stimulating energy of hormones, but science cannot explain its origin in the bodily being. Science cannot explain the chemical enhancement of the capability of sexual expression and enjoyment in the brain. Neither can science explain asexual love—not yet. That twinkle in the eye in our close friendships, that marvellous thrill of desire for unity with another being in our intimate spousal sexuality, is in the genes. It has yet to command rational explanation. And by assumption, divine love has primacy and has the quality of enduring, because divinity is infinite, and divinity has sole possession of perfect love, transcending all human thought. Jeremiah spoke of it:

> The Lord hath appeared of old unto me, saying, *Yea, I have loved thee with an everlasting love:* therefore with lovingkindness have I drawn thee. (Jer. 31:3, KJV; emphasis added)

More incisive and to the point, and putting it into the historical perspective of Creation, is the Jewish translation:

> The Lord revealed Himself to me of old. *Eternal love I conceived for you then;* Therefore I continue My *Grace* to you. (Jer. 31:3, *The Jewish Study Bible*; emphasis added)

How marvellous is grace—unmerited favour, unmerited perfect love. It is another view of redemption, and it reflects a reclamation, a restoration. It was conceived of old by God. Grace was in the eternal Torah of the mind of God.

Robert Browning has immortalized this love affair between God and humans on a very tender personal basis, in his poem:

God, Thou Art Love

> If I forget,
> Yet God remembers! If these hands of mine
> Cease from their clinging, yet the hands divine
> Hold me so firmly that I cannot fall;
> And if sometimes I am too tired to call
> For Him to help me, then He reads the prayer
> Unspoken in my heart, and lifts my care.
>
> God, Thou art love! I build my faith on that.
> I know Thee Who has kept my path, and made
> Light for me in the darkness, tempering sorrow
> So that it reached me like a solemn joy:
> It were too strange that I should doubt Thy love.

No one can adequately challenge the closeness Robert Browning had with his God. It recalls Jacob and God clinging tenaciously to each other at the Brook Jabbok (Gen. 32).

The Jewish poem Hadamut, in the Aramaic language, was composed in the year 1096 in Germany by Rabbi Mayer, son of Isaac Nehoral. Nehoral was a cantor in the city of Worms, Germany. Hadamut praises God as the creator and ruler of the world, and he names Israel as the chosen people to propagate that love. Hadamut extols the giving of the Ten Commandments on Mount Sinai. Hadamut is recited or sung on the first day of the Feast of Shavuot, celebrated seven weeks after Passover. In this poem, Hadamut captured the imagination of the German Christian named Frederick Martin Lehman, who was born in Mecklenburg, Schwerin, Germany. He used its history and theme, which encapsulates the following poem, the third verse of which is excerpted from the Hadamut poem:

> The Love of God is greater far, Than human tongue or pen can tell.
> It goes beyond the highest star and reaches to the lowest hell.
> The guilty pair, bowed down with care, God gave Himself to win;
> His erring child, He reconciled and pardoned from his sin.
>
> When years of time shall pass away, And earthly thrones and kingdoms fall,
> When men who here refuse to pray, On rocks and hills and mountains call,
> God's love so sure, shall still endure, All measureless and strong;
> Redeeming grace to Adam's race—The saints' and angels' song.
>
> "Could we with ink the ocean fill and were the skies of parchment made,
> Were every stalk on earth a quill and every man a scribe by trade;
> To write the love of God above, Would drain the ocean dry;
> Nor could the scroll contain the whole, Though spread from sky to sky."

> O love of God, So rich and pure, So measureless and strong
> It shall forevermore endure, The saints' and angels' song.[49]

The Eden story written by Moses explains the dialogue between God and humanity, and it is a love story indeed. It can be described as the original devekut (meaning communion with God).

Inspiration is a substitute at best, but it is all we have left of a much greater and closer communion with God. It can still be a close and rich communion through the continued ministration of the Ruach Hakodesh. The beginning of earthly Torah in human existence was face-to-face, which God relished, and to which humanity responded with a sense of belonging to Him and a voluntary immersion in His divine love. There were conditions to it. The conditions were the proper exercise of free will. This gave humanity choice. The cohabitation with God had to be one of choice, and Adam and Eve had to refrain from eating of the Tree of Knowledge of Good and Evil to consolidate that choice. Their loyalty was a means of expressing their love for God. This was lost with humanity's choice of the knowledge of evil. Finiteness was embraced as death passed upon all humans. Inspiration became the substitute for the achievement of authenticity. Voice to ear, mind to mind, and visions and dreams are substitutes. Inspired people such as priests, judges, kings, and prophets became intermediaries between God and humans. The motivation came largely from divine endeavour, but it also fulfilled the longing in many human hearts. The command "Let them make me a sanctuary that I may dwell among them" was a very pushy request. There was one huge reason for God's persistence: He wanted the face-to-face, two-party love relationship to be restored, and that had to come through God's own plan—the plan of redemption, mediated by Ruach Hakodesh and Ha-Mashiach. These were measures to restore the Edenic perfection. This is the root of Judaism as a redemptive religion. It was expressed at the Gates of Eden, enshrined in the Abrahamic Covenant, and beamed from Mt. Sinai. These were all harbingers of the promised Messiah. God's deep longings of love to again be in face-to-face communion and love relationship with humans burned intensely in His bosom.[50]

The Tanak, a document produced by many authors (and editors) who were inspired, was compiled by an inspired Sanhedrin and invested with such great authority that it was labelled "inspired and sacred." A further quality was bestowed on it by "closure." In the case of the Tanak, closure bound, protected, sealed, and insulated it. Closure bars addition to or subtraction from the Tanak, and this enhances its authority and standing.

The Tanak is the document produced by God's love and human inspiration. It has become the dominant governing authority for those who live by it. It is interpreted as the voice of God; this attribute is so strong that its interpretation has led to plurality and divisiveness. Agreement concerning its meanings and intentions has become so varied that the uninitiated have to rely on others for reliability of the proposed interpretation, and they make decisions based on those interpretations. The variability has led to the rise of groups who have agreed with certain interpretations in the name of religious liberty. The lack of agreement can lead also to aggression and violence between the groups. To me, the Tanak is communication from God, clothed in the earthly garb of its inspired but human authors. I bow to the wisdom of the authors, editors, and compilers, and to the authoritative body that instituted closure. Its basic concept of redemption, when realised, binds humans together and destroys divisiveness and its ensuing chaos.

Inspiration does not mean that the authors, editors, and compilers were infallible and that every clause is fixed in one expounded meaning. The Tanak must bear a sensible and reasonable interpretation that does not contradict itself, and that can be made for my time, even though written several thousand years ago. That is why it is an enduring document. Unity is absolutely essential, conceptually and contextually, in interpretation. The direction of travel cannot seek diversion or deviation from the primary aim, which is to restore a face-to-face love relationship with the Creator. God's intention is redemption. There is no other reason for the existence of Judaism and the authority of the Tanak. In this divine link it cannot be compared to any other epic composition in existence. A humble fisherman, excited and captivated by Yeshua of Nazareth, declared the Tanak to be the writings of "Holy men of God who were moved by the Holy Spirit" (2 Pet. 1:21, KJV). A very erudite member of the Sanhedrin, Saul of Tarsus, also imbued by Yeshua of Nazareth, agreed: "All Scripture [the Tanak] is given by inspiration of God, and is profitable for doctrine, for reproof, for correction, for instruction in righteousness, that the man of God may be perfect, thoroughly furnished unto all good works" (2 Tim. 3:16-17 KJV). That is good advice despite its source. All they had in their minds and hands was the Tanak and its Messianic fulfilment as they saw it, after the arrival of Yeshua of Nazareth; there was no B'rit Hadasha for them to follow. The Tanak was their precious and esteemed document, the written product of inspiration and God's love. It was composed of primitive Judaism and Jewish history.

Jacob Neusner, a distinguished research professor of religious studies at the University of South Florida, wrote the preface to Abraham Cohen's *Everyman's Talmud* in the 1995 reprint. He clearly and massively errs when he states that "the Torah—comprising the Hebrew Scriptures or Old Testament AND the oral traditions ultimately preserved in the Talmud—by the faithful of Judaism."[51] He has absolutely no personal or corporate authority to elevate the Talmud into equality with the Tanak into an envelope called the Torah. The Talmud is not Torah. No Sanhedrin has elevated it to such loftiness. The Torah is closed with the Tanak. The Talmud cannot be joined on equal footing to the Tanak. Plato's *Republic*, Aristotle's *Politics*, the Koran, *The Iliad* and *The Odyssey*, the Mahabharata, the Ramayana, and the Talmud may all be great epics—but only Tanak is Torah, the authentic and hallowed conversation of God with humanity.

Several factors determine what the Tanak means to me. It is sacred, by which I mean I regard it as commanding respect and authority and God's expression of love. Its divine concepts encapsulate divine love. It is a message from God, but I must allow for some garbling in its human expression. It is ancient in that it was written in a long, bygone generation and civilization, but it retains its application for my time. The nuances of the language in which it was written must be regarded. And I must pay utmost respect to the concepts and context involved, in order to avoid proof-texting and deviation. A. J. Jacobs, writing in his wonderful book *The Year of Living Biblically*, has warned that God did not sit at his carved oak desk in Heaven and dictate the Tanak to a group of flawless secretaries.[52] The Tanak is also a very human and terrestrial document. Interpretation of the Tanak must pay attention to the goal of the entire book. It must be conceptual and contextual. It must be understood in terms of the age in which it was written, and then applied in our time. And it must be true to the intent of the meaning of the language in which it was written. Its principles are eternal. The timelessness of the applications of the Tanak span the entire human existence.

I arbitrarily divide the Tanak, dating it[53] as being a five-part document concerning five key men. These men were inspired and greatly loved by God. They were all given the same message. Who are they?

1. **Adam:** At the creation of the world, together with his wife, Eve, they were created immortal, endowed with free will, and enjoyed face-to-face communion with God. They were in a solid love relationship with God. This was lost, and mortals needed redemption. The restoration, mediated by the Ruach Hakodesh, became the responsibility of the Patriarchs to follow, culminating in Messianic intervention and redemption.
2. **Noah:** (dated many generations before Abraham): He was entrusted with a brand-new beginning to the redemptive plan after the Flood. Abraham was a descendent from Shem, the son of Noah, through the line of Arphaxad.
3. **Abraham:** (ca. 2165-1990 BC): The call of Abraham and the covenant he made with God started the Jewish story. His journey to Canaan was a far-reaching act of faith.
4. **Jacob:** (grandson of Abraham): He wrestled with God at Jabbok and clung tenaciously to God, to assure himself of his resolve to carry out the Abrahamic Covenant. Because of his faith, God changed his name, and God would cling

to Israel on His own terms, much more tenaciously in the future.

5. **Moses:** (born ca. 1525 BC): His call at the burning bush was a call to lead the Hebrew slaves to the Promised Land. His writings laid down the blueprint of Judaism, the Book of Job and the Pentateuch. Job was likely written while he tended his father-in-law's sheep in Midian, while on self-exile from Egypt, a fugitive from Egyptian justice. The Pentateuch was written at Mt. Sinai.

The history of the children of Israel followed. That history was wayward and stormy. The Tanakian part endured to the time of Malachi, who lived about 424 BC, and comprises the rest of the Tanak. This entire period of writing occupied one thousand years.

These five men were inspired by God to lead in the plan to restore face-to-face communion with God. All five men pointed to the Messiah. The Tanak has the complete story; it is sufficient to bring to pass God's desired plan. The principles and practice of modern Judaism must be subordinated to the Tanak, which God imparted, to guide the Jews in implementing the restoration. Defining the practice of primitive Judaism exemplified by the lives of these men is essential to realising how far current Judaism has strayed.

The result of the combined inspired human talent and divine revelation brought the terrestrial Torah, the Tanak, into existence. It is generally accepted by scholars that the Tanak was completed about 400 BC, compiled by the "men of the Great Assembly." It was not added to after that, and scholars consider that it became closed between 200 BC and AD 200. Some scholars, on the basis of rabbinic utterances, propose the date AD 70 as the official closure of the Tanak. This subject will be discussed in greater detail in the chapter titled "The Tanak."

The veracity of the Tanak has been reinforced by "the discovery in the 1940s and 1950s of a preserved library (the Dead Sea Scrolls) of the so-called Qumran community which must have been part of the Essene movement (formed as an idealization of poverty, celibacy and asceticism). Here were almost all the texts of the Hebrew scriptures, some in multiple copies, dating from a thousand years before any other known Biblical manuscript."[54]

The great love story between God and perfect humanity had its inception in Eden. Following the Fall, inspiration became the substitute for a loss of face-to-face expression of love and connection, outside the gates of Eden. That great love story intensified deeper than it is possible to plumb, when He locked the Gates of Eden with them standing there, staring longingly back at Him with a heartbreak all of their very own. The Tanak is the wondrous document expressing this love story between God and humanity. It contains the definition of that intensified love that broke God's own heart in response. God was now willing to pay the highest price to win humanity back to His bosom. In Isaiah's words, it would "crush" the Ha-Mashiach. Mighty and stupendous is Elohim, the Lord our God is one. Blessed be He.

CHAPTER 6

THE JUDAISM OF THE PATRIARCHS (THE JUDAISM OF THE BLOOD)

Could the religion of the Patriarchs be called primitive Judaism? If it came down from Eden to Abraham in the "primitive oral Torah" and was incorporated by Moses in the Pentateuch, it certainly is primitive Judaism. Who were the Patriarchs? From Adam they were Abel, Seth, Enosh, Kenan, Mahalalel, Jared, Enoch, Methuselah, Lamech, and Noah (Gen. 5). There possibly were gaps of generations here, and despite Ussher's attempt to date the creation of the world, the timeline is difficult to soundly argue. Assuming that the list of named patriarchs is incomplete, the age of the earth exceeds Ussher's attempt to limit time. Despite this, the nature of Torah from Adam to Abraham is not difficult to consolidate. People and events matter more than time. "For a thousand years in Thy sight are but as yesterday when it is past, and as a watch in the night" (Ps. 90:4).

Adam and Eve were created perfect by God. They were immortal, were sinless, and had intimate "face-to-face" communion with God. God's love for them, and their love for Him and each other, were the supreme principles and the exhilarating enjoyment of their existence. Their endowment with willpower and freedom of choice was guaranteed. They loved God in reciprocity because they chose to do so. The great magnetism of love is that it begets love. When their wrong choices separated them from God, they became mortal. They were heartbroken. They were driven from Eden, and then God's plan was laid out to restore them to perfection and immortality. He had planned for a future redeemer who would release them from eternal death, bear their punishment, and restore them to perfection and immortality. There was nothing mystical about this plan, which was to be implemented by their Messianic redeemer God. They were asked to offer a sacrificial lamb as a symbolic substitute, to die on the altar as a burnt offering. They understood perfectly that this was a redemptive act that would be carried out by the coming of the Messiah. They hoped it would be soon because they longed to be back in Eden in the magic of the love relationship with God. That was the deep longing in their souls. This was the basic religion of Adam and Eve, and after they were driven from the Garden, it constituted their reason to go on living; it brought them hope, solace, and happiness. This is a deep-seated quality they discovered in themselves, placed there in their makeup by a compassionate God. God Himself longed for their embrace in a greater and cosmic sense, as well as being a deep, personal emptiness that needed to be filled. Moses saw this, experienced it, and included this story in the first written Torah, which was God's communication, continuing connection, and will for them.

It is fair to say that the glorious future for Adam and Eve centred around the person of Ha-Mashiach, an "anointed one" anointed to be their ticket back into Eden, restoring immortality.[55] Adam and Eve's firstborn was Cain. Eve thought he was the promised Ha-Mashiach, and when she gave birth she said, "I have gotten *the man* from the Lord" (Gen. 4:1; emphasis added). She was anxious to get back to the Edenic state of perfection and love relationship with her God, and she was bitterly disappointed that Cain was not the Ha-Mashiach. The turn of events resulted in Cain becoming the first murderer. He was a tiller of the soil, a farmer, and a fruit tree grower. He was proud of his work and the produce of his fields. He decided that his personal efforts as a farmer should be respected by God, and he found it inconceivable that he should deign to ask his brother Abel, a keeper of sheep, to give him a lamb without blemish to offer as a sacrifice for the propitiation of his sins. He tried to forge a substitute, the work of his hands, as a symbolic Messianic offering. He refused to accept that deity should be his propitiation, and he resolved to do it through his own efforts. God did not accept the offering of the fruits of his field. It was not God's plan for humanity to find substitutes for salvation. God had decided from eternity that He would do it Himself. Some of the rabbinic sages in the Talmud support this realization.[56] Cain got intensely angry, and he rose up and slew his brother. Abel's lamb without blemish was accepted and consumed from on high by God Himself. God does not accept our own righteousness, our own accomplishments of law keeping, which are as filthy rags. He requires that we present His substitutionary Messianic redemption.

> And the Lord had respect unto Abel and to his offering; But unto Cain and to his offering He had not respect. (Gen. 4:4b)

God insists that He will be our redeemer. Here is the earliest example that we cannot keep God's law perfectly and require a substitutionary provision by the Messiah's sacrifice. God's preference of an animal sacrifice to the fruits of the soil *must be explained,* or else we must admit that Cain had an injustice done to him, in that his offering was not respected. It was a big blow to Cain, but it was not unexpected. *The Jewish Study Bible* translates this succinctly.

> The Lord paid heed to Abel and his offering, But to Cain and his offering He paid no heed. Cain was much distressed and his face fell. And the Lord said to Cain: Why are you distressed, And why is your face fallen? Surely, if you do right, There is uplift, But if you do not do right Sin couches at the door; Its urge is towards you, Yet you can be its master. (Gen. 4:4-7)

The situation explained to Cain here by God is very deliberate and points out the abrogation by Cain of the plan God had laid down. "But if you do not do right, Sin couches at the door." So Cain's act of bringing fruits and vegetables was a deliberate act of defiant sin, a rejection of Messianic intervention, and the implication is that Cain knew he was bringing the wrong offering. His attitude to God was, "Take it or leave it, and you'd better take it if you want my worship." Cain's act was one of rebellion. It is very clear that God is saying here that the shedding of the blood of the sacrificial animal pointed to the Messianic propitiation for sin, and it was a defiant and rebellious act of pride to offer fruits and vegetables instead of the required blood.

The entire Aaronic priesthood and Tabernacle Temple services instituted at Mt. Sinai was built on the offering of blood. The spot occupied by the Most Holy Place of the Temple on the Temple Mount is deeply stained with the blood of the animals without blemish offered there. This was indeed the requirement outlined to Adam and Eve and their children. This was Torah, this was primitive Judaism, this was the religion of the Patriarchs. Those who try to substitute the offering of blood are contravening the Messianic sacrifice, and like Cain they become "Ceaseless wanderer[s] on earth . . . and leave the presence of the Lord" (see Gen. 4:8-11, *The Jewish Study Bible*).

Contrary to what the Talmud implies, God does not prefer shepherds to tillers. Since God Himself, blessed be He, is the Messiah, any substitute is a rejection of God. His plan was the offering of the blood, that sin should be punished by the shedding of blood, that the blood of deity is that blood that will be shed. The commentary in *The Jewish Study Bible* recalls Genesis 3, with reference to Cain's disobedience; the primal sin is disobedience of the Torah. Torah calls for propitiation by the shedding of blood. Rejection of the blood was that primal sin outside Eden.

The offering of blood would stand as the great act for the propitiation for sin in the Temple service until the destruction of the Second Temple in AD 70. It was the religion of the Patriarchs. It is heartening that the Day of Atonement is still celebrated and is the holiest day of the Jewish calendar. And the Day of Atonement enacts the carrying of the blood into the Most Holy Place by the high priest. It was splashed on the Mercy Seat and the Ark of the Covenant. The blood cleansed all the sins of all the people. Their repentance led to forgiveness and cleansing by the symbol of the blood, which prefigured the Messianic sacrifice. This is the whole basis of primitive Judaism. The loss of the Second Temple caused the great falling away from Messianic redemptive primitive Judaism and its replacement by Talmudic philosophy. If used as a substitute for the blood, this is a Cain-like substitution, a rebellion against the primitive Judaism proclaimed in the Pentateuch. It is a massive error of Talmudic teaching that the offering of the blood is to be set aside and replaced by "acts of benevolence."[57] This is not a Tanakian teaching—Torah cannot be set aside.

Adam and Eve's next born son was Seth. Again, Eve thought that she had given birth to the Ha-Mashiach. She said, "For God hath appointed me another seed." She wanted the Messiah to appear in her lifetime. Eve was recalling the promise by God made to her after her sin: "I will put enmity between thee and the woman, between thy seed and her seed. It shall bruise thy head and thou shalt bruise its heel" (Gen. 3:15-16, KJV). *The Jewish Study Bible* states this more starkly, intoning deeper meaning.

> I will put enmity between you and the woman, And between your offspring and hers; They shall strike at your head, And you shall strike at their heel.

The Messianic redemptive power would destroy the Serpent.

Seth was a good man and brought up his son Enosh uprightly, whose influence was righteous. The record says that under Enosh's influence, "then began men to call upon the name of the Lord" (Gen. 4:25-26). Men call upon God's name when they require absolution for their sins, and the sacrificial lamb without blemish again provides the blood for the forgiveness of sin.

Subsequently the record mentions the succession of the Patriarchs to Enoch. Enoch lived righteously for 365 years. "And Enoch walked with God, and he was not; for God took him." He was translated to Heaven to be with God eternally. Enoch was granted eternal life on the merits of the Messiah. Judging from the foregoing patriarchal history, the sacrificial lamb provided the symbolic propitiation for his sins, and God took him prematurely. This was the first occasion of God's borrowing against His own plan to pay for sin with Himself. He was using a credit card issued by the eternal riches of the Bank of Heaven! He would borrow again when He took Elijah up to glory. On both occasions God was magnifying the cleansing by the blood of the sacrificial animal. Enoch and Elijah were allowed into heaven by the symbol. God had confidence in Himself—He was to be the Messianic sacrifice, and He would pay the debt.

The patriarchal witness of Enoch, the solid religion of the blood, was a huge triumph of the power of primitive Judaism: The intent of the Torah and Messianic intervention was to restore the perfect Edenic state and immortality.

When we come to Noah, we find that wickedness did abound, and the thoughts of men's hearts were evil continually. They had stopped relying on the blood. "And the Lord regretted that he had made man on the earth and His heart was saddened. The Lord said, I will blot out from the earth the men who I created . . . [But] Noah was a righteous man; he was blameless in his age; Noah walked with God" (Gen. 6:6,8,9). The record says, "And God remembered Noah" (Gen. 8:1, *The Jewish Study Bible*). *The Jewish Study Bible* comments, "The statement that God remembered Noah is the turning point of the whole Flood narrative, marking the triumph of *mercy* over *judgement*" (see margin of p. 23; emphasis added). Messiah is God's vehicle of mercy. Repentance, forgiveness, and propitiation constitute the mechanics of the eradication of sin. Noah built an altar and sacrificed a sin offering, the blood of the lamb without blemish. God made a covenant with Noah, never again to destroy the earth by a flood. He set the rainbow in the rain cloud as a sign (Gen. 8:20-22; 9:8-18).

The religion of all these Patriarchs was redemptive. There is no indication that the primitive Torah outlined salvation and perfection through law keeping, but through the redemptive blood of the animal sacrifice, which symbolized Messianic redemption. In fact, the early example of Cain is abundant evidence that God rejects any attempt at a "do it yourself" religion. There is great merit in benevolence for the praise of our God, but not an atom of it is salvific. Not one subatomic particle underpins or substitutes for Messianic deliverance. God does it all Himself.

CHAPTER 7

THE JUDAISM OF ABRAHAM

Abram was the final patriarch in the line up to come on the scene after Noah. Civilization had again forgotten God, and idolatry was pervasive like the waves on the ocean. Abram cleansed his father's house of idols and preached monotheism. The Abrahamic Covenant is born as God's plan to bring back Edenic perfection and immortality for all humanity. It will be accomplished by the blood. The Abrahamic Covenant is the foundation of Abraham's religion. It embraces land, Torah, and Messiah, and it is repeated here.

> The Lord said to Abram, Go forth from your native land
> And from your father's house To the land that I will show
> you. I will make of you a great nation, And I will bless you;
> I will make your name great, And you shall be a blessing I
> will bless those who bless you And curse him who curses
> you; And all the families of the earth Shall bless themselves
> by you. (Gen. 12:1-3, *The Jewish Study Bible*)

The Jewish Study Bible, commenting on this covenant, states it was born "As an act of God's Grace alone" (p. 30). Here Abram is highly favoured. He is getting a tract of land, his multiplied seed becomes the keepers of the Torah, and his progeny (specifically Messiah) brings happiness to all nations. The covenant is accepted by Abram, who then packs up and leaves Ur of the Chaldees, deep in Mesopotamia, and journeys to the Promised Land. God changes his name to Abraham, and the rite of circumcision becomes the seal of the covenant agreement. The multiplication of his progeny is still a fairy tale to Abraham because he and Sarah are old and childless. Their futile attempt to ensure the future of the covenant by Ishmael is refused by God, who promises that the covenant will be produced through their own fleshly son (Gen. 17). They are still doubtful, and the record says, "Abraham fell on his face and laughed" (Gen. 17:17, KJV). God promises Ishmael a good future also, but the covenant will be with the fleshly son of Abraham and Sarah. The old couple are still in a state of innocent disbelief, and so God actually visits them (in the person of Michael, according to the Talmud) and verbally promises the son. Sarah heard the promise while concealing herself behind the tent door: "Therefore Sarah laughed within herself . . . And the Lord said unto Abraham, Wherefore did Sarah laugh? Then Sarah denied, saying, I laughed not; for she was afraid. And he said, Nay, but thou didst laugh" (Gen. 18:13, KJV). What beautiful banter between creator and creature, caught in the innocent human reality of the frailty of old age. And Isaac was born of old age in the Promised Land. And Sarah laughed again in the realization that she had borne and nursed an infant in her old age. They circumcised Isaac on the eighth day as God had commanded, and Isaac became a signatory to the Abrahamic Covenant. That was the entire reason for circumcision, and nothing more.

But Abraham did not understand the full significance of the covenant until the Mount Moriah experience. What happened on Mount Moriah? To answer this question, one needs to look at the antecedent history of Jerusalem, since the focal point of this city down through the ages is Mount Moriah. It is the drama that occurred here that has made the city of Jerusalem the most sacred on the planet, the centre of Monotheism, and the holiest of places for Judaism and Christianity. For the Jews it began with Abraham and the sacrifice of Isaac.

When Abraham arrived in the Promised Land, one of the first contacts he had was with Melchizedek, King of Salem (Gen. 14). At this point Abraham was still childless. His nephew Lot had gotten into trouble by living in Sodom and was taken captive by the invading kings. These kings had sacked Sodom and Gomorrah and had taken Lot and his family as prisoners. Abraham mustered an army and went after them, defeated them, and brought back his relatives and all the loot the invaders had taken from these cities.

Victorious Abraham was welcomed back by the grateful King Bera of Sodom. Melchizedek, King of Salem, was also in the welcoming committee, providing a feast of bread and wine. Melchizedek is described as "a Priest of God Most High." He blessed Abraham, saying,

> Blessed be Abraham of God Most High, Creator of heaven and earth. And blessed be God Most High, Who has delivered your foes into your hand.

> "And Abraham gave him [Melchizedek] a tenth of everything" (Gen. 14:1-24, *The Jewish Study Bible*).

Melchizedek was the temporal king of Salem and also a priest of the monotheistic God Most High. In Psalm 110, David sings about this Abrahamic victory and contact with Melchizedek. *The Jewish Study Bible* translates the words "malki-tzedek" as "a rightful king," but the margin discussion is convincing that the allusion is to Genesis 14:18 and King Melchizedek (see *The Jewish Study Bible*, p. 1,408). The King James Version translates "malki-tzedek" as Melchizedek. There is a discussion in the Talmud about Melchizedek; he was a Shemite, and as such he was present in Noah's Ark "in the loins of his forefather." The Talmudic discussion is about kindness to animals.[58] The Jerusalem Targum also records this lineage of Melchizedek. Melchizedek was a Shemite, monotheist King of Salem and a priest of God Most High. Salem was the parcel of land that became the nucleus of Jerusalem, and it was a stronghold of monotheism before Abraham arrived there. Abraham acknowledged these facts by paying him tithes, and it is believed he became heir to the parcel of land called Salem, and that is where Abraham would meet his Waterloo. At the time of Abraham, Melchizedek is the only other monotheist the Tanak identifies; they were conjoined as the monotheistic evangelisers of the world. Abraham started by cleansing his father's house of idols and now aimed to wipe out idolatry from the Promised Land. Other scholars imply this as well.[59]

To Abraham, Salem became a sacred place where Mount Moriah was situated. Then Isaac was born and became the precious child through whom all God's promises were to be fulfilled. It seemed cruel to Abraham to reject Ishmael, but Sarah wanted Ishmael and Hagar (the runaway implementation substitute of her own concoction) cast out of the household. Strangely, God approved.

> And God said unto Abraham, Let it not be grievous in thy sight because of the lad and because of thy bondwoman, in all that Sarah hath said unto thee, hearken unto her voice: *for in Isaac shall thy seed be called.* (Gen. 21:12, KJV; emphasis added)

Ishmael and Hagar were sent into the wilderness. God had a future for them, but that is a discussion pursued elsewhere.

Abraham's skirmish and agreement over a well with Abimelech followed, and then came Abraham's Waterloo. *The Jewish Study Bible* best captures the astoundingly dramatic, deeply meaningful, and heartfelt cosmic event.

> "Some time afterward, God put Abraham to the test . . . Take your son the favoured one, Isaac, whom you love, and go to the land of Moriah, and offer him there as a burnt offering, on one of the heights I will point out to you [God is particular about land]. So early next morning, Abraham saddled his ass and took with him two of his servants and his son Isaac. He split the wood for the burnt offering, and he set out for the place of which God had told him. On the third day Abraham looked up and saw the place from afar. Then Abraham said to his servants, You stay here with the ass. The boy and I will go up there, *We will worship and we will return to you.*
>
> Abraham took the wood for the burnt offering and put it on his son Isaac. He himself took the firestone and the knife; and the two walked off together. Then Isaac said to his father Abraham, Father! And he answered, Yes, my son.

And he said, Here are the firestone and the wood; but where is the sheep for the burnt offering? And Abraham said, God will see to the sheep for His burnt offering, my son. And the two of them walked on together. They arrived at the place of which God had told him. Abraham built an altar there; he laid out the wood; he bound his son Isaac; he laid him on the altar, on top of the wood. And Abraham picked up the knife to slay his son. Then an angel of the Lord called to him from heaven: Abraham! Abraham! . . . Do not raise your hand against the boy, or do anything to him. For now I know that you fear God, since you have not withheld your son, your favoured one, from Me . . . . And Abraham named that site Adonai-yireh, whence the present saying, On the mount of the Lord there is vision. The angel of the Lord called to Abraham the second time from heaven, and said, by Myself I swear, the Lord declares: Because you have done this and have not withheld your son, your favoured one, I will bestow My Blessing [My Son] upon you and make your descendants as numerous as the stars . . . . All the nations of the earth shall bless themselves [with My Blessing, My Son] by your descendants, because you have obeyed My command. (Gen. 22:1-18; emphasis added)

Human sacrifice was a cruel, disgusting, heathen practice in the time of Abraham. The Tanak has a lot to say about it. *The Jewish Encyclopedia* summarizes the matter well. The god to whom human sacrifice was made was Molech in the Masoretic text, and Moloch in the Septuagint. Molech is first mentioned in Leviticus 18:21: "Do not allow any of your offspring to be offered up to Molech . . . I am the Lord." The prohibition is repeated in Leviticus 20:1-6: "Anyone among the Israelites, or among the strangers residing in Israel, who gives any of his offspring to Molech, shall be put to death." In 1 Kings 11, Solomon's great sin was outlined, for which the punishment was the division of Israel into two kingdoms, which greatly weakened Israel and resulted in the slide into national oblivion; Israel did not recover till AD 1948.

At that time Solomon built a shrine for Chemosh the abomination of Moab on the hill near Jerusalem, and one for Molech the abomination of the Amorites. And he did the same for all his foreign wives who offered and sacrificed to their gods.

Second Kings 23 tells of Josiah's reforms when he destroyed the shrines Solomon had built for his foreign wives' gods, particularly Molech. *The Jewish Study Bible* confirmed these dreadful abominations in numerous places.

- Jeremiah 32:35 "They placed their abominations in the house which bears My name and defiled it, and they built the shrines of Baal which are in the Valley of Ben-hinnom, where they offered up their sons and daughters to Molech."
- Jeremiah 7:31: "And they have built the shrines of Topheth in the Valley of Ben-hinnom to burn their sons and daughters in fire—which I never commanded, which never came to My mind."[60]
- Ezekiel 20:26: "When they set aside every issue of the womb" indicate links to God requiring dedication of their firstborn to Him in Exodus 22:28 and 34:19.[61]
- Amos 5:26 (KJV): "But ye have borne the tabernacle of your Moloch and Chiun, your images, the star of your god, which ye made to yourselves. Therefore will I cause you to go into captivity beyond Damascus, saith the Lord, whose name is The God of hosts."

God never condoned human sacrifices. Human sacrifices in Israel might have been perceived as "extraordinary offerings to YHVH," according to some critical scholars.[62] The motive of these sacrifices is not far to seek. It is given in Micah 6:7: "Shall I give my firstborn for my transgression, the fruit of my body for the sin of my soul?" In the midst of the disasters which were befalling the nation men felt that if the favour of YHVH could be regained it was worth any price they could pay (*The Jewish Study Bible*).[63]

It is quite clear that God's request of Abraham for the sacrifice of Isaac was not a condoning of human sacrifice to Himself. Abraham

did not recognize it as such. Abraham appears very definite that no
harm would come to Isaac, that he would never kill and burn his
son. His faith in God was colossal. He told the two servants to tarry
with the ass at the certain spot while he and his son went further on
to worship. He said quite emphatically, "We will worship and we
will return to you." It is so satisfying to repeat it:

"We will worship and we will return"

Great was Abraham's faith, and when Isaac asked where the
sacrificial sheep was, Abraham replied, "God will see to the sheep
for His burnt offering." But he dared God to the last second,
bound his son, placed him on the altar, and raised the knife of
death. Rembrandt has immortalized that moment in time with his
extraordinarily beautiful painting of deep spiritual meaning, *The
Sacrifice by Abraham.*

For millennia the rabbinic sages of Israel have been wondering why
this deed is recorded by Moses, and none has come to a satisfactory
conclusion from the Jewish point of view. It is a mind boggling
enigma to Jews with no agreed spiritual meaning, and it does not
fit into "nonheathen," clear Jewish thinking. Some are so perplexed
that they wish Moses had not recorded such a story. The attempted
Talmudic explanation is extremely poignant: Abraham Cohen in
Everyman's Talmud discusses it under the heading of "God and the
Universe," in the subsection of "Angelology." The Talmud labels
Satan as a fallen angel, one who repeatedly challenges God. This
story in the Talmud best explains Abraham's handling of God's
"unreasonable" request. I quote Abraham Cohen.

> The Scriptures relate, "Abraham made a great feast on the
> day that Isaac was weaned" (Genesis 21:8). On this verse
> the Talmud tells: "Satan said before the Holy One, blessed
> be He, 'Sovereign of the Universe! Thou didst graciously
> bestow offspring on this old man [Abraham] at the age
> of a hundred years; and of all the feasts he made [at the
> weaning] he did not offer a single dove or pigeon [the
> cheapest of sacrifices] unto Thee!' He [God] replied to him,

'Did he not do it all for the sake of his son? If I were to tell him to sacrifice his son unto Me, he would immediately obey'" (Sanh. 89b).

Having in this way been responsible for the test, Satan proceeds to make it fail in its purpose. Samael came to see our father Abraham and said to him, "Old man, old man, have you lost your senses? Are you going to slay a son who was granted to you when you were a hundred years old?" "Certainly," said Abraham. "And should God impose still severer tests upon you, will you be able to endure them?" "I will," he answered, "even stronger than this one." "But tomorrow He will say to you, Shedder of blood! You are guilty of having shed the blood of your son!" "Even so," said Abraham, "I must obey."

Seeing that he [Satan] could not succeed with him, he went to Isaac and said, "Son of an unhappy mother, your father is going to slay you." Isaac replied, "Nevertheless I must submit." Then Satan said, "And all the beautiful garments which your mother made for you will pass into the possession of Ishmael, the enemy of your house; do you pay no attention to that?" Although the whole of it did not enter (Isaac's mind), part of it did; so it is written, "And Isaac spoke unto Abraham his father and said, My father" (Genesis 22:7). "Father" is mentioned twice, indicating Isaac's wish that Abraham should be filled with compassion towards him. (Gen. R. LVI. 4).[64]

This story from the Talmud tells us a lot. It is a tantalizing altercation occurring between God and Satan, possibly in some level of heaven or the nether region. But it does not tell us of the divine significance there is to Abraham's sacrifice of Isaac. For that we must go to the prophet Isaiah. His whole book is oriented to Messianic redemption by the divine redeemer. The birth of the redeemer is announced as the birth of an earthly infant, but lo and behold the infant turns out to be divine.

> For unto us a Child is born, unto us a Son is given. And the government shall be upon His shoulder; And His name shall be called Wonderful, Counsellor, The Mighty God, the Everlasting Father, the Prince of Peace. Of the increase of His government and peace there shall be no end, Upon the throne of David, and upon his kingdom To order it, and to establish it. With justice and with righteousness From henceforth even forever. (Isa. 9:6-7, KJV)

The Messiah is deity, very God, the Lord our God is one Lord. Messiah is not a separate entity. He is God, and He comes in His Messianic power, the function to restore immortality and perfection to the human race. And "He is brought as a Lamb to the slaughter" (Isa. 53:7). The Messiah will lay down His life for the human race, to cleanse and reinstate us to Edenic perfection. That was the message God wanted to impart to Abraham. He was not requesting a sacrifice as to Molech. He was enunciating His coming as the lamb without blemish, the blood sacrifice for sin. The message to Abraham was: Abraham, I will spare your son but my son, deity's penetrance of humanity, will die to save the human race. The father and the son are one and the same in deity. They are not separate in identity. Isaiah 53 is sheer beautiful poetry describing the glorious, loving, pitiful, and powerful divine condescension and agony. Such beautiful musical poetry does not exist anywhere else. King David danced to it. Although I love the King James Version translation, *The Jewish Study Bible* does the better rendition:

> Who can believe what we have heard?
> Upon whom has the arm of the Lord been revealed?
> For He has grown, by His favour, like a tree crown,
> Like a tree trunk out of arid ground.
> He has no form or beauty that we should look at Him.
> No charm that we should find Him pleasing.
> He was despised, shunned by men,
> A man of suffering, familiar with disease.
> As one who hid His face from us
> He was despised, we held Him of no account.

Yet it was our sickness that He was bearing,
Our suffering that He endured.
We accounted Him plagued,
Smitten and afflicted by God;
But He was wounded because of our sins,
Crushed because of our iniquities.
He bore the chastisement that made us whole,
And by His bruises we were healed.
We all went astray like sheep,
Each going his own way;
And the Lord visited upon Him
The guilt of all of us.

He was maltreated, yet He was submissive,
He did not open His mouth;
Like a sheep being led to slaughter,
Like a ewe, dumb before those who shear her,
He did not open His mouth.
By oppressive judgement He was taken away,
Who could describe His abode?
For He was cut off from the land of the living
Through the sin of my people, who deserved the punishment.
And His grave was set among the wicked,
And with the rich, in His death
Though He had done no injustice
And had spoken no falsehood.
But the Lord chose to crush Him by disease,
That, if He made Himself an offering for guilt,
He might see His offspring and have long life,
And that through Him the Lord's purpose might prosper.
Out of His anguish He shall see it;
He shall enjoy it to the full through His devotion.

My Righteous Servant makes the many righteous,
It is their punishment that He bears;
Assuredly, I will give Him the many as His portion,
He shall receive the multitude as His spoil.

> *For He exposed Himself to death*
> And was numbered among the sinners,
> Whereas *He bore the guilt of the many*
> *And made intercession for sinners.*

Most Jewish rabbinic sages miss Isaiah's Messianic intent of this chapter. There are those who would impute this description to King Hezekiah, and others who contend that Hezekiah was the Messiah's forerunner.[65] But Rabbi Judah the Prince, redactor of the Mishnah, is the only one of the great sages who identifies the Messiah in Isaiah 53. How marvellous! I quote Abraham Cohen:

> Biblical passages which were interpreted in a Messianic sense afforded a variety of names by which He would be called. Certain rabbinic* students even exercised their ingenuity to discover for Him [Messiah] a name similar to that borne by their teacher. What is the Messiah's name?
>
> The School of R. Sheila said, Shiloh (Genesis 49:10)
>
> The School of R. Jannair declared, Jinnon (Psalm 72:17)
>
> The School of R. Chaninah said, I will show you no favour (Jeremiah16:13)
>
> Others [schools] contend . . . Menachem son of Hezekiah (Lamentations 1:16) as it is said, The Comforter that should refresh my soul is far from me. *The Rabbis maintain that his name is "the leprous one of the School of R. Judah the Prince," as it is said "Surely he hath borne our griefs and carried our sorrows; yet we did esteem him stricken, SMITTEN OF GOD, and afflicted" (Isaiah 53:40).*[66]

In his notes Cohen explains the term "leprous" used for the Messiah's name.

> The verse therefore foreshadowed a Messiah who would suffer from leprosy. It is told of R. Judah the Prince that

though he was grievously smitten with illness for thirteen years, yet he used to say, 'Beloved are sufferings', as a sign of God's mercy (B.M. 85a). Accordingly it was remarked that the Messiah, as prophesied by Isaiah, would belong to the type exemplified by this Rabbi.[67]

Leprosy in the Tanak is frequently equated with sinfulness—for example, Miriam in Numbers 12:10, Gehazi in 2 Kings 5, and Uzziah in 2 Chronicles 26:19. Therefore it is totally appropriate that the Messiah of Isaiah is burdened with leprosy, the leprous sin of the whole world. R. Judah the Prince believed totally in Isaiah's Messiah. The Lord chose to crush Himself with the disease of leprosy, the leprous sin of the whole world.

Cohen further states:

> Mention is made of a rather mysterious figure called Messiah son of Joseph. The passage reads: 'Messiah son of Joseph was slain, as it is written, "They shall look unto me whom they have pierced; and they shall mourn for him as one mourneth for his only son (Zechariah 12:10).[68]

This is explained as in "Son of David," as meaning the ancestral Joseph, son of Jacob. Both David and Joseph are Messianic type figures who saved their people. Therefore this reference in the Talmud should not be concluded as applying to Joseph, the husband of Mary, mother of Yeshua of Nazareth. Zechariah, however, presses the piercing as an injury inflicted on the Messiah.

Did Abraham on Mount Moriah understand that he was linking heaven and earth in the challenge he posed to God's unreasonable request? Did he realise he was enacting God's penetration of humanity with his divinity, which would be the propitiation for the sins of the whole world? Abraham and God dared each other, and they both demonstrated the total unselfishness of each other. Every time he offered the blood of a lamb without blemish for the propitiation of his sins, Abraham was enacting redemptive, primitive Judaism. Abraham, the last of the chain of Patriarchs before the Jews were installed as the chosen people, was steeped in redemptive primitive Judaism, the Judaism of the blood. It is no wonder that God loved Abraham so much. Abraham is called the friend of God (2 Chron. 20:7; Isa. 41:8).

The religion of the Patriarchs was indeed redemptive. They extolled the Torah, but they relied on Messianic redemption for salvation. Abraham did not seek salvation by good works. Nor did he ever contend that perfect obedience to the Torah for salvation was humanly possible. If it were possible, why would God need to implement Messiah? Abraham achieved perfection through the forgiveness of sin by placing his sin and guilt on the sacrificial Lamb Without Blemish, the atonement by the blood.

As pointed out already, Abraham (Gen. chapters 11-30) did not concoct a religion to start the Jews off. He already had embraced a primitive oral Torah, inherited from the foregoing Patriarchs. His religion was redemptive. Recognising his sins, he made animal sacrifices to atone, as did his ancestors Adam and Abel and all the others in the line to Noah. Abel's murder in defending the ritual, which pointed to the Messianic sacrifice, is incontrovertible. A substitute sacrifice—in this instance Cain's fruit and vegetables, a product of the sweat of his brow—was not representative of the promised Messianic deliverance. Abraham clearly understood the Messianic propitiation, and he decisively built an altar wherever he went and sacrificed the substitute animal without blemish, a symbol of the Messiah. His religion was one of "atonement by the blood."

It is difficult to understand the faith and zeal of Abraham in view of the idolatry of his father and grandfather. To be blunt, he was living in a stronghold of idolatry. But he considered himself the heir of the primitive oral Torah passed to him through the Patriarchs from Adam to Noah. These Patriarchs were monotheistic. Abraham may be dubbed as the father of monotheism, and he deserves the honour, but he was not the originator of it. The orally passed Torah from the ancestral Patriarchs was totally monotheistic. In their minds there was only one God, the creator and redeemer. Early in his life, Abraham, despite the idolatry of his parents and grandparents, had decided that he would be a champion of the primitive Torah that had come down to him. He embraced monotheism. He had cultivated a dialogue with and ardently worshipped Jehovah. How this happened, we do not know, but it is the foundation for the entire Jewish reason for existence.

The primitive oral Torah that had come down to Abraham was the Torah originating in the Garden of Eden. In face-to-face communion with Adam and Eve, the original devekut, God Himself had professed his eternal love for them. He had given them the Garden, which he Himself had planted "Eastward in Eden." He had given them each other in the love relationship of marriage; He had given them the workweek of six days and the seventh day Sabbath, in which to celebrate creation and worship Him in that close communion, which He prized very much. He had also given them eternal life and freewill so that they were free individuals with their own personalities. Worshipping Him was to be voluntary. His great love for them was to be the motivating factor to preserve their love towards Him. He warned them that there was an alternate pathway that could lead them to death. They unfortunately chose to know evil and were driven from the Garden. Their telomeres began to deteriorate, and the deterioration towards death commenced. Outside the Gates of Eden, they wept bitterly because they lost their face-to-face communion with their beloved creator and the enjoyment of their beautiful Garden. They found themselves on an earth that was now blighted.

But God did not leave them sorrowful and hopeless. He gave them the hope of redemption, and He told them that He Himself would redeem them, restore the gift of eternal life to them, and bring them back to face-to-face communion and fellowship with Him. He told them that He would actually vanquish death, that He would shed His blood for them in their restoration. They could not understand this, and so He gave them an inkling of the reality of the experience that the Messiah would undertake for them. They were to kill a sacrificial animal without blemish and shed his blood to enact the Messiah's sacrifice, which would assure them of the forgiveness of their sins and keep alive the hope of restoration to eternal life and face to face communion with God. Abel's sacrifice of a lamb was the first recorded human sacrificial act, but no doubt he had learned to do this from his parents. The promise of the Messiah was so real to Eve that when she gave birth to her firstborn, Cain, she exclaimed, "I have gotten the Man from the Lord." She thought Cain was the promised Messiah. And so the sacrificial animal became the forgiveness and release from sin for all Jews in Judaism until AD 70. This was the gist of the primitive oral Torah that had been passed down by the Patriarchs and had been embraced by the young Abraham. This story created a miracle in his life; God spoke to him and made the covenant with him.

The Talmud records a story that I believe to be true. Abraham's father was a trader in idols in the city of Ur of the Chaldees, a bastion of idolatry. His father manufactured idols and had a shop where idols of every description were sold. He was asked to tend the shop one day and took the opportunity to smash all the idols except the largest and placing the hammer, which he had used to destroy them in the hands of the remaining largest idol. When his father returned and viewed the mayhem, Abraham calmly announced that the largest idol had done it. When his father did not believe him, stating that the idols had no life and were powerless, Abraham posed the question, "Then why do you worship and facilitate others to worship these powerless idols?" It cost his father a lot of money to relearn the lesson of monotheism and return to the worship of the one true God. And God, looking down from His Heaven, saw the altercation and decided, "Here is the man for whom I have waited so long. I will go into business with him." And so God spoke to Abraham and made a covenant with him. The Abrahamic Covenant was the great and mighty plan with which to win humanity back to face to face communion and love relationship with Himself.

Abraham lived in Ur of the Chaldees. He had established an active lifestyle as a tender of flocks and herds. He has been called a wandering Bedouin, but he was also an inhabitant of a very idolatrous city. His business had prospered because he had multiple employees to tend his animals and be a supplier of food, milk, and meat—and no doubt a clothing business with the skins of the animals. Ur of the Chaldees benefited from his dwelling there, so he did not just wander off to Canaan as a wandering Bedouin looking for pasture. He had to engineer his own exodus out of Ur of the Chaldees, a wicked, idolatrous city (Gen. 12:4; 13:1-3).[69] His family was full of idolators, steeped in the heathen practices of Ur. He had to wrest his family from the enthralling atmosphere of big city life.

This was a prototype of the Exodus from Egypt. No doubt he sacrificed a lamb and conducted an exit from Ur with its idolatry. This represented an escape from slavery, but it was not as dramatic and endangered as the Passover instituted at the Exodus from Egypt. He had a massive entourage as he tracked his way to the Promised Land. In Padan-Aram, he and Sarah conducted a proselytizing campaign. He later was able to organize an army to rescue his wayward nephew Lot from the entanglement into which he had gotten. It was unfortunate that his grandson Jacob's family faced starvation in a severe and prolonged drought. They had to transplant to Egypt and delay the occupation of the Promised Land by almost 500 years as a result of their losing focus on the Abrahamic Covenant, while sojourning in Egypt. But Abraham was very knowledgeable in the primitive Torah and practiced his ritualistic religion, established at the Gates of Eden. Genesis 12:7-8 states, "And there he built an altar." Genesis 26:4-5 says, "And in your Seed all the nations of the earth shall be blessed; Because Abraham obeyed My voice and kept My charge, My commandments, My statutes, and My laws." This primitive Torah brought atonement for sin, recognised the lost immortality, and became the instrument of God in reclaiming the lost Paradise in the Messianic dream. He firmly practiced a redemptive religion. He also looked forward to a resurrection from the dead. One of his first acts in Canaan was to buy the Cave of Machpelah for a repository of his bones, to symbolically await the resurrection from the dead (Gen. 23:1-19; 25:7-11).[70] I thrilled at standing at the mouth of the Cave of Machpelah, firmly locked by the Moslems in charge, who assured me I was only a few feet from Abraham's bones. Because the resurrection would require divine intervention, he had the long sight to have faith in the reality of a redemptive Messianic future.

Abraham's religion was basic to the founding of the Hebrew nation. It came as a covenant between God and himself. There were three great pillars in the covenant, and these are the supports on which the legitimacy and mission of Israel rest: land, Torah, and Messiah.

CHAPTER 8

THE JUDAISM OF MOSES

This topic is the most complex in this book. It is a big task to consider the contents of the Book of Job and the Pentateuch, both authored by Moses. His Judaism is not "Talmudic post-Second Temple destruction" Judaism. His Judaism had three basic doctrines: the Doctrine of God, the Doctrine of Man, the Doctrine of the Chosen People.

The background of Moses needs to be discussed. He grew up in Pharaoh's palace, the adopted Hebrew child of the Pharaoh's daughter, who rescued him from the Nile. Those very waters carried all the drowned male children born in the slave camp of the Hebrews out into the Mediterranean Sea. The lucky Moses had a Hebrew nursemaid for his early years, who happened to be his mother. She instilled the oral Torah into his brain in those early years, and he never forgot who he really was. He was blessed with a prince's university education, which entailed both brain and brawn education. He was groomed as Egyptian royalty to succeed to the Pharaoh's throne. But he was living a dual life, which led to clandestine activities on behalf of the Hebrew slaves. He murdered a high-ranking Egyptian who was beating a Hebrew slave and buried the body in the sand. He was betrayed by the Hebrews for this defensive act and was forced into self-exile to escape Egyptian justice. He absconded to Midian, where he sojourned for 40 years. During this time he married Zipporah and tended sheep for his father-in-law. In his spare time he wrote the story of a man named Job, who he had met in Uz, a village in proximity to Midian; that is another wonderful story that will be alluded to in this book. But the detectives of heaven pursued him and found him there. The Divine Pharaoh of Heaven would make him face his supplanter on the Egyptian throne, to get justice for his enslaved people and implement the Abrahamic Covenant. The oral Torah was ringing in his head; its dominant theme was the Garden of Eden story of a lost perfection and immortality. He related it steadfastly to the Abrahamic Covenant. His primitive Judaism was exposed at the burning bush, and he was made to take his shoes off and stand barefoot before God. He was given his mission. As a stammerer he refused to accept it, but he was told to take his older brother Aaron along. Aaron was a good speaker but a rather weak character. Moses had a character of steel, a Hebrew heart steeped in the oral Torah, and a pharaoh's brain, and God took advantage of all that.

The task was immense. He had to take the economic lifeblood of energy away from Egypt because the Hebrews were hardworking slaves. The story is well-known. He managed to wrest a group of uneducated, unruly, idolatrous sun worshippers who loved the fleshpots of Egypt out of their abject misery and out of the forgetfulness of their calling. He was not 100 percent successful, but he got the majority out. They needed a lot of discipline—they needed to be taught Judaism. Most were not fortunate enough to have parents like Amram and Jochebed. They all spoke fluent Egyptian, and some spoke a faulty Hebrew. There were no Torah scrolls, and they had no synagogues to attend; the illiteracy rate was high. Moses knew he had a massive task.

Here was a man with a university education, strength of character, determination, knowledge, and wisdom. Predominant was the weight of the Abrahamic Covenant on his shoulders. The release from slavery and the extraction of the maladjusted, miserable, and motley crew from Egypt were colossal tasks. He was the architect of the immortal Passover Festival, which was a triple triumph: release from the bondage of slavery, release from the bondage of sin, and teaching them basic primitive Judaism. He replaced the bonds of slavery with the eternal bonds of the Abrahamic Covenant. He convinced them that they were a chosen people who belonged in the Promised Land, and they had an oral Torah to govern them, of which they were mostly ignorant. They had no inkling of the Messianic mission God had planned from eternity. The oral Torah had been strong enough to make Moses discard his adoption into Egyptian royalty. The Hebrew slaves were thus straddled with a Messianic message for the world, which they scarcely understood. Messianic blood, symbolised by the blood of the Passover lamb, would first sever them from Egypt. That blood was splashed on their doorposts and lintels. They escaped the sword of the Angel of Death by that symbolic blood. They had a great and happy future ahead of them. But they also took a great penchant for idols out of Egypt with them. In fact, when they got to Mount Sinai, they were in idolatrous withdrawal, and they wanted the golden calf in a hurry. They threatened Aaron who folded in cowardice and made it for them. God was about to wipe them off the face of the earth and make of Moses a great nation. No wonder that at Mount Sinai, Moses wrote down rules for virtually every aspect and detail of their lives so that they would stay on the straight and narrow. The spirit of this Mosaic disciplinary stringency never left them; later, it inspired the rabbinic schools that arose in the diaspora to major in Halachah. Halachah also became their insurance against assimilation. Halachah gave them a false trust in their "keeping of the law" for redemption, and when they lost the Second Temple and no longer shed blood for remission of sin, they began to feel forgiven by Halachah. Their religion morphed into a dry set of precepts with no excitement whatsoever, and void of Messianic blood. They began to think that law-keeping would transform them and qualify them for immortality. But those with vision would endure. The development of the Tanak on the foundation of the Pentateuch was miraculous. Unfortunately the Talmud majored in philosophy and precept, and the excitement of Messianic redemption was almost lost.

But Moses had a strategy, which was written down at Mount Sinai. The Ten Commandments were given, and this was the basis for the moral law. With the establishment of the Aaronic Levitical Priesthood, both the moral law and the ceremonial law were given detailed expression in the Tabernacle Sanctuary, where the Shechinah dwelt. God had to request "Let them make Me a sanctuary that I may dwell among them" (See Exod. 25:1,8). God still had a modicum of faith in them and felt He should be with them all the time. The foundation of the Temple service gave dual foci. The Ark of the Covenant cradled the Decalogue written with God's finger on the tables of stone, and it was the great moral standard. Absolute perfection was required. The sacrificial blood sprinkled on the Mercy Seat recognized their frailty and brought repentance and forgiveness and they stood perfect before God only through that Messianic blood. This dualism in the Most Holy Place where the Shechinah dwelt represented the totality of primitive Judaism, law and blood. "Knowing their frame and remembering that they were dust," He set up the system of repentance and forgiveness by the sacrifice of the lamb without blemish, whose blood was shed and life taken as a symbol of Messianic redemption. Here was God's mercy. Messianic perfection was required as a substitute for the perfection they could not achieve, and Messianic blood provided propitiation for their sins. The holiest day of the year was the Day of Atonement, when the high priest proffered the burnt offering for his own sins, and then the burnt offering for all the sins of all the people, taking the blood of the animal without blemish into the Most Holy Place, where it was sprinkled. This was an awesome task for the high priest, and it prefigured what the Messiah would do for them. Is there any other explanation? Why was blood needed at all in the Most Holy Place? And when they lost the Second Temple, Israel lost sight of Messianic redemption by the shedding of blood, which would restore the whole world to immortality. That was the proclamation outside the Gates of Eden, and amply portrayed by Abel's sacrifice. That was the proclamation on Mount Sinai. Is there any other explanation? That was the reason for the Tent Tabernacle and later Solomon's Temple. That was the reason for the Second Temple, and it is the reason why the Third Temple needs to be rebuilt. God wants to dwell among them. It is the focus for the law and the blood.

Moses was extremely strict with the exaction of behaviour in keeping the moral law, with instant death by stoning for the "heinous" sins. These are listed, (See Exod. 31, Lev. 20, 24, Deut. 13, 17, 22). Here is the list for instant stoning: Those who make sacrifice of humans to Molech, those indulging in spiritualism, those consulting "familiar spirits" and "wizards," children who curse their parents, adulterers, those committing incest (including sex between siblings and with uncles and aunts and their siblings' spouses), homosexuals, sexual threesomes (which include the mother-in-law), bestiality, men who have sex with menstruating women, children (of Israelite mothers) who blaspheme or curse God, murderers, false prophets and false dreamers of dreams, people who incite to idolatry, those knowingly bringing "blemished" animals for sacrifice, people who disobey the rulings of priests and judges, women who marry pretending to be virgins, and rapists. The stoning of Sabbath breakers was mentioned separately in Exodus 31. Eternal damnation appeared to be the fate of those who were stoned to death as instant punishment. There were cities of refuge where lawbreakers could hide and plead their case. Moses differentiated between "heinous" sins and "not so heinous" sins. But all sin was transgression of the law and required the application of the blood for absolution.

The quality of the animal sacrifice was of enormous importance. Firstborn animals also appeared to be of significant value. The symbol stood for perfect Messianic sacrifice. The symbol for the Messiah had to be perfect. The fact that those who tried to pass off sickly or lame sacrificial animals were to be put to death was therefore protection of the symbolism of the perfect Messiah, because the Messiah was deity. This particular sin of offering sickly or deformed animals was said to be a markedly tolerated abomination in the years prior to the destruction of the Second Temple; all one had to do to sidestep this rule was to pass a small bribe to the priest.

The abrogation of the moral law embodied by the Decalogue called for severe punishment. The severity of the death penalty by stoning inflicted so summarily by Moses is considered just as appalling by many modern thinkers and moralists. The death penalty is on the way out in modern jurisdictions. The death penalty lingers in some jurisdictions in the modern world only for first-degree murder. It has largely been displaced by life imprisonment in today's justice systems. Modern jurisprudence is much more lenient than that of Moses. Many of the laws of Moses were clothed in the "Thus saith the Lord" garb, as if God was speaking. Some thinkers feel that Moses used God's frontline authority to sanction his severest retributions because he wanted to be taken very seriously and could not tolerate any slippage back into Egypt and idolatrous heathenism. The prophets, priests, judges, and strong men and women of the Tanak were reformers who totally condemned idolatry. They portrayed Israel's loss of nationhood, and all their catastrophes, as judgements from God for their idolatry. Moses's severity could be therefore considered as a drastic preventive measure to keep Israel secure and strong. The stoning of transgressors was likely not a common occurrence. Moses was severe because he was obsessed with the survival of Israel. God had threatened to wipe them out in favour of him. Three thousand men died in punishment after the golden calf episode. Women died, too, but they were not enumerated.

The ceremonial law was a little more fun, so to speak, and the feasts were definitely fun. The Talmud abounds in discussion of these, what they meant, and why they were good.

Everyone agrees that the dietary and other health laws were the best rules Moses knew, both by inspiration and education, to keep Israel in good health and prevent people from dying. Disease abounded, and there were no modern medical and surgical treatments. There were some Ayurvedic applications, but most of the health rules were oriented to prevention rather than cure. It is reasonable that some have suggested that pork was infested with trichinosis and was bad to eat, hence the prohibition. Even if modern pork is not infested with trichinosis, the amount of fat that is consumed with pig meat in modern society is extremely hazardous to good cardiovascular health and to the prevention of cancer. It is also suggested that the menstrual impurity rules should really be described as the prevention of pelvic inflammatory disease, because hygiene was so poor, making sexual intercourse very hazardous when the mucous lining of the female genital tract was being renewed. All dermatoses were called leprosy until there was healing and the priests could say the patient was cured (the disease had run its course, or else the body had overcome it) before allowing them back in the camp. True leprosy could not be cured. And so we could discuss the health rules imposed by Moses as being very reasonable for his time. No doubt health and wellness had been part of the curriculum in the universities of Egypt. Were he writing the rules today, Moses would still emphasize preventive medicine. Full marks to Moses; he was certainly inspired by God to proceed with the rules he made, although there are some aspects which some might consider questionable. A. J. Jacobs, in his book *A Year of Living Biblically* has the right attitude.[71] His opinion is certainly of value and is to be seriously considered. He has the essential approach to the inspiration of the Bible that does not disappoint when some find "flaws" and their faith gets derailed.

> The Bible may have not been dictated by God, it may have had a messy and complicated birth, one filled with political agendas and outdated ideas—but that does not mean the Bible can't be beautiful and sacred.[72]

And again:

> The challenge is finding meaning, guidance, and sacredness in the Bible even if I don't believe that God sat behind His big oak desk in heaven and dictated the words verbatim to a bunch of flawless secretaries.[73]

This is the correct approach to the Tanak that we need in this modern world of critical thought, discovery, and invention. Life finds us in the universe, and we must define our place in it. The Tanak has the empiric explanation. *The Stanford Encyclopedia of Philosophy* states, "Like 'rationalism' and 'empiricism', 'existentialism' is a term that belongs to intellectual history. Its definition is thus to some extent one of historical convenience."[74] It credits people like Jean-Paul Sartre and his philosopher associates in post-war Germany, France, and Spain for defining it. Existentialism is considered a modern idea and is defined as a philosophy "Stressing the importance of personal experience and responsibility and the demands they make on the individual, who is seen as a free agent in a deterministic and seemingly meaningless universe."[75] But Moses established reality-bound existentialism linked to God, creation, and the universe in the Pentateuch. Nothing equals it.

The story of Moses from his birth to his death tells you why he existed and what exactly was his religion: it was primitive Judaism. His Torah included the Garden of Eden and the story of disobedience that led to the loss of immortality. He clearly understood the Messianic plan to restore the Edenic perfection, and the Pentateuch spells it out. The religion of Moses was implicitly bound with the history of Israel from Egypt to the Promised Land. The keeping of the law, moral and ceremonial, was extremely important, and discipline was the watchword in his guidance of Israel. But realizing that no one kept the law perfectly, Moses saw that repentance and forgiveness were needed. God could only accept perfection, so a perfect substitute was needed, and forgiveness was accomplished by the death of the sacrificial lamb without blemish, which was a symbol of the Messianic propitiation. The greatest witness to this belief of Moses is the Day of Atonement and all it means.

The Talmud magnifies the Pentateuch by microscopic dissection. Abraham Cohen has given a clear explanation of reality-bound existence in his book *Everyman's Talmud*. The basic concepts of the doctrine of God and His universe, and the doctrine of man and his world, are owed to Moses. Cohen summarizes the Talmud's dissection of the Pentateuch, which essentially is the conversation of God with His people. The Tanak evolves in terms of Mosaic revelation. The Talmud is a discussion between people. Then Cohen further divides that discussion into the compartments of domestic life, social life, moral life, physical life, and jurisprudence. All this has to do with the everyday governance of a wayward people who needed to be constantly disciplined and made to behave in a civilised and godly manner. Finally, Cohen artfully links the doctrine of God and man with the hereafter that was implicit to Moses. This discussion of the hereafter contains a dissection of the redemptive aspects of primitive Judaism, and it is here that the coming of the Messiah and the final Tanakian eschatology of Israel is fulfilled. Redemptive Judaism is fully explicit in the Talmud, it is but poorly understood and not clearly explained by the Talmudic philosophers. Sadly, some rabbinic sages relegated the redemptive aspects of Moses's religion to mysticism.

Primitive Mosaic Judaism will now be discussed in terms of pure Tanakian theology, with references to the Talmud. The shortcomings of the Talmud are clearly defined by Jacob Neusner in his preface to Cohen's *Everyman's Talmud*. He credits Cohen with overcoming these shortcomings in the tenor of his book. Nonetheless, many Talmudic utterances are complicated in its jargon and do often wander from the essential structure and context of the Tanak. The Talmud also contains many gems of truths that blend with the theology of the Tanak. But its great weakness is that it can wander away from Tanakian theology. Neusner states:

> Talmudic scholarship at that time concentrated on the meaning of words and phrases, the exegetical task overshadowing questions of meaning and value. A technical vocabulary obscured the traits and sense of the documents . . . . The issue was . . . what is it we want to know about this vast, ancient, influential writing, and why do we want to know it?[76]

Neusner bestows on the Talmud an unwarranted primacy, which equates it with (and sometimes supersedes) the Tanak. This cannot be allowed, because Tanak alone is Torah and is supreme. Neusner links Hermann Strack's *Introduction to Talmud and Midrash* and Solomon Schechter's *Some Aspects of Rabbinic Theology* to Cohen's success, and he credits Cohen with overcoming these stated shortcomings. He is correct in this opinion. Therefore Cohen is highly valued for the Talmudic understanding, sorting, and clarification that he provides in his book. This chapter of my book will attempt to clarify the Tanakian teaching, which is the basic theology of Moses found in the Tanak, and relate it to the Talmud. The Talmud does not restrict its scope of discussion to the Pentateuch, but it does include significant reference to the rest of the Tanak. Talmudic doctrines that are at variance with the Tanak must and will be rejected. The treatment of Talmudic themes will be followed as occurs in Cohen's book. I find the Talmud useful when it agrees with and exalts the Tanakian theology.

A. The Doctrine of God

Moses is the source of our basic knowledge of the God of Judaism. The following is a presentation of this theology of Moses, with additional comments from the Talmud. The Talmudic template is taken from Abraham Cohen's *Everyman's Talmud*.

1. God the Creator

Moses is the sole source for the knowledge of God in primitive Judaism. "In the beginning God created the heavens and the earth." Genesis 1:1 establishes God's eternal pre-existence and creatorship. Cohen cites the Midrashic account of the first interview that took place between Pharaoh and Moses and Aaron. The existence of God is regarded as an axiomatic truth for which no proof is needed, or offered by the Tanak and the Talmud.[77] "For He spoke, and it was, He commanded and it endured" (Ps. 33:9) was David's description of Creation.

2. God's Unity

Moses was a firm believer in monotheism. "It has been clearly demonstrated to you that the Lord alone is God. There is none beside Him" (Deut. 4:35). And again the SHEMA: "Hear O Israel the Lord our God is one" (Deut. 6:4). God's name Elohim, which Moses used in describing the Creator, is plural and indicates the plurality of His action with humanity in terms of Ruach Hakodesh, by which He nourishes us and is instrumental in providing repentance, and Ha-Mashiach, by which He redeems us.

3. God's Incorporeality

Moses describes God as Father (see the attribute of fatherhood, discussed later, and Ps. 103:13), Spirit (Ruach, Gen. 6:3), and Redeemer (Ha-Mashiach, Job ch. 19 Moses equates redeemer with God).

Ezekiel (in the Chayyoth) describes God as a glory: "Blessed be the GLORY of the Lord from His place" (Ezek. 3:12b KJV). This is discussed further under His transcendence and immanence, but it is of importance here to describe God's Shechinah glory that was in the Tabernacle and Temple.

Moses wanted to scrutinize this glory in more tangible detail.

> I beseech Thee, show me Thy GLORY. And He said, I will make all my goodness pass before thee . . . . [But] Thou canst not see My face; for there shall no man see Me and live . . . . And it shall come to pass, while My GLORY passeth by, that I will put thee in a cleft of the rock, and will cover thee with My hand while I pass by; and I will take away My hand, and thou shalt see My back; but My face shall not be seen. (Exod. 33:18-23, KJV)

God admits here that He has face and hands; He has feet (He walked in the Garden of Eden); He has a voice, and hence vocal cords; He thinks, so He has a brain; He sees and weeps, hence has eyes, optic nerves, tear ducts, and lacrimal glands; He breathed into Adam's nostrils, so He has a mouth and a trachea and lungs. So, in human terms God has a physical body. The Talmud, however, fairly unanimously insists on the incorporeality of God:

> Rabbinic literature contains numerous passages which rather startle the reader by reason of their strong anthropomorphic ascriptions.[78]

In his book *Aspects of Rabbinic Theology*, Solomon Schechter accounts for this as "the humanizing of the deity and endowing

Him with all the qualities and attributes which tend towards making God accessible to man" (p. 36). In summary, Moses, the Talmud, and many Jewish scholars understand God in human terms, and they deny His corporeality. The exception is in God's penetration of humanity in the expression of His redemptive power. This will be discussed later in this chapter, under the heading "God's Justice and Mercy."

4. God's Omnipresence

Scholars agree that Job 38 declares the omnipresence of God. The Talmud deduces that the Shechinah is in every place. This is an acceptable belief, but the Shechinah was specifically tangibly manifest in the Tent Tabernacle, Solomon's Temple.[79]

5.God's Omnipotence

Moses declares this attribute in Job 39. The Talmud deduces "Blessed art Thou O Lord our God, King of the Universe, Whose strength and might fill the world."[80]

6. God's Omniscience

Genesis 6:6 states that God was fully aware by His omniscience that evil pervaded the whole antediluvian world. The Talmud deduces that the Torah existed before the Creation, declaring that God knew of the impending evil to befall His earthly creation. "From the beginning of Creation, the Holy One, blessed be He, foresaw the deeds of the righteous and the wicked,"[81]

7. God's Eternity

"In the beginning God," Genesis 1:1, indicates that He was there before everything that had a beginning. It is the same as infinity, which by definition is limitless. The Talmud uses Jeremiah 10:10 to deduce God's eternity: "The Lord is the true God; He is the living God and an everlasting king." "So it is with our God Who lives and endures for all eternity."[82]

8. God's Justice and Mercy

Moses gives primacy to Abraham's view of God: "The first Hebrew patriarch addressed the Deity as 'The Judge of the whole earth' Genesis 18:25, and the Talmud regards Him in the same light. As the Creator of the world and of the human race, He HOLDS HIS CREATURES TO ACCOUNT for the manner of their living" (emphasis added).[83] With all the evil in the world Abraham challenged God in pleading for Sodom "Shall not the Judge of all the earth do justly?" Genesis18:25.

Deuteronomy 10:17, Jeremiah 32:18, and Daniel 9:4 all declare that God is great, mighty and terrible. Then came Nehemiah and insisted that God keep the covenant and mercy in His dealings with humans:

> Now therefore, our God, the *great*, the *mighty*, and the *awe-inspiring* God, Who keepest Covenant and Mercy, let not all the trouble seem little before Thee, that hath come upon us, on our kings, on our princes, and on our priests, and on our prophets, and on our fathers, and on all Thy people, since the time of the kings of Assyria unto this day. Howbeit, Thou art just in all that is brought upon us; for Thou hast done right, but we have done wickedly. (Neh. 9:32-3 KJV, emphasis added).

The Talmud deduces:

> This is the *greatest manifestation of His might that He subdues His anger* and shows longsuffering with the wicked; and it is likewise the manifestation of His terrible

101

acts, without which how could a single nation be allowed to continue in existence?[84]

The attribute of grace, it was taught, exceeds that of punishment (i.e., justice) by "five-hundredfold." This is a deduction from the Second Commandment of the Decalogue, and the Talmud further declares:

> Retribution, therefore, extends at most to four generations, whereas mercy extends to at least two thousand generations (Tosifta Sot. IV. I). 'Even in the time of His anger He remembers mercy' (Pes. 87b) . . . . Much use is made of the prophetic doctrine, "I have no pleasure in the death of the wicked, but that the wicked turn from his way and live" (Ezekiel 33:11). Upon it is based the Theory of Repentance which occupies so prominent a place in Rabbinic thought . . . . While believing, therefore, that He is the Judge of the Universe, the Rabbis delighted in calling Him Rachmana (the MERCIFUL) and taught that *"the world is judged by grace."*[85]

The law condemns and demands judgement and punishment, but saving grace is accomplished by God's Ha-Mashiach power, emanating from Himself. This is the source of the summum bonum of human behaviour in Micah 6:8 (KJV): "What doth the Lord require of thee, but to do justly, and to love mercy, and to walk humbly with thy God." Here is the highest standard supported by the Decalogue. Humans must achieve this perfection to satisfy God's requirement as a condition for re-bestowal of immortality. But because no human attains to this standard of lawkeeping despite all his genuine striving, God's Ha-Mashiach power bestows it as a gift. Redemption by the Ha-Mashiach power is a *gift*. It is here that His justice and mercy blend for the accomplishment of renewed immortality.

9. God's Fatherhood

Moses declared in Deuteronomy 14:1, "Ye are children of the Lord your God," thus firmly defining God's fatherhood. Moses links this to the Creation: "Let Us make man in our own image, after our likeness" (Gen. 1:26, KJV). This likeness is not in bodily form, for God is incorporeal. This likeness is in the love relationship of which humans became capable. Love is the likeness ingredient, which is the mighty quality of God's fatherhood. David the psalmist amplifies this: "As a father pitieth his children, so the Lord pitieth them that fear Him, For He knoweth our frame, He remembereth that we are dust" (Ps. 103:13-14, KJV). *The Jewish Study Bible* says it more emphatically: "As a father has compassion for his children, so the Lord has compassion for them that fear Him. For He knows how we are formed; He is mindful that we are dust."

The Talmud exalts the idea:

> The Fatherhood of God is synonymous with His love for the human family. Every creature is living proof that the Father of all is a God of love. The best expression of this idea is found in the aphorism of R. Akiba: "BELOVED IS MAN, for he was created in the image of God; but it was by a special love that it was made known to him that he was created in the image of God; as it is said, 'For in the image of God made He man."(emphasis added).[86]

Jeremiah 4:22 says that God calls His wayward children stupid: "For My people are foolish, they have not known Me; they are stupid [sottish] children" (KJV). The Talmud also emphasizes the aspect of humans being children in this relationship of love. R. Judah, commenting on Deuteronomy 14:1, said:

> At the time that you conduct yourselves as dutiful children, you are called God's children, implying that if you are not dutiful, then you are not God's children. R. Meir however " . . . declared that in either case the name of 'God's

children' applied; and he urged in favour of his contention that in the Scriptures there occurs such phrases as 'they are sottish children' (Jeremiah 4:22) and 'children in whom is no faith' (Deuteronomy 32:20), thus proving that although they were unworthy they were still called 'children.'"[87]

One may conclude that God is the "Everlasting Father" (Isa. 9:6) not only because He is eternal, but also because He is eternally our Father. We are separated only when we ourselves break the relationship, which remains anyway, pending restoration of that relationship of love. God never stops loving us. He is indeed "Our Father."

10. God's Holiness and Perfection

Moses exhorted holiness, quoting God: "Ye shall be holy for I am holy (Lev. 19:2). Ezekiel elaborates on the holiness of God:

And I will sanctify My great name, which was profaned among the nations, which ye have profaned in the midst of them; and the nations shall know that I am the Lord . . . when I shall be sanctified in you before their eyes (Ezek. 36:22-33)

Joshua exhorted the people: "He is a Holy God" (Josh. 24:19). Human holiness is achieved by God cleansing us from all our filthiness. This requires our repentance and His forgiveness and the Holy Spirit's regeneration. He gives us a new heart and a new spirit: "And I will put My Spirit within you, and cause you to walk in My statutes, and ye shall keep My ordinances, and do them" (Ezek. 36:27). God has original holiness, but we need sanctification. Humanity cannot fathom the perfection and holiness of God. We have a duty to strive for holiness, but because we are erring human beings, the Talmud adds, "My holiness is higher than any degree of holiness you can reach."[88] Therefore it is certain that human perfection is achieved only as a gift from God's Mashiach power. Nonetheless every human must strive to be sanctified. It is a betrayal of the Ha-Mashiach gift if one does not strive to keep the law and be sanctified. We must weep but not lose hope when we fail.

11. God's Ineffable Name

Moses received the Decalogue on Mount Sinai. The third commandment of the Decalogue states: "Thou shalt not take the name of the Lord thy God in vain, for the Lord will not hold him guiltless that taketh His name in vain" (Exod. 20:7, KJV). This demands reverence. The Collins Dictionary defines ineffable as "incapable of being expressed, indescribable or unutterable."[89] According to the Talmud, the uttering of God's name was originally restricted to

> the High Priest on the Day of Atonement, after he had made the threefold confession of sins on behalf of himself, the priests, and the community. The third occasion is described in this manner: "Thus did he say: O JHVH, Thy peoples, the House of Israel, have committed iniquity, have transgressed, have sinned before Thee. I beseech Thee by the name JHVH, make Thou atonement for the iniquities and for the transgressions and for the sins wherein Thy people, the House of Israel, have committed iniquity, have transgressed and sinned before Thee; as it is written in the Torah of Thy servant Moses, saying: 'For on this day shall atonement be made for you, to cleanse you; from all your sins shall ye be clean before JHVH' (Leviticus 16:30). And when the priests and people that stood in the court heard the glorious and revered name pronounced freely out of the mouth of the High Priest, in holiness and purity, they knelt and prostrated themselves, falling on their faces, and exclaiming: Blessed be His glorious, sovereign name for ever and ever."[90]

The Talmud makes the holy name of God implicit with the Day of Atonement and redemptive Judaism.

12. God's Place in the Cosmos

This topic will be dealt with in the chapter of this book titled "The Population of Heaven and the Origin of Evil." Moses defines God's centrality in the cosmos, and the Talmud has added rabbinic thought and imagination to that description. Suffice it to say here that God is the central figure in the existence of the cosmos, animate and inanimate.

13. God's Immanence and Transcendence

Immanence refers to the divine presence within an individual. It is defined as indwelling and inherent, the state of being within.[91] The word "inherent" means that it is an inseparable and intrinsic part. This is not allowable in Judaism and smacks of pantheism. But the divine presence can indwell as an invited presence. In the theology of Judaism, this is only able to take place by Ruach—that is, indwelling by God's Holy Spirit. By God's own deity Ruah, God is able to have access to humanity. Moses understood this very well, and it was a vital part of his theology. In Numbers 11:26-30, there is the story of two men, Eldad and Medad, who were filled with the Spirit and who prophesied. Since they were unknowns, Joshua, the son of Nun, reported them to Moses. Joshua requested that Moses forbid them from prophesying. Moses answered, "Enviest thou for my sake? Would God that all the Lord's people were prophets, and that the Lord would put His Spirit upon them" (Num. 11:29, KJV). The Hebrew word "Ruah" can also mean "wind," but *The Jewish Study Bible* translates it specifically to mean "Spirit."

The Holy Spirit was powerful in the theology of Moses. In selecting a craftsman for the building of the Tabernacle, God directed Moses to choose Bezalel because he was "filled . . . with the Spirit of God" (Exod. 31:1-5, KJV). *The Jewish Study Bible* translates it as "Divine Spirit." This choice of Bezalel is reinforced by Moses because "He [God] hath filled him with the Spirit of God" (Exod. 35:31, KJV). *The Jewish Study Bible* translates it again as "the Divine Spirit." David rejoiced in the communion of the Divine

Spirit. In his darkest hour after committing adultery with Bathsheba and murdering her husband, he fortunately found repentance. He begged, "Cast me not away from Thy presence and Take not Thy Holy Spirit from me (Ps. 51:11, KJV). Isaiah reinforces the Mosaic theology of the Divine Spirit: "I will pour My Spirit upon thy seed" (Isa. 44:3, KJV), and again in the Mashiach prophecy:

> The Spirit of the Lord God is upon me, because the Lord hath anointed me to preach good tidings unto the meek; He hath sent me to bind up the broken-hearted, to proclaim liberty to the captives, and the opening of the prison to those who are bound. (Isa. 61:1, KJV)

Joel looked forward to the day when "It shall come to pass afterward, that I will pour out My Spirit upon all flesh" (Joel 2:28, KJV). Wondrous things happen when the Holy Spirit indwells, when God has access into people's lives.

Transcendence appears to be the opposite of immanence. The Song of Moses, "I will sing unto the Lord, for He is highly exalted" (Exod. 15:1), describes God as so majestic that He is far above the abode of humans. The Talmud sees His throne in the seventh heaven. Ezekiel's Chayyoth is invoked, and the king, the living and eternal God, high and exalted, abides above them.[92] And yet the rabbinic sages were stressed to imply that God was also a very close and personal God: "However high He be above His world, let a man but enter a synagogue, stand behind a pillar and pray in a whisper, and the Holy One, blessed be He, hearkens to his prayer. Can there be a God who is nearer than this, Who is close to His creatures as the mouth is to the ear?"[93]

B. The Doctrine Of Man

The condition of man in relation to God has been carefully spelled out by Moses.

1. Creation of the Body and Soul

For the pattern for the creation of man Moses said that God took His own image (Gen. 1:27; 9:6). For the raw material, He took the dust of the ground (Gen. 2:7). For the gift of life God breathed into the creature's lungs His own breath. (Gen. 2:7). And man became a living soul. Body and breath of life constituted a living soul. And He bestowed immortality on that living being, to be maintained on the fruit of the Tree of Life. Immortality was conditional on the obedience of the Torah. The Tree of Knowledge of Good and Evil was the test of obedience (Gen. 2:9, 15-17). The story is very simple, although miraculous. Moses makes no mention of a creation of a duality within man, of obedience and disobedience in Adam and Eve, as is implied in the Talmud and Kabbalistic teachings.[94] Moses clearly states that the Serpent had access to the Garden of Eden to cause disobedience (Gen. 3:1). In the Book of Job, Satan occupies a prominent place in the population of Heaven and the Nether World.[95]

The theology of Moses does not allow humanity to own divinity. "For in the day that thou eatest thereof thou shalt surely die" (Gen. 2:17). Ezekiel reinforced this: "The soul that sinneth, it shall die (Ezek. 18:20). The soul is not intrinsically immortal; immortality is a bestowment and in the case of humans was conditional to obedience. There is no evidence in the Pentateuch or in Job for intrinsic immortality of the soul. When the body dies, the soul dies with it because they cannot exist apart. Humanity's past or future as created beings has no measure of divinity (deity) whatsoever. Divinity belongs only to God, and if it belonged to any other being in Judaism, monotheism is shattered and no longer a principle of the universe. The Talmud states that man's soul is from heaven, and therefore man is partially divine. The Talmud uses as proof Psalm 82:6-7" "I said, ye are gods, and all of you sons of the Most High."[96] The Talmud is in great error if it teaches that man is partially divine. Only God is deity; only He is divine. Not even the angels, who are created beings, are divine. The Holy Spirit and Ha-Mashiach alone are divine, but they are God, intrinsic and one with Him. "They" are Elohim (plural) but are God Almighty and should not be referred to as "they." "They" is used only as a convenience of language to refer to functions of deity. The Lord our God is one, blessed be He.

To conclude from this verse that humanity was endowed with divinity is a misapprehension. It is noncontextual and contrary to the entire Tanak. *The Jewish Study Bible* renders this passage, which is about poverty and social injustice, quite correctly:

> They [wicked judges who judge perversely] neither know or understand, they go about in darkness; all the foundations of the earth totter. I had taken you for divine beings, sons of the Most High, all of you; but you shall die as men do, fall like any prince. (Ps. 82:6-7, *The Jewish Study Bible*)

It is a gross error to interpret this scripture as teaching that humans are partially divine. The Talmud makes a gross error in this connotation.

Likeness to the image of God was resident in and intrinsic to humanity's ability to love God and each other. Humanity can aspire to love as He does to show that likeness. Humanity has no other likeness to God. Even the act of forgiving a fellow human for a slight is part of the love mechanism, which gives us a likeness to God. The Talmud emphasizes this correctly:

> That the human being was created in the image of God lies at the root of the Rabbinic teaching concerning man. In that respect he is pre-eminent above all other creatures and represents the culminating point in the work of Creation. "Beloved is man, for he was created in the image of God; but it was by a special LOVE that it was made known to him that he was created in the image of God; as it is said, 'For in the image of God He created man.'"[97]

Love gives the Tanak and the universe meaning and cohesion. "Yea, I have loved thee with an everlasting love; with loving kindness have I drawn thee" (Jer. 31:3-4). The comparison is made to the intense love and desire a man has for his virgin bride. God loves and humanity reciprocates. "And thou shalt love the Lord thy God with all thine heart, and with all thy soul, and with all thy might" (Deut. 6:4-5, KJV). Moses links love to God with "Hear, O Israel: The Lord our God is one Lord." Love to God should be the dominant and governing principle in our existence. We cannot truly love God if we do not love our fellow humans, even the ones who slight us. The Talmud makes another excellent point here about love. Because God loves and regards humans so highly, they should love each other as highly. This idea emanates from the commandment: "Thou shalt love thy neighbour as thyself" (Lev. 19:18, KJV).[98] If humanity has any resemblance to the likeness of God, it is in the ability to love, and in the demonstration of that love. Humanity's likeness to God resides in the ability to love and be loved and not in sharing divinity, which is the sole possession of a monotheistic God, the sole deity of the universe.

2. The Bestowment of Free Will

Love cannot be forced. With love, humanity was given free will so as not to be puppets. Moses takes great care to spell out that Adam and Eve were free agents in the Garden. The Tree of Life would ensure their immortality. The Tree of Knowledge of Good and Evil would test their free will, love, and obedience. Choice was emphasized by Moses as he led the bunch of freed slaves to the Promised Land.

> See, I set before you this day life and prosperity, death and adversity. For I command you this day, to Love the Lord your God, to walk in His ways, and to keep His commandments, His laws, and His rules, that you may thrive and increase, and that the Lord may bless you in the land you are about to enter and possess. But if your heart turns away and you give no heed, and are lured into the worship and service of other gods, I declare to you this day that you shall certainly perish . . . . I have put before you life and death, blessing and curse. Choose life—if you and

> your offspring would live—by loving the Lord your God, heeding His commands, and holding fast to Him. (Deut. 30:15-20, *The Jewish Study Bible*)

See, This day I set before you blessing and curse: blessing, if you obey the commandments of the Lord your God . . . and curse, if you do not obey the commandments of the Lord your God. (Deut. 11:26-28, *The Jewish Study Bible*)

Because God is invested with divine foresight so that He foresaw the entrance of disobedience but still chose to go ahead and create humankind, the rabbis were in consternation. Nonetheless, they believed, "Everything is foreseen by God, yet freedom of choice is given."[99] The enmity between the Serpent and the woman would culminate in the head wound to the Serpent by the Ha-Mashiach. The Tanak again records, "Behold, man is become as one of us to know good and evil" (Gen. 3:22).

3. The Entrance of Sin and Death

Originally endowed with immortality, humanity lost it in Eden and must depend totally on Ha-Mashiach to restore it. When immortality is restored, humanity will continue to worship the great God of the multiverses. Ha-Mashiach the redeemer will one day restore immortality to the human soul, but never will endow divinity as an intrinsic characteristic. There is only one divine God; the Lord our God is one. Moses quoted God: "For in the day that thou eatest thereof, thou shalt surely die" (Gen. 2:17, KJV). The great lie of the Serpent was "Ye shall not surely die" (Gen. 3:4-5 KJV). *The Jewish Study Bible* translates this very succinctly: "And the Serpent said to the woman, 'You are not going to die, but God knows that as soon as you eat of it your eyes will be opened and you will be like divine beings who know good and bad." The Serpent uttered two big lies: "You are not going to die," and "You will be like divine beings." Both lies have been the curse of humanity. The Talmudic teaching that "God helps the good to advance in goodness, and the wicked to advance in their wickedness" as a single principle of His government is quite erroneous. For instance: "In the way in which a man wishes to walk he is guided."[100] And again, "If one goes to defile himself, openings are made for him; and he who goes to purify himself, help is afforded him."[101]. And yet again, "If a man defiles himself a little, they (i.e., God) defile him much; if he defile himself here below, they defile him for the World to Come."[102] This is gross error and cannot be sustained in the context of the Tanak. The Tanak speaks of the Holy Spirit indwelling and guiding those who choose to welcome Him into their lives (Isa. 61:1-2). But it is grossly erroneous to give the Holy Spirit the work of advancing evil in people's hearts and lives. Satan, the Serpent, does that.

Cohen is emphatic that "The conviction that man's will is unfettered is therefore seen to be the foundation of Rabbinic ethics."[103]

This status of being unfettered is totally incompatible with the above Talmudic teaching that God advances defilement in people's lives. Humanity is free to choose, and humans exercise that choice every day.

The human body is the greatest scientific marvel in the universe. As with Moses in the Pentateuch, the Talmud's foray into anatomy and physiology of the human body does not fit into our present advanced scientific knowledge. Cohen has a good explanation: "With the limited physiological knowledge at their command the Rabbis were evidently anxious to demonstrate how every function of every organ had been designed by God for the well-being of the individual and the prolongation of life."[104] This is a splendid judgement. All past eras must be looked upon in such a manner, including the medical knowledge of Moses, and the scientific knowledge as recently as that of AD 2012. The frontiers of our understanding of the human body are always advancing, and because they were not accurate last year does not mean that we should lose confidence in the people on whose shoulders we stand.

Moses defined sin as disobedience to Torah. Sin can exist as sin committed in ignorance and known wilful sin (Lev. 4:13-14, KJV). Moses teaches that the entrance of sin caused death. An Edenic, sinless state would have ensured that humanity continued in immortality. The loss of immortality and the onset of death as a result of disobedience is clearly outlined by Moses. Eve was tempted by the Serpent and succumbed. Adam dragged himself down with her because he loved her and feared separation from her. How did this happen? It was sheer disobedience to Torah. In the days of the evolution of the Talmud, the sages struggled with the mechanism of the entrance of sin. The schools of Hillel and Shammai could not agree with the idea that it would have been better if man had not been created because of sin and suffering:

> Then I accounted those who died long since more fortunate than those who are still living, and happier than either are those who have not yet come into being and have never witnessed the miseries that go on under the sun. (Eccles. 4:3, *The Jewish Study Bible*)

Cohen states:

> At the root of the discussion was the agreed opinion that man is essentially a sinful creature who is bound during his lifetime to do many deeds which earn for him the condemnation of God.[105]

The Talmud erroneously teaches that Elijah did not sin and therefore was allowed into heaven.[106] Cohen admits that the rabbinic literature gives contradictory answers to the question whether it is possible for any person to be perfectly sinless. No one born of the seed of the primal couple has been sinless, no matter how saintly. The Talmud has great difficulty with the mechanism of the entrance of sin into the world. Moses taught it was disobedience to Torah that had occurred by succumbing to temptation by the Serpent. The existence and role of the Serpent was a very difficult subject for the rabbinic sages. Denying the influence of temptation by Satan the Serpent, the sages therefore invented the Two Impulse Theory. Cohen states:

> The belief that in every human being there are two urges—one to evil [acquired at birth] and the other to goodness [acquired at adolescence]—figures prominently in Rabbinic ethics. Having to find a basis for the doctrine in the text of the Bible, the Rabbis deduced it in this way: "What means that which is written, 'The Lord God formed man' (Genesis 2:7), the word 'wajjitzer' (and He formed) being spelt with two letters j? THE HOLY ONE, blessed be He, CREATED TWO IMPULSES. The Hebrew word for 'impulse' is Jetzer: hence the two j's were taken to indicate two—the Jetzer Tov, 'good impulse,' and the Jetzer Hara, the 'evil impulse.'" (emphasis added).[107]

Even allowing for the fact that Hebrew is a sacred language, this is the weakest argument possible for such an important doctrine as the origin of evil. It flies in the face of what Moses plainly stated that the Serpent beguiled Eve. Moses clearly stated that God made man perfect—and now the Talmud attributes God with the creation of built-in evil tendencies to sin. It negates God's goodness and glory, and it destroys His redemptive plan. It destroys the Messianic triumph of the restoration of sinlessness and immortality. God will have to sit in judgement on Himself, and convict Himself, for creating evil and misery and death in the world. This rabbinic doctrine stains God's character. The topic of the origin of evil is dealt with in this book in the chapter "The Population of Heaven and the Origin of Evil."

Cohen believed that wrongdoing results from the loss of self-control. The Talmud states:

> A man does not commit a transgression unless a spirit of madness has entered into him.

> Important safeguards against sinning were suggested by Rabbi Judah the Prince and his son Gamaliel. The first,

> Rabbi Judah said: "Reflect upon three things and you will not come within the power of sin: Know what is above you—a seeing eye, and a hearing ear, and all your deeds are written in a book." The second said: "An excellent thing is the study of the Torah combined with some worldly occupation, for the labour demanded by them both makes sin to be forgotten."[108]

Common with this dictum is the belief that "Satan finds mischief for idle hands [and minds] to do." This quote is attributed to Charles Dickens, but a discussion of it had the outcome that Satan also finds mischief for busy hands to do![109] This idea is a better opinion and comes with good advice, than believing that God built the tendency to evil in the human heart.

Eve chose to believe the Serpent instead of God's warning. The loss of immortality and the onset of death as a result of disobedience to Torah must be recognized as a personal choice and the exercise of free will. Nowhere in the Pentateuch does Moses attribute to God the creation of an evil tendency in humanity. Moses, quoting God after the disobedience in Eden, said, "By the sweat of your brow shall you get to eat, until you return to the ground—for from it you were taken. For dust you are and to dust you shall return" (Gen. 3:19, *The Jewish Study Bible*).

The Talmud is elaborate and lengthy in its discussion of death.[110] An "Angel of Death" is invoked, whose special action was seen in Egypt at the first Passover. Cohen says that the sages believed that death was a consequence of sin.[111] In considering the soul in Genesis 2:7, the Hebrew word is "nephesh." This has multiple meanings but the one that suits the context best is "a breathing creature[s]," which is what Adam and Eve became when God breathed His life-giving breath of air containing oxygen into their nostrils. The same happens to a newborn. While the creature is alive, he is called a living soul; when breathing ceases irreversibly, death supervenes, and the subject then becomes a dead, nonbreathing creature, or a dead soul. God is the sole source of life, so that life that He gave by His breath ceases. What lives on is the personality of the dead individual, as a memory. This memory is a relationship, which was shared with God and with humans. When death supervenes, there is no remaining physical or spiritual identity of that individual that flits to heaven or hell. There is no persisting existence. There is no evidence in the Tanak that there is a residue of the living soul that lives on. The body goes back to dust, and the breath expires. "We must needs die, and are as water spilt on the ground, which cannot be gathered up again" (2 Sam. 14:14, KJV). "Many of those that sleep in the dust of the earth will awake, some to eternal life . . . others to everlasting abhorrence" (Dan. 12:2, *The Jewish Study Bible*). Here Daniel invokes the resurrection of the dead, which will take place in the Messianic age. Daniel sees the Messianic intervention of the great prince, Michael. Moses, in the Book of Job, establishes a resurrection that will take place after death. "I know that my Redeemer liveth and that He shall stand at the latter day upon the earth. And though . . . worms destroy this body, yet in my flesh shall I see God" (Job 19:25-26 KJV). So death is a sleep from which all will be awakened. "The living know they will die. But the dead know nothing; they have no more recompense, for even the memory of them has died [eventually]. Their loves, their hates, their jealousies have long since perished; and they have no more share till the end of time in all that goes on under the sun" (see Eccles. 9:1-6, *The Jewish Study Bible*). Solomon indicates here the resurrection at "the end of time."

4. The Facing of Judgement

After the living soul becomes a dead soul, there will be a judgement. "Shall not the Judge of all the earth deal justly?" (Gen. 18:25, *The Jewish Study Bible*). Abraham was pleading for the sparing of Sodom and was reminding God that He must be sparing to be seen as just. The final verses of the Book of the Ecclesiastes state, "Revere God and observe His commandments, for this applies to all mankind: that God will call every creature to account for everything unknown, be it good or bad" in his life (Eccles.:

12:13-14, *The Jewish Study Bible*).The Tanak teaches throughout its pages that there will be a final judgement for all.

After setting destiny as the outcome of following obedience to the Torah or disregard for the Torah, the first Psalm clearly sets the inevitable judgement as the fate of all humanity. "Therefore the wicked will not survive judgement, nor will sinners, in the assembly of the righteous. For the Lord cherishes the way of the righteous, but the way of the wicked is doomed" (Ps. 1:5-6, *The Jewish Study Bible*). Having outlined the coming judgement by which all will face an accounting of their lives, the Psalmist in the next chapter trumpets the coming of the Ha-Mashiach power of God. The psalmist clearly spells the "Sonship" of this Ha-Mashiach power of God.

> Why do nations rage, and the peoples imagine a vain thing? The kings of the earth set themselves, and the rulers take counsel together, against the Lord, and against his Anointed, saying, Let us break their bands asunder, and cast away their cords from us. He who sitteth in the heavens shall laugh; the Lord shall have them in derision. Then shall he speak unto them in his wrath, and vex them in his great displeasure. Yet have I set My king upon My holy hill of Zion. I will declare the decree: The Lord hath said unto Me, *Thou art My Son: This day have I begotten Thee.* Ask of Me, and I shall give thee the nations for thine inheritance, and the uttermost parts of the earth for thy possession. Thou shalt break them with a rod of iron; thou shalt dash them in pieces like a potter's vessel. Be wise now, therefore, O ye kings; be instructed ye judges of the earth. Serve the Lord with fear, and rejoice with trembling. *Kiss the Son,* lest he be angry, and ye perish from the way, when his wrath is kindled but a little. Blessed are all they who put their trust in him. (Psalm 2:7-12, KJV; emphasis added)

The Jewish Study Bible comments on this psalm in the margin and points out that the word "anointed" denotes Ha-Mashiach. The Hebrew words are "al-Adonai v'al-meshicho," which refers to Mashiach ben David, the greater Son of David.[112] Al-Adonai (Master) is one of the names of God in Judaism.[113] Psalms 1 and 2 are clearly implicated in judgement with the intervention of the Mashiach or Messianic power of God.

The Talmud states that judgement will result in a reward of Gan Eden for the righteous and Gehinnom for the wicked. This is carefully explained by Cohen, quoting the Talmud in his book (see pp. 370-389). So how does God separate the righteous from the wicked? Isaiah first describes the state of Israel in contrast to all the mighty acts of God recited in chapter 63.

> We have all become like an unclean thing, And all our virtues as a filthy rag. We are all withering like leaves, and our iniquities, like a wind carry us off. (Isa. 64:5, *The Jewish Study Bible*)

> Verily every man at his best state is altogether vanity. (Ps. 39:5, KJV)

If God deals justly, He must send *all* to Gehinnom, because *all* are guilty of disobedience to Torah. So how do some escape and get counted as righteous? It is by divine intervention. Isaiah cries out from the depths of despair, "Where is He who brought them up from the sea?" (Isa. 63:11, *The Jewish Study Bible*). This passage recalls the deliverance from Egypt and passage through the parting of the Red Sea. The commentary in the margin rightly makes the observation that this passage (Isa. 63:11-14) refers to "God's movement from *wrath to grace* in judgement"[114] (*The Jewish Study Bible*, p. 909, emphasis added). Isaiah pleads, "Surely You are our Father; . . . from of old, Your name is 'Our Redeemer'" (Isa. 63:16, *The Jewish Study Bible*). Repentance leads to forgiveness and absolution. According to the Day of Atonement service, the blood of the sacrificial lamb without blemish, sprinkled in the Most Holy Place of the Temple, attains absolution. And what does that blood signify if not the Ha-Mashiach expression of God? Despite variant views expressed in the Talmud, the sages stated that one of the big questions asked in the final judgement is, "Did you hope for the salvation of the Messiah?"[115] The only hope in the judgement, where all are judged as "filthy rags," is Messianic intervention. God provides it:

- YHVH is the Divine Goel, redeeming His people. The law (Torah) holds all in because they cannot keep it perfectly (Isa. 63:16).
- YHVH is El Shaddah, Adonai, the saviour in the escape from Egypt (Exod. 6:2-3).
- YHVH is the redeemer who delivers Israel from "the clans of Edom," who seek to destroy them (Exod. 15:13).
- YHVH is the redeemer who gathers Israel from the ends of the earth in judgement (Ps. 107:2-3).
- YHVH is majestic in His role as deliverer (Isa. 62:11; 63:1).
- YHVH is a vindicator, a redeemer, a judge conducting judgement at the latter day upon the earth (Job 19:25). The Hebrew names of God all intone redemption.
- YHVH is Haggoel, the redeemer (Job 19:25, Ps. 19:14).
- YHVH is Goel, kinsman redeemer (Num. 5:8).
- YHVH is Goel Yisrael, the redeemer of Israel (Lev. 25:2; Isa. 39:7).
- YHVH is Goel Haddam, avenger of blood (1 Sam. 6:20).
- YHVH is Adonai Tsuri v'go'ali, Lord, my rock and my redeemer (Ps. 19:14).
- YHVH is Tsidkenu (Sid-qe-nu), "The Lord our Righteousness" (Jer. 23:5-6).[116]

It is true that following the entrance of sin, a controversy ensued between humanity and the Serpent: "I will put enmity between thee and the woman, between thy seed and her seed" (Gen. 3:15, KJV). God was not going to let humanity go and clearly planned to rescue them, and that is the tug of war that began between God's Holy Spirit and the Serpent. It was to be a fierce and bruising battle between God and the Serpent, in which the latter would be dealt a lethal head wound. God as the Ha-Mashiach divine power would inflict that head-wound on the Serpent. That was God's redeemer function, and that is why repentance and forgiveness were implemented as the sacrifice of the lamb without blemish. That was the symbolic meaning of the Day of Atonement. We cannot face judgement and live without redemption.

5. The Plan of Redemption and the Hereafter

Sin, the transgression of the Torah, was followed by death and judgement. Immortality was lost, and humanity was separated from God. Obviously corrective measures were necessary; therefore Messianic redemption was implemented. The sacrificial system was instituted with the advocacy of the Aaronic priesthood (Exod. 28, 29).

Death had to be conquered to restore immortality, and that was God's personal Messianic function. On the Day of Atonement, the congregation of Israel was not divided into two groups of those who had kept the law perfectly and those who had not. No one had kept the law perfectly, and the Day of Atonement sacrifice was for all the sins of all the people. No pious group was exempted. Absolution is not attained by piety; it is accomplished by deity. Our righteousness is as filthy rags. The prerequisite to forgiveness was repentance. Moses had instructed that the sinner must acknowledge his guilt and seek forgiveness and expiation. The act of repentance was signified by the placing of both hands of the penitent one on the sacrificial animal without blemish, whose lifeblood symbolically provided the expiation that followed. The Talmud adds meaning and colour to this process. Repentance is held as a gift from God, and

> was one of the things which were designed by God even before the world itself was formed. "Seven things were created before the Universe came into being. They are: Torah, Repentance, Paradise, Gehinnom, the Throne of Glory, the Sanctuary, and the name of the Messiah."[117]

If by the statement "were created" the Talmud means "thought of" or "planned for," then the statement is acceptable as being in agreement with the Tanak. But the objection would be to the Messiah being defined as a created being. The Ha-Mashiach power of God is a role played by deity or God Himself, and is therefore divinity itself, intrinsic to God, the Lord our God is one. God Himself resides in His Ha-Mashiach role. The Talmud declares further,

> Great is repentance, for it reaches to the Throne of Glory. Great is repentance, for it makes the Redemption (by the Messiah) to come near. Great is repentance, for it lengthens the years of a man's life.[118]

Abraham Cohen puts repentance gently and tenderly into the context of the great love story between God and humanity.

> Since, as the Bible declares, God delights not in the death of the wicked but that he turn from his evil way and live (Ezekiel 33:11), it follows that He is anxious for man to repent and facilitates his endeavour to do so " . . . When a human being is conquered He grieves; but when He is conquered [By having His anger overcome by means of repentance] He rejoices." The words of Ezekiel, "They had the hands of a man under their wings" (Ezekiel 1:8), refer to the hand of God which is extended beneath the wings of the Chayyoth to receive penitents from the power of judgement.[119]

That hand of God is His Ha-Mashiach extension to save. The penitent are protected "under the wings" of the Almighty God. "He shall cover thee with His feathers and under His wings shalt thou trust" (Ps. 17:8; 91:4 KJV). And the Talmud further says: "As the sea is always accessible, so is the hand of the Holy One, blessed be He, always open to receive penitents."[120]

Therefore, the righteous are deemed righteous because they are penitent, and not because they have obeyed Torah perfectly. They stand sinless because their sins are forgiven. The blood of the lamb without blemish has brought them absolution. On the night of the Day of Atonement, all of Israel stands perfect before God.

This great excerpt from Abraham Cohen needs to be read by the whole world.

> With the fall of the Temple and the cessation of the Atonement offerings, the importance of repentance as a means of expiation became inevitably enhanced. This is also true of the efficacy of the Day of Atonement. Even when the sacrificial system was in operation, the Rabbis assert, contrition was essential before an offering could prove acceptable to God. There is the explicit teaching: "Neither sin-offering nor trespass-offering nor death nor the Day of Atonement can bring expiation without repentance."[121] Tosifta Joma v.9) . . . . "The sacrifices of God are a broken spirit" Psalm 51:17).[122]

King David, that ugly adulterer and murderer, understood the importance of repentance, and with the Ruach Hakodesh working on his heart, he grasped the gift of repentance to proclaim, "The sacrifices of God are a broken spirit; a broken and a contrite heart O God, Thou wilt not despise" (Ps. 51:17, KJV). After repentance and forgiveness brought him a "clean heart and a right spirit," he acknowledged with his animal sacrifice the Messianic accomplishment on his behalf. He was given a clean slate.

Repentance is born as the gift of the Holy Spirit working upon the heart of the sinner. Forgiveness and expiation are accomplished by the Ha-Mashiach power of God Himself. The Lord our God is one, blessed be He.

Moses believed in God; it was easy for him because he talked with God everyday. This belief led him into four great, overwhelming, definitive religious convictions. The rest was all rules and regulations for the everyday governance and education of an uneducated and unruly people who he rescued from slavery. The four great religious convictions were derived from the Abrahamic Covenant.:

(i) **Torah**—The law of God. It was perfect. However, Moses had the conviction that no one kept it perfectly.

(ii) **The Conviction of Sin**—Because no one kept the law perfectly, everybody needed repentance, confession, and expiation so that they could again stand perfect before the law.

(iii) **Atonement of Sin**—This was built into God's plan of redemption: Repentance would come as a gift by the mediation of Ruach Hakodesh, but confession and expiation were necessary. God would shed His own blood, thereby defeating eternal death, which resulted from disobedience of the law. This would be accomplished by the penetration of humanity by Ha-Mashiach. Therefore Moses implemented the symbolism of the sacrificial animal without blemish (because God is perfect, the symbol must be without blemish), whose blood was shed in lieu of God's future act. The penitent sinner placed both his hands on the sacrificial animal while the priest slit its throat and shed the blood. It was gruesome, but that is what sin does—it causes death. The sinner left the altar of sacrifice, again perfect before God.

To implement these above three convictions, God had convinced Moses that Ha-Mashiach would come. He told the people:

> The Lord your God will raise up for you a prophet from among your own people, like myself, him you shall heed. This is just what you asked of the Lord your God at Horeb, on the day of the Assembly, saying, "Let me not hear the voice of the Lord my God any longer or see this wondrous fire anymore, lest I die." Whereupon the Lord said to me, "They have done well in speaking thus. I will raise up a prophet for them from among their own people,

like yourself: I will put My words in his mouth and he will speak to them all that I command him; and if anybody fails to heed the words he speaks in My name, I Myself will call him to account." (Deut. 18:13-19 *The Jewish Study Bible*)

How was he to be like Moses? Moses had freed them from slavery; Ha-Mashiach would free them from sin. The margin comments on this prophet in *The Jewish Study Bible* state that later Jewish interpretation provides for a "Messianic Prophet at the end of time." And Ha-Mashiach would come in the form of a man. God would mask His fiery majesty of which they were sore afraid. So Moses was secure in the belief that the Ha-Mashiach would be divine, would arrive in the future, and would accomplish the atonement.

What did Moses teach would happen after judgement? He knew that judgement could not have a good outcome without redemption. Judgement is about the law, the Torah. Judgement is a decision about how one performed. God can only tolerate perfection in the obedience to Torah. If His standards were lower, He would not have driven Adam and Eve out of Eden. So He interposed His own Ha-Mashiach power in reclaiming his erring children by His perfection and His blood, the blood of the lamb without blemish. God has no blemish, and He is the only one who can interpose Himself to satisfy the demands of the law, the Torah. God is the author of Torah, and He will also be the author of redemption. The Messiah will be God the redeemer. He provides repentance by His Ruach Hakodesh power and forgiveness and expiation by His Ha-Mashiach power. That is what the Day of Atonement is all about.

Moses's fourth overwhelming conviction was:

(iv) *Judgement and Resurrection*—At the end of time, there would be a resurrection. He had trumpeted this message in the words of Job.

I know that my Vindicator [Redeemer] lives. In the end He
will testify on earth—This after my skin has been peeled
off. But I would behold God while still in my flesh, I
myself, not another would behold Him. (Job 19:25-26 *The
Jewish Study Bible*)

Abraham Cohen states:

No aspect of the subject of the Hereafter has so important
a place in the religious teaching of the Rabbis as the
doctrine of the Resurrection. It became with them an article
of faith the denial of which was condemned as sinful;
and they declared: "Since a person repudiated belief in
the Resurrection of the dead, he will have no share in the
Resurrection."[123]

The Talmud relied heavily on Isaiah, Ezekiel, and Daniel for proof
of the resurrection in the challenge that came from the Sadducees,
who did not believe in the resurrection.

Isaiah states:

Oh, let your dead revive! Let corpses arise! Awake and
shout for joy, you who dwell in the dust!—For your dew
is like the dew on fresh growth; you make the land of the
shades come to life (Isa. 26:19, *The Jewish Study Bible*)

Ezekiel states:

Thus saith the Lord to these bones: I will cause breath to
enter you and you shall live again. And you shall know that
I am the Lord . . . . And He said unto me, "O mortal, these
bones are the whole House of Israel." . . . Thus saith the
Lord God: "I am going to open your graves, and lift you
out of the graves, O My people and bring you to the land of
Israel." (Ezekiel 37:11, *The Jewish Study Bible*)

Daniel states:

> At that time the great prince, Michael, who stands beside
> the sons of your people, will appear. It will be a time of
> trouble, the like of which has never been since the nation
> came into being. At that time, your people will be rescued,
> all who are found inscribed in the book. Many of those that
> sleep in the dust of the earth will awake." (Dan. 12:1-2, *The
> Jewish Study Bible*)

The Tanak clearly associates the resurrection with the end of time.
In the books of the prophets are grand final scenes where the
Tanakian eschatological events play out. As the Tanak abounds
in pictures of Messianic intervention, it also abounds in the final
scenes, which restore immortality to humanity. Again it is by
divine intervention. *Immortality is restored at the resurrection of
the dead and the transformation of the living who have trusted in
Ha-Mashiach.*

The last day events in the Tanak with regard to Messiah are of
two kinds. As explained above, the Messiah was to come as a man
("Son of Man"'). Malachi talks about a forerunner introducing
the Messiah, who will then provide cleansing from sin: "For He
is like a smelter's fire and like fuller's lye. He shall act as a purger
of silver . . . and he shall purify" (Malachi 3:2, *The Jewish Study
Bible*). His entrance and fate as a man is beautifully and solemnly
declared in the Book of Isaiah. But He would also come as a king.

The Talmud discusses His coming as 'The Son of Man' in terms of
the suffering servant.

> The Rabbis maintain that his name is "the leprous one of
> the School of R. Judah the Prince," as it is said, "Surely he
> hath borne our griefs, and carried our sorrows; yet we did
> esteem him stricken, smitten of God, and afflicted," Isaiah
> 53:4 [KJV]. Rab declared, The Holy One, blessed be He,
> hereafter raise up for Israel another David, as it is said,
> "They shall serve the Lord their God and David their king,

whom I will raise up unto them" Jeremiah 30:9 [KJV]. It is
not stated "has raised'" but "will raise" (Sanh. 98b). Other
designations suggested for him [Messiah] are given in these
extracts: "R. Joshua b. Levi said, His name Tzemach ('the
branch', cf Zechariah 6:12). R. Judah said, it is Menachem.
R. Aibu, said, 'The two are identical since the numerical
value of the letters forming their names is the same' (p.
Ber. 5a). R. Nachman asked R. Isaac, 'Have you heard
when Bar Naphle (son of the fallen) will come?' He said
to him, 'Who is Bar Naphle?' He answered, 'The Messiah.'
The other asked, 'Do you call the Messiah Bar Naphle?' He
replied, 'I do, because it is written, In that day will I raise
the tabernacle of David that is fallen.'" Amos 9:11 [KJV]
(Sanh. 96b). Mention is once made of a rather mysterious
figure called Messiah son of Joseph. The passage reads:
"Messiah son of Joseph was slain, as it is written, 'They
shall look unto me whom they have pierced; and they
shall mourn for him as one mourneth for his only son'"
(Zechariah 12:10 [KJV]), (Suk. 52a).[124]

Cohen repeatedly quotes the King James Version of the Tanak. *The
Jewish Study Bible* translates Zechariah 12:10 as, "But I will fill
the House of David and the inhabitants of Jerusalem with a spirit of
pity and compassion; and they shall lament to Me about those who
are slain, wailing over them as over a favourite son and showing
bitter grief as over a first-born." The marginal comment allows that
the Hebrew here is ambiguous, but if verse 10 is linked to verse 9
preceding it, the meaning would be better translated as a Messianic
piercing, as the Talmud declares.[125]

It is worth continuing the quote, which the Talmud makes from
Isaiah 53 with reference to the "suffering" or "leprous'" Messiah:

Who can believe what we have heard?
Upon whom has the *Arm of the Lord* been revealed?
For He has grown, by His favour, like a tree crown,
Like a tree trunk out of arid ground.
He had no form or beauty, that we should look at Him:

No charm that we should find Him pleasing
He was despised, shunned by men,
A man of suffering, familiar with disease.
As one who hid his face from us,
He was despised, we held him of no account.
Yet it was our sickness he was bearing,
Our suffering that he endured.
We accounted him plagued,
Smitten and afflicted by God;
But he was wounded for our sins,
Crushed because of our iniquities.
He bore the chastisement that made us whole,
And by his bruises we were healed.
We all went astray like sheep,
Each going his own way
And the Lord visited upon him
The guilt of all of us.
He was maltreated, yet he was submissive,
He did not open his mouth;
Like a sheep being led to the slaughter,
Like a ewe, dumb before those who shear her,
He did not open his mouth.
By oppressive judgement he was taken away
Who could describe his abode?
For he was cut off from the land of the living
Through the sin of my people, who deserved the punishment.
And his grave was set among the wicked,
And with the rich in his death
Though he had done no injustice
And has spoken no falsehood.
But the Lord chose to crush him by disease,
That, if he made himself an offering for guilt,
He might see offspring and have long life,
And that through him the Lord's purpose might prosper.
Out of his anguish he shall see it;
He shall enjoy it to the full through his devotion.

My righteous servant makes the many righteous,
It is their punishment that he bears;
Assuredly, I will give him the many as his portion,
He shall receive the multitude as his spoil.
For he exposed himself to death
And was numbered among the sinners,
Whereas he *Bore the Guilt* of the many
And *Made Intercession for Sinners.*
  (Isa. 53:1-12, *The Jewish Study Bible*, emphasis added)

The School of Rabbi Judah the Prince recognises Isaiah 53 as a description of the Messiah, "the leprous one," as it is said, "Surely he hath borne our griefs and carried our sorrows. Yet we did esteem him stricken, smitten of God, and afflicted"—Cohen uses the KJV here. Only the Messiah, the lamb without blemish, can bear human griefs and carry human sorrows. The entire chapter describes sin-bearing. It is a description of what happened on the Day of Atonement. The sacrificial animal without blemish, who bore all the sins of all the people, was slaughtered, and the blood carried into the Most Holy Place, where cleansing occurred. The Messiah was to be "leprous"—that is, laden with the sin of the human race. "But the Lord chose to crush him by disease, that if he made himself an offering for guilt, he might see offspring and have long life."

Here is the restoration of Eden and immortality. Look at the declaration of the Messianic redemption in the statement: "My righteous servant makes the many righteous, it is their punishment that he bears." Some Jewish scholars argue that the servant in this passage is a specific individual; the Targum and various Midrashim identify the servant as the Messiah. Others have strained to prove that this servant signifies the suffering of collective Israel at the hands of their enemies. Still others have equated the servant with Moses, or Jeremiah, or "the righteous minority of Israel." Some rabbis deny that there is the "notion of vicarious suffering" in this chapter of Isaiah.[126] The entire animal sacrificial system is oriented to the Messianic sin bearer, so it cannot be denied. Rabbi Judah the

Prince eminently believed that this passage depicted the sin-bearing Messiah.

As stated above, Messianic penetration in the Tanak is of two types. One type has the common thread of Messianic entrance as a low-key affair; it happens in the garb of a common man in humility. It is, as above in Isaiah's description, "the suffering servant." But it had cosmic significance. In Malachi's words, "But who may abide the day of his coming, or who shall stand when he appeareth. For He is like a refiner's fire" (Mal. 3:2, KJV). He comes as a lamb to the slaughter, as a sin bearer, as a purifier from sin.

But there are also grand scenes of Messianic entry that are associated with the resurrection of the dead, where there is divine majesty and kingship—for example:

> O gates, lift up your heads! Up high, you everlasting doors, so the King of glory may come in! Who is the King of glory?—the Lord, mighty and valiant, the Lord, valiant in battle. O gates, lift up your heads! Lift them up, you everlasting doors, so the King of glory may come in. Who is the King of glory?—the Lord of hosts, He is the King of glory. (Ps. 24:7-10, *The Jewish Study Bible*)

Daniel 12:1-2 have already been alluded to, and it is another majestic entrance of Messiah the King and is associated with the resurrection.

Ha-Mashiach will first provide redemption "as a lamb to the slaughter," and then he will usher in immortality and an everlasting kingdom. This is the great hereafter. Thus is accomplished the return to the Edenic state, where Adam and Eve were first installed before the great disobedience.

C. The Doctrine of the Chosen People

1. The Abrahamic Covenant

Moses understood this very well. Everything hinged on the Abrahamic Covenant, but it must be viewed in the entirety of God's relationship with humanity. It is a sacred part of God's plan for the world. It must be viewed as a special love relationship with Israel, but it was symbolic of God's eternal love relationship with all humanity, God's greatest joy and burden. Besides being a love relationship with Israel, it was a business relationship. Those who do not feel that Israel is special or that Israel has no part to play deceive themselves, if they believe the denouement of the Tanak. Besides classing Israel as special, the business relationship of Israel with God placed upon them a massive responsibility. Having been accepted by Abraham, the children of Abraham cannot sidestep the issue. They are not in the land of Israel for a purely political or national reason. They are there because God expects them to achieve "the blessedness of all nations." They can only do this if they understand the gravity and the expectation of the Abrahamic Covenant. Moses believed it and laid the groundwork (a great accomplishment) to get them ready for the job. The time element in God's plan is incomprehensible; retrospectively, it looks like a massive waste. The suffering of humanity in the sequence is massive, and the suffering of Israel is also colossal. There should be no assignment of blame here because it has not been easy. But now Israel has another opportunity.

Israel's history, in retrospect, makes the matter clearer. Here we must rely again on the Abrahamic Covenant.

1. The occupation of the Promised Land is sacred and very important—but to the Covenant. A modicum of land is now restored. It is willed by God and must be guarded, prospered, and protected.
2. The magnification of the Torah is primary to the Covenant. It must be deemed as Tanak, Israel's only canon, and must

be Israel's sole guide. Torah contains the eschatological blueprint.

3. The Messianic promise, the 'Seed of Abraham' is the most essential part of the covenant. "In thy Seed shall nations of the earth be blessed" needs to be grasped for success. The blessedness of all nations is the receiving of the Messiah and is still to be achieved.

At this juncture, there must be a discussion of the great body of Halachah that has developed out of the Torah written down at Mt. Sinai. Of necessity, the Torah needs to be deciphered into moral, redemptory, and what has been defined as Halachah. The Christian world has appropriated the moral law in the Torah, the redemptory function of Torah, and selected aspects of the body of Halachah that was part and parcel of the written Torah. This body of Halachah has further defined the Israelites as a nation. It has also defined Judaism starting at Mt. Sinai. The Aaronic priesthood was established at the onset and, with the building of the Tabernacle, the Tabernacle became the centre of worship. The sacrificial system was composed of redemptive, thanksgiving, and cultural sacrifices. When the First Temple, or Solomon's Temple, was built on the Temple Mount, Jerusalem became the centre of worship in Judaism and the centre of the Jewish world. The focus of Judaism was oriented to the Temple services. This was temporarily lost when the Babylonians destroyed it, but on being rebuilt as the Second Temple, it again functioned as the centre of Judaism. But when the Second Temple was destroyed by the Romans and the diaspora occurred, attention was paid solely to Halachah. With the definitive development of the Talmud, the nature of Judaism totally changed. Having lost the redemptive sacrificial system in practice, only Passover and the Day of Atonement remained as reminders. The schools of the rabbis and sages would make of Halachah a virtually new Judaism that did not concentrate on redemption but rather on the Torah or law. The Talmud took ascendancy away from the Tanak and became the supreme focus of rabbinic Judaism.

I have written extensively in this book about the neglected redemptive aspects of Judaism, which are mentioned in the Talmud.

But I have not focussed on the rest of Halachah. A description is necessary. Abraham Cohen has conveniently classified the body of social Halachah, and I now draw attention to it:

2. Talmudic Influence[127]

The following classification (points 1-6) is excerpted from Cohen's *Everyman's Talmud*, pages vi-viii.

1. Domestic Life:
   This concerned a discussion of Woman, Marriage and Divorce, Children, Education, and Filial Piety
2. Social Life:
   This concerned The Individual and the Community, Labour, Master and Workman and Peace and Justice.
3. Moral Life:
   This defined aspects of The Imitation of God, Brotherly Love, Humility, Charity, Honesty, Forgiveness, Temperance, and Duty to Animals.
4. Physical Life:
   Care of the body, Rules of Health, Dietetics, The Treatment of Disease.
5. Folk-Lore:
   Demonology, The Evil Eye, Magic and Divination, Dreams, and Superstitions.
6. Jurisprudence:
   (a) Criminal Law
       The Courts, Judges and Witnesses, The Trial, Modes of Punishment.
   (b) Civil Law
       Torts, Found Property, Bailment, Tenancy, Sale and Delivery, Prescriptive Right, and Inheritance.

The practice of Halachah varied in the chronological history of Israel. Primitive Judaism suffered greatly. Idolatry, the great traumas of the destruction of the First and Second Temples, the forced exiles in foreign lands, the expulsions from countries where they had settled, the persecutions by pogroms and holocausts, the havoc created by the forces of assimilation—all these events took their toll on what was original, primitive Judaism.[128]

Current Judaism is significantly focussed on the above Halachah,[129] which has been confused by the Talmudic departures from Tanakian Judaism. With the various denominations representing the great variation in modern Judaism as a philosophy, variations in religious practice and disunity in Israel is massive. The excessive pluralism is more of a warring diversity. It is highly divisive and destroys a necessary unity in Israel. Great energy is spent on the differences, rather than the unity that is so essential in modern Israel. My book *The Fair Dinkum Jew* is a call for reformation, and mine is not a lonely voice.

3. The Task of Moses

It was Moses's job to get Israel out of Egyptian slavery, place them back in the Promised Land, and make them aware of the Abrahamic Covenant. This was very difficult. Horeb (Mt. Sinai) accomplished reformatory guidelines:

1. **Moral,** and applied to all humanity. This included the Decalogue.
2. **Redemptory,** and again applied to all humanity. Messiah comes for all humanity. This included the daily sacrifice for sin and individual penitence. It also included the Day of Atonement, which is applicable to all humanity
3. **Halachah,** deduced from the **Ceremonial** laws of feasts and thanksgiving, and local governance, for the everyday life of the Israelites as an ethnic people. It contains many rules, some of which could benefit all humanity but were especially necessary for the reformation of a group of idolatrous and unruly slaves.

The Aaronic priesthood was installed to manage it all. Moses went a little bit to the extremes in some of his rules and summary punishments. Some of the great rabbis and sages in Israel also went to extremes; this is reflected in the production of the Talmud and its elevation to the erroneous, giddy heights of being salvific. This extremism has changed Judaism into a philosophy instead of the redemptive Judaism, which was the religion of Moses. Moses found that he could not take the unruly, idolatrous Hebrews into the Promised Land. Forty years in the desert resulted in the deaths of most of these unruly, rebellious, and idolatrous slaves. God equated them with the antediluvian wicked whom He destroyed by the flood, when He wanted to destroy them at Mt. Sinai and make of Moses a great nation.

4. The Task of Joshua

Joshua was able to take them across to possess the land. Joshua succeeded in establishing them there. In a chapter in this book, a brief history of Israel in the Promised Land has been told.

5. The Task of King David

Israel reached its peak as a religious, political, and national entity and power in David's tenure, and it appeared to be poised to carry out the Abrahamic Covenant under the reign of David's son Solomon. But Solomon failed miserably with the introduction of idolatry and the slide of the nation into heathenism. The Babylonians eventually destroyed the First Temple.

6. The Task of Inspired Prophets

Reformation has been the focus of the history of Israel, from David to the rise of modern Zionism. The major and minor prophets were reformers. But Israel was steeped in idolatry and corruption.

7. The Task of Modern Zionism

Theodor Herzl, Chaim Weizmann, Vladimir Jabotinsky, and David Ben-Gurion appear to stand out as giants in modern Zionism in the successful achievement of the return to the Promised Land. Theodor Herzl, in his dream of the Jews returning to the Holy Land, stated:

> The Jews who will it shall achieve their State. We shall live at last as free men on our own soil, and in our own homes peacefully die. The world will be liberated by our freedom, enriched by our wealth, magnified by our greatness. And whatever we attempt there for our own benefit will redound mightily and beneficially to the good of all mankind.[130]

Israel must now see the great wealth to be reaped by the realization of the Abrahamic Covenant. Indeed, it will secure and benefit Israel as a nation and "will redound mightily and beneficially to the good of all mankind." There, is the fulfilment of the Abrahamic Covenant. There, is the cleansing of Israel and all humanity. There, is the triumph of the resurrection. Moses the Patriarch would heartily endorse the prophecy of Herzl.

8. Israel's Task Today

The survival of Israel is the task in hand today, and it should be viewed in terms of the Abrahamic Covenant and a return to the redemptive Judaism of Moses. The Third Temple needs to be rebuilt. God must return to live amongst His people. We cannot forget His request: "Let them make Me a Sanctuary that I may live among them." In my book *The Fair Dinkum Jew*, I have written extensively about the reformation necessary. It is imperative that Israel needs to believe in and defend its political, national, and religious integrity.

9. Tanakian Eschatology

Tanakian eschatology requires Israel to accomplish the Abrahamic Covenant; the Messianic Age needs to be ushered in. The Messianic Age is not mysticism. A glorious future is still in store for Abraham's children. The Messianic shedding of blood and the resurrection will usher in immortality. God's great desire to be reunited with His loved ones (all humanity) will have been achieved. He will do it Himself through His Ruach and Mashiach power. Hear, O Israel, the Lord our God is one.

CHAPTER 9

A BRIEF RELIGIO-POLITICAL
HISTORY OF ISRAEL

The history of Israel starts with Abraham at about 2100 BC. The precedent history recorded by Moses has application to the Jews, and there is no doubt that the Creation story of the beginning of the universe also belongs to them. The Garden of Eden and Adam and Eve are solid cornerstones in the original foundation of Judaism. To them also belongs the patriarchal lineage along which the Oral Torah was passed from Adam to Noah and thence to Shem, his son. Ultimately it came to Abraham from Shem through the line of Arphaxad, Abraham's ancestor. But the ethnicity and legitimacy of the Jews begins with Abraham. Why should any nation be entitled to legitimacy? It is because God gave the Jews a mission, a cause for them to endure. The covenant that Abraham made with God unequivocally establishes their legitimacy. Abraham lived in Ur of the Chaldees, a thriving city deep in Sumerian Mesopotamia with its idol worship and heathen culture. But Abraham had championed monotheism and cleansed his father's house of idols. It was then that God called him and made the covenant with him. This covenant was recorded by Moses in Genesis 12:

> The Lord said to Abram, Go forth from your native land And from your father's house To the land that I will show you. I will make of you a great nation, And I will bless you; I will make your name great, And you shall be a blessing. I will bless those who bless you. And curse him that curses you; And all the families of the earth shall bless themselves by you. (Gen. 12:1-3, *The Jewish Study Bible*)

The covenant was reinforced in Genesis 17, and God changed Abram's name to Abraham. In addition, circumcision was introduced as a tangible sign of the validity of the covenant.

> Such shall be the Covenant between Me and you And your offspring to follow, which you shall keep: Every male among you shall be circumcised. You shall circumcise the flesh of your foreskin, And that shall be the sign of the Covenant Between Me and you . . . . Thus shall My Covenant Be marked in your flesh As an everlasting pact. (Gen. 17:10-13)

There is no doubt that the Abrahamic Covenant was interpreted in terms of land, Torah, and Messiah. As the lives and the writings of the leaders of Israel unfolded, the judges, prophets, and kings of Israel were concerned with the covenant. All were inspired to challenge Israel to the task of the covenant. Their national existence stood or fell as they upheld the sacredness of land, Torah, and Messianic expectation. The inspired writings that recorded the foundation and history of the Jewish nation became enshrined in the Tanak. Malachi, the last book of the Tanak, was written around 425 BC. The era of the production of the Tanak closed around 400 BC, and the Tanak became Israel's inspired guiding light and collective Torah. Israel's history to that point in time was recorded in the Tanak.

Not long after Abraham arrived in Canaan, famine drove him and his large retinue to a short sojourn in Egypt, but then he returned to Canaan. His grandson Jacob became the heir to the covenant (see chapter 22, "The Dream of Jacob"). Jacob had 12 sons from two wives and two concubines. Jacob's favourite son, Joseph, was sold by his jealous brothers into slavery and ended up in Egypt. Joseph prospered there, eventually becoming prime minister of Egypt and rescuing the country from seven years of drought that came after seven years of plenty. He had had divine revelation that seven years of prosperity would precede the drought and made provision for the drought years. Jacob and his other 11 sons and families ended up in Egypt because of the famine in Canaan; they met with Joseph and settled in the Land of Goshen, a fertile part of the Nile Valley. They prospered there, multiplied, and were perceived as a threat to the Egyptians of the time of the pharaohs. The Egyptian nation was indigenous to Africa with a home-grown people who had arrived from the Western Desert. (The Arabs did not Arabize Egypt till after AD 600.) Jacob's children, who were now a virtual nation, became very visible in Egypt. They were enslaved by the pharaohs to reduce the threat perceived from their presence—a slavery that lasted for 430 years. Moses was raised up by God to bring Israel back to Canaan. Moses was born around 1525 BC.

Moses is considered the greatest of the prophets in Israel. He was responsible for the organization of the uneducated, unruly, idolatrous, ex-slave Israelites into a disciplined and religious nation—a formidable and daunting task. Fortunately, as has been demonstrated over the entire Jewish history, the Oral Torah had been preserved. This primitive Torah, which had come down from Adam via the Patriarchs to Noah and thence to Abraham, Jacob, and Joseph, had survived. Moses benefited from a pharaonic university education. He was educated in all of the martial arts and governing and leadership abilities, which befitted and qualified an heir to the throne of the pharaohs. He was fully aware of Hammurabi and educated in the history of the then known world. He was also endowed with the knowledge of the Oral Torah, which had come down from Adam, and which had been instilled in him by his nurse and early educator (who also happened to be his mother), Jochebed. She had given him a awareness of his Hebrew ancestry, and he became acutely aware of the Abrahamic Call of God. The Abrahamic Covenant was the challenge that most governed his thinking. This was a major factor in his behaviour as he made a conscious decision to eschew the Throne of Egypt in preference to the leadership of a people through whom the blessedness of all nations would come. His people would be the ancestors of the Messiah, whose kingdom would be forever and ever. He had a difficult time trying to broker a release of the Hebrew slaves. Many of them were already steeped in the sun worship of Egypt and were not ready to be dislodged from slavery. Despite slavery, they were enjoying the flesh pots of Egypt. Many decided to stay in Egypt, having become idolators and intermarried with Egyptians—they had lost their Jewish heritage. Moses's youthful enthusiasm resulted in his murdering of an Egyptian, which he thought he had hidden by burying the body in the desert sand. But the news had spread because he was betrayed by his own kith and kin, and he had become a fugitive from Egyptian justice. He ran away to Midian, where he got married, fathered some children, and made a living tending his father in law's sheep for 40 years. But God did not leave him there at peace. While there he wrote the Book of Job (my belief, buttressed by the Talmud), which spans the scope of the relationship of God with his created universe.

Eventually Moses faced up to the task of his life at the Burning Bush. He became a fearless and fierce spiritual and military leader. He had a huge task of re-educating an idolatrous group of unruly and uneducated slaves. This education was not only in the oral Torah but also in governing them on a local and national basis. He organized them in maintaining education, justice, and health care. When he wrote everything he had in his mind, and with the promptings from God, the Pentateuch spurted from his pen. Mount Sinai gave him the inspiration, which would harness his knowledge of the primitive Oral Torah as well as the knowledge he had obtained in his university education in Egypt. He became a zealot with the fierce ambition of establishing his people as a nation in the Promised Land. Eventually he did not get to do that final task of entering and possessing the Promised Land. He passed the baton to Joshua, the son of Nun, and laid the groundwork for the judges and prophets and kings in Israel who followed him. The Book of Genesis mainly contains the story of Creation and the Patriarchal history of the world to his time. Exodus is chiefly concerned with the exit from Egypt and receiving the law at Sinai. The Book of Leviticus tells of the Tabernacle and the priestly ministry. Numbers records the wanderings in the wilderness. The Book of Deuteronomy contains a summary of everything important to Israel in their past, present, and future; it ends with the dire warning that Israel's loss of the vision of the Abrahamic Covenant would result in punishment. The plan is spelled out.

> That thou shouldest enter into Covenant with the Lord thy
> God, and into His oath which the Lord thy God maketh
> with thee this day; That He may establish thee today for a
> people unto Himself, and that He be unto thee a God, as
> He hath said unto, and as He hath sworn unto thy fathers,
> to Abraham and to Isaac, and to Jacob." (Deut. 29:12-13,
> KJV)

And what happens if they do not keep the Covenant of Abraham?

> And the Lord rooted them out of their land in anger, and in
> wrath, and in great indignation, and cast them into another
> land. (Deut. 29:28, KJV)

> Even all the nations shall say, Wherefore hath the Lord done
> thus unto this land? What meaneth this great anger? Then
> men shall say, Because they have forsaken the Covenant of
> the Lord God of their fathers . . . For they went and served
> other gods. (Deut. 29:24-25, KJV)

And what happens if they repent and seek to keep the Covenant of
Abraham?

> That then the Lord thy God will turn thy captivity, and have
> compassion upon thee, and will return and gather thee from
> all the nations where the Lord thy God hath scattered thee.
> (Deut. 30:3, KJV)

Nothing could be clearer; Israel's future was lucidly spelled out.
There would be no surprises. The plan of the covenant was to beget
the Messiah, who would restore immortality.

Moses could not have been more absolute in his warning about
what would be the consequences of abrogating the Abrahamic
Covenant. Israel would be punished severely. Idolatry was their
besetting sin. Their national standing would be devastated by their
idolatry and rejection of the worship of Jehovah.

After Moses, from about 1400-1050 BC, Israel struggled on under the rulership or guidance of the judges and prophets. The significant names that are traced in the Tanak, in somewhat historic chronological order, are Joshua, Othniel, Ehud, Deborah, Barak, Gideon, Abimelech, Tola, Jair, Eli, and Samuel. Joel, Abijah, and Samson are also mentioned latterly with some spiritual leadership. Judges, prophets, and high priests played their part, but Samuel was the most powerful leader to the time of the establishment of the monarchy.

Following the partial acquisition of the Promised Land, the initial theocratic government of Israel deteriorated in the days of Eli, the high priest. Idolatry and anarchy prevailed. The evil sons of Eli typified the rotten atmosphere in Israel. Israel was worshipping Baalim and Ashtaroth, the heathen gods. The Torah scrolls penned by Moses had been misplaced and lost. The Philistines captured the Ark of the Covenant and placed it in their idolatrous Temple of Dagon. That news caused the death of Eli. The grandson of Eli was born shortly after and was named Ichabod, which meant "The glory has departed from Israel" (1 Sam. 4:21-22, *The Jewish Study Bible*). Israel sank to an all-time low. Before the Ark of the Covenant was returned to Israel after 20 years, 50,070 men had died in punishment by God. The Philistines could not cope with the Ark. God had already called Samuel, when he was still a child. When he took office he secured Israel again with a strong theocratic management. But his two sons, like those of Eli, also became corrupt. The bright lights in Israel became dissatisfied with the priestly leadership and demanded a monarchy, like the surrounding nations. Samuel became very agitated and refused, but God ordered him to comply. "It is not you they have rejected, it is Me" (1 Sam. 8:7, *The Jewish Study Bible*). Saul was chosen as king, and a disastrous period followed.

But the people's choice was not God's choice. God had willed that Judah was to be the ancestor of the Messiah, and the kingdom was passed to David, the son of Jesse, of the tribe of Judah. He was "a man after God's own heart" (1 Sam. 13:14). The glorious expansive reign of David followed, and Solomon his son succeeded him.

Solomon was a man of peace. David viewed the Tent Tabernacle as a relic of their miserable wilderness existence. David's wish to build a temple to replace the Tent Tabernacle, which had housed the Levitical Priesthood and had carried out the religious life of Israel, was disallowed by God. God gave the task to Solomon. He built the glorious First Temple on Mount Moriah. The Holiest of Holies was situated over the very exact spot where Abraham offered Isaac, enacting the sacrifice of the Messiah. The reign of David represents the zenith of the splendor of the Israelite nation. Solomon was responsible for the downward slide—downhill all the way from there until AD 1948. Solomon had many wives and concubines. Many foreign, idolatrous women whom he loved had undue influence over him; 1 Kings 11 tells us all about it. Despite all his wisdom and all his glory and closeness to God, he allowed his wives to turn away his heart after other gods. He went after Ashtoreth, idol of the Sidonians, and Milcom, idol of the Ammonites. He built high places with altars for Chemosh, the abomination of Moab, and for Molech, abomination of the children of Ammon. He did likewise for all his foreign wives, who burned incense and sacrificed to their gods. The record says:

> *And the Lord was angry with Solomon* . . . . Wherefore, the Lord said unto Solomon . . . I will surely tear the kingdom away from thee and will give it to thy servant . . . but will give one tribe to thy son . . . for David thy father's sake. (1 Kings 11:9-13 The Jewish Study Bible, emphasis added).

The kingdom was divided between Jeroboam and Rehoboam, into the northern kingdom called Israel and the southern kingdom called Judah. Judah was comprised of the Tribe of Judah, some Benjaminites, and some Levites, which included the high priesthood.

The northern kingdom, called Israel, had a disastrous history during the reigns of kings from Jeroboam I to the last king, Hoshea. The northern kingdom was destroyed when attacked by Assyrian Shalmaneser V at about 722 BC. He carried most of the people to

Assyria, and they never came back. They are referred to as the Lost Ten Tribes.[131]

The southern kingdom of Judah was ruled by a succession of kings from Rehoboam to Zedekiah, a period from about 925 BC to 588 BC. In that year Nebuchadnezzar II inflicted the Babylonian captivity on the kingdom of Judah; Jerusalem and Solomon's Temple were destroyed.

During the period of the monarchies of both kingdoms, God sent prophets to reform the Israelites, who were plagued by idolatry. The penchant for idolatry by Israel was very strong. After Samuel, the prophets Elijah, Elisha, Obadiah, Joel, Jonah, Amos, Hosea, Isaiah, and Micah appeared in that chronological order, but with some overlap; they had influence on both kingdoms. Nahum, Zephaniah, Jeremiah, Habakkuk, and Daniel arose as the idolatry and waywardness in Israel mounted to huge proportions, engulfing Israel in massive iniquity. Israel was almost totally given over to idolatry. God was in a state of despair. Zerubbabel arrived back from captivity in 536 BC to rebuild the Temple; the captives Ezra and Nehemiah followed. During this period the prophets Zechariah and Haggai had immense influence. The final Tanakian prophet Malachi had influence at the time of Nehemiah. The prophets were all reformers and rose independently of the mostly corrupt ordained priesthood. The chief priests during the monarchy were not god-fearing leaders; they had lost sight of the Torah and the redemptive religion of primitive Judaism. However, the prophets were great reformers and did their best to get Israel to return to the worship of the true God. Their vision of the Abrahamic Covenant sought to reclaim Israel. They railed against idolatry. Simon Sebag Montefiore, in his astounding book *Jerusalem—The Biography*, gives an excellently researched detailed account of this dreadful period in Jewish history.[132] Part one in his book titled *Judaism* is the best reliable account and commentary I have found about this period; serious students of Jewish history should read this work. I do not agree with all his opinions and conclusions, but I heartily endorse the majority of his work dealing with the Tanakian period. I quote from his preface:

> There was surely scant prospect that David's little citadel, capital of a small kingdom, would become the world's cynosure. Ironically it was Nebuchanezzar's destruction of Jerusalem that created the template for holiness because that catastrophe led the Jews to record and acclaim the glories of Zion. Such cataclysms usually led to the vanishing of peoples. Yet the Jews exuberant survival, their obstinate devotion to their God and, above all, their recording of their version of history in the Bible laid the foundation for Jerusalem's fame and sanctity.[133]

Make no mistake, this account does not ascribe or credit the pre-captive Jews for Jewish "exuberant survival, their obstinate devotion." It is the travail of the Jews in the resultant captivity that proved their remarkable resilience. The Jewish dross was consumed in the fires of the captivity. It was a remarkable reformation that must be lauded. Also, the foundation for "Jerusalem's fame and sanctity" was not laid in the record of the writings in Babylon, but in the meeting of Abraham and Melchizadek in their embrace of the Abrahamic Covenant long before. However, the resilience of the Jews does certainly reinforce it. Unfortunately, we must sadly but loudly lament the demise of the nation of Israel after King David. Solomon and the idolatry he introduced must be blamed. It was the loss of dedication to the Abrahamic Covenant. Israel's besetting penchant—nay, addiction—to idolatry was the destructive catastrophe. We have therefore to credit the Jewish resilience to a small minority who "recorded and acclaimed the glories of Zion." Strong nationhood went down the drain, and the Abrahamic promise to be as the numbers of stars of the firmament became the characteristic of the discarded Abrahamic son, Ishmael. The Moslem faith, with which God made no Abrahamic Covenant, is professed by more people today than those professing the current brands of Judaism. Abraham had given Ishmael a separate blessing. Unless you count Christianity as a sect of Judaism, you do not get the numbers. Unfortunately again, one must concede that current Christianity bears little resemblance to the primitive Christianity of Yeshua of Nazareth, just as current Judaism bears little resemblance to the primitive Judaism of Abraham, Jacob, and Moses. Both Abraham and Yeshua of Nazareth would heartily but sadly agree. Montefiore's astoundingly honest book is a sad and highly lamentable account of Jerusalem and Mount Moriah, down through the ages. Thank God that 1948 took place, and nationhood is back. The Jews have another chance to implement the Abrahamic Covenant, continue their special communion and conversation with God, and bring peace and blessedness to all nations. This is a very daunting task.

Montefiore has an understanding of the Abrahamic Covenant. He recognizes land, Torah, and Messiah. Tracing the early history of Jerusalem, he states:

> The Bible took the place of the Jewish state and the Temple became, as Heinrich Heine put it, the "portable fatherland of the Jews, the portable Jerusalem." No other city has its own book and no other book has so guided the destiny of a city. The sanctity of the city grew out of the exceptionalism of the Jews as the Chosen People. Jerusalem became the Chosen City, Palestine [Canaan] the Promised Land, and this exceptionalism was inherited and embraced by the Christians and the Muslims.[134]

Again, Montefiore must agree that the cause of the devastation and loss of the Temple and Jerusalem was the result of Israel's forsaking of the Abrahamic Covenant. It was Israel's preference for idolatry that destroyed the Temple and Jerusalem. Israel needs to embrace some repentance here. The Christians and Moslems who invaded the Holy Land were an unruly, cruel, and unholy lot who did nothing but desecrate it—especially the Christians, who paid more attention to relics than to the ethics of Yeshua of Nazareth. The Moslems tried desperately to stamp out the legitimacy of Isaac and Jacob. Building a mosque on the site of the Jewish Temple has desecrated Mt. Moriah. World Jewry is now faced with the responsibility of eschewing idolatry and keeping the covenant.

147

What else will they talk to God about? Without the Abrahamic Covenant and Messianic deliverance, Judaism is a purposeless religion. Embracing the Abrahamic Covenant tells God that His desire to reinstate immortality is their priority. Scholarly discussion of the Talmud is not a substitute for redemptive Judaism. The Jewish state must rebuild the Temple and renew its redemptive service in order to fulfil the Abrahamic Covenant. No "portable fatherland" or "portable Jerusalem" will suffice now that they are back in the Holy Land. The principle of the lamb without blemish must be reclaimed. It is no longer necessary to bleed the animals to death, but the symbolism of the blood is the essence of Israel's Day of Atonement. It must be symbolically carried again in principle, into, and splashed in the Most Holy Place. The Shechinah is waiting for it. The deep, redemptive meaning of atonement has been lost in current Judaism. Circumcision is remembered, but the Covenant it forgotten. The sign has eclipsed the covenant.

The time of Malachi needed significant reformation. The opening complaint of his book is Israel's disregard for the perfection of the symbolic Messianic animal sacrifice. This disregard accelerated over 400 years to AD 70.

> The prophetic tradition roundly condemns those who substituted the offering of sacrifices for true penitence, but at the same time the prophets never objected to sacrifices as such and denounced those who spoiled sacrifices by choosing flawed animals.[135]

From the time of Eden the sacrificial animal was to be without blemish, because it signified the Messiah, who was deity. Yet Israel was bringing defiled food to the temple. Blemished animals—the sick, the lame, the blind, the stolen, and deformed—were being sacrificed. God said, "If only you would lock My doors, and not kindle fire on My altar to no purpose! I take no pleasure in you . . . and I will accept no offering from you" (Mal. 1:10, *The Jewish Study Bible*).

God preferred that the doors of His Temple be locked, rather than blemished and profane sacrifices be offered. The perfection of the Messianic sacrifice was ignored, and God was insulted. God also railed against the common practice adopted in Israel of divorcing their Judahite wives and taking heathen, idolatrous wives (Mal. 2:10-16, *The Jewish Study Bible*).

The strident proclamation in this short book of Malachi is the trumpet announcement of the coming Messiah.

> Behold I am sending My messenger to clear the way before Me, And the Lord whom you seek shall come to His Temple suddenly. As for the angel of the Covenant that you desire, he is already coming. But who can abide the day of his coming, and who can hold out when he appears? For he is like a smelter's fire and like fullers lye. Lo, I will send the prophet Elijah to you before the coming of the awesome, fearful day of the Lord. (Mal. 3:1, *The Jewish Study Bible*)

Many Jewish scholars and commentators agree that Malachi calls for reformation. The coming of the Messiah was to be ushered in by the spirit of the prophet Elijah, which was a divine call for reformation from idolatry. Witness the events on Mount Carmel. Now the Tanak teaches that Elijah did not die but had been taken by God into paradise. Israel expected him, as the forerunner, to come back to the earth to usher in the coming Messiah.

The history of Israel after Malachi was again downhill after the reformation wrought by Zerubbabel, Ezra, and Nehemiah. There was no king in Israel after Zedekiah, who was vanquished by Nebuchadnezzar II. The world powers that ruled after the Babylonian kings kept Israel in subjugation. Medo-Persia, Greece, and Rome would hold Israel in subjugation. Israel would continue as a depressed and sinful people with no real independence and nationhood until AD 1948. After Malachi, the period dubbed the Silent Period ensued. But Jews as a people were restive and resilient. Tanakian Judaism would be replaced by a complex philosophy with the development of the Mishnah, and the Talmud.

Kabbalah is an attempt to derail primitive, redemptive Judaism. Ask Gershom Scholem for his opinion (see the chapter "The Ha-Mashiach of Israel"). Theological schools would be established with the appearance of great sages, rabbis, and scholars. These centres were responsible for the writing of the Mishnah, Gemara, and Kabbalistic writings. The Tanak was the textbook for the composition of the Mishnah. It then would be virtually ignored, with attention being paid to the Mishnah, with major departures from the redemptive Judaism of the Tanak. The Talmud focussed on Mishnah and created its own devisings. Midrashi would become occupied with the confusion in the Talmud.

With the loss of the Second Temple, Judaism drastically changed. The 2,000 years of the diaspora that followed were dark days indeed. The Tanak was lost as the guiding source of belief and practice, and Judaism gave way to the Talmud as the source of guidance for religious practice. Israel would become pluralistic in belief, mostly with the preoccupation of their religious focus on the minutiae of halachah. This has developed into a high degree of disagreement and a warring divisive and deluded disunity. The Abrahamic Covenant would be lost as the fundamental and focal foundation and cornerstone. Belief in the Messiah became largely relegated to mysticism. Judaism is no longer a unified religion based on the Tanak alone. The loss of focus on the Abrahamic Covenant threatens Israel's ethnicity and legitimacy. The Jews would wander the world as a people without a homeland for 2,000 years until modern Zionism was born and fuelled by Theodor Herzl, Chaim Weizmann, Ze'ev Jabotinsky, and Ben Gurion. Since AD 1948 the nation of Israel has been a secular state, and more Jews still live outside the state of Israel, in a comfortable and preferred diaspora. There is no tinge of Zionism that can be traced in the current diaspora except by proxy. Modern idolatry is taking shape in world Jewry. Assimilation, secularism, humanism, religious superficialism, and religious extremism are the new idols. Where is the primacy of primitive, redemptive Judaism? Where is the Third Temple? Where is the Shechinah? Where is the longing for the redemptive Messiah?

CHAPTER 10

THE SHECHINAH—GOD WITH US

The Torah is defined as God's communion with humanity. Initially the Jews were not involved because they did not exist at Creation. The primal divine-human interaction began at the Creation and was a face-to-face dialogue that Adam and Eve had with God (original primal devekut). Adam and Eve were not Jews by definition. After the entrance of sin, this communion became a more distant interaction, but still a dialogue continued between God and humanity. It began in the oral or spoken form, committed to memory and passed down from generation to generation. Therefore Torah is not primarily a Jewish invention.

In the context of continued connection with God, it is of value to consider the Hebrew concept of devekut (communion with God). Devekut has been magnified, expanded, and detailed by both Kabbalah and Hasidism, but it is not original with them. In its original and purest definition, it is what occurred in Gan Eden between God and the primal couple and which was intended to continue on into eternity between God and humanity. It was interrupted by the entrance of the disobedience of the primal couple. God has initiated a persistence with it in terms of imparting His love through inspiration. His desire to "Dwell with Israel" in the Temple services was signified by the Shechinah in the Most Holy Place. God works eminently through the Ruach Hakodesh to be with humans; these influences are His efforts in maintaining devekut. Both Kabbalism and Hasidism have put devekut into a straitjacket by defining their own rules for it, as well as detailed, invented consequences of the breakage of those rules. Gershom Scholem has written very tersely and with clear thinking about devekut. His essay "Devekut, or Communion with God" is very instructive and highly valued for all devotees of a companionship with the Almighty. Devekut became a important necessary force as the gates of Gan Eden shut behind the guilty pair.[136]

The oral Torah in its human context commenced with the instruction given to Adam and Eve in the Garden of Eden. God finished creation of the sun, moon, and stars, as well as the animal and vegetable kingdoms. The human species was the pinnacle of His work. He placed them in the special spot, Eden. They were given sexuality, thus instituting marriage and procreation. They were given physical work tending the Garden, which produced food and drink. They were given the Sabbath in order to rest and commune with God. Their first Sabbath was not a rest, because they had just been created, and they had not worked physically as yet. Later the Sabbath would become a day of rest, but initially it was a celebration. It was God's rest from His labour of Creation. It was more a cessation of His work of Creation, because He is omnipotent. More specially, it was a celebration of His satisfaction with His handiwork. The first Sabbath for Adam and Eve was a special day when they formed a love relationship with God. He was their Father, and forever He would be a Father to the human race. The acknowledgement of God as our Father is the greatest celebration of the Sabbath. That celebration would be extended to God's intervention as our redeemer. The Sabbath was to be an enduring institution providing multiple benefits for both God and humanity. The weekly cycle, determined by seven rotations of the Earth, was an institution peculiar and specific to the Earth. God wanted one-seventh of humanity's time for devekut, to commune with them, to invigorate them with His love, to enjoy them. and to love them back. The added benefit for them was their rest from labour. One cannot desert a normal life for the implementation of total devekut without becoming an ascetic. God meant for humans to labour six days. Practicing the presence of God in our lives during those six days, as long as one does not have to be locked up into asceticism, is not an impossibility. The Torah should always be in our minds without the need to wear phylacteries or become ascetics.[137]

On that first Sabbath, He gave them a tour of the Garden and showed them the Tree of Life, which would provide them with continuing immortality. He also showed them the Tree of Knowledge of Good and Evil. Here was the first recognition of the existence of evil already in the universe. They were to stay away from it because they would lose their immortality if they were to eat of it. He introduced the idea of death to them: death would be an eternal cessation of existence. They were thus endowed with free will. They had to enter a constant decision to voluntarily choose God and eternal life, and to reject evil and eternal death. Eden was the commencement of the oral Torah. All this was Torah. It must have been somewhat overwhelming for Adam and Eve. The Garden was their home, but it also became God's home away from His usual abode. Being omnipresent, He could be with them continually. This was by the institution of the Shechinah (literally, "dwelling"'). He also got into the habit of walking in the Garden "at the cool of the day," and continuing His communion with the primal couple. He had a presence in the Garden. The perfect world had an overt presence of God, the Shechinah. Here is an introduction to the knowledge of God's immanence (God *with* us, not intrinsically *in* us), and transcendence (God is in the highest plain of existence, to which no created being can attain). God's glory was manifest in Eden. It was the first manifestation of the Shechinah.

Moses was the recipient of this story of the Creation, and the institution of the oral Torah from his parents Amram and Jochebed. He did not tell us for how long this state of Edenic perfection continued. Unfortunately, the primal couple ate of the Tree of Knowledge of Good and Evil, and disobedience, sin, and death entered the human world. Immortality was lost, Eden was removed, Shechinah was withdrawn, and immanence was darkened to the view of fallen humanity. It spelled separation from face-to-face communion with God (Gen. 1-3). God's special presence with Moses was manifest at the Burning Bush.

Shechinah would return again during the time of the journey of Israel from slavery in Egypt to the Promised Land. It was first manifested as the pillar of cloud by day and the pillar of fire by night (Exod. 13:21-22), and when the Tent Tabernacle was built at God's specific request: "Let them make Me a sanctuary that I might live among them" (Exod. 25:1, 8) His Shechinah enveloped the Tabernacle, and His presence was manifest continually in the Most Holy Compartment. The Shechinah also graced the Temple of Solomon. God has a constant desire to live with humanity. He created us for His pleasure and He longs to be constantly with His loved ones. The Shechinah is the manifestation of His great love and presence.

The Talmud amplifies the story of the Shechinah. God is transcendent because He is infinite and is everywhere in the universe. Under the heading of transcendence and immanence, Abraham Cohen extensively discusses the Talmudic presentation of this topic.

> When they [the rabbis] reflected upon the ineffable Majesty of the Creator, His absolute perfection and boundless might, they reverently spoke of Him as a Being immeasurably removed from the limitations of the finite world. But they, at the same time realised that such a transcendent God was of little use to the human being who was grappling with the problems of life and yearned for communion with a Helper and Comforter and Guide amidst his perplexities and struggles. They, accordingly stressed the doctrine that God was immanent in the world, and was very near to all who call on Him in sincerity . . . . "However high He be above His world, let a man but enter a synagogue, stand behind a pillar and pray in a whisper, and the Holy One, blessed be He, hearkens to his prayer. Can there be a God nearer than this, Who is close to His creatures as the mouth is to the ear?" (p. Ber. 13a) . . . . And the priestly benediction, "The Lord make His face to shine upon thee" (Numbers 6: 22-27) is interpreted, "May He give thee the light of the Shechinah" (Num. R. xi. 5). The Divine Presence brings God . . . into the most intimate contact with human beings, so that He even shares their sorrows. (Chag. 15b)[138]

When there is no physical manifestation of God's presence with humanity, such as light, smoke, or fire, He is even closer. In another very cogent pronouncement in the Talmud, Cohen states:

> Another Rabbinic concept to indicate the nearness of God and His direct influence on man is that of Ruach Hakodesh (the Holy Spirit). Sometimes it seems to be identical with the Shechinah as expressing the divine immanence in the world as affected by what transpires there. (Lament. R. 1. 45)[139]

The Talmud does not always present a scriptural message. In connection with the Ruach Hakodesh, there is described a period of absence of the prophetic gift after Malachi, which is interpreted as the withdrawal of the Holy Spirit from Israel. Instances then are quoted for the role of Bath Kol, or "daughter of a voice." There are times when God has said, "My Spirit shall not always strive with man" (Gen. 6:3), as in connection with the Flood. But God has not withdrawn His Holy Spirit from the earth, nor will He ever. Perhaps Bath Kol is a fainter perception of the Ruach Hakodesh, invented by the rabbinic scholars to be a substitute for what they perceived as a withdrawal of the Ruach Hakodesh. It will be glorious to be in the actual presence of the Holy One, blessed be He, and to be able to praise Him for the majesty and immanence (God with us) that we will enjoy forevermore.

Ruach Hakodesh is God, blessed be He. The Lord our God is one. Ruach Hakodesh is not another being with independence from the God we call Father. The rabbis did not recognise a separate entity or deity. Ruach Hakodesh is God Himself, manifest in a closeness to us, constantly there to assure us of His love and caring. David recognised the Ruach Hakodesh in the twenty-third psalm.

> Yea though I walk through the Valley of the Shadow of Death, I will fear no evil; for Thou art with me; Thy rod and Thy staff they comfort me. (Ps. 23:4, KJV)

Just as the shepherd uses his rod and staff to guide the sheep, so is the Ruach Hakodesh, Almighty God, by our side to be our companion and guide, if we only let Him.

The great prophet Elijah, who was taken by God into glory, was at a very low ebb in his life. Having risked his life to challenge Ahab and Jezebel, who caused Israel to plunge into idolatry, Elijah found himself with his tail between his legs, hiding in a cave in the mountains and fearing a wicked woman. God sent an earthquake and a fire, which did not bring Elijah any assurance. And then the Ruach Hakodesh spoke to him in the "still small voice." He was reassured that there were seven thousand in Israel who had still not bowed the knee to Baal. The Ruach Hakodesh got through to Elijah. The Ruach Hakodesh is God Himself, blessed be He, the Lord our God is one (see 1 Kings 19).

The Ruach Hakodesh is still God's way of getting close to us, concealing His majesty but penetrating our world of sin and woe. Moses knew he was going to his death as he climbed to the top of Pisgah in the mountain of Nebo. He turned to bless the tribes of Israel, and this is what he said.

> There is none like unto the God of Jeshurun, Who rideth upon the heaven in thy help, and in His excellency on the sky. The eternal God is thy refuge, and underneath are the everlasting arms; and He shall thrust out the enemy from before thee, and shall say, Destroy them. (Deut. 33:26, KJV)

The Ruach Hakodesh is God Himself, concealing His majesty so that He can access us. We are carried in "His everlasting arms," and many of us do not know it. The Talmud appears to wholeheartedly accept the concept that Elohim's plurality embraces the Ruach Hakodesh, but is reluctant to accept Elohim's oneness with Ha-Mashiach. It is because the Talmud describes Ha-Mashiach as a created being and expressed as a son. But the Tanak expresses the Ha-Mashiach as being in eternity as the redemptive name and function of Elohim. His divinity creates the penetrance of humanity, and He will come as "the Mighty God, the Everlasting Father" (Isa. 9:6). Divine Messianic Elohim is expressed in terms of human sonship.

God with us functionally and in reality is Ruach Hakodesh and Ha-Mashiach. Blessed be He, the Lord our God is one.

CHAPTER 11

THE TANAK

Guiding Principles of Discussion:

1. *Eternal Torah in the Mind of God*
2. *Definition and Evolution of Earthly Torah*
3. *The Primitive Torah*
4. *The Written Torah*
5. *The Collective Closed Torah, the Tanak.*
6. *The Interpretation of Torah*
7. *The Triumph of the Tanak*
8. *The Evolution of the Mishnah and Gemara*
9. *The History of the Use of Torah*
10. *The Emergence of Tradition*

1. Eternal Torah In The Mind Of God

God's immutable laws for the universe (multiverses) existed from eternity and pre-existed the creation of humans. This fact is defined as the will of God and is assumed in the writings called the Tanak. God's motives cannot be fathomed by human measures, but they are detectable by His creative acts and His handling of His created energy and matter. These are existent in both the physical and spiritual manifestations that are apparent. God must be assigned a mind that has been active in what He has created and in His relationships with the created matter and spiritual existence. Ideas of His character and behaviour are formed by understanding His created objects, solid, liquid, energy, scientific principles, and indeed His expressed thoughts, motives, feelings, and desires. God is both complex and simply understood, and the limitations of plunging the depths of understanding are human limitations. The concept that God's mind existed from eternity, and that Torah has also always existed from eternity as part of His machinations, is a mighty principle. The terrestrial side show has been at least one of His working plans in which humans are involved. But it is realised that this side show has been invested with such importance that it was and is His continuing eternal preoccupation. He has made a huge investment of Himself in the side show. This concept is acceptable, and it is compatible with Tanakian theology and is reinforced by the Talmud.[140]

God is not constrained by time, and neither were his perfect creatures Adam and Eve—until they disobeyed the Torah that existed from eternity. After he made them, "God saw that everything that He had made . . . was very good" (Gen. 1:31). The genetic determinants of free will were never meant to die. The telomeres and telomerase were built for eternity. Since their disobedience, humanity passed into the time mode very stringently, and death accessed their bodies. Death became an impending phenomenon on this planet (Gen. 2:17). God foresaw this, and His objective to reinstate the immortal condition first bestowed must be regarded as the prime and most important aspect governing His relationship with mortals. The side-show is His major preoccupation and is sealed in the eternal Torah in the mind of God.

Therefore it must be conceded that nothing is more important in eternal Torah than the redemption of fallen humanity. The terrestrial status quo is not acceptable to the eternal Torah. It is the nagging irritant in the mind of God. It is the source of frustration and sorrow in the eternal mind of God. Here is where Talmudic thought, although agreeing with the existence of the Eternal Torah of the Mind of God, has diverted from it. Redemption, the most prominent factor in the mind of God, has been relegated to mysticism, and post-Second Temple Judaism is no longer in sync with eternal Torah. Post-Second Temple Judaism is a runaway train that has derailed, and it is off the tracks of the eternal Torah. God's measures to deal with this catastrophe have precedence in His mind.

2. Definition and Evolution of Earthly Torah

The word "Torah" is best defined as the conversation of God with humanity. God had made and found Himself a love object. The conversation was first preoccupied with this love relationship, one of pure enjoyment and delight for both parties. But after the Fall, humanity separated itself from that love, and the conversation became preoccupied with mortality. There was great sorrow in heaven. Torah became involved in dealing with time, suffering and death, and resurrection.

In carrying out His desires for the side show defined above, it is apparent that God waits for key people to come along as His instruments, through whom He works. The sparseness of the occurrence of key people is restrictive to His purposes. The Patriarchs were obviously key people. Abraham and the Jews were key people. The Jews still are key people. It has been a major consternation why God tolerated polygamy, slavery, sexism, and racism in Tanakian times. He was waiting for key reformers to turn up to help Him to correct these evils. He endowed humanity with free will, and He is not about to rescind it. Human impatience with God for the current suffering and misdemeanours of humanity is understandable, but it is unfair and short-sighted. His dependence on key people is His decision, not His shortcoming. Humans are misled by but are mostly adverse to dictators. God takes every opportunity to effect reformation. His aversion to humanity's worship of other gods has been colossal, and He will go to strange lengths to punish any sort of idolatry. He admits to jealousy as any jilted lover.

The terrestrial oral Torah started with God's conversation with Adam and Eve. All that happened in Gan Eden, and after expulsion from it, formed the oral Torah. Meir ben Gabbai, a rabbi in Turkey, wrote these words in 1581.

> The highest wisdom [the sofia of God, which is the second
> sefirah] contains as the foundation of all emanations
> pouring forth out of the hidden EDEN the true fountain
> from which the Written and the Oral Torah emanate.[141]

The subsequent events culminating in the arrival of Moses became part of the primitive oral Torah. Gabbai refers to it above as the written Torah. It had been passed from memory to memory, from one generation to the next, from Adam to Moses. It became the foundation and guiding information of Judaism. The Pentateuch authored by Moses was the original *written* document, written in Hebrew. This segment was largely embodied in the Book of Genesis, documenting the history of the beginning of the world. It told the story of Adam and Eve and the Garden of Eden at the Creation of the world, a perfect world—until the disobedience of the primal couple and the loss of immortality. The redemptive plan to win back innocence, immortality, and face-to-face communion with God was outlined in the sacrificial system taught to Adam and Eve. It was the atonement for sin. Sin was defined as the transgression of the Torah.

God put Himself into the job of redemption through the Ruach Hakodesh and the Ha-Mashiach, integral parts of Himself, Elohim. Hear, O Israel, the Lord our God is one, Blessed be He. The first murder occurred over the symbol of the sacrifice, when a substitute symbol for the Messiah was made. Cain wanted God to recognise his works, his accomplishments as a farmer, as being "good enough" for him to be accepted by God. Cain wanted to bypass Ruach Hakodesh and Ha-Mashiach intervention with his own plan. Abel saw his guilt when he looked back at what had happened in Eden and at his own acts of disobedience. He was repentant by the gift of the Ruach Hakodesh and needed forgiveness. His parents had taught him that the shedding of the blood of the Messiah would take away his guilt and make him right with God. He brought the symbolic lamb without blemish from his flock to acknowledge Messianic salvation. Abel's offering for the eradication of his sins was accepted by God. But God rejected Cain's nonsymbolic, self-concocted offering. This scenario will be elucidated further in this book.

3. The Primitive Torah

The word "Torah" needs some further definition. The primitive Torah was the communication between God and humanity that started with the Creation. The conversation between God and humans, in the Garden and after, constituted God's guidelines for their lives. Adam and Eve taught this to their children, and that is how Cain and Abel learned their spiritual duties, which Abel accepted but Cain decided to challenge. Disobedience to the Torah had dire consequences. God's continuing effort to reach after His erring children—giving them further messages for their worship of Him, for instruction in the conduct of their lives, and for dealing with sin as it occurred—constituted the primitive oral Torah. This conversation became a living and growing relationship. This oral Torah passed down to the Patriarchs all the way to Moses, who wrote it down at Sinai.

The rabbinic dynasty never contended that Torah started with the Jews. Examination of the pre-Israel oral Torah is vital in order to trace the denouement of God's dealings with humanity. The story of the Patriarchs from Adam to Noah gave details of life after the entrance of sin; it is a summary of the early history of the world. There is a further discussion in this book of patriarchal Judaism, and it describes how humanity deteriorated from the pristine status of Eden to the utter wickedness of the antediluvian world:

> The Lord saw how great was man's wickedness on earth, and how every plan devised by his mind was nothing but evil all the time. And the Lord regretted that He had made man on earth, and His heart was saddened. The Lord said, I will blot out from the earth the man who I created. (Gen. 6:5-9, *The Jewish Study Bible*)

There is no doubt that God tried hard and long to reform antediluvian humanity; this was done through the power of Ruach Hakodesh, through Noah's witness under the Holy Spirit's guidance while building the Ark: "And the Lord said, My Spirit shall not always strive with man" (Gen. 6:3, KJV). God destroyed that civilization with the Flood, sparing Noah and his family. As He had with Adam and Eve, God made a covenant with Noah. Noah's first act as he exited the ark was to build an altar and make an animal sacrifice with the shedding of blood, emphasizing again the Messianic redemptive nature of God's effort to reinstate humanity to the perfect creation status of Eden.

But after the Flood, humanity went on the downward path again, and the Tower of Babel became the archetype of rebellion. The confounding of language occurred, and the dissatisfaction of God with the recurrent deterioration of the human race continued (Gen. 11).

Abraham then became the instrument in God's hand to be the father of a special people, to bring to pass the will of God to restore the original Edenic perfection that had been lost. In this effort the Abrahamic Covenant became the centrepiece of the book of Genesis. The other four books of the Pentateuch tell the story of Abraham's descendants being disciplined on their journey to the Promised Land, where they were to carry out the Abrahamic Covenant.

4. The Written Torah

Moses led the Israelites out of Egypt and brought them to Mt. Sinai, where he organized them into a religio-political nation. There is no doubt that the lawlessness—which characterized the antediluvian world, the Babel world, and the idolatrous world of the Israelite slaves in Egypt—made Moses very conscious of the propensity to lawlessness in humanity. He saw it as an incorrigible condition in his own people, and he tried to root it out by every means possible. He was extremely severe in his treatment of breaking the law, sometimes hardly giving them a chance for repentance. Cities of refuge were built for sinners to hide in, pending his judgements; many sinners were summarily put to death. As a result he built a most massive system of moral and ceremonial laws to govern them and prevent a recurrence of wickedness. Isaiah Horovitz wrote about Moses.

> In the days of our teacher Moses the only prohibitions were those he had expressly received at Sinai. Nevertheless, he added ordinances here and there for special purposes as they arose; and so did the prophets after him, and the scribes, and every generation after him with its scholars.[142]

To deal with sin, defined as the transgression of the law of God, God had already ordained the animal sacrificial system pointing to Messianic redemption. Moses officially instituted the Aaronic Priesthood to lead and implement the animal sacrificial system on an organized basis. Moses was consumed with the prevention and punishment of sin. At times he appeared merciless with the propensity of Israel to break God's law. Talmudic writings interpret the entire scenario painted by Moses as being in the mind of God prior to the creation of the world (Cohen discusses this on p. 347). Unfortunately the rabbinic dynasty post-destruction of the Second Temple concentrated on law keeping and forgot to factor in the work of the Ruach Hakodesh and Ha-Mashiach in the acts of repentance, confession, restitution, forgiveness, and atonement.

Everyone agrees that the primitive oral Torah was greatly expanded and magnified by what happened at Mount Sinai. Much of it was given to organize and govern a chosen people. The colossal task of Moses was the disciplining of a band of unruly and idolatrous slaves whom he had released from Egypt. He had to change them into a lively spiritual and God-fearing nation. After the writings of Moses became their guidelines, Torah continued to expand by God's guidance. The writings of the judges, prophets, kings, and others were added to the existing written Torah, as an account of Israel's historic vicissitudes in which God was intimately involved. That is how the Tanak grew. Written about humanity from Adam to

Moses to Malachi, the governing document for Israel also contains the essence of God's will for all humanity.

Initially the five books of Moses were the detailed standard to govern the behaviour of the Jewish people. Together with the Decalogue as its centre, the Torah outlined by Moses became the law in Israel. Many of its aspects were rules, some of which, if broken, had immediate dire punishment, namely death. Sabbath breaking (Num. 15:32-35), as well as the offering of children as sacrifices to Molech, homosexuality, bestiality, adultery, blasphemy, and idolatry (Lev. 20; 24; Deut. 13; 17; 22), were summarily punished by death by stoning. Most transgressions of the law, however, were leisurely forgiven by the timely symbolic sacrifices of animals without blemish, a practice that had come down from the disobedience of Eden.[143] Note that Steinsaltz and the Talmudic references he quotes do not relate the sacrifice of the sin offering to Messianic redemption for the atonement for sin. But it is obvious that the Temple services foreshadowed the Messianic redemption, which God had planned for the rescue.

And so the Pentateuch spelled out a code of behaviour and a system of governance for the chosen people. Moses was almost besotted with the sensitivity of Israel's propensity to sin and the fact that it was constantly strong and luring. The Aaronic priesthood was installed, which spelled out the redemptive nature of God's plan. Its beauty and responsibility were sealed together with the dire consequences by the sacrificial system. Sacrifices were made to deal with individual sin on an occurrence basis. Repentance and restitution preceded the animal sacrifice, which brought forgiveness. Atonement was accomplished by the shedding of blood. As the Passover festal lamb immortalised the celebration of deliverance from Egypt, so did the mighty Day of Atonement—instituted at Sinai, when the blood was taken into the Most Holy Place where the Shechinah dwelt—bring expiation and deliverance from sin. All the sins of all the people on a collective basis were forgiven on the Day of Atonement. The animal died on their behalf, and that animal without blemish represented the Messiah.

God's request, "Let them make Me a sanctuary that I may dwell among them," became the greatest challenge to Israel and the whole world (Exod. 25:8, *The Jewish Study Bible*). It was like one built a house, and God had the person install a "supervisory granny flat" for Himself within it. This flat was the Tent Tabernacle, at first in the wilderness wanderings and replaced later by the glorious Temple of Solomon (1 Kings 6:13). God said to Solomon, "And I will dwell among the children of Israel, and I will not forsake My people, Israel." And did He ever move in! He dramatically filled the Tent Tabernacle and then Solomon's Temple with His fiery presence, the Shechinah. Some biblical scholars claim that God has an exact similar abode in Heaven that supplied the pattern, which He had shown to Moses on the mountain for the copy built on Earth (Exod. 25:40). A scene in Heaven describes God's throne and fiery presence (see also Dan. 7:9-15).

There were times in Israel's history when Israel evicted God from the Tabernacle and the Temple. During Eli's high priesthood, his evil sons used the Ark of the Covenant illegally to fight the Philistines. The Ark was captured by the Philistines, and there was a great slaughter of Israelites by the Philistines. Eli died of shock, and his daughter-in-law, also in a state of shock, went into premature labour caused by an abrupt delivery of her pregnancy. She also died after naming the infant son that survived "Ichabod, saying, The Glory is departed from Israel" (see 1 Sam. 4-7). It took the supplanting of King Saul and the reign of King David to restore the Ark to the Most Holy Place in the Tent Tabernacle. (2 Sam. 6). When Solomon's Temple was built, the Shechinah transferred to it (2 Chron. 5:14; 7:1-2). It was a glorious day in Israel.

But Solomon built idolatrous shrines all around the Temple, and God allowed the Egyptians to spoil the Temple (1 Kings 14:25-26). Two hundred sixteen years later, King Ahaz desecrated it further (2 Kings 16:7-9, 17-18; 2 Chron. 28:24-25). Finally Babylonian King Nebuchadnezzar II destroyed the Temple completely. The God of the universe then became a homeless vagabond on earth. The side show in the eternal Torah in the mind of God appeared to be in ruins. The purpose of the Tabernacle and Solomon's Temple was the enactment of His Edenic plan to restore immortality and face-to-face communion with humanity. God was no longer supervising His plan of redemption on-site in Jerusalem. When the Second Temple was built and grandified by King Herod the Great, the Most Holy Place lay empty and there was no Shechinah. Leading up to AD 70, it became the greatest place of corruption in Israel, with the total devastation of the plan of Messianic redemption. This corruption of the priesthood came to a head during the time of the prophet Malachi, and it progressed to the Second Temple's destruction (See Mal. 1 and 2). With the destruction of the Second Temple 2,000 years ago, God has been a homeless person on earth.

To summarize the redemptive features of the Pentateuch, the essence of the law, the Ten Commandments, reclined in the Ark, in God's inner sanctum, the Most Holy Place. It was the standard He required. But realising that humanity could not reach that standard perfectly, He placed the Mercy Seat in the Most Holy Place. The sacrificial system with the shedding of the blood of the lamb without blemish would symbolically expiate for sin. He had pointed out the significance of this to Abraham on Mount Moriah. The perfect deity required a perfect standard of law keeping. But that was beyond the reach of sinful beings. Messianic blood would be shed for the expiation of sin, which was the transgression of the law. Perfect Messianic character would substitute in the time of judgement. On the Day of Atonement, that blood would be carried into the Most Holy Place and sprinkled on the Ark of the Covenant containing the law and the Mercy Seat; all the sins of all the people would be forgiven and wiped out. That is the whole meaning of Israel's holiest day of the year, the most important event in the Jewish calendar. God's abode in the Most Holy Place was designed to receive that blood and show mercy. The law, justice, and mercy met together in God's presence on the Day of Atonement in the Most Holy Place. The built-in Messianic mission is thus accomplished in symbolism. There is no greater urgent task for Israel than to rebuild the Temple, so that God can again live among us. Judaism has been a hopelessly fractured philosophy ever since the destruction of the Second Temple. The redemptive function of the Temple is no longer physically present in Israel. The spiritual highlight of redemption survives only in the Day of Atonement service, but Israel does not recognize it as symbolic Messianic redemption.

5. The Collective Closed Torah—The Tanak

The upheavals caused by the weakness of Israel led to national crises one after another. The reformers came one after another. The good times and the bad times, the glories, the backslidings, the punishments, and the reformations created a mass of writings, which became the "collective" and "final" earthly Torah of Israel. It became classified as:

1. Torah—The Pentateuch, including Job, because the evidence is that it is the oldest book of the Tanak, and based on the evidence available, it was authored by Moses.
2. Nevi'im—Joshua, Judges, First and Second Samuel, First and Second Kings, Isaiah, Jeremiah, Ezekiel, and the Twelve Minor Prophets.
3. Kethuvim—Psalms, Proverbs, The Scrolls (Song of Songs, Ruth, Lamentations, Ecclesiastes, Esther), Daniel, Ezra, Nehemiah, First and Second Chronicles.

The idea that additions would be made to the Tanak may have been contemplated, but the Council of the Elders in Judaism, as it was practiced at that time, wisely prevented this by closing the Tanak. This magnified its authority and sacredness. This Council of Elders was none other than the Sanhedrin (see Sanhedrin.org). This point illustrates how powerful the Sanhedrin was during some periods of Jewish history. The closure of the Tanak was accepted and gradually solidified. It did not render Judaism as a closed religion; it did not consign it to the end of the spiritual aspirations of the Jews. Neither did God stop searching after humanity in an attempt to "live among them." The Tanak is brimming with all the future events to take place in the implementing of His side show. God speaks eloquently through the Tanak, and it is up to the Jews and all humanity to listen. The Tanak has evolved into the greatest epic religious tract produced upon the earth. Its treasures are colossal. There is only one religion in the Tanak.[144] By definition as the conversation of God with the Jews, it cannot be a multiplicity of religions. There is only one God, blessed be He, so there can be only one religion. It is Tanakian Judaism.

6. The Interpretation of Torah

The methods of interpretation of the Tanak have produced a plethora of literature that is very valuable and instructive.[145] The Jewish Publication Society must be complimented for this tremendous translation by modern scholars. Numerous essays are included in *The Jewish Study Bible* document and are worth reading. Attention must be paid to interpretation because the treasures of the Tanak need to be properly deciphered and applied.

There is great unity in the Tanak; its parts are all congruent. There is no internal disagreement within it because its writers adhere to the same theses. Its foundation story is Gan Eden, and its central theme is redemption. There are no dissensions or contrary opinions in the Tanak, such as there are in the Talmud between the School of Hillel and the School of Shammai.[146] The Tanak is basically a history book of a people in conversation with God, and it is not difficult to understand. It is not considered a word perfect document or a strictly scientific treatise.[147] Today's scientific "facts" often are disproved tomorrow, but the Tanakian theology does not change. Its understanding can change with expanding wisdom and knowledge—but that is a human trait. Prophetic utterances are a very challenging area and must be carefully handled without dogmatic predictions.

Deciphering the inner meaning of many of its recorded events, such as King David's naked dance, must be governed by two powerful principles. They are foundational to the Tanak and must be oriented to the eternal Torah in the mind of God, discussed initially in this chapter. First is the great conceptual principle. The very basic plan in God's mind in that the eternal Torah must be obeyed. A simple question answers the matter. What was in God's mind when He conceived Creation, what went wrong, and what did He do to repair it? Surely no Jew or Gentile will ever settle for the status quo on this planet. Despite the beautiful scenery and the love relationships enjoyed on the Earth, the pathetic sorrow and suffering of all humanity is too overwhelmingly sad and intolerable to God. It cannot continue ad infinitum; change must come. God intends it, no matter how mystical it looks. The Tanak is a convincing witness to it.

The second great principle for interpretation is the contextual principle. If interpretations are out of the context of the passage being studied, they must be discarded. Concept and context must be obeyed. Some passages have multiple applications and fulfilments, but they must coincide conceptually. There is only one story in the Tanak: It is the story of the redemption of the Jews, and through them all humanity.

With the giving of the law and the institution of the priestly sacrificial system for the expiation of the sins caused by breaking of the law, God had dealt fairly with the problem of disobedience on the planet. He had preserved free will while furthering His goal to bring back immortality, the major thrust of the eternal Torah in the mind of God. But with the loss of the Second Temple, a duality became prominent in Israel. Israel would cultivate personal piety, which has always been a goal instilled by Moses and the reforming prophets. But Israel's rabbinic schools began to teach the idea that one could keep the law perfectly and achieve immortality in a resurrection initiated by the claim of perfect law keeping. This is totally non-Tanakian. The rabbinic schools relegated the sacrificial system to an ethereal mysticism in which few rabbis invested. They preserved the Day of Atonement as Israel's greatest national holiday while totally divesting it of its intended meaning, which the sacrificial system sought to teach: a symbol for Messianic intervention. Faith in the atonement service for the forgiveness of sin ceased to have any meaning. The rabbis substituted it with faith in good works and law keeping. They turned a blind eye to the realisation that no human could keep God's law perfectly, as the law demanded. The rabbis wrongly interpreted the Prophet Micah. Sacrifices had become the outward sign of a religion that had no inward change. God despised such a religion; it was like the Papal sale of indulgences centuries later. There was no repentance in the heart. The sacrifice had become the indulgence bought with money.

> With what shall I come before the Lord, and bow myself before the High God? Shall I come before Him with burnt offerings, with calves of a year old? (Mic. 6:6. KJV)

If repentance did not precede the sacrifice, there would be no humility in the heart of the sinner. The sacrifice can never be the substitute for repentance. The sacrifice was the symbolic expression of confession, forgiveness, and expiation. Repentance was the work of the Ruach Hakodesh. Forgiveness and expiation was the work of the Messiah as redeemer.

> He hath shown thee, O man, what is good; and what doth the Lord require of thee, but to do justly, love mercy, and to walk humbly with thy God. (Mic. 6:8, KJV)

This is just as succinctly expressed in *The Jewish Study Bible*:

> He has told you O man, what is good And what the Lord requires of you: Only to do justice And to love goodness, And to walk modestly with your God. (Mic. 6:8)

The interpretation of Torah needs always to keep in mind the big picture. For instance, in elucidating law keeping, sin, and expiation, the interpretation of the Tanak must always be conceptual.

Despite the realisation that the law would never be perfectly kept, supreme human effort should be expended in trying to keep the law. This effort sanctifies but is never perfect. God required an unblemished accomplishment; that is why the sacrificial animal had to be without blemish: it represented the unblemished Messiah, the golden standard. The Messianic provision was clearly in the mind of God, a great provision in the eternal Torah. In his early days of teaching, Rabbi Hillel had sought to set aside Messianic provision. His idea had the later support of Rabbi Jochanan b. Zakkai.[148]

Another Hillel, a fourth century rabbi, declared, "Israel had no Messiah (yet to come) since he [Israel] had already enjoyed Him [Messiah] in the days of Hezekiah."

Abraham Cohen comments:

> He [Hillel] was taken to task for his remark . . . . As will be seen, there was considerable variety of opinion about the identity of the future Redeemer. The belief was general that the sending of the Messiah was part of the Creator's plan at the inception of the Universe . . . . "Seven things were created before the world was created: Torah, repentance, the Garden of Eden (i.e. Paradise), Gehinnom, the Throne of Glory, the Temple [Heavenly], and the name of the Messiah" (Pes. 54a). In a later work [of Hillel] there is the observation: "From the beginning of the creation of the world king Messiah was born, for He entered the Mind of God before even the world was created." (Persikta Rab 152b)[149]

It is astounding that the Talmud generally denies the divinity of such a Messianic figure, despite Cohen's protestation: "On one point the Rabbis were unanimous, viz. he would be just a human being divinely appointed to carry out an allotted task. The Talmud nowhere indicates a belief in a superhuman Deliverer as the Messiah."[150] Cohen is wrong. He ignores all the scriptures referring to the Son. Cohen does not clearly define the "allotted task" he ascribes to the Messiah. In his continuing dissertation, however, Cohen goes on to enumerate the Messiah's many names, and these implicate divinity with redemption. He also cites Rabbi Judah the Prince's endorsement of a "suffering" and "'leprous" Messiah. This idea will be further elaborated elsewhere in the book.

The Tanak was dealt a disastrous blow by Emperor Titus. As history bears out, with the destruction of the Second Temple, the sacrificial Messianic redemptive part of the duality died out. As a result of this loss, Israel focussed completely on the law. The magnification of the law would expand in Eretz Israel and in the diaspora, in the great schools of the sages and their disciples. This would result in the production and redaction of the Mishnah and the Gemara (the Talmud), and Israel would become more concerned with the minutiae of the law. The exercise of faith in the Messianic redemption was forgotten, and Judaism became a philosophy. A divisiveness arose with opposing schools of thought, which gave rise to multiple Jewish sects; extensive pluralism resulted. The Judaism practiced during the subsequent 2,000 years (and continuing) has lost its resemblance to the Abrahamic and Mosaic primitive Judaism. The sacrificial redemptive religion, required in the knowledge that the law could not be perfectly kept, would be lost. The Day of Atonement would be a constant, yearly reminder that the breaking of the law required forgiveness of sin, but the mechanism for it, the Messianic redemption, was forgotten. Interpretation of the Tanak must harken to Judaism before the destruction of the Second Temple. This is perhaps the greatest disaster to befall primitive Judaism.

7. The Triumph of the Tanak

But first the Tanak would become the greatest volume of religious literature. The Torah (the Pentateuch, recognised as Jewish scripture about 450 BC) progressed to join up with the Nebhiim (the writings of the Prophets of Israel, recognised as Jewish scripture about 201 BC) and the Kethubhim (the other writings, recognised as Jewish scripture not long after the Nebhiim). Hence the name TNK, or TaNaK. If Sinai occurred at about 1445 BC, and the Book of Malachi was written about 400 BC, then the Tanak was written over a period of 1,000 years. This is a marvellous and cosmic occurrence, and it illustrates the resilience, tenacity, and dedication of the Jewish people to their God. The Tanak is indeed a stupendous document from which three great religions draw inspiration: Judaism, Christianity, and Islam. The great account of the communication between God and humanity shows the divine guidance and sacredness of the Tanak. The word "Torah" then became applied to the only written scripture in Jewish possession—the collection comprising the Pentateuch, the Nevi'im, and the Kethuvim. Collectively they were called the Jewish Bible, and in the Christian era they became referred to as the Old Testament. The Tanak must retain its definition as God's conversation with Israel with whom He lived (off and on). Through them He has redemption for the whole world.

Cohen states that the Torah reflects the divine mind and is perfect in every respect. He likely refers to the earthly Torah. But its human writers were not perfect, and there is a need to emphasize that fact.[151] The authorship of the Tanak is discussed in the Talmud,[152] which outlines it as follows: Moses wrote the Pentateuch and Job. Joshua wrote his book and the last eight versus of Deuteronomy. Samuel wrote his books, Judges, and Ruth. David wrote the Psalms with the collaboration (inspiration?) of Adam, Melchizedek, Abraham, Moses, Heman, Jeduthun, Asaph, and the three sons of Korah. Jeremiah wrote his book, Lamentations, and Kings. Hezekiah and associates wrote Isaiah, Proverbs, Song of Songs, and Ecclesiastes. The men of the Great Assembly wrote Ezekiel, the Twelve, Daniel, and Esther. Ezra wrote his book and the genealogy of Chronicles down to himself, and Nehemiah completed it.[153] Christian scholars accept the Tanak unreservedly as the Old Testament part of the Christian Bible. Some disagreements over authorship exist. The strongest disagreement appears to be the authorship of Isaiah. As stated in the book, Christian scholarship identifies Isaiah as being the son of Amoz, as a prophet during the reigns of the four kings of Judah—namely Uzziah (known also as Azariah), Jotham, Ahaz, and Hezekiah.[154] The Jewish acceptance of the books for inclusion was very controversial among the rabbinic sages according to the Talmud. Particularly, the Song of Songs, Ecclesiastes, Esther, and Ezekiel caused several sages a lot of consternation.[155] But eventually the inclusions were solidified as part of the Tanak. When finally there was consensus, the men of the Great Assembly closed the Tanak and prohibited any addition.[156]

The Tanak is the only document in existence that seeks, as its sole aim, to restore the perfection of Eden and immortality. It is the will of God planned in eternity, to be in a love relationship with humanity. It wonderfully outlines the rescue of humanity, God's supreme love object. It clearly spells out the deity's Elohim role of Ruach Hakodesh and Ha-Mashiach. He is the supreme creator, redeemer, and glorifier, one divine being. Hear, O Israel, the Lord our God is one; blessed be He.

8. The Rise of the Mishnah and Gemara

The evolution of the Mishnah and Talmud must be considered as the conversation of the Israelites with each other. There is no indication in the Talmud that it is an inspired and sacred document. Mishnah and Talmud make no claims to be revelations from God; they are not canon. The Mishnah purported to be a commentary on the Tanak. The Gemara were commentaries on the Mishnah. The latter two were compounded as the Talmud.

The Talmud lays down conditions for the study of Torah.[157] One special condition was that a man should not exclusively study Tanak and not do income-producing work as well, to earn a living. But then exceptions were made, granting loopholes. The Tanak was held in awe as inspired.

> But great latitude was allowed in the matter of interpretation, and no check was placed on the ingenuity which read into, or out of, the text meanings which seemed poles asunder from the literal intention. "Is not My word like a hammer that breaketh the rock in pieces?" (Jeremiah 23:29)—as the hammer causes numerous sparks to flash forth, so is a Scriptural verse capable of many interpretations.[158]

But this latitude, which often paid no heed to the conceptual and contextual meanings of the intent of the Tanak, would get the adherents into a lot of trouble. The word Torah also came to be too loosely used, especially when it began to be used to include Mishnah and Gemara. The accumulation of new discussions and philosophies, the Midrashim, began to be referred to as a new oral Torah. The argument is being made that these new Midrashim are justified because the Tanak and Talmud need to be brought into modern times. This is an extremely important happening and is very necessary. But we cannot call this reinterpretation Torah. The Tanak must be reinterpreted for modern times. Moses's concepts need to be adapted to modern times. The halachah derived from Moses needs updating and modernising, but the Tanak is sacrosanct and owns the term Torah.[159] If another oral Torah is recognized and comes into existence, the Talmud sees it as a progressive step:

> The [new] Oral Torah, which, being unwritten, remained in
> a flexible state, allowed the written ordinance to be adapted
> as the conditions of succeeding ages changed.[160]

Reinterpretations are a dime a dozen in the Talmud. It is important that reinterpretations be contextually true and be in harmony with the great conceptual principles of Creation, redemption, and glorification. These cannot be compromised. This is the Almighty God's side show, perhaps the most important part that occupies attention, in the infinity and eternity of God.

9. The History of the Use of Torah

Cohen emphasizes the vitalizing power of the Torah.[161] The rabbinic sages saw special merit in keeping the law, and that is laudable. But they also taught that that merit earned would be used for acceptance in place of Messianic redemption.[162] That concept negates the Tanakian principle of the provision of redemption by the Messiah. If acceptance to God and resumption of immortality are determined by Torah keeping, then the accusation of legalism stands. The magnification of the law certainly is honourable but is not salvific: "The Lord is well pleased for His righteousness sake; He will magnify the Law, and make it honourable" (Isa. 42:21, KJV). "Oh, how I love Thy law! It is my meditation all the day" (Ps. 119:97, KJV) reflects the rejoicing that comes from the sanctification that is acquired by law keeping. "Great peace have they who love Thy Law and nothing shall offend them" (Ps. 119:165). *But no one keeps the law perfectly,* and one must depend on Messianic redemption to obtain repentance, forgiveness, and eternal life. Elijah and Enoch did not go up to Paradise on the basis of their own law keeping. They are up there on a credit note from Messianic redemption.

Nationhood was absent after the last king, Zedekiah, about 600 BC. The last prophet Malachi is dated 400 BC. The Hasmoneans cannot be considered as constituting dynastic nationhood in Israel. The Seleucids were in power over Israel, and the apparent semi-autonomy the Hasmoneans enjoyed during their short period was because of the waning power of the Seleucids. The Jews were politically rudderless and were ruled by foreign powers until AD 1948, a period of 2,548 years. But their survival as an influential and gifted people during this period is monumental. Their spiritual evolution showed disturbing trends, but their dedication to monotheism and maintaining an identity were colossal. During this period in the proverbial wilderness of political and national nothingness, the spiritual leadership of the Jews did great things. They assembled and closed the sacred Tanak, they wrote and redacted the Mishnah, they composed the Gemara, and they assembled the Talmud. These were monumental accomplishments and will be discussed again in this chapter. Modern Western civilization is built on the Tanak, which remains God's sacred Torah and the foundation on which all Jews and Christians stand.

The Tanak was written in Hebrew. God wrote the Decalogue in Hebrew with His finger. This makes it a very sacred language. The Hebrew language was in use in 1400 BC. The Tanak

employs 8000 different Hebrew words (of which 2000 appear only once), but of course this was not the whole vocabulary at the disposal of the Hebrew speaker in Biblical times. His vocabulary no doubt amounted to 30,000 or over,

> but the authors of the various books of the Bible [Tanak]
> had no reason to use most of these words.[163]

The Targums are translations of the Tanak into Aramaic, the language spoken by Aram, the fifth son of Shem. Old Aramaic is dated 975-700 BC and was spoken in Padan-aram.

> By the 8th Century BC it was the major language from
> Egypt to Asia-Minor . . . . It was employed by the great
> Semitic empires, Assyria and Babylon . . . . The language
> of the people of Palestine shifted from Hebrew to Aramaic
> sometime between 721-500 BC.[164]

Aramaic was the language of the Jews in the time of Yeshua of Nazareth. South Indian converts of St. Thomas still worship in the Aramaic language as Syrian Christians.

The Tanak was translated into Greek in 250 BC by the Jewish diaspora in Alexandria, Egypt, which at the time was a Hellenistic community. This community used Greek as their everyday language. This translation was named the Septuagint. The Vulgate is a fourth-century AD Latin translation.

It was a natural consequence, out of the legal atmosphere of Israel spawned by attention to the law, that a religious culture arose that greatly honoured personal piety and obedience to the Torah or law. The intent of the laws and how they should be obeyed became a challenge to the thinkers and studious minds in Israel. Even the rank and file were imbued to please their God and went to extraordinary lengths to magnify the law. Out of homelessness, dispossession, and national sadness, a contemplative, religious atmosphere solidified in Israel, and great theological schools were established. Great sages and their disciples emerged who thought deeply and became leaders in the interpretation of the law. These schools arose not only in Palestine but also in the diaspora, notably Babylon. This intense and studious culture appears to have started from the time of Zerubbabel, Nehemiah, and Ezra, commencing about 537 BC. They were pioneers, being returnees from Babylon who came back to rebuild the Temple and Jerusalem. The religious culture pioneered by these young men became the hotbed of dedication to magnifying Torah; this inspired the rise of the theological schools that sprang up. Rabbinic leaders and sages taught in these schools, which attracted the best and brightest of the Jews.[165]

The Jews continued to focus on the study of the Tanak and demonstrated an intense desire to plumb its depths. There was a compelling yearning to decipher and obey its precepts. But the Talmudic reinterpretation of the legal system laid down by Moses has eclipsed Judaism as a communion with God and mostly concentrated on a rather dry, legalistic, and philosophical "wandering in the desert" conversation. The idea that salvation could be attained by their perfect law keeping was delusional. The redemptive function of primitive Judaism was abandoned, and there was no general and pervasive depth in the friendship with, dependence on, and yearning for God. The exceptions were the development of Kabbalah and Hasidism, which wandered away from Tanakian theology.

In summary, all the Jewish kings that arose after David and Solomon were weak. They were in a state of vassalage, mere satraps who paid taxes and indemnities to stronger foreign powers. After the last king, Zedekiah (who reigned around 600 BC) and the destruction of Solomon's Temple by the Babylonians, the Jews lost national status. Despite the so-called dynasty of the Hasmoneans, the Jews remained nationally weak and rudderless, under foreign domination, until the glorious dawn of AD 1948. No one would admire their intermittent subjugation, often extremely and devastatingly cruel, by the powers of Assyria, Babylon, Medo-Persia, Greece, and Rome. During this politically and nationally weak status, the Jews became a nation at study. Studious introspection of the Mosaic law gave rise to the development of the Mishnah and the Gemara. There is no current, logical explanation as to why God did not raise up prophets and patriarchs during this time of political and national weakness and wandering in the desert, unless one looks to the rise of Christianity. The eschatology of the

Tanak holds the answer to that question, and the Tanak remains as God's great communication with Israel and all humanity. The Tanak remains the source of Israel's future.

The eschatology of the Tanak is briefly discussed in the Talmud, but the great focus is legalistic. The Tanakian eschatology is bound up with the redemptive function of primitive Judaism and Messianism, but sadly it was greatly neglected since the loss of the Second Temple in AD 70. Messianic contemplation concentrated on obtaining political and national status, and it neglected the salvific redemptive Tanakian theology. The understanding of God's Messianic thrust in the Tanak has not been a priority and was relegated to the metaphysical and mystical. That eschatology deteriorated into the alternative of mysticism and Kabbalistic teaching. The Mishnah and Gemara do recognise a Messianic future, but they do not develop and elucidate this future. The Abrahamic Covenant became the most neglected centrepiece of Judaism. The eschatological hope of Israel embedded in the Tanak was eclipsed by attention to the spurious possibility of salvation by benevolence and perfect law keeping. Political machination overtook Messianic effort. The pious Jew had one supreme consuming desire: to study to know the will of God expressed by Moses so as to obey it. This consuming desire became an introspection and fixation into which the Jews poured all their energy. To live an upright life, to be recognized by their fellows as being pious, to be valued by God for this, and to be worthy of God's attention became their entire devotion.

Looking to the future, when the Third Temple will be built, what kind of service will be practiced in it? In the absence of the appearance of the Messiah in Israel, will there be a return to the sacrificial system, which prefigured the Messianic mission to provide the expiation for sin and guilt in Israel?

There is no question that the destiny of the Jews, their Tanakian eschatology, is tied up with the Messiah and the blessedness of all nations. Nothing is more Abrahamic. It is the Messiah who will set up his everlasting kingdom in Jerusalem. For what kind of a

Messiah are the Jews looking in their deepest desires? Are they looking for a national political leader who will guarantee their physical survival in the current world for the rest of eternity? Or are they looking for a Messiah who will be the mechanism of forgiveness and absolution from their breaking of the law? If they have no guilt and feel expiated by their "perfect" law keeping, why flock to the synagogue on the Day of Atonement? Do they not ask for forgiveness for having broken the law when they get to the synagogue? Has not repentance brought them there? Are they not standing in a state of expulsion outside the Gates of Eden and longing to enter back in? What exactly did Moses and Aaron tell Israel had happened on the Day of Atonement? Was it not that the blood of the animal without blemish sprinkled on the Mercy Seat in the Most Holy Compartment that brought them forgiveness, and they left the synagogue on the Day of Atonement with a clean slate?

The study of the Tanak was seriously in place long before the destruction of Jerusalem and the Second Temple by the Romans in AD 70. It began after the prophet Malachi composed his book around 400 BC. Malachi had dire warnings for Israel about the consequences in store, if the Torah was disregarded. Malachi singled out the Levitical priesthood that had become corrupt. Malachi's great theme was the Messiah. He prophesied about the coming forerunner and the Messiah coming after that forerunner; this caused great excitement.

> Behold I am sending My messenger to clear the way before Me and the Lord whom you seek shall come to the Temple suddenly. As for the Angel of the Covenant that you desire, he is already coming. (Mal. 3:1, *The Jewish Study Bible*)

> But who may abide the day of His coming? And who shall stand when He appeareth? For He is like a refiners fire. (Mal. 3:2, KJV)

This scripture warns of the coming deity (the forerunner will "clear the way before Me"), but first He will send His messenger to "clear the way" ahead of Him. The warning from Malachi was stupendous. Messiah is deity but is coming as a human, and He will be heralded by Elijah. Messiah is also "the Angel of the Covenant." The word "angel" is better translated as messenger (the Hebrew words are o-mal'ak, which in English are "and the messenger'"). It is the Abrahamic Covenant. There was no other covenant in Israel. Messiah is also like a refiner's fire: He is going to subject you to fiery cleansing, where your dross is consumed. He will do the powerful work of cleansing you from sin, for that is His Messianic job. His coming brings the final Day of Atonement.

Despite the return from Babylonian captivity (empowered by Cyrus), Israel as a nation was weak and feeble, both politically and nationally. This has already been discussed but needs emphasis here. No powerful kings arose to inspire and unify them as a nation in Messianic longing. Israel was subject to the Medo-Persian Empire; Greek civilization then dominated. The Romans would then place Israel in a state of devastation for 2,000 years. But the study of Torah prospered, and the sages and their disciples focussed with great zeal on the Tanak, particularly the Pentateuch. It was this voluminous commentary on the Tanak, again named the oral tradition, that travailed during the almost 500 years of the Second Temple. This prolonged study gave birth to the Mishnah. It is important to review this post-Malachian period of about 500 years, which culminated in the terrible destruction of Jerusalem and the Second Temple in AD 70. In this period, Hellenism became the dominant power affecting Israel and the diasporic Jews:

> On the eve of the invasion of the Persian Empire by Alexander of Macedon, Judaea was a small insignificant province within Darius' domain . . . . Judaea was allowed to conduct its own cultural and religious affairs . . . . Alexander and his Macedonians marched across the Hellespont, defeated Darius' army at Issus and marched south along the coast to Egypt . . . . In the remote hills of Judaea Hellenism came face to face with deeply rooted Jewish traditions.[166]

A large majority of Jews in Judaea and the diaspora absorbed Hellenism; this was particularly prominent in Alexandria. After Alexander's death and after the Greek Empire was divided among his four generals, the Jews became significantly Hellenised under Ptolemy's influence, especially the numerous influential Jews in Egypt. That is how the Septuagint originated in Alexandria. Philo Judaeus (Philo of Alexandria) "believed Judaism to be a universal religion and that it did not achieve this universality by any abandonment of its beliefs or practices."[167] Flavius Josephus also records much about the Hellenistic influence on Judaism. Seleucus established himself in Babylon and extended his kingdom over the Levant, and eastward to India. Thus in the second century BC, Judaea was under the influence of the Ptolomys of Egypt and the Seleucids of Syria. Antiochus IV Epiphanes, the Seleucid king, lived about 215-164 BC, and he interfered severely with Judaism and the practice of Torah and the appointment of high priest in the Second Temple.

> Antiochus pillaged the [Second] Temple . . . [he] attacked Jerusalem . . . [and] pursued a zealous Hellenizing policy. He made possession of the Torah [The Tanak] a capital offence and burned the copies he could find. He banned many traditional Jewish religious practices: Jewish sacrifices were forbidden . . . . Altars to Greek gods were set up . . . [and] The idol of Olympian Zeus was placed on the altar of the Temple.[168]

This set the stage for the revolt of the Maccabees. The first book of the Maccabees tells of the revolt of Mattathias and his sons Judas, Jonathan, and Simon Maccabaeus. They organised a military campaign against Antiochus Epiphanes, and despite great loss of life, they succeeded against the Seleucids. In 165 BC the Temple was cleansed and reconsecrated. Hanukkah was set up as a festival of celebration, and Simon Maccabaeus started the Hasmonean dynasty. But because he was not of the royal line of David, even the Jews did not recognise him. The Hasmoneans ruled from 140-37 BC according to Aidan Steinsaltz,[169] but it is known that Pompey invaded Judaea in 63 BC. From about 140 BC to

Pompey's invasion, Judaea had semi-autonomy, and the Seleucids began to collapse with the rise of the Roman power. Hellenism had a general and widespread deleterious effect on Judaism in Israel, but more so in the diaspora.

Pompey invaded Judaea in 63 BC and made it a part of the province of Syria. Rivalry with Julius Caesar ensued, and with Pompey's defeat the Romans set up a client kingdom controlled by the Herods. The Jewish-Roman War, which culminated in the destruction of Jerusalem and the Second Temple in AD 70, is blamed on the rebellion of the Jews against taxation by the Romans. Titus and Vespasian succeeded in crushing the Jews and initiating the diaspora that would last 2,000 years.

During the 200 years leading up to the Roman devastation of Israel, the spiritual power of Israel was wielded by the high priest and the Sanhedrin. The first high priest was Aaron (Exod. 28; 29), and the first Sanhedrin consisted of Moses and the seventy elders he had chosen at Sinai (Num. 11:16). This was a landmark precedence. The power invested in the Sanhedrin (also called the Great Assembly) waxed when there were no kings, judges, or prophets wielding great reformatory influence, and it waned when there were. The Roman Pompey disbanded the Sanhedrin in favour of his puppet appointments. The conclusion is that at this time the Sanhedrin was contemporary with the backsliding of Israel into idolatry. Its reformatory influence was poor. There were significant periods of corruption of the priesthood and the Sanhedrin, as in Malachi's time. Nevertheless, at times the high priest and the Sanhedrin preserved the spiritual bulwarks of Israel. The Sanhedrin took steps at various times to preserve the Torah (the Tanak) as well as the mounting volume of oral Torah.[170] But the spiritual limelight soon became the property of the great sages, and their disciples ensconced in the great schools that arose both in Israel as well as in the diaspora. During the almost 500-year hiatus in the period of Israel's political and national poverty, culminating in the utter devastation that occurred in AD 70 and its aftermath, these great schools flourished. Persecution and political poverty produced great spiritual strength. The Jews would survive.

The Tanak was the great foundation document (Torah) of the Jewish people. After the commencement of the Christian era, it became the foundation document of Christianity as well. But Christianity went on to produce its own supplementary document, the B'rit Hadasha, which was necessary to document its rise and record the life of Yeshua of Nazareth. It is significant that the early disciples of Yeshua of Nazareth and the authors of the B'rit Hadasha were all Jewish.

As the Mishnah and Gemara became more prominent, the Tanak took a back seat with the Jewish sages and their disciples. The collective Talmud became the main document of Judaistic philosophy, and it would determine the direction of the Jewish people's contemplation.

The Talmud credits the Holy Spirit with imbuing every one of the Tanakian judges, prophets, inspired kings, and other leaders. Cohen says that the Pentateuch was supreme:

> Of the Hebrew prophets, Moses was pre-eminent and stands in a class by himself . . . . His comprehension of the divine message was more intimate than theirs. The revelation granted to him was the source from which all the later prophets drew. "What the prophets were destined to prophesy in subsequent generations they received from Mount Sinai". (Exodus R. 28:6, cited in Cohen, p. 123) . . . . It followed from this that nothing spoken by a later prophet could in any way be in conflict with, and add to or detract from, the writings of Moses. "Forty-eight prophets and seven prophetesses spoke prophecies for Israel, and they neither deducted from nor added to what was written in the Torah [Pentateuch], with the exception of the law to read the Book of Esther on the Feast of Purim". (Meg. 14a, cited in Cohen, p. 123) . . . . Different grades of inspiration were recognized. "The Holy Spirit which alights on the prophets only does so by measure . . . .". (Lev. R xv.2) . . . . "When the latter prophets Haggai, Zachariah and Malachi died, the Holy Spirit departed from Israel". (Sanh. 11a, cited

by Cohen, p. 124) . . . . The supreme message of Hebrew
prophecy was the call to erring men and women to retrace
their steps to God. *"Every prophet only prophesied for the
days of the Messiah and the penitent* . . . . It shall come to
pass afterward that I will pour out My Spirit upon all flesh;
and your sons and your daughters shall prophesy, your old
men dream dreams, your young men shall see visions."[171]

10. The Emergence of Tradition

This topic has been repeatedly referred to above. There was
good reason for this. With the Holy Spirit presumed to be gone,
the Shechinah departed, the prophetic gift silenced, and later the
Second Temple destroyed and the sacrificial system rendered
impractical, all that was left of primitive Judaism were the Torah
(Tanak) and the shell of the Day of Atonement. The rabbinic
sages would go on to create the Talmud and develop a philosophy.
Redemptive Judaism was forgotten as they majored in legalism
and relegated the Messiah to mysticism. The Promised Land was
lost, the Torah was confused, and the Messiah was banished to
imprisonment in the mysticism of the city of Safed. The Tanak
needs to be restored to its rightful place in Israel. There needs to be
a refocus on Messianic redemptive Judaism. The side show in the
Torah of the eternal mind of God needs completion. The Abrahamic
Covenant needs to be kept.

The emergence of tradition needs to be discussed. The esteemed
Gershom Scholem has written significantly about this. I lean very
heavily on him in explaining the emergence of tradition. He terms
the Tanak "revelation" and pays due respect to it. Scholem states:

> In all religions, the acceptance of a divine revelation
> originally referred to the concrete communication of
> positive, substantive, and expressible content. It never
> occurred to the bearers of such revelation [the authors]
> to question or to limit the specific quality and closely

delineated content of the communication they [the authors] had received [from God].[172]

But it must be pointed out that the Sanhedrin who closed the Tanak forbade any changes or additions to be made. This has mostly been faithfully adhered to, but the changes and additions came thick and fast as an extended oral Torah.

Scholem goes on to say:

> Where, as in Judaism, such revelation is set down in holy writings and is accepted in that form, it initially constitutes concrete communication, factual content and nothing else. But inasmuch as such revelation, once set down in Holy Scriptures, takes on authoritative character, an essential change takes place. For one thing, new historical circumstances require that the communication, whose authoritativeness has been granted, be applied to everchanging conditions. Furthermore, the spontaneous force of human productivity seizes this communication and expands it beyond its original scope. "Tradition" thus comes into being . . . . At this point begins the process in which two questions gain importance: How can revelation be preserved as a concrete communication? . . . And, with ever greater urgency: Can this revelation be applied to all, and if so, how? With this second question, spontaneity has burst into nascent tradition. In the process of this renewed productivity, Holy Scriptures themselves are sometimes enlarged, new written communications take their place alongside the old ones. A sort of no-mans-land is created between the original revelation and the tradition. *Precisely this happened in Judaism, for example, as the Torah, to which the quality of revelation was originally confined, was "expanded to include other writings . . . the boundaries often shifted: the Canon, as Holy Writ, confronted tradition . . . ."*

> The process which is considered here occurred in Judaism at the time of the Second Temple . . . . But changed circumstances, especially the impact of the Hellenic world . . . . Tradition now asserted itself ever more emphatically as a new religious value and as a category of religious thought . . . . In the process, the original meaning of revelation as a unique, positively established, and clearly delineated realm of propositions is put in doubt—and thus a development as fruitful as it is unpredictable begins which is highly instructive for the religious problematic of the concept of tradition.[173] [emphasis added]

Without a doubt Scholem is describing what became a new Judaism comprised of tradition, one no longer obedient to the revelation. He goes on to explain how this occurred.

> The understanding of tradition as a process that creates productivity through receptivity can now be seen clearly. Talmudic literature recognizes two types of men who preserve the tradition. One . . . who could recite from memory the texts of all the old traditions of the schools—[a] mere receptacle(s) . . . [and] The truly learned man . . . who is bound to tradition through his inquiries. So far as the consciousness of future generations is concerned, only men of the second type are the true carriers of tradition, for tradition is living creativity *in the context of revelation*. Precisely because tradition perceives, and unfolds that which lives in the word, it is the force within which contradictions and tensions are not destructive but rather stimulating and creative.[174] [emphasis added]

With all due respect, Scholem is presuming far too much! First, he presumes that the "tradition" conceived in the guise of creativity is "in the context of revelation." Second, he overlooks the contradictions that destroy the revelation (The Tanak) by substituting the new thinking in its place. These are significant criticisms of his thinking. He himself has accused Kabbalism and Hasidism of destroying what he believes is "acute Messianism," and what he has formulated as the "catastrophic apocalypticism" of Isaiah and Daniel. He has done this in an essay titled "Neutralization of Messianism in Early Hasidism."[175] He also destroys the conception of the idea developed by Kabbalah and Hasidism on their interpretation and development of "Devekut, or Communion with God" in an essay by that title in the same book.[176] I commend and laud him for doing this on both counts, because I believe he is being faithful to Tanakian theology in his concepts of Messiah and Devekut. The rabbis depart in so many instances from what Scholem defines as revelation, clearly the Tanak. What is significantly bad about such liberty to produce tradition is that the rabbinic sages who did this assumed they were getting it all from Mt. Sinai. Scholem quotes Meir ben Gabbai and Isaiah Horovitz, who made this assumption.[177] Scholem seems uncomfortable to go along with this philosophy that the rabbinic sages "uttered in the context of the messages Moses received from God." He reconciles the controversies of the Schools of Shammai and Hillel with the idea that everything will be cleared up in the long run. But at the same time, he definitely is uncomfortable with the idea of the license tradition takes with revelation.

> It is the Oral Torah of which is written at the beginning
> of the "Ethics of the Fathers" in the Mishnah: "Moses
> received the Torah from Sinai and transmitted it to Joshua,
> and Joshua to the elders, and the elders to the prophets, and
> the prophets transmitted it to the Great Synagogue" . . .
> We do not know whether the dogmatic concept of a *"fence
> around the Torah"* (preventive measures intended to assure
> observance of the Torah) is ascribed to it.[178]

It seems that there is uncertainty as to the connotation of the designation here as oral Torah, but it appears that it is tradition that is meant. There seems to be an attempt here by the rabbinic sages to imply that tradition began with Ezra and Nehemiah and Haggai, Zechariah and Malachi.

Scholem goes on to say:

> In any event, reference to the Oral Law is already common
> in the first century in the Common Era. The content and
> range of this most important concept fluctuated, and with
> advancing consolidation of Rabbinic Judaism it underwent
> an expansion. At first this tradition, appearing as Torah,
> was limited to statutes or ordinances not contained in the
> Torah [the Tanak] available to everyone . . . . Thus in the
> course of generations, many statutes circulated which
> were designated as "Halakhah to Moses from Sinai"
> (Cf. the compilation of these statutes in Wilhelm Bacher,
> "Tradition and Tradeten," Leipzig, 1914, pp. 33-46)
> Soon, however, the scope of the concept's application was
> enlarged. Everything that was discussed by the scribes and
> transmitted to the academics—whether legal, historical,
> ethical, or homiletic—was implanted into the fruitful
> realm of tradition . . . . The Oral Torah no longer simply
> runs parallel to the Wriiten; the task now is to derive it and
> deduce it from Scripture.
>
> The unfolding of the truths, statements, and circumstances
> that are given in or accompany revelation becomes the
> function of the Oral Torah [tradition], which creates in the
> process a new type of religious person.[179]

It appears from the account of Scholem in the foregoing statements
that the early rabbinic sages desired to link the written Torah [the
Tanak, or "revelation"] with the oral Torah ["'tradition'"]. Scholem
describes an evolution that occurred as follows:

> A creative process begins to operate which will permeate
> and alter tradition—the Midrash: the more regulated
> halakhic and the some-what freer aggadic exegesis of
> Scriptures, and the views of the Biblical scholars in their
> various schools are regarded as implicitly contained in the
> Written Torah [revelation] . . . .

This leads to the viewpoint expressed daringly in Talmudic writings, namely, that the total substance of the Oral Torah [tradition], which had in fact been the achievement of the scholars, comes from the same source as the Written Torah [Tanak or revelation], and that it was therefore basically always known. The saying "turn it . . ." reflects this viewpoint. But underneath this fiction . . . there lies a religious attitude which is interesting and which had significant results. I refer to the distinct notion of revelation including within itself as sacred tradition the later commentary concerning its own meaning. This was the beginning of a road which . . . was to lead to the establishment of mystical theses concerning the character of revelation as well as the character of tradition.

Here we immediately encounter a significant tension in the religious consciousness of the scholars themselves . . . . On the one hand, there was the blossoming productivity of the academies . . . . On the other hand there arose the claim . . . . That all this was somehow part of revelation [the Tanak] itself—and more: not only was it given along with revelation, but it was given in a special, timeless sphere of revelation in which all generations were gathered together; everything had been explicit to Moses, the first and most comprehensive recipient of Torah. The achievement of every generation, in its contribution to tradition, was projected back into the eternal present of the revelation at Sinai. This, of course, is something which no longer has anything in common with the notion of revelation with which we began, namely, *Revelation is unequivocal, clear, and understandable communication.* According to this new doctrine, revelation comprises everything that will be legitimately offered to interpret its meaning.

The *patent absurdity of this claim* reveals a religious assumption that must be taken all the more seriously. The rabbis did not hesitate to express this assumption in rather extravagant formulations.[180]

And so the rabbinic sages made a religion out of tradition and Halachah, but it turned out to be a philosophy instead. It left a vacuum and the great longing for Messianic realization continues. The Tanak has the answers but is not given attention. The Messiah of the Tanak is awaiting Israel. The exciting, energizing, and salvific primitive redemptive Judaism needs to be rediscovered.

CHAPTER 12

THE MISHNAH

The second great document to come out of the religious atmosphere of Judaism, after the sacred Tanakian Torah canon, was the Mishnah. The Mishnah developed as a commentary on and discussion of the Tanak, more particularly the Pentateuch where resided the LAW. The word Mishnah means 'study', and the study of the Tanak produced a very complex legal body of material, passed from the sages in the schools to their disciples, who held it in their memory. And this body of material also became known as the new 'Oral Torah.' There were many sages and rabbis who produced material that became part of the Mishnah. The Mishnah was written in Hebrew.

Five great rabbinic sages came into prominence at the turn of the era (BC to AD, or BCE to CE). They were more or less contemporaries.

Rabbi Hillel (?60 BC-AD 10) was a Babylonian Jew who migrated to Israel where he became prominent as President of the Sanhedrin. He produced and presided over a great deal of material that was incorporated in the Mishnah.

Rabbi Shammai was born in Israel (50 BC-30 AD) and was very active as a leader of the interpretation of the Law. He and Hillel had major differences of opinion. Like Hillel, he also contributed and presided over interpretation of the Mosaic Law, which material was included in the Mishnah.

Rabbi Akiva (AD 50-135) lived through the destruction of Jerusalem and the Second Temple. He also was a teacher and contributor of inclusions in the Mishnah.[181]

Rabbi Yochanan Ben Zakkai (?AD 30-90) was a pupil of Hillel. He was trapped in Jerusalem when the Zealots were holding it. The Zealots had slaughtered many of the rabbinic sages who were pacifist towards Rome. Zakkai was a pacifist, and to escape being killed, he was smuggled out of Jerusalem in a coffin. He was quite prominent because he received permission from Vespasian to start the rabbinic school in Yavneh, which became the leading centre of Jewish learning for centuries.[181]

Rabbi Judah the Prince (AD 135-219) Because the Mishnaic material of study existed in fragmentary and mostly memorised form, there was a danger that this material would be lost. It was Rabbi Judah, the Prince, the Lion, who decided to codify it and write it down.[182]

Adin Steinsaltz has the best concise commentary to hand, which is very illuminating regarding the constitution of the Mishnah. But he barely discusses the theology of the Mishnah in his book *The Essential Talmud*. For that, we will go elsewhere. Steinsaltz wrote:

> As the Oral Law [Mishnaic writings] was transmitted from teacher to disciple over the centuries through oral instruction, the need for some sort of arrangement and editing of the material became evident . . . . In earlier generations when the oral law adhered closely to the written law [The Pentateuch] the latter served, inter alia, as an instrument for reminding the student of the halachah derived from each verse. This use of the biblical text not only as the legal and logical basis for oral law but also as a mnemonic aid, was carried over to talmudic literature and Jewish literature in general. It created the concept of asmakhta (support), that is, citing a biblical text that is not the direct source of the halachah but that is combined, by some exegetic method, with a known halachah to serve as a

mnemonic aid. Use of this method was so widespread that sometimes it is almost impossible to distinguish between the authentic commentary and that which serves merely as a asmakhta.[183]

This is a remarkable insight of Steinsaltz. It shows how loosely and noncontextually the halakhah could be related to the original biblical text to which it was attached. Therefore, the degree of accuracy of the exposition of the Tanak by the Mishnah (and later the Gemara) is questionable. The relationship of the deduction to the original Tanakian text is very suspect. Although this may look like a triviality in a literary or mnemonic prop sense, this kind of linking has the potential to devastate the original conceptual and contextual meaning and intent of the Tanak. It also gave the particular halachah derived undue weight, and the unwarranted authority of the Tanak. One can see that Talmudic philosophy had a great license to wander away from the Tanak and yet demand and receive undue theological weight and homage. There is evidence that this did happen in many citations and decisions the sages made, especially when there was dissension and variations in opinion. But there are also some fantastic and erudite interpretations that are true to the intent of the Pentateuch. In a discussion of many of the subjects in the Mishnah, this book will enthusiastically point to these erudite interpretations. But I will also pointedly refer to the non-Tanakian variant views of the sages. It is always good theology to stay close to the great concepts of the Tanak. This tactic preserves primitive Tanakian Judaism.

Steinsaltz says further:

> Many areas of oral law, however, developed far beyond the isolated verses that served as their substantiation. In these spheres it was deemed necessary to classify numerous details into more general categories. Initially this was apparently done by simple means and was meant to facilitate memorization and study.[184]

Here is a method of developing and remembering deduced halachah, which is "far beyond the isolated verses [from the Tanak] that served for their substantiation." It is here that serious issue is taken to uphold the Tanak far above the deduced and interpretive Mishnah, and the subsequently deduced and interpretive Gemara. It should therefore be a rule that while the Tanak is kept at the highest level as the sacred and divine word of God, the Mishnah and the Gemara are the philosophy of men. No one in Judaism should be held in higher and more sacred esteem than Moses and the other writers of the Tanak. Also, if the Mishnah and the Gemara are not in conceptual and contextual harmony with the Tanak, then the idea or belief being touted must be replaced by what the Tanak is saying. The Talmud must not be elevated to the level of the Tanak, no matter how erudite or venerable their authors were. Besides, many of the developed halachot, mishnayot, and midrashim were not unanimously held at the times they were deduced. They came often as struggles of opinions from different sages and different schools.

Steinsaltz summarizes this as follows:

> The vast amount of material accumulated over several generations began to constitute a problem at a time when Jewish religious and judicial institutions maintained a certain hierarchy and employed uniform methods of legislative ruling, all matters in dispute being submitted to the Great Sanhedrin in the Temple for unequivocal judgement. But breaches began to appear in the wall of uniformity in the Hasmonean era, and open controversy erupted in the days of Hillel and Shammai, when the existence of two different schools of thought was officially recognised.[185]

The Hasmonean period gave rise to a great profusion in the multiplication of sages, different schools, and vast numbers of disciples. The destruction of Jerusalem and the second Temple dampened this multiplication. After the devastation in AD 70, the school at Yavneh survived, and the Sanhedrin took refuge there, but moved back and forth to the city of Usha in Galilee.[186] Rabbi Judah, who was born in AD 135, settled in the school of Usha. Rabbi Akiva's disciples resided in Usha. Rabbi Judah decided to summarize the Mishnah. The Mishnah then became the centre of attention, and with it the major writings of veneration. From the viewpoint of primitive Judaism, it is a pity that all this scholarly energy was expended in the study of the Mishnah instead of the Tanak. This study emerged as the Gemara; attention was diverted from the redemptive religion of the Tanak. There is no doubt that the discussion began in the interpretation of the Tanak, but it often continued in esoteric directions, especially when there was divergence of opinions and controversy. There is a great need to decipher Moses in terms of his humanity (Egyptian education) and in terms of his inspiration (what God told him). Because of the dissension in the philosophies emanating from the sages and their schools, there is a great need to further decipher the writings of the Pentateuch in order to be able to apply the true and practical Mosaic intent for the 21st century. This concept will be discussed elsewhere in this book.

As the editor and classifier of the Mishnah, Rabbi Judah himself "sometimes changed his opinions on certain issues and consequently introduced amendments into the mishnayot."[187] Rabbi Judah arranged the Mishnah writings into six orders: Zeraim, Moed. Nashim, Nezikin, Kodashim, and Toharot. These orders dealt with various collections of Mosaic law, and they will be discussed further in this chapter. But it is not the objective of this book to discuss this immense body of work and assess its total validity or otherwise. It is sought here to describe that it should not occupy greater authority than the Tanak or replace the basic doctrines of the Tanak. No matter how erudite the sages were who produced the Mishnah and Gemara, they cannot reinterpret or replace the original meaning of the Tanak to arrive at a variant view. Any new ideas or interpretations made in the Mishnah and the Gemara must be in conceptual and contextual harmony with the entire Tanak, or else it must be discarded. They cannot nullify or supersede the clear and foundation teachings of the Tanak.

Steinsaltz further summarizes:

> The Mishnah is a large body of material pertaining to the opinions of the sages of the generation immediately preceding Rabbi Judah's, but there is also a detailed record of the disputes of his own generation, and his own view is sometimes noted as an isolated opinion opposed to the general consensus . . . . He sometimes changed his opinion on certain issues and consequently introduced amendments into the mishnayot.
>
> At times he was unable to introduce certain of his new formulations or theories into the work, since a previous ruling had already been accepted, and sometimes additions contradicting his own previous decisions were made. Similarly, a new formulation occasionally rendered previous mishnayot superfluous, but since it was the rule that "a mishnayot does not move from its place," both statements were retained . . . . He succeeded in completing the Mishnah and endowing it with its permanent form and character, thus rounding off the period of the tannaim [those who study] . . . . but in any case it was now a complete and sacred work.[188]

Steinsaltz's last sentence is the tragic one that tells us that the Mishnah was "a complete and sacred work." Generally speaking, Jews probably agree with him, but this is what has led to the confusion of "'current Judaism," which has become a philosophy rather than a religion. There is only one sacred and complete book in Judaism, and that is the Tanak. The Mishnah and the Gemara are not communications with God (as was the Tanak), but communications between men. Therefore the claim to sacredness is not valid. These great sages contributing their opinions were not claiming their opinions came from God. They often quarrelled about their opinions, and there was no sacred clarity whatsoever.

The great weakness of the Mishnah is that it concentrated on the law (the legal part of Torah). There is no doubt that Moses gave the Israelites the law at Sinai. He had the massive task of bringing a horde of unruly and idolatrous slaves out of Egypt. Some of them cursed and swore at him, and after the golden calf episode, which occurred simultaneously with the giving of the Ten Commandments at Sinai, 3,000 died as a judgement from God (Exod. 32:28). The massive task that Moses faced was getting them into shape and controlling them so that he could make of them a God-fearing nation. But at the very same moment, the great Day of Atonement and the sacrificial system of the Tent Tabernacle and the Aaronic Priesthood were instituted at Sinai. The enshrined law was sprayed with blood on the Day of Atonement. But while this majestic redemptive service was being installed, this wretched group of loathsome, idolatrous, but pitiable people were worshipping the golden calf. The Day of Atonement ordained a Messianic animal without blemish sacrifice, the propitiation and forgiveness of all the sins of Israel. This was the most important tenet in primitive Judaism.

The Mishnah does not explain and magnify the great Abrahamic Covenant. Both Mishnah and the Gemara kept the focus on law. Israel thus thought that their acceptability to God would come from how holy they could become, by obeying the minutiae of the law. But it was the blood of the sacrificial animal without blemish that was carried into the Most Holy Place and sprinkled on the Mercy Seat and Ark, which contained the Ten Commandments that would bring them acceptability to God. It was not their righteousness that was carried by the chief priest into the Most Holy Place. It was the blood that brought them forgiveness and holiness and acceptability with God. The law demanded perfection, which not one genetic, adopted, or converted Jew ever born on the planet could achieve. If that was possible, then there was no need for the Day of Atonement. Israel would then be in the embarrassing situation of atoning for its own sins. In other words, a Jew could say to himself, "I'm such a virtuous fellow, I forgive myself." That idea was definitely not what Moses taught.

The story is often told that it was not fair that God hated Esau because of his love of idolatrous women, and He loved Jacob instead (Mal 1:1-3), when Jacob was so full of deceit and subterfuge. Neither of them were great law keepers, but it was Jacob who showed repentance and took hold of the Abrahamic Covenant to fulfil it. Acceptance with God, according to the Tanak, is not by keeping the law, but by admitting its breaking, being repentant, and pleading the blood of the sacrificial lamb without blemish, the Messianic figure. It is the blood that will save Israel. That does not mean that we can ignore the law. It is extremely important to strive with blood, sweat, and tears to keep it, but none will be able to be perfect before God, and all will need the blood on the Day of Atonement. Kabbalah borrows from Buddhism when it states that some will need several reincarnations before they can reach the stage that they, by keeping the law, conquer death. It is the deity that conquers death and imparts immortality. The redeemer of Job in the land of Uz, the one who imparted immortality to him (Job 19:25-27), is the redeemer of us all. That came from the belief and pen of Moses the Patriarch. At the same time that God gave the law at Sinai, He gave Israel the machinery to obtain forgiveness for breaking it. That is not antinomianism of any stripe—it is grace. King David, who was described as "A man after God's own heart" (1 Sam. 13:14), was one of the most dreadful sinners of all time. He was a lascivious coveter of his neighbour's wife, with whom he committed adultery, and then he murdered her husband so that he could take her as wife. He broke three commandments of the ten in that massive sin. But he repented first and then offered the sacrificial lamb to atone, shedding its innocent blood to expiate for his sin. Listen to David's admission of guilt:

> Have mercy upon me, O God, according to Thy loving
>   kindness,
> According unto the multitude of Thy tender mercies,
> Blot out my transgressions.
> Wash me thoroughly from mine iniquity,
> And cleanse me from my sin . . . .
>
> Against Thee only have I sinned and done this evil in Thy
>   sight,

That Thou mightest be justified when Thou speakest,
And be clear when Thou judgest
Behold I was shaped in iniquity and in sin did my mother
    conceive me . . . .

Purge me with hyssop, and I shall be clean;
Wash me and I shall be whiter than snow . . . .

Hide Thy face from my sins, and blot out all mine
    iniquities.
Create in me a clean heart O God, and renew a right spirit
    within me.
Cast me not away from Thy presence and take not Thy
    Holy Spirit from me.
Restore unto me the joy of Thy salvation . . . .

Deliver me from blood guiltiness O God, the God of my
    salvation . . . .
For Thou desirest not sacrifice, else would I give it:
Thou delightest not in burnt offering.
The sacrifices of God are a broken spirit;
A broken and a contrite heart, O God, Thou wilt not
    despise . . . .
Then shalt Thou be pleased with the sacrifices of
    righteousness,
With burnt offering and whole burnt offering;
Then shall they offer bullocks upon Thine altar.
(Ps. 51, selected verses, KJV)

Here is the great enunciation that repentance precedes sacrifice
and forgiveness. Without repentance, sacrifice is an indulgence,
a blasphemy. God loathes sacrifice that is offered without
repentance.

Listen again to David as he feels clean after the expiation of his
sins by the offered blood on the altar.

Bless the Lord, O my soul, and all that is within me,
Bless His holy name.
Bless the Lord O my soul, and forget not all His benefits,
Who forgiveth all thine iniquities, Who healeth all thy
    diseases.
Who redeemeth thy life from destruction,
Who crowneth thee with loving kindness and tender
    mercies,
Who satisfieth thy mouth with good things
So that thy youth is renewed like the eagle's.

The Lord executeth righteousness and judgement
For all who are oppressed.
He made known His ways unto Moses,
His acts unto the Children of Israel.

The Lord is merciful and gracious,
Slow to anger, and plenteous in mercy.
He will not always chide,
Neither will He keep His anger forever.
He hath not dealt with us after our sins,
Nor rewarded us according to our iniquities.
For as the heavens are high above the earth,
So great is His mercy toward them that fear him.

As far as the east is from the west,
So far has He removed our transgressions from us.
As a father pitieth his children,
So the Lord pitieth them that fear Him.
For He knoweth our frame,
He remembereth that we are dust.
(Ps. 103:1-14, KJV; emphasis added)

David could write this because he had experienced it. The Tanak
does not forgive sins by requesting the law be kept. The law is the
great standard that accuses the sinner, that points out his guilt. Sins
are forgiven by the Messianic blood, of which the animal sacrifice
is only a symbol. Since the advent of sin into the world in Eden,

God who made us from dust and gave us immortality (which we squandered) still remembers that we are dust, now mortal dust. Our only hope is the restoration of immortality by the deity. Pretending to keep the law perfectly does not restore immortality.

When discussing Mishnah and the Gemara, several names become prominent in their exposition:

Herbert Danby translated the entire Mishnah into English, finishing in 1958. This facilitated its study by those not fluent in Hebrew. In his preface he said:

> The Mishnah has considerable value, whether for the study
> of comparative religion, or for the study of the civilization
> of the Near East during the first and second centuries of our
> era, or for the study of Christian origins, or for the study of
> the development of Judaism and the conditions of Jewish
> life during the final stages of its association with the soil of
> Palestine.[189]

Interestingly and miraculously, the fatalism in that last clause has been abrogated by the marvellous resilience of the Jewish people and the power of Jehovah to bring them back to the "soil of Palestine." In 1948 God granted a miracle to His chosen people. Danby was so wrong to imagine that Israel no longer was linked to the soil of Palestine. The word "final" was the wrong word to use.

Abraham Cohen published his remarkable *Everyman's Talmud*, which appears to have been printed first in 1931, for that is the date of his first preface. The second preface to the revised edition is dated 1948. Schocken Books first published it in 1975; it was republished in 1995 with a preface by Jacob Neusner. Neusner is profuse in extreme praise of the Mishnah and Gemara, which he collectively calls the Talmud. He is also very profuse in praise of Abraham Cohen for making the Talmud accessible to the ordinary person. This book makes the Talmud intelligible to the layperson who is unlikely to wade into the original document in the original language, or even into the tome that is the English translation.

Neusner states in the preface, "Cohen succeeded in answering the question, what does the Talmud in particular say about the important issues of religion, theology, ethics, and jurisprudence?" That is exactly how I see his *Everyman's Talmud*, and I use Cohen in this book to solidify what I have to say about Tanakian Judaism.

Jacob Neusner has written eloquently in his four volumes of *The Talmud of Babylonia: A Complete Outline*, and also in his book *The Talmud: An Academic Commentary*.

Adin Steinsaltz is outstanding in providing an analysis of the Talmud in his book *The Essential Talmud*. Without being involved too much with the theology of the Talmud, he provides the interested person with a balanced view of what happened in the formation of the Talmud. Steinsaltz very ably relates the Mishnah to the Gemara in his book, but he rightly points out that relating the Talmud to the Tanak is a complicated task, because the connection drawn can often be farfetched.

In my opinion, the Mishnah commenced its recognisable cumulative growth at about 536 BC and took shape as the oral traditions of the Jews and used the name oral Torah (reminiscent of what Moses received from the Patriarchs preceding him from Adam to Abraham). However, Danby suggests that it started around the second century BC.[190]

Danby goes on to say:

> Although the Mishnah was compiled in its present form at the end of the 2nd Century [AD], it deals fully with phases of legislation and religious practice which for more than a hundred years had ceased to have any practical bearing on Jewish life. The destruction of Jerusalem in AD 70 made an end of the last vestiges of national self-government, and it marked also the extinction of the [Aaronic] priesthood and the Temple worship.[191]

Danby makes a further cogent observation:

> When we turn to the Mishnah's religious importance . . .
> within a generation of its compilation we find it described
> as "the iron pillar of the Law. Citing Leviticus Rabba,
> 21,4 reporting Joshua ben Levi, early 3rd Century [AD]),
> and according to a later teacher *the study of it was as*
> *meritorious as offering sacrifice.*[192]

Danby has another relevant statement:

> In the most exact sense the Mishnah is the final expression
> of the Jewish nation's unimpaired religious life: whatever
> modifications may have since arisen in the observances of
> Judaism have arisen out of conditions of exile, conditions in
> which the religion indeed persisted, but persisted as a thing
> incomplete, as a maimed survival. Approximately the half
> of the Mishnah has no longer any practical bearing on the
> present religious practice of Judaism.[193]

These are major indictments of post-AD 70 Judaism by Danby,
and they need to be analysed for their validity or otherwise. These
opinions or indictments will affect the Gemara as well, when
dealing with any post-AD 70 tractates of the Gemara. Danby was
correct to make these judgements in view of the dreadful wound
inflicted on the Jews and Judaism by the destruction of Jerusalem
and the quasi "Jewish nation," and especially the destruction of the
Second Temple. Here is the huge divide between the Judaism prior
to AD 70 and the Judaism afterwards: *the destruction of the Second*
Temple was perhaps the greatest tragedy to have befallen the Jews.
The loss of the symbolic sacrificial system left the Jews as a people
celebrating the Day of Atonement without an understanding of
how the atonement is accomplished. As Danby says so eloquently,
Judaism "persists as a thing incomplete, as a maimed survival."
A comparison of these two kinds of Judaism on either side of this
date is certainly in order. They are different. The brands of Judaism
with and without the Temple were bound to be different. I dedicate

a chapter in this book to this consideration. Messianic Judaism (Tanakian Judaism) was replaced by rabbinic Judaism. This replacement took the vitality, reality, and sustaining excitement out of Judaism; it has become a esoteric, moribund, dry, and fossilized religion. Many centuries later, comparing the benefits of the Enlightenment that impacted Europe after the French Revolution, Walter Laqueur's assessment was similar to this conclusion. Making a comparison with what the Enlightenment had to offer as an alternative, Walter Laqueur stated:

> The German-Jewish Haskala (enlightenment) led many Jews away from Judaism and it has come in for bitter attacks from both the orthodox and the latter-day Jewish national movement . . . . The great decline in faith had set in well before the turn of the century. Judaism had been undermined from inside; the Haskala was not the cause of this crisis but its consequence. Orthodox Jews naturally expressed their horror at the progressive Christianization of the synagogue, for this, not to mince words, is what it amounted to. But the reform movement was only the reaction to the chaotic state of religious life . . . . The sad truth which most defenders of traditional Judaism have always been reluctant to face was that it had become meaningless for many people . . . . Much of the influence of the Enlightenment was shallow and its fallacies were demonstrated only too clearly in subsequent decades. But in the clash between secularism and an ossified religion based largely on a senseless collection of prohibitions and equally inexplicable customs elaborated by various rabbis in the distant past, there was not the slightest doubt which would prevail. It was a conflict between a modern philosophy and a moribund religion.[194]

Gershom Scholem is not so pessimistic because his focus was on the Tanakian blueprint. He was excited by Messianic intervention and a cataclysmic apocalypticism (see chapter 21, "The Ha-Mashich of Israel"). Without these essential elements, to which Laqueur was not exposed, the Judaism restricted to Halachah was indeed the husks of Judaism. Halachic Judaism will never move the secular masses that call themselves Jews. But the Messiah will. Today, 55 percent of Israelis and probably 95 percent of American Jewry are secular.

The Mishnah is the first major work of rabbinic Judaism. To reiterate, it was redacted about AD 220 by Rabbi Judah HaNasi, the Prince, the Lion[195] when the possibility that it might be forgotten was perceived. Rabbi Judah deserves great thanks and recognition for the immense work that went into the redaction. Jewry should value his immense effort.

As stated already, the Misnah consisted of 6 orders containing 63 tractates. The orders are as follows:

1. Zeraim (Seeds)
2. Moed (Festivals)
3. Nashim (Women)
4. Nezikin (Damages)
5. Kodashim (Holy Things)
6. Toharot (Purities)

Steinsaltz has very ably given the Mishnah chapters with the parallel pages discussed by the Bavli and the Yerushalmi in an appendix at the end of his book. This is of great value in its study.[196] :

In the Zeraim Order, the Bavli comments only on the Berakhot, which is the section on prayers and benedictions, while the Yerushalmi comments on all the topics regarding the subject titled "Seeds," which deals with the laws about agriculture in Israel.

In the Moed Order, the Bavli ignores the discussion on the Shekalim, but otherwise they both discuss all the other topics in this section of the Mishnah on festivals.

In the Nashim Order, which deals with the subject of women, both Bavli and Yerushalmi discuss all the topics.

In the Nezikin Order, dealing with damages, both Bavli and Yerushalmi do not discuss Avot, which is the section on ethics and derekh eretz, and Eduyot, which is the section on "A collection of testimonies on various subjects."

In the Kodashim Order, the Bavli discusses all the sections except the topics Midot and Kirim. The Yerushalmi ignores this whole order.

The only topic discussed in the Tohorot Order by both Bavli and Yerushalmi is Nidah, which deals with the ritual impurity of Women. They both ignore all the other topics in this Order of the Mishnah.

Although all the Orders of the Mishnah deal with extensive commentary on moral, ceremonial, and judicial laws instituted by Moses, it is reasonable to note that only the Moed (Yomah and Peshaim), Nashim (Eduyot), and Kodashim (Zevahim and Tamid) deal with theological subjects such as God, Creation, the Fall of humanity and the loss of immortality, Messianic redemption, and glorification. Abraham Cohen, in his book *Everyman's Talmud*, has been extremely diligent in helping the unschooled in the collective Talmud to come to grips with their relationship with God and their personal eternal hereafter.

Jacob Neusner wrote the copyrighted foreword to the 1995 reprinting of Abraham Cohen's book, and he states:

> Cohen's *Everyman's Talmud* is the right place to begin not only to learn about Judaism in general but to meet the substance of the Talmud in particular. Here we find out what the Talmud says about all of the important issues of theology, law and jurisprudence comprised in Judaism, or the Torah.[197]

Although it is understandable that Neusner should make the claims that Judaism's best apologetics are in the Talmud, and that Talmud is Torah, Neusner *is not correct*. He has no spiritual license to ignore the Tanak and equate Talmud with Torah. The Judaism of Abraham, Jacob, and Moses is in the Tanak. These patriarchs knew no Talmud, and the conversation God had with Israel in the Tanak is the ultimate source from which to learn primitive Judaism. The Talmud is commentary and not the sacred canon. Neusner is out of order. Has he tested every clause in the Talmud to be in synch with the Tanak? He is relying very heavily on tradition and assuming that the Talmud has replaced the Tanak as the sourcebook for Judaism. Multiple scholars feel that the Talmud has rendered Judaism a philosophy and it is no longer a redemptive religion.[198] The Talmud is a great work and must be respected, but it is only a commentary and discussion by the sages. The Tanak, which is the only document in Israel's foundation that deserves the title of Torah, is their conversation with God. Mishnah is commentary on the Tanak, and the Gemara is commentary on the Mishnah. Neusner is elevating the commentaries to "inspired" Torah status, which they are not.

After lauding the Talmud to equality with the Bible (he likely means the Tanak or Old Testament), Neusner settles down to a more sensible definition of the Talmud:

> The Talmud is made up of a philosophical law code, the Mishnah, and an extensive analysis of and commentary upon the Mishnah. That commentary extends to the laws and the principles of the laws contained in the Mishnah. It is intellectually ambitious but economical and not prolix: a few questions occur throughout. That briefly defines the document.[199]

This is an excellent definition, and it is most heartening to see his admission that it "is made up of a philosophical law code, the Mishnah. And an extensive analysis of and commentary upon the Mishnah." Neusner goes on to be more erudite when he states:

> But the definition misses the key to the document and what makes it open-ended, a writing to which every generation makes its contribution. The Talmud is open-ended and

invites you to join in its discussion. The main trait of the
Talmud is its argumentative character, its argument, back
and forth.[200]

This kind of document is a legal treatise, an argument in the law
courts, an excellent debating society. Judaism is not a perennial
debating society to go on ad infinitum. The sacred canon is God's
conversation with us to procure our redemption. That is Judaism,
and that Judaism is in the Tanak. It is not to be subjected to the
vicissitudes of an indecisive argument back and forth, down
through the ages. It is a fixed plan, a redemptive religion in which
humanity was schooled outside the Gates of Eden. It concerns
the Abrahamic Covenant, which is God's agreement with us to
restore immortality via the means of land, Torah, and the Messiah.
Judaism was laid down by Moses as a redemptive religion perfectly
explained in the sacrificial system, the Day of Atonement, and
Messianic expectation. We can debate with God, but we cannot
renege on the Abrahamic Covenant. *We cannot refuse the coming
of the Messiah.* We cannot escape God's plan to restore immortality
to the human race. All Jewry and humanity must see that their
salvation is to re-enter the Gates of Eden through the sacrifice of
the lamb without blemish. The law reminds us that we are sinners
and are unacceptable to God. The law cannot save us; it only
condemns us as sinners. The Talmud tells us that God planned the
giving of the Messiah before the creation of the world.[201]

> The belief was general that the sending of the Messiah
> was part of the Creator's plan at the inception of the
> Universe . . . . From the beginning of the creation of the
> world King Messiah was born, for he entered the mind (of
> God) before even the world was created.[202]

We are to rejoice in the Messianic salvation God has provided.

In conclusion, the Mishnah is a great literary work, an erudite
discussion among the Jewish thinkers who gave birth to it. But
this discussion is not sanctioned by inspiration and does not have
the imprint of "Thus saith the Lord." It cannot and must not be

regarded as sacred; it must not be called canon. It must also be responsibly stated that the Talmud (Mishnah and Gemara) has little if any meaning for the large majority of Jews alive today. To them it is a dry, moribund religion. Judaism needs to take hold of its Messiah. In this venture excitement, redemption, and immortality are waiting to be found.

CHAPTER 13

THE GEMARA

The Gemara is the name by which the two Talmuds are known: the Bavli, or the Babylonian Talmud, and the Yerushalmi, developed in Jerusalem. Although they are dated after the turn of the era, they had been in the mill almost parallel with the development of the Mishnah. They are mainly a commentary on the Mishnah, but the writings were put together after the Mishnah had jelled through Rabbi Judah the Prince's efforts, at about AD 200. Basically, the Mishnah is the official commentary on the Tanak, and the Gemara is the official commentary on the Mishnah. And the right-wing Jews regard all as Torah. The Mishnah and the Gemara (collectively the Talmud) get all the analytical attention and the religious devotion of the majority of the observant Jews in this day and age.

Adin Steinsaltz, a renowned Israeli rabbi and scholar, has great insight into the Talmud and defines it as follows.

> The formal definition of the Talmud is the summary of Oral Law that evolved after centuries of scholarly effort by sages who lived in Palestine and Babylonia until the beginning of the Middle Ages. It has two main components: The Mishnah a book of halachah (Law) written in Hebrew, and the commentary on the Mishnah, known as the Talmud (or Gemara), in a limited sense of the word, a summary of discussion and elucidations of the Mishnah written in Aramaic—Hebrew jargon.[203]

Erudite schools of Jewish scholars arose in Palestine and Babylon, and they created a massive contemplation of Halachah.

The Bavli was produced by the Babylonian Jews, was written in Babylonian Aramaic, and was a distinct dialect. It commenced with the Babylonian captivity inflicted by Nebuchadnezzar II at about 588 BC. It served as the constitution and bylaws of rabbinic Jews.[204] The Bavli is composed of 37 tractates and had, as its deduced collective aim, the task of uncovering the truth that God manifested in the Torah (presumably the Pentateuch or written Torah) and the Mishnah (which was classified as the oral Torah). Rabbi Judah had not written down the Mishnah as a single written document until about AD 200, and this must have been a very difficult task, because the Bavli and the Yerushalmi were already developing alongside an as yet unredacted Mishnah. There had to be a focus on oral Torah to give the Bavli and Yerushalmi substance. The Babylonian and Yerushalmi rabbinic succession had a difficult task, and Rabbi Judah did a marvellous scholastic job to bring the Mishnah together as a written document. A good question to ask would be, "How did Rabbi Judah the Prince keep the Mishnah from mixing with the Gemara that was developing alongside it, in oral form?" Another good question would be, "How did the rabbis pouring out the Gemara not get it entangled with the main body of the Mishnah before Rabbi Judah's redaction feat?" As already mentioned, Adin Steinsaltz provides an appendix at the end of his book *Orders and Tractates of the Mishnah and Talmud*.[205] In that appendix he orientates the reader to a parallel study of the three documents. The Babylonian rabbinic succession continued the composition of the Bavli from as early as the year 588 BC to the year AD 600. As mentioned above, the Mishnah was redacted about AD 200. This is remarkable and shows how enterprising and resilient the Jews were in exile, in producing a document that jelled together over a thousand years. The conclusion is that the Bavli and Yerushalmi focussed on a fluid and oral Mishnah until the latter was redacted and written down by Rabbi Judah. After this, it must have become easier to note the parallels.

The Yerushalmi or Palestine-developed Talmud is considered older than the Bavli. It was written in Palestinian Aramaic, a variant dialect that was somewhat different from the Babylonian Aramaic. The Bavli is considered more authoritative. This distinction probably came about by the sheer prominence of Babylon and the veracity of the rabbinic sages who lived there. The Encyclopedia Britannica scholars summarize the three documents well:

> "If we compare the way in which the two Talmuds read the same Mishnah, we discern consistent differences between them . . . . The Yerushalmi talks in details, the Bavli in large truths; the Yerushalmi tells us what the Mishnah says, the Bavli, what it means [is]:
>
> 1. The Yerushalmi analyses evidence, the Bavli investigates premises;
>
> 2. The Yerushalmi remains wholly within the limits of its case, then vastly transcends the bounds of the case altogether.
>
> 3. The Yerushalmi wants to know the rule, the Bavli asks about the principle and its implications for other cases.
>
> The Yerushalmi provides an exegesis and amplification of the Mishnah; the Bavli, a theoretical study of the law in all its magnificent abstraction, transforming the Mishnah into testimony to a deeper reality altogether: to the law behind the laws.[206]

This summary does excellent justice to the meaning and significance of these works not only for devotees and students of Judaism, but as instruments that attempt to plumb and plunge the depths of the Tanak. The collective Talmud is the product of the Jews in the millennia of their national weakness and ineffectuality, and during their diasporic persecution and introspection. It represents their struggle to understand and preserve their religion, and as an expression of Jewish pent-up mental brilliance and giftedness. There is no doubt that they are the most energetic people on earth individually and theologically (which credits the great rabbinic dynasty). Plainly, they were a recognizable and pitiable, abject, political and national failure, from the downward slide after the zenith of national splendour achieved by King David and King Solomon. But that slide stopped in AD 1948 when a powerful national rebirth occurred, energized by Zionism and the will of God. Five wars that could have all been national collapses have proved them to be the most powerful tiny nation on earth. But it is unfortunate that the religion developed by the formulation of these documents took Judaism off the rails and snared it in a philosophical, esoteric aimlessness. Aimlessness is not too harsh a word, because no sensible person will admit to perfect law keeping in their whole lives. Their need for absolution from law breaking is undeniable and puts them on the same level as everyone else born on the planet. The belief that Torah is the ticket back to immortality devastates the redemptive Judaism of Abraham, Jacob, and Moses.

Theoretically, Mishnah, Bavli, and Yerushalmi developed as discussion of and commentary on the Tanak. But these documents are conversations and verbal battles amongst the rabbinic sages; they do not represent messages from or conversations with God, and they do not equal or supersede the Tanak. There has to be a repetition here. The Tanak is a sacred document because it is a conversation with God, and it must be viewed as its theological denouement of God's will. It is the complete record of the story of human existence on the planet Earth. The Jews and Gentiles are simply repeating the previous history of the Hebrews. Moses is very explicit in the Pentateuch: humanity was created perfect and immortal by the hand of God. Perfection and immortality were lost by disobedience to Torah by the wrong use of the will, and so death passed upon the human race. God implemented Messianic intervention to provide a correction and to restore perfection and immortality; He chose the Abrahamic Covenant to be the instrument through which to provide the Messianic intervention. It is all there in the primitive Torah of the Tanak. Christianity, in all its confusion, cannot depart from this basic plan. The Tanak tells the story of the repeated failures of the chosen people to embrace Messianic redemption. All the judges, prophets, and Tanakian sages call for reformation. In the Tanak, one can read for hours the pleadings of God for a happy relationship with Israel. Malachi, the last prophet of the Tanak, declares the arrival of Elijah to prepare the way for the Messiah. The world is waiting. Israel has a glorious and stupendous future for the asking; the era of the Third Temple is imminent.

Solomon Schechter has written some very thoughtful and disciplined volumes called *Studies in Judaism*, but he follows the strange rabbinic line that tries to separate the redemptive theology of Judaism under a label called mysticism. Mysticism implies the notion that it is ethereal, cloudy, ill understood, and perhaps so "out of this world" that it is not practical and perhaps not deserving of serious belief. This does a travesty to the Tanak, which does not recognise a mysticism as such. This is an unwitting, semantic negative on Schechter's part because he is otherwise most erudite in pronouncing what was important in Judaism. Looking at Ezekiel and Daniel, one finds passages that are difficult to understand, especially in the description of extraterrestrial, heavenly scenarios, and dreams and visions of future prophetic events. But these difficult to understand passages are not so mystical that they prohibit the reader from getting their meaning. They require further delving and clarification. In his introduction to his volumes of *Studies in Judaism*, Schechter states:

> Those who are at all familiar with old Rabbinic literature hardly need to be told that "the sea of the Talmud" has also its gulf stream of mysticism, which, taking its origin in the moralizing portions of the Bible, runs through the wide ocean of Jewish thought, constantly co-mingling with the icy waters of legalism, and unceasingly washing the desolate shores of an apparently meaningless ceremonialism, communicating to it life, warmth, and spirituality.[207]

It is very rewarding to hear Schechter describe the Talmud as "the icy waters of legalism." Legalism does not feed the masses of

Jews who define themselves as secular because they find no joy in it. The gulf stream of the Talmud is not mysticism but is the redemptive provision that is primitive Judaism, which the Talmud has relegated to the ethereal realm. The School of Kabbalah has taken the subject of Jewish mysticism and turned it into a religion more akin to Buddhism. The miracle needed is for Judaism to be redefined as the salvific redemptive religion that it is, which can provide the restless majority of Israelis and American and other diasporic Jews with the hope of redemption. The law only tells them they are sinners and condemns them to die. Messianic redemption tells them that they are forgiven and that they will live forevermore. Even those religious, legalistic, extremist Jews find their religion largely ceremonial, phylacteric, restrictive, choking, and lacking assurance. The Day of Atonement does provide forgiveness and release from their guilt, but they have not realized from whence comes their redemption. And all that the Kabbalistic adherents have to look forward to is the hopeless realization that after several reincarnations, they might have the chance of being perfect enough to be acceptable to God. There is little doubt that they have the inner conviction that they will never achieve that status, but they are numbed—as Schechter says so aptly, numbed indeed by the "icy waters of legalism." They shiver and freeze in legalistic Judaism; there ceases to be the warm, exciting, and life-giving circulation that Messianic deliverance has to offer. To the Jews who realise this, the legal document is like icicles in their blood vessels carrying no life-giving oxygen, and it is a premonition of eternal death.

Schechter realizes this as he further says:

> To draw attention to this fact [quoted above] a humble attempt has been made in the ninth essay, "The Law and Recent Criticism, a subject which I have essayed to expound in a series of essays on "Some Aspects of Rabbinic Theology."[208]

Schechter later stated in his book that he was not describing the mysticism in Judaism as theosophy or occultism:

> But as a manifestation of the spiritual and as an expression
> of man's agonies in his struggle after communion with
> God, as well as of his ineffable joy when he receives the
> assurance that he has found it.[209]

Schechter has identified what the masses of secular Jews need in their lives. They need the ineffable joy when they receive the assurance that they have a personal communion with a loving, forgiving, and redeeming God who receives them into His bosom. That is the same experience that Jacob had that night at the Brook Jabbok. He felt so vulnerable to the hatred in his brother Esau's heart. Esau sought to kill him for his deception and thievery, but in wrestling with the Almighty and embracing Him so tightly, Jacob would not let go until he had the assurance that he was solidly in the bosom of his loving, forgiving, merciful, and redeeming God. That was his ladder to heaven, and that is what all the secular and observant Jews need. That is what the whole world needs. They see themselves as law breakers and long for the assurance, which the law cannot give, of that ineffably joy. And that is not the message they are getting in the synagogues, nor from the rabbis who constantly dangle the law in their faces.

An exalted opinion of the Talmud makes it very difficult for the rank and file Jews to feel the emotion of primitive Judaism. That emotion is the release that comes from knowing repentance, forgiveness, acceptance, and atonement; it is the Brook Jabbok experience. All these come from being right with God. Most Jews get a fleeting taste of it on the Day of Atonement, and that is why the synagogues are full on the Day of Atonement. The law only tells of where and how the adherent has failed. Atonement gives absolution and freedom. The Passover lamb and the Day of Atonement ox have been sacrificed as the symbolic atonement of the Messiah.

Contemplate the status of the Jews, Israelis, and diasporic (American and others). At last count there are over five and a half million Israelis.[210]

- 50 percent are secular and do not worship in synagogues or consider themselves religious
- 30 percent are religious Zionists
- 15 percent are ultra-Orthodox or Haredim
- 5 percent are Messianic Zionists or Gush Emunim, Messianic Jews, and Karaites Jews
  (See *Beirut to Jerusalem* by Thomas Friedman, p. 288 and on.)

How many of these Jews have a redemptive religion? How many have the "ineffable joy" of knowing they are right with God?

At last count there are over six and a half million diasporic Jews. In America, where the vast majority of these live, a 2003 Harris Poll revealed that:

- 54 percent consider themselves secular.
- 46 percent belong to a synagogue, and of this 46 percent:
- 38 percent are members of reform
- 33 percent are conservative
- 22 percent are Orthodox
- 2 percent are reconstructionists
- 5 percent are other types of religious Jews

Consider the kind of Judaism on offer.

Adin Steinsaltz states:

> Historically speaking, the Talmud is the central pillar of Jewish culture. This culture is many faceted, but each of its numerous aspects is connected in some way with the Talmud . . . . Halachic literature, is of course, based entirely on the Talmud . . . . It is impossible to approach Biblical

exegesis or Jewish esoteric philosophy without knowledge
of the Talmud literature.[211]

This idea is very erroneous because it places a fence around the
Tanak, which he feels is impenetrable without knowing the
Talmud. Biblical exegesis does not depend on Talmudic "esoteric
philosophy" and "self-contradictory sacred intellectualism" to bring
it meaning. Jacob's and David's redemptive religions were lived in
total absence of the Talmud. How he ascribes "intrinsic sanctity"
to such a defined document is beyond logic. Steinsaltz exalts the
Talmud to giddy heights.

> A man with expert knowledge of the Bible [Tanak] or even
> the Bible and Mishnah is not yet considered a scholar; in
> order to win that title he must know the Talmud as well.[212]

However, Steinsaltz admits that the Talmud is in a constant state of
flux.

> Talmudic scholarship is to a certain extent self-contradictory,
> a type of "'sacred intellectualism." It places unparalleled
> emphasis on the theoretical, analytical, and critical aspects
> of human thought. No individual can study Talmud without
> being an eternal sceptic; the form of study itself is based
> on a series of questions, and the student himself is expected
> to submit his own questions and voice his own doubts and
> problems. At the same time, Talmudic study is not regarded
> merely as a secular exercise in developing the mind or
> abstract capacity for thought, but as a subject of intrinsic
> sanctity.[213]

The study of the Talmud is mental and legal discipline. The rank
and file majority of Jews cannot obtain sanctity or sacredness
from it. This kind of religion does not forgive sins and provide
restoration to the bosom of the Father. The clear injunction at Eden
(and firmly fixed in the minds of the Patriarchs from Adam to
Abraham and indeed in the minds of Jacob and Moses) was that
the sacrificial lamb constituted symbolic atonement to be provided

by the Messiah. The identification of Ha-Mashiach remains the unfulfilled task of the children of Abraham in their mission of bringing blessedness to themselves and all nations. Redemption is not through the erudite interpretation of the law expounded in the Talmud; it comes from Messianic fulfilment to be obtained from prayerful contemplation of the Tanak and the realization that Jews have a redemptive loving God. The experience of King David after he had coveted his neighbour's wife, committed adultery with her, and then murdered her husband so he could take her to wife was a series of disastrous actions flouting God's law. David could not continue to enjoy the bosom of his heavenly Father until he had absolution. What a beautiful rendition Psalm 51 is of the repentance and forgiveness that David was able to find in the Messianic redemption waiting for him in his contrition. The law had broken his spirit with its accusing finger, which is what it does. But the Brook Jabbok experience was there for him to tightly embrace his God, and the Father received him with the assurance of forgiveness.

There is no greater provision for sinful human beings, all breakers of the law:

> All we like sheep have gone astray, we have turned everyone to his own way. And the Lord has laid on him the iniquity of us all. (Isa. 53:6 emphasis added)

Jacob and David had no Talmudic legal document in which to seek absolution. They had the Messianic sacrificial symbolism, which was provided outside the gates of Eden. The masses of Jewry need that Messianic forgiveness too. In 1948, the era of the Third Temple arrived.

In Isaiah 66:1, God asks a question. "Thus saith the Lord: The heaven is My throne, and the earth is My footstool. Where is the house that ye build unto Me? And where is the place of My rest?" When will people of the nation of Israel, now back in their homeland, build the ladder of Jacob's dream to scale that western wall? When will the Jewish nation's political leaders and rabbinic dynasty point the "unforgiven masses" of secular Jews who stand "accused by the law" to Messianic forgiveness and redemption? Year after year we celebrate the Day of Atonement, but there is no assurance. Without Messianic assurance, Yom Kippur is only a hollow ritual.

Do not discard the Talmud. It is useful to discuss aspects of theology and realize the limits there are to our ideas, because they are measured by the Tanak. I use the Talmud extensively in this book. But dream Jacob's dream, climb Jacob's ladder, and tightly embrace Jacob's God at Brook Jabbok. The glorious morning dawns! Israel will fulfil its Messianic dream, and Israel will wrestle with God. Israel will get the blessing of the eternal God. We will limp up the banks of Brook Jabbok and find healing and rejoicing.

CHAPTER 14

KABBALAH

Kabbalah is classified as a mystical part of the philosophy that is Judaism. Primitive Redemptive Judaism is defined as a religion based on the Tanak, and therefore Kabbalah is not strictly part of the religion of Abraham, Jacob, and Moses. Plainly, Kabbalah does not conform totally to the teaching of the Tanak. It certainly arises out of Judaism because it does use the foundation story of the Garden of Eden. Its ideas are quite diffuse, however. The presentation of Kabbalah is varied and can be so mystical and ethereal that it is at times difficult to comprehend intellectually. But it has some substance to it and is worthy of study. Historically, Kabbalah became prominent in the 12th Century and increased its prominence after the expulsion of the Jews from Spain in AD 1492. The city of Safed in Israel is situated in Galilee and is one of the four sacred cities in Judaism, the other three being Jerusalem, Hebron, and Tiberias. Safed enjoys the highest elevation in Israel at 2,953 feet and was originally founded by one of Noah's sons, according to tradition. The area in which it is situated was assigned to the tribe of Naphthali according to the Tanakian Book of Judges.[214]

Kabbalah is developed from two compositions that must be defined as apocryphal and not part of the Hebrew canon, because if they were existent before the Tanak was closed, it was the decision of the Sanhedrin to exclude them.

1. The Sefer Yetzirah (Book of Formation), purportedly written by Abraham, would make it the oldest extant writing in Judaism. Its ideas derive from the 22 letters of the Hebrew alphabet.

2. The Zohar (Book of Splendour), according to Gershom Scholem, was composed late in the 13th Century in Castile, Spain by Moses ben Shem-Tov de Leon. He credited it to Rabbi Shimon bar Yochai who lived in the 1st and 2nd centuries, who stated he received it from Moses. It consisted of dialogues between masters and students concerning incidents in the Bible and other spiritual, non-Tanakian topics.

Rabbi Shimon was likely the founder of the community from which the Kabbalah Centre in Safed arose. In the centuries that followed, he was succeeded by other famous rabbis. Prominent among them were Rabbis Luria, Moses Cordovero (of the Thirteen Principles fame), Joseph Karo, and Yehuda Ashlag. More recently Rabbi Brandwein has been in charge and was succeeded by Rav Berg.[215] Scholem is an authority on Kabbalah. For my purposes I find the book by Michael Berg (the son of Rav and Karen Berg) titled *The Way* to be the most comprehensible and illuminating, and is my main source for the Kabbalistic ideas that I discuss here. In his introduction he states, "The wisdom of Kabbalah is a five thousand-year-old tradition whose purpose is to bring an end to all pain and suffering in the world."[216] This is very noble indeed.

The most prominent feature of Kabbalah—and one that is most deeply appealing—is that it is based on the Genesis account of Creation and the story of Adam and Eve and the Garden of Eden. This idea is pure Torah, but departures from the Tanakian Creation story and variant views are also expressed. Basic Kabbalah sees the Edenic story and the entrance of sin because of the wrong use of the will. It recognizes the human race as one big family, transcends the ethnicity of the Jewish race, and wants salvific healing to be available to all. Indeed, it aspires to the Abrahamic Covenant and blessedness of all nations, which it hopes to achieve by a specialized inward devekut. This is contrary to the Tanak which achieves that blessedness by the arrival of a human Messiah.

Lurianic Kabbalah is a major variant and steps outside the basic Kabbalah and the Tanak. It reinvents Creation with the idea of Tzimzum, or contraction of God's essence to allow space (which

God vacated) for Adam and a finite independent world to exist, where free will could be exercised. This idea predicates:

> a ray of Light, [God being defined as Light] from God's hidden essence (Ein Sof) entered the empty space and acted upon the existing mixture of reshimu [residue] and Din [judgement]. This illuminating ray serves as a permanent link between Ein Sof and the empty space. The form of the divine Adam produced by this first ray of Light is termed the "Primordial Man (Adam Qadmon) . . . described with vivid anthropomorphic detail. The . . . light issuing from the 'eyes' [of Adam] emanated in . . . atomised or separated into different sefirot so as to require their containment in special vessels or qelim . . . . Some of these vessels were unable to contain the fight within them, and consequently shattered . . . . This event is known in the Lurianic texts as 'shevirot ha-qelim,' or the 'breaking of the vessels.'"[217]

The 'breaking of the vessels' was the wrong exercise of the will, and resulted in a 'scattering of sparks'. This caused the 'Galut', which started as an uprooting of Adam, and later the Jewish diaspora. Rabbi Luria implicated a Galut of 'the divine' as well, which was termed a scattering of the 'sparks of the Shechina'. Rabbi Luria also envisaged forces of evil and darkness which are called 'shells' and 'offscourings' which strangely are attributed to God.

Lurianic Kabbalah sees the only way out of this mess to be Tikkun olam ("fixing or repairing the world"), the 'lifting of the sparks'. This is an individual matter. Scholem stated this as: "Every man amends his own soul, and by the process of transmigration that of his neighbour . . . . In this system, redemption is synonymous with emendation or restoration."[218] This is an individual achievement. The Tanakian view is that this is achieved by Messiah, a force from God, of His own volition, emanating from heaven. Messiah provides atonement and initiates a catastrophic, apocalyptic cessation of history and restores perfection and immortality to the human race. Kabbalah reinvents Messianism as "devekut," where the Baal Shem implied that Messiah is to be found personally in communion with God and can be achieved anywhere at any time by anybody. Gershom Scholem calls this a "neutralizing of Messianism," which was seen as a belief of early Hasidism, as well as being a major belief in Lurianic Kabbalah.[219] The brokenness of every individual is repaired through their sanctification of physicality.[220] This idea is "do it yourself" salvation and departs from the blueprint of the Tanakian Mosaic substitutionary achievement of a Messiah emanating from God, first to achieve atonement and then culminating in the catastrophic, apocalyptic arrival of a Messianic new earth and immortality. Gershom Scholem embraces this latter idea. In other words, God Himself rescues fallen humanity. Therefore, this Kabbalian idea is not the Tanakian redemptive religion, which was clearly outlined in the Temple Service in the primitive Judaism of Moses.

The idea of Tikkun olam originated in the rabbinic period. Rabbi Shimon bar Yochai and later Rabbi Yochanan believed that the Jewish people will be redeemed when every Jew observes Shabbat twice in all its details. Presumably, when the repairing process is completed by self-accomplishment, the Messianic Age is achieved. The Messiah then comes as a glorious age. According to Lurianic theory, he does not come as a provider of redemption, which has already been achieved by the performance of ritual mitzvoth, commandment keeping and fulfilment of religious obligations.[221]

The other problem here is the mechanism of Creation set forth by Lurianic Kabbalah. Adam is divine in that he emanates from God and occupies a space vacated by God but still in continuity with God. This is contrary to the Genesis account of Adam being formed from the dust of the ground and then given life by the breath of God. The Genesis account of the entrance of sin is not by the "breaking of vessels" inside a "divine" Adam. Eve gets left out of their primary story. The initial disobedience of Adam and Eve was caused by their acceding to temptation by the Serpent. The Genesis account is contrary to a divine Adam having an experience of "breaking of the vessels" inside him. This designates the entrance of sin as originating from inside Adam. Lurianic Kabbalah does not exactly give a mechanism for this breakage, except perhaps that God left His "dross" behind in the space He vacated and isolated for Adam. If that is the explanation, then God is responsible for the entrance of sin. The other objectionable feature is that God has "dross" in Him. This entire theory appears to obviate a previous origin for evil, and the presence of the Serpent in the Garden.

It is important at this juncture to discuss the towering, modern colossus of Gershom Scholem, and his journey in Kabbalah. His personal stance in Judaism is somewhat difficult to define. He tried to be sympathetic to all the prevailing facets that Judaism had spawned or espoused, many of them veering in directions in which Tanakian theology could not accompany them. Gershom Scholem was an academic authority on Kabbalah, as well as a professor of Kabbalah at Hebrew University in Jerusalem. He authored many books on Kabbalah and is highly respected. He has written a very good summary of the progression of Kabbalism from early to modern times. His essay titled "The Messianic Idea in Kabbalism" gives an excellent synopsis of Kabbalah. He clearly points out the departures of Kabbalistic thought from traditional Judaism (Talmudic), occasionally also mentioning a few departures from the Tanak ("revelation") as well. He discusses Lurianic Kabbalah as a nontraditional and non-Tanakian idea.[222] These pages do not reveal specifically the aspects of the Lurianic Kabbalah he endorses, but he is emphatic about what he rejects. Arthur Hertzberg from New York University wrote the preface for the posthumous republishing of the book cited above by Scholem, in 1995. In this preface, Hertzberg states that Scholem gave a lecture entitled "Reflections on Jewish Theology," offering perhaps his own views at the end of the lecture. Scholem subordinated Kabbalah to Halachah:

> I am convinced that . . . Zionism contains within its religious content (and) a religious potential that is far more fundamental than anything that is expressed by the existing "religious parties of the State of Israel." In the dialectic of Jewish life, the religious tradition continues to be the challenge, and the fundamental element in that tradition is the Halachah.[223]

Hertzberg points out that in his earlier years Scholem had regarded Halachah as a fossil. But Halachah had now become to Scholem:

> the central element of religious continuity. Mysticism is the refresher and corrective, but one can detect a progression in Scholem's later years of growing worry about its [Kabbalah's] "anarchic tendencies."[224]

From my viewpoint of reading Scholem, he goes further in a disapproval of Kabbalah for rejecting what he regarded as his own firm belief in the Gan Eden promise of the "restorative force" and "utopian factor" and the timing or occurrences of these Gan Eden promises, which are basic to Tanakian theology. Scholem espoused the Prophet Daniel's "Last Days" events, and Isaiah's apocalypticism (chapters 1-2), which are also basic to Tanakian theology. Again, from my reading of Scholem, I see him embracing the coming of the Messiah as king and ruler of the world, which is embodied in the great apocalyptic events of the Tanak. Kabbalah unequivocally rejects apocalypticism in its view that the Messiah is not a person but an impersonal force that inspires humanity to work out its own salvation by pure living, good deeds, and benevolence. This Kabbalism is totally un-Tanakian. The Tanak clearly emphasizes Messianic atonement and redemption all the way through. I do not read Scholem as rejecting apocalyptic events in favour of Kabbalism's directional course, of a future lacking the apocalyptic ushering in of Messiah. There is no doubt in my mind that Scholem embraced the apocalyptic Messianic event and the Resurrection.[225] Scholem's contributions are further discussed in chapter 21, "The Ha-Mashiach of Israel."

In summary, Kabbalah clearly departs from the Tanakian Creation and redemption story of Moses the Patriarch, Israel's greatest guru and Sinai colossus. As a devotee of Tanakian theology, one is incumbent to reject this Lurianic reinvention of the Creation and the distorted Messianic idea which substitutes for the redemption story of the Pentateuch.

But Kabbalah has much to commend it. The roots of Kabbalah are deeply implanted in the communion God had with Adam and Eve in the Garden of Eden, and soon after they were driven from it. The barriers that disobedience (the wrong use of the will) brought to the divine-human communion spoiled the happiness of God and humanity. God became more distant because of the awe that is deity. The big realization was that humanity had lost immortality:

> If immortality is not available to us now, Kabbalah assures us—guarantees us—that the death of death is indeed on its way. How soon it arrives is entirely up to us.[226]

The reattainment of immortality is therefore the great goal of Kabbalah. The loss of immortality was the great tragedy that overtook the human race "in the Beginning." For how long a period of time Adam and Eve enjoyed immortality before their disobedience is up for conjecture; it may not have been a long time. No children were present in Eden ("I will make most severe your pangs in child bearing; in pain shall you bear children"—Gen. 3:16, *The Jewish Study Bible*), so this mitigates against it being a very long time. Kabbalah dwells on this portion of time as being a wonderful communion between the light (the preferable name in Kabbalistic writings for God) and Adam and Eve. Kabbalah assigns to this portion of time an explanation that is understood as the composition of perfectly created humans. The thinking for this is likely the nature of God and the nature of perfect humans. Genesis 1 states,

> And God said, Let us make man in our image, after our likeness . . . . And God created man in His image, in the image of God He created him; male and female He created them and God said to them: Be fertile and increase. (Gen. 1:26-28 'The Jewish Study Bible')

Kabbalah has a lot to say about the nature of humans as being fashioned in the image of God, and Lurianic Kabbalah seems to be the dramatic departure from the more pervasive beliefs of Kabbalah in this respect. The creation of humans in the image of

God is not proffered as a theory that Adam and Eve were "little gods" or sub-gods. Kabbalah is firm on monotheism and has respect for one God. However, when God uses the plural "Us," He is clearly stating that He manifests Himself in different functions. The Tanak subscribes to the idea of God being in the form of the Holy Spirit (Ruach Hakodesh), and that the Holy Spirit is indeed deity. Again, Almighty God manifests as Ha-Mashiach in His redemptive function. Messiah will appear in Israel as a human as well as deity, and nothing less. He will not be a flash in the pan. There is nothing in Kabbalah that assigns a resemblance of the bodily form of humans to the form of God. God does not have a human-like frame, and Kabbalah firmly rejects the idea that God has a body. But God's power is expressed sometimes in the human idiom—for example, Deuteronomy 33:27 states, "The ancient God is a refuge, a support are the arms everlasting." In that same passage, He is also described as a shield and a sword.[227] The alikeness of God and humans comes in the form of the ability to love, share, and empathise. Does the Kabbalah dictum "We are partners with the Creator in the great ongoing process of creation" have any bearing in this respect? It is difficult to know, but it seems to be implied. The genetic, built-in apparatus that gives humans the ability to replicate (procreate) may also be a resemblance, but this characteristic is also present in lower forms of life. It is a reproductive endowment and does not denote that we can create like God created. Kabbalah does not discuss this physical feature, to my knowledge. Kabbalah affirms that God is Ein Sof, or "the Infinite," who is Creator. "Kabbalah teaches that a distinction does exist between male and female energies." When "He" is used to describe God (the Creator), "He" encompasses both forms of energy:

> The Creator is an infinite force of positive energy . . . the essence of hope, peace, contentment, mercy, and fulfilment; the source of everything in Creation that opposes the forces of confusion and chaos and suffering and pain; an endless source of Light and an unnameable timeless presence. [This] . . . energy of the Creator is carefully and lovingly

distributed in our world, because the Creator's deepest intention is to *share* with us peace, joy, kindness and love.[228]

Logically, if God "opposes the forces of confusion and chaos and suffering and pain," then these opposite forces are not His nature and are against His will. In defining the existence of good and evil in the world (or universe), Kabbalah is ethereal in the explanation that it proffers. In explaining the existence of evil, Kabbalah recognizes that temptation to do evil is a very vital force and surrounds us constantly. But how it came into existence in the perfect world of the Creator is not adequately or logically explained by Kabbalah. Kabbalah is not true to the Tanakian context. The Lurianic concept of the origin of evil has already been discussed above. The explanation Kabbalah offers, which is from the School of Safed, is incomprehensible when considering and defining the character of God.

> Kabbalah teaches that evil resides in our perception of evil. If we understood its true origin and purpose, it would be revealed as another manifestation of the Creator's wisdom.

> For many people, humanity's own ultimate responsibility for suffering is perhaps the most difficult of all Kabbalah's precepts.[229]

This Kabbalistic teaching is not logical and is not compatible with the Tanak. God allowed free will and choice to the Eden couple in their perfect, unfallen state; they were certainly not His puppets. In the endowment of free will at Creation, there was an alternative choice. The Tanak's explanation for the existence of evil is different to that spawned by Kabbalah. Rabbinic Judaism also spells out a variant of the origin of evil. If the tendency toward evil as a proclivity was a part of the make-up of the perfect couple, they could not be considered perfect—they would be flawed indeed when they came from the Creator's hands. But they were not. The Tanakian concept of the origin of evil has been discussed elsewhere in this book in detail and will be briefly stated here.

Kabbalah envisions "the death of Death" as a solution to all the miseries of this life. The spiritual longings in Kabbalah are deep and heart-rending. The longings of the individual soul and the collective soul of humanity are well expressed in Kabbalah. The complaints of the spirit are stark and far from ethereal. How does the teaching of Kabbalah guarantee us the death of Death and the restoration of immortality? Unfortunately, Kabbalistic teaching departs from the teaching of the Tanak and adopts a "Do it yourself" technique. The Tanak accomplishes a Messianic conquest of eternal death, whereas Kabbalah sees it occurring as an accomplishment of the individual in Kabbalistic halachah. Kabbalah sees the soul of a righteous man dwelling on a "higher plain" (whatever and wherever that is, is a value judgement) and the soul of a wicked man dwelling in the netherland, a "lower plain." When earthly life comes to an end, the 'righteous man' undergoes a transformation that occurs as he ascends to a spiritual plain in a oneness with God, a closer proximity to the Creator, and presumably he thereby conquers death. The wicked man faces death only to be told he has to go back; he has accumulated negative energy to high levels and has to go for "another revolution" in another incarnation.[230] Higher spiritual plains in Kabbalah have to be earned. Kabbalistic thinking asks the question:

> For what purpose . . . did the Creator let everything get so complicated? Why does spiritual transformation have to be so difficult? If there is no limit to God's power, why doesn't God just instantly reinvent us as a species of . . . fully enlightened human soul[s] . . . . *We cannot achieve fulfilment without doing the spiritual work of earning fulfilment.*[231]

Here is a total departure from primitive redemptive Judaism as typified and practiced in the sacrificial system in the Levitical Aaronic priesthood in the Temple services laid down by Moses. The Aaronic priesthood is based on a substitutionary mechanism. This is deeply embodied in the Day of Atonement service instituted at Sinai. God's Messiah *is* God Himself and will be the ultimate sacrifice and the conqueror of eternal death. The Messiah is part and parcel of God Himself. But Kabbalah teaches a "do it yourself" way of overcoming eternal death.

> Our essence is of the Creator, whose nature is to give and to share, and for whom the whole concept of "free gifts" is inadmissible. There is a Hebrew phrase in the Talmud that is pertinent to the idea—nahama dichisufa, which can be translated as "bread of shame." It refers to wealth or sustenance that, because it is unearned, brings us pain and regret rather than joy and fulfilment. Rabbi Ashlag called attention to this phrase as a way of describing the dangers of unmerited abundance. On a spiritual level, and psychologically as well, it's against our interests and against our nature to "'accept something for nothing."[232]

This statement devastates Tanakian redemptive theology. It is utterly erroneous. One must ask the question, What is the underlying principle of the Day of Atonement? On the holiest day of the calendar, in Judaism in the time of the Jewish Tabernacle in the desert, and then in Solomon's grand and glorious Temple, and in current spiritual observance in the synagogues, it is still substitutionary. The high priest offered the sacrificial animal as a burned offering. The blood was taken into the Most Holy Place where the Shechinah dwelt, and it was sprinkled on the Ark of the Covenant and the Mercy Seat. This blood cleansed the entire nation of Israel of her sins. Repentance (a gift of the Ruach Hakodesh), confession, and restitution were followed by forgiveness from God. The sins of all the people were placed on the head of the sacrificial animal without blemish. Here was a substitution symbolizing the Messianic expiation. Forgiveness was given for nothing, for free—a gift of God, shifting the guilt of all Israelis off their shoulders. And Israel walked away from that service cleansed from all sin, standing perfect before God. Here was the gift of repentance and forgiveness for free, a totally unmerited favour.

How can Kabbalah overlook this great act of God and tell the world that everyone must earn forgiveness and find acceptability with God by study and hard work at appeasing their base natures, by works that can never be perfect? It is contrary to the whole plan of God commissioned at the Gates of Eden and again at Sinai. As if any person, in any number of lifetimes, can become perfect enough to reach the standard of perfection required by God so that he can reinvest mortals with immortality. No one, no matter how earnest and yearning they are, can keep the law of God as perfectly as that law requires. The free gift from God is compatible with His great love and is not inadmissible, as Kabbalah declares. Quotations from the Talmud should not be allowed to override the great principles of the divine provision of the Tanak.

According to the Tanak, the origin of evil is well outlined by Moses in the Books of Job and Genesis. It also is well described in several other books of the Tanak. Isaiah and Ezekiel add their inspired voices. Job, the oldest book of the Tanak (which bears the imprint of authorship by Moses), offers the first explanation for the origin of evil. "The Adversary" or "Accuser" is presented as the great inciter of evil, the one who seeks to overthrow God. The Hebrew word Ha-Satan is differentiated from the word Satan by some Hebrew scholars, but the qualities of the Adversary (Ha-Satan), which are described in the Book of Job, fit in well with the tempter Satan in 1 Chronicles 21. Here Satan incited King David to enumerate the army of Israel to gauge Israel's strength instead of trusting in God (See Book of Job and 1 Chronicles 21, *The Jewish Study Bible*). In Ezekiel 28, the prophet rails against the King of Tyre, who had challenged God and exalted himself to be a god. The prophet uses the imagery and rhetoric reminiscent of the Fall of Lucifer—the Adversary, the Accuser, Satan. He was created by God as a perfect cherub, and he was present with God in the preparation of Eden. Ezekiel adds his voice in this enunciation of the originator of evil. "Iniquity was found in him" (Ezek. 28:15, KJV). "You were blameless in your ways, from the day you were created, until wrongdoing was found in you" (Ezek. 28:15, *The Jewish Study Bible*). Although the primary target of this address is the King of Tyre, the rabbinic sages allow for multiple applications. This is especially so when a behaviour matches another behavioural instance. In the Eden story, the reality of the Garden must be believed. Lucifer, the Adversary, the Accuser, Satan, now in the guise of the Serpent, beguiles the primal couple and causes the Fall of humanity (Gen. 3, *The Jewish Study Bible*). Their disobedience divests them of their innocence and immortality, and it becomes a barrier to the personally bestowed great love and communion enjoyed with God. But now God loves them to death! Their loss of immortality now ensures that death will overtake them. And so, outside the Gates of Eden, God teaches them that He Himself will come to their rescue. He teaches them that He will be the propitiation for sin. Symbolic of this God requires them to offer sacrifices. The offering of the sacrificial lamb symbolically cleansed them from sin foreshadowing what the Messianic God will do for them. Moses will enshrine this great deliverance in the symbolic institution of the Passover as they flee Egypt, and in the great Day of Atonement at the fiery encounter with God on Mount Sinai. Kabbalah is remiss in contravening this great truth and in not celebrating and teaching this basic Tanakian doctrine.

Contrast the intervention of God by His personal function of deity to redeem sinners, with this commentary of *The Jewish Study Bible* when discussing this scripture.

> In Judaism, the estrangement caused by the innate human appetite for evil does not require an act of Messianic redemption to be healed. Rather, the practice and study of Torah renew intimacy with the God of Israel and lead to eternal life.[233]

> The Holy One (blessed be He) created the Evil Inclination. He created Torah as its antidote.[234]

This comment and this extract from these Jewish scholars repudiates the Judaism of the Tanak, the same Judaism of Abraham, Jacob, Moses, and David. The sacrifice of Isaac by Abraham on Mount Moriah enshrined the act of Messianic redemption. The Judaism that was enshrined in the Aaronic priesthood of the Tent Tabernacle and then Solomon's Temple needs to be brought back. O God, we need the Temple to be rebuilt to remind us of Messianic redemption. The Judaism of the Tanak is redemptive, and that redemption is not earned by the practice of Torah. Who on God's planet can practice Torah absolutely perfectly? Let him stand up! The study of Torah does not cleanse or procure remission for sin, but the blood of the sacrificial lamb does. Worldwide Jewry does not enter a study session of the Torah for forgiveness on the Day of Atonement, but it invokes the blood of that ox without blemish that symbolises Messianic redemption. Israel sacrificed animals for this purpose until AD 70. What a devastation to the Tanakian concept of redemption is this erroneous substitution!

Kabbalah introduces another feature that is not supported by the Tanak. Reincarnation is not taught by the Tanak—on the contrary, God offers humanity only one lifespan. Reincarnation has been borrowed from Buddhism.

Moses wrote of Cain's murder of Abel in terms of God's reaction. "What have you done? Hark, your brother's blood cries out to Me from the ground" (Gen. 4:10, *The Jewish Study Bible*). Abel had only one life span, which Cain snuffed out. Cain went out with the curse of separation from God, with no promise of multiple lifetimes to perfect acceptance with God. All that was proffered was the expiation Cain could achieve with the burned offering of the lamb without blemish, symbolic of the Messiah's sacrifice. This was something that Cain had already rejected. God did not offer him reincarnation, so he could achieve regeneration in another life.

Job recognized this. In Job 14, he talks of the limit of time allotted in the one life God bestows.

> "Man born of woman is short-lived and sated with trouble.
> He blossoms like a flower and withers;
> He vanishes like a shadow and does not endure . . . .
> His days are determined;
>
> You know the number of his months
> You have set him limits that he cannot pass.
> Turn away from him, that he may be at ease
> Until like a hireling he finishes out his day . . . .

If a man dies, can he live again?
All the time of my service I wait
Until my replacement comes.
You would call and I would answer You;
You would set your heart on Your handiwork.
Then You would not count my steps,
Or keep watch over my sin.
My transgressions would be sealed up in a pouch;
You would coat over my iniquity.
(Job 14, *The Jewish Study Bible*)

Here is a repudiation of reincarnation. The only way a human can escape the wrath of God for his disobedience is to accept the mercy of God's forgiveness. His replacement must come to take over and bear his guilt. At the end of his one allotted lifetime, his sins can only disappear "sealed up in [the] pouch" of forgiveness, and God "coats over [his] iniquity" with the Messianic expiation. It is a totally free gift, thanks be to God. Job looked forward to the day of resurrection.

For I know that my Redeemer liveth, and that He shall stand at the latter day upon the earth; And though after my skin worms destroy this body, yet in my flesh shall I see God. (Job 19:25-27, KJV)

The Jewish Study Bible says it just as succinctly:

But I know that my Vindicator lives;
In the end he will testify on earth—
This, after my skin is peeled off.
But I would behold God while still in my flesh,
I myself and not another, would behold Him;
Would see with my own eyes:
My heart pines within me.

Not only did Job have a vindicator ("go'el" means redeemer), but that redeemer was the go'el of Israel. To Job, the Messiah, his redeemer, was God Himself ("shall I see God").

King David's Naked Dance

Solomon was not in any hesitation of his view of the human lifespan.

> For he who is reckoned among the living has something to look forward to . . . since the living know that they will die. But the dead know nothing; they have no more recompense, for even the memory of them has died. Their loves, their hates, their jealousies have long since perished; and they have no more share till the end of time in all that goes on under the sun . . . . Whatever is in your power to do, do with all your might. For there is no action, no reasoning, no learning, no wisdom in Sheol, where you are going. (Eccles. 9:4-6, 10, *The Jewish Study Bible*)

> The law of the Lord is perfect, converting the soul; the testimony of the Lord is sure, making wise the simple. (Ps. 19:7)

Halachah is mighty and is a good disciplinary action to make humans long to obey and be more in tune with the Creator. But it does not make anyone good enough to re-enter the Garden, where the Creator is waiting with outstretched arms to receive His children in face-to-face relationship with them. To enable that, the Creator provided Messianic redemption.

Kabbalah is devotional and serves to foster devotion to and communion between God and humanity. It recalls and tries to recapture that wonderful communion between God and humans in that great love relationship between humanity and their Creator, the original devekut, that existed in the Garden of Eden.

The strength of Kabbalah is its dedication to devotion; there is no substitute for personal devotion to God. This is where the human expresses love to his God, and where God reciprocates by embracing His beloved child. That is what happened at the Brook Jabbok (Gen. 32:25-32). True worship of God occurs in that divine embrace. That divine embrace motivates humans to pour out themselves in love toward their fellow humans. Kabbalah emphasizes this as sharing and the generation of the electricity of positive energy.

Kabbalah has much to offer. In the expression of love to one's fellow humans, in the provision of charity, we see the value of its teaching. Kabbalah enhances prayer life. Kabbalah emphasizes the true significance and celebration of the Shabbat (Sabbath). But it needs to recognize the spiritual rest that the Shabbat provides. Striving all the six days of labour to earn a living, and worrying all week to meet the requirements of halachah, makes the Shabbat a necessity. The Shabbat brings the spiritual realization of rest in the sacrifice of the Messiah as their redeemer. Nothing else on earth brings more peace, calm, and total rest. This brings the great reassurance, despite the human effort of obeying halachah having fallen short of the mark. Torah requires perfect obedience to the standard required by the justice of God. On the Shabbat we can rest in Messianic redemption and not be in doubt of the assurance of forgiveness and salvation, even though we have fallen short of perfect obedience to the law. Shabbat is terrestrial and will endure terrestrially eternally. "From one Shabbat to another shall all flesh come to worship before Me, saith the Lord" (Isa. 66:23).

Kabbalah gives us insight into the miracles of God. The contemplation of the miracle of life, DNA, and the genetic code is massively miraculous. Every breath inhaled, every heartbeat, and every chemical reaction in the cells of the human body to maintain and promote life is fantastic in the extreme. The act of procreation and the propagation of human and all other life is a study of miracles.

Kabbalah teaches the practical value of meditation. There is great amelioration of the restive human spirit in meditation and in the contemplation of God. The Psalmist knew the importance of tranquillity to the soul.

> Desist! Realise that I am God! I dominate the nations; I dominate the earth. (Ps. 46:11, *The Jewish Study Bible*)

The King James Version translates it more meditatively: "Be still and know that I am God." What wonderful peace and security there is in the heart in this contemplation. The meditation of God is the bulwark against mental disequilibrium and provides strength to cope with the vicissitudes of life. It is the anchor of the soul and brings stability for practical living. It brings joy to the spirit, and its happiness is contagious. It is the balm of Gilead. No one who contemplates the great love of God need be depressed no matter what the irritating pathology. And if they do become depressed, there is help.

Kabbalah's call for transformation of nature needs to be viewed seriously. Humans need to study the holiness of daily living, which God wants them to achieve, so that they can be seen to value the Edenic perfection from which they have fallen. But unfortunately, this transformation will never be perfect and cannot qualify for the right to allow humanity to walk back through the Gates of Eden and into immortality. For that, the symbolic sacrifice of the lamb without blemish, the Messianic provision, is necessary. Kabbalah needs to realise this important Tanakian doctrine. Kabbalistic teachings must not deny this important, redemptive provision; it is the redemption of Israel and the whole world.

The sin of David in coveting and committing adultery with Bathsheba and murdering her husband so that he could take her to wife is a case in point that illustrates the redemptive power in Tanakian Judaism. Having recognised his sin and having realised his true repentance, he approaches God. He does not say, "Please give me another reincarnation so that I can work this iniquity out of my system and achieve the transformation you require to restore immortality to me." He does not say, "Please allow me some time to study Torah and do a bunch of good deeds. I will try to keep two consecutive Shabbats perfectly." Instead he pleads for mercy. "*Have mercy* upon me, O God, as befits your faithfulness; *in keeping with your abundant compassion* . . . . Purge me with hyssop till I am pure, wash me till I am whiter than snow . . . . Hide Your face from my sins; *blot out all my iniquities*" (emphasis added). Here is David pleading for an outside power to rescue him:

He begs for mercy, compassion, purging, washing, and blotting out of his sins. These are all outside influences that God must dispense to procure his forgiveness. These outside powers he cannot earn. He will never achieve that on his own merit because "Indeed I was born with iniquity; with sin my mother conceived me" (Ps. 51:5, *The Jewish Study Bible*). David could never achieve escape from that status with "obedience to the law." The law is forever his accuser because at no point in his life could or would he be perfectly compliant. The law wants him dead (Ezek. 18:4, 20: "the person who sins shall die"). David wanted the Messiah's blood splashed on the Ark and Mercy Seat.

Then David goes on to realise that offering sacrifices to appease God without the prior true repentance was a travesty. The "True sacrifice to God is a contrite spirit; God, you will not despise a contrite and crushed heart" (Ps. 51:19, *The Jewish Study Bible*). The sacrifices follow the contrition as a symbol of the Messianic provision: "Then you will want sacrifices offered in righteousness, burnt and whole offerings; then bulls will be offered on Your altar" (Ps. 51:19, 21, *The Jewish Study Bible*). David did not plead with God for several more reincarnations (because his sin was indeed very heinous), to work the wickedness out of himself and eventually arrive transformed by halachah at the Gates of Eden. Instead he was granted immediate forgiveness and reinstatement in the eyes of God. It became possible indeed by the symbolic animal sacrifice, which followed the contrition (Ps. 51:21, *The Jewish Study Bible*). David was quite aware of the fact that the status of animal sacrifices had deteriorated. The Roman Catholic indulgences, which agitated Martin Luther, were sold to excuse intentional sins in the Papal Middle Ages! Israel massively indulged in those sacrificial animal indulgences in their history. The several hundred years prior to AD 70 were indulgence years, which God said he detested. The Jews were sacrificing blemished and deformed animals with no repentance in their hardened and perverse hearts. No wonder God allowed the destruction of the Second Temple, and the diaspora to occur. There was no sign of contrition and crushed heart in the majority of sacrificial offerings in the time of Herod's Temple. The Temple had become primarily the site of trade and cash profit from those sacrificial indulgences sold. The Temple was grossly desecrated at that time by the indulgent profiteering on blemished and sick animals, not representative of Messianic deity. The priests looked the other way in exchange for bribes.

The inventions of Kabbalah—with its self-earned forgiveness and salvation—is thankfully not what is taught in the Tanak. God's great love and provision of Himself in Messianic deliverance is what is firmly offered by Moses. Neither does the Kabbalah of Safed teach the redemptive atonement taught by Moses. Kabbalah has many good aspects in promoting communion with the wonderful God of Israel, and understanding and enjoying His love affair with them. But they must not forget that the Day of Atonement provides the repentance from Ruach Hakodesh as well as the forgiveness and redemption from Ha-Mashiach. Hear, O Israel, the Lord our God is one. Blessed be He.

CHAPTER 15

THE IDOLATRY OF ISRAEL

The definition of idolatry in the Jewish context is the preference of an object or desire to be worshipped other than the monotheistic God YHVH. This is a definition tailored for the worshipper who knows the monotheistic, true God. Idolatry began in Eden when Eve showed her desire for the Serpent's fruit, which represented a disobedient challenge to the God she knew and loved. Adam's first idol was his wife, with whom he preferred to share the doom of her action. Cain's first idol was himself, because he felt he could get God to respect his prowess as a agriculturalist; he wanted this as a status symbol to be a redemptive feature in the place of Messianic deliverance.

Since Creation, idolatry, though unchanging in its defined material existence in the history of the Jews, has taken very subtle forms. Idolatry as a desire can exist even as a state of mind. Thus motives can be construed to be idolatrous when they work against the great principles for living set out by YHVH. In this manner, a benign disregard for Torah is idolatrous.

Chaim Weizmann gave idolatry a very wide definition. In a speech at the seventeenth Zionist Congress, he made a plea for restraint from violence by Jews, which was being advocated against the British Mandate. For this he was called a demagogue. In personal anguish, he replied,

> I warn you against bogus palliatives, against short cuts, against false prophets, against facile generalisations, against distortion of historic facts . . . . If you think of bringing redemption nearer by un-Jewish methods, if you

> lose faith in hard work and better days, then you commit
> idolatry and endanger what we have built. Would I had a
> tongue of flame, the strength of prophets, to warn you
> against the path of Babylon and Egypt. Zion shall be built
> in Judgement—and not by any other means.[235]

Idolatry comes to the fore in biblical Jewish history with Abraham, but it long existed in the world before him. As stated above, idolatry in Israel has come to include any special desire within a Jew, or object or power in that Jew's environment, that is preferred to the worship of YHVH. This is a very wide dragnet. After the fall of humanity the primacy of the Creator in the lives of humans was jealously guarded by God Himself. History and archaeology bear evidence that the most elaborate system of worship, directed away from YHVH, first achieved a sophisticated development in Egypt. Every country in the world has been discovered to have multiplicity of gods in its historical and archaeological revelations. The revival of monotheism cannot be truly traced to any culture or civilization other than the Hebrew race, which possesses the story of the Garden of Eden and has the Torah. A claim has been made that monotheism did exist in Egypt, in para-Hebrew Egyptian history and archaeology, but a close examination of this claim reveals that the pharaoh who is credited for this merely decided that he and his court would restrict their attention to the sun god, choosing him in preference to the other gods of Egypt.[236] Akhenaten, who ruled from 1379 BC to 1362 BC, made the sun god the sole object of his devotion. He reigned during the 430 years the Hebrews were enslaved in Egypt. This restrictive worship of one god is not the same as the belief that other gods truly do not exist, and therefore it cannot be labelled monotheism. The Patriarchs from Adam to Abraham were monotheists. The monotheism of the Hebrews is unequivocal about this, as the Tanak bears out in their conversation with YHVH. He clearly states this, and gives the warning that humanity must not conjure up other deities because He is extremely jealous. YHVH labels this a serious iniquity, and the first two commandments of the Decalogue are dedicated to this warning and advise serious retribution to those who disobey. Any departure from monotheism is a very serious matter in Hebrew thought and history. "The Lord our God is One, blessed be He."

Idolatry is usually associated with an image made of wood, stone, clay, metal, or a synthetic substance. It is also tangible when an element, object, or manifestation in nature or the cosmos is chosen for obeisance. It is more difficult to identify or isolate when it is a concept, characteristic, or motivation within a person, but nonetheless that is a very real option.

The drama regarding idolatry in the Tanak begins on a very serious note with Abram of Ur of the Chaldees, the progenitor of Hebrew ethnicity. His whole life was so involved with YHVH that he had no tendency to seek other gods that he knew did not exist. It was not the same with many of his descendants, who were weak-kneed. The very attractive story in the Talmud may be apocryphal, but it truly depicts Abram's sterling character. There was no point in his life where he wavered. He smashed all the idols in his father's shop as a youth, except for the largest one whom he blamed for the mayhem, and then he argued the futility of idolatry with his father. He convinced his father and grandfather that any part in the propagation of idolatry was very sinful.

The first two commandments of the Decalogue deal specifically with idols being substituted for God:

- Commandment I: "You shall have no other gods besides Me."
- Commandment II: "You shall not make for yourself a sculptured image, or any likeness of what is in the heavens above, or on the earth below, or in the waters under the earth. You shall not bow down to them or serve them. For I the Lord your God am an impassioned God, visiting the guilt of the parents upon the children, upon the third and upon the fourth generations of those who reject Me, but showing kindness to the thousandth generation of those

who love Me and keep My commandments." (Exod. 20:1-6,
The Jewish Study Bible)

The dragnet here cannot be wider: "any likeness of anything"
(KJV). The retribution meted out is difficult to fathom. Idolators
are severely dealt with by God. The genetic weakness of the
human frame is no respecter of persons. Genetic strength comes
from the racial mixture of genes; being inbred is not an advantage.
Environment and luck also play a part in survival. The Tanak
elsewhere (Job 1:12) decries the fact that often the good and
the evil people can both prosper and suffer, perhaps with equal
distribution, and because there is none who keeps the law perfectly,
we are all sinners. Natural catastrophes and the vicissitudes of
modern civilization are also no respecters of persons. The favoured
nature of monotheistic worshippers can be argued quite strongly,
but God's mercy, compassion, and forgiveness are so prevalent and
pervasive that He Himself complicates the logic of the argument
by bending the rules when He forgives. His mercy has been far
greater than His jealousy and retribution; He rushes to forgive.
"He remembers that we are dust." God is happiest when His
anger is appeased, and the Talmud gloats about this. His whole
plan is to rescue all humanity with His Messianic intervention
and redemption. His love is bigger than the universe, bigger than
the infinity in which He resides. Nonetheless, the threat is in the
commandment, and it must therefore be recognised as a deterrent.
Abrogation of the law is totally dependent on His mercy.

Idolatry was widely prevalent in the Promised Land when
Abraham arrived there with his retinue. He specifically sent for
a wife for his son Isaac to where his monotheistic relatives lived
in Haran. Rebekah came untainted and showed a major aversion
to idolatry by her intolerance of Esau's idolatrous women and her
anxious urging of Jacob's going to Haran to find a wife. She likely
did not know of Laban's penchant for idolatry. Isaac's older twin
son, Esau, lost the birthright because of idolatry: he was a victim
of the idolatrous women he loved. He did not strictly embrace
monotheism and did not qualify to be the father of the chosen
people (Gen. 27). Jacob was unwavering. He had a very strong

involvement with God in his life, reminiscent of Abraham's walk with God (Gen. 28). But his father-in-law Laban was a part-time idolater, and Jacob's favourite wife Rachel stole some of her father's idols, taking them with her (Gen. 31). It is suspected that Rachel was also a part-time idolater, but Jacob cleaned his own household of idols after he realised some of them in his retinue possessed a few idols (Gen. 33).

When the family went to Egypt to escape the famine, they discovered Joseph was prime minister of Egypt and was the saviour of Egypt from the famine. The intended short sojourn in Egypt turned out to be a long one of 430 years, partly in prosperity and then in slavery. During this time many of the Hebrews intermarried with the Egyptians and adopted the worship of idols and other gods in the cosmos. Many of these people remained behind in Egypt and did not follow Moses to the Promised Land, but many did, and some of them were the instigators of the worship of the golden calf at Mt. Sinai. God was very upset, and 3,000 men died in the retribution that followed; the number of women who died is not mentioned. Most of the gold that went into the making of the calf came from their earrings and other jewellery. The weakness of Aaron was colossal in being the instrument to do their bidding and making the golden calf, which they worshipped in a frenzy of heathenism. Moses and God were both in a state of shock. God wanted to destroy them all on the spot and make of Moses a great nation, but Moses would not allow it.

> Moses said unto the people, Ye have sinned a great sin; and now I will go unto the Lord; I shall make an atonement for your sin. And Moses returned unto the Lord, and said, "Oh, this people have sinned a great sin and have made them gods of gold. Yet now, if Thou wilt forgive their sin; and if not, blot me I pray thee, out of Thy book." And the Lord plagued the people, because they made the calf, which Aaron made. (Gen. 3, KJV)

The Hebrews who left Egypt were a motley crew. Most were uneducated and unruly, and they likely knew not their God. Ezekiel gives us significant insight into the condition these Hebrew slaves were in when they left Egypt.

> Thus saith the Lord God: In the day when I chose Israel, and lifted up Mine hand unto the seed of the house of Jacob, and made Myself known unto them in the land of Egypt, when I lifted up Mine hand unto them, saying, I am the Lord your God; In the day that I lifted up Mine hand unto them, to bring them forth from the land of Egypt, into a land that I had searched out for them, flowing with milk and honey, which is the glory of all lands; Then said I unto them, Cast ye away every man the abominations of his eyes, and defile not yourselves with the idols of Egypt, I am the Lord, your God. But they rebelled against Me, and would not hearken unto Me; they did not every man cast away the abominations of their eyes, neither did they forsake the idols of Egypt.

> Then I said, I will pour out My fury upon them, to accomplish Mine anger against them in the midst of the land of Egypt. But I wrought for My name's sake, that it should not be polluted before the nations, among whom they were, in whose sight I made Myself known unto them, in bringing them forth out of the land of Egypt. Wherefore I caused them to go forth out of the land of Egypt, and brought them into the wilderness. (Ezek. 20:5-10, KJV)

They were in the wilderness for 40 years. Moses had the unenviable task of curing them from idolatry, as well as educating them and disciplining them into a nation. The events at Mount Sinai were designed to marshall them and teach them the Torah, which had been neglected through those years of slavery. Unfortunately, their tendency to idolatry remained strong.

Israel had a bad time wandering in the wilderness. They were thirsty; God quenched their thirst miraculously. They were hungry; God gave them manna to eat. But they complained about the manna as they longed for the fleshpots of Egypt. They screamed at

Moses, "Wherefore have ye brought us up out of the land of Egypt to die in the wilderness? For there is no bread, neither is there any water; and our soul loatheth this light bread [manna]" (Num. 21:5, KJV). Because of this, God sent poisonous serpents to sting them, and many died. God instructed Moses to make a bronze serpent as an instrument of healing. The medical profession has taken the serpent on the cross as their symbol of healing. Those who were bitten were healed by simply looking at the symbol. It is very important to note that the serpent symbol was not worshipped; the look simply exercised their faith.

When they arrived in Canaan to take the land, they were given explicit instructions.

> Neither shalt thou make marriages with them . . . for they will turn away thy son from following Me, that they may serve other gods; so will the anger of the Lord be kindled against you, and destroy thee suddenly. But thus shall ye deal with them. Ye shall destroy their images, and cut down their idols, and burn their carved images with fire. For thou art an holy people unto the Lord thy God; the Lord thy God hath chosen thee to be a special people unto Himself, above all people who are upon the face of the earth . . . . Because the Lord loved you and because He would keep the oath which He had sworn unto your fathers. (Deut. 7:3-8, KJV)

Repeatedly God gave Israel warnings against idolatry as they settled the land of Canaan. Pagan customs were forbidden. Intermarriage with the idolatrous tribes was strictly forbidden because it was a steppingstone to idolatry.

Solomon was granted the task of building the First Temple. David had earnestly desired to do this, but God had denied him the privilege. David was a man of war, but Solomon was a man of peace. It is fair to say that in the history of Israel, the zenith of the nation had been reached, both militarily and spiritually, during the reign of David. Redemptive Judaism was practiced in the Temple. Messianic expectation was high. The highlights were the daily sacrifice for sin made by the priest, the joyous escape from Egypt celebrated by the Passover festival, and the greatest event of the Jewish calendar, the yearly Day of Atonement, which was celebrated in the First Temple, a triumph for the worship of the true God. Besides having the reputation for being the wisest man, Solomon was also the most foolish. He had many foreign wives, and now he built altars to their several gods.

> For Solomon went after Ashtoreth, the goddess of the Sidonians, and after Milcom, the abomination of the Amorites . . . . Then did Solomon build an high place for Chemosh, the abomination of Moab, in the hill that is before Jerusalem, and for Molech, the abomination of the children of Ammon. And likewise he did for all his foreign wives, who burned incense and sacrificed unto their gods. And the Lord was angry with Solomon, because his heart was turned from the Lord God of Israel . . . . Wherefore, the Lord said unto Solomon, Forasmuch as this is done by thee . . . I will surely tear the kingdom away from thee, and will give it to thy servant. (1 Kings 11:5-11, KJV)

As a result of the stupid, wilfull mistake of Solomon's leadership, Israel was overwhelmed in the punishment that followed. The downward slide continued with the division of Israel into two kingdoms, which greatly weakened Israel. Idolatry devastated both kingdoms. The prophets sent from God groaned with the foolishness of Israel, and God Himself wept bitterly. There is no more sorry a sight than the most privileged and enlightened nation in history becoming so enfeebled and degraded. From the ethereal and exalted high of communion and fellowship with God to the depths of idolatry, immorality, and sinfulness, was a long way to fall. Writing in his magnificent book *Jerusalem—The Biography*, Simon Sebag Montefiore writes:

> Solomon's magnificence may be exaggerated, but his decline only rings too true: the king of wisdom became an unpopular tyrant who funded his monumental extravagances through high taxes and the "chastisement of whips." To the

disgust of the monotheistic biblical authors, writing two centuries later, Solomon prayed to Yahweh and other local gods, and furthermore he "loved many strange women." Solomon faced rebellions . . . . The Israelite kingdom was tottering.[237]

On the death of Solomon, Israel became divided into the northern Kingdom of Israel, ruled by his general Jeroboam. Solomon's son Rehoboam became king of the southern Kingdom of Judah. The idolatrous depravity continued (2 Kings 17:1-24). Eighteen kings reigned in the northern Kingdom after Jeroboam, years mostly spent in idolatry. In a nutshell, here is what happened to the northern kingdom.

> And the Lord rejected all the seed of Israel, and afflicted them, and delivered them into the hand of the spoilers, until He had cast them out of His sight. For He forcibly removed Israel from the house of David; and they made Jeroboam, the son of Nebat, king; and Jeroboam drove Israel from following the Lord, and made them sin a great sin. For the children of Israel walked in all the sins of Jeroboam which he did; they did not depart from them, until the Lord removed Israel out of His sight, as He had said by all His servants, the prophets. So was Israel carried away out of their own land to Assyria unto this day. (2 Kings 17:20-23, KJV)

That occurred in about 721 BC, and it was the end of the northern kingdom. Samaria was settled by foreigners, who mixed with the few remaining poor, straggling Jews.

The evil of idolatry in the southern Kingdom of Judah was mitigated by the good kings Asa, Hezekiah, Joash, and Josiah. On the death of Solomon, 19 kings and one queen (Athaliah) reigned in the Southern Kingdom. Idolatry was greatly diminished by the reforms of the good kings, but it was not completely wiped out of the land. The reforms of good King Josiah are worth mentioning.

The king had the idols burned in the Kidron Valley, and expelled the male prostitutes in the Temple; he smashed the child-roasters of the Valley of Hell and killed the idolatrous priests, grinding their bones into their altars.

(*Josiah's reforms were a vital step in the development of Judaism. Two tiny silver scrolls were found in a Valley of Hinnom tomb of this period: inside was etched the priestly prayer of Numbers 6:24-26 which remains part of the Jewish service today, "For YHVH is our restorer and rock. May YHVH bless you and keep you and make His face to shine [upon you]."[238]

But finally the cup of iniquity of the Kingdom of Judah was filled, and during the reign of Jehoiachin, the Babylonian captivity occurred. Nebuchadnezzar placed Zedekiah, the last king of Judah, on the throne. But Zedekiah did not last long because of his noncooperation with the Babylonian king. Zedekiah's sons were killed in front of him, and then his eyes were excised from their sockets, and he was taken captive to Babylon. Jerusalem and the Temple were plundered and burned (2 Kings 24) in 586 BC. Such was the dalliance of the Hebrews with idolatry during the reigns of their kings.

Idolatry was Israel's greatest besetment and tragedy, and this is clear in the Tanak. In the entire history of Israel, God pleads for them to repent and to return to Him. It is no wonder that many Christians like to imply that God has totally and irrevocably rejected Israel as His chosen people. *But he has not,* and Israel is now back in their land and must turn to Him.

When we start at Creation and the Garden of Eden, the great lie of the Serpent, "Ye shall not surely die . . . and ye shall be as God" (Gen. 3:4-5, KJV), was believed and brought degradation and death. The Serpent kept lying to the human race, and they learned all the ramifications of evil, and it was easy to neglect the good. God's face was hidden from them, and so Torah was not so desirable because of the discipline required in obeying God; it was

252

easier to indulge the fleshly lusts to which they were now subject. The antediluvian world had deteriorated to the fullest extent: "And God saw that the wickedness of man was great in the earth, and that every imagination of the thoughts of his heart was only evil continually. And it repented the Lord that He had made man on the earth, and it grieved Him at His heart" (Gen. 6:5-6, KJV). He ended probation for the antediluvian world but saved the family of Noah. After the golden calf episode at Mt. Sinai, God wished to similarly destroy Israel and make of Moses a great nation, but Moses would not agree.

Take a closer look at the event of the worship of the golden calf.

> Early next day, the people offered up burnt offerings and brought sacrifices of wellbeing; they sat down to eat and drink, and then rose up to dance. The Lord spoke to Moses [who was with Him in the mountain], Hurry down, for your people, whom you brought out of the land of Egypt, have acted basely. They have been quick to turn aside from the way that I enjoined upon them. They have made themselves a molten calf and bowed down to it, and sacrificed to it, saying: This is your god, O Israel, who brought you out of the land of Egypt . . . . Thereupon Moses turned and went down from the mountain [collecting Joshua on the way down] bearing the two tablets of the Pact. When Joshua heard the sound of the people in its boisterousness, he said to Moses: There is a cry of war in the camp. But he answered: . . . It is the sound of song I hear. As soon as Moses . . . saw the calf and the dancing, he became enraged . . . He took the calf . . . ground it to powder and strewed it upon the water and so made the Israelites drink it. (Exod. 32:6-20 *The Jewish Study Bible*)

This sort of behaviour continued in the wilderness, which God willed as a prison for these idolaters. They were not allowed to enter Canaan with Joshua; their carcases fell in the desert. But Israel continued in idolatrous parley in the Promised Land.

In the history of Israel after Solomon, there were several prophets who tried to put Israel back on the rails.

Amos wrote:

> Have ye offered unto Me sacrifices and offerings in the wilderness forty years, O house of Israel? But ye have borne the tabernacle of your Moloch and Chiun, the star of your god, which ye made to yourselves. (Amos 5:25-26, KJV)

Jeremiah adds his voice in specific clarity:

> Look at the high places. Is there any place you have not acted like a prostitute? . . . When Josiah was king, the Lord said to me, have you seen what Israel, that unfaithful woman, has done? She has turned away from Me, and on every high hill and under every green tree she has acted like a prostitute. I thought that after she had done all this, she would surely return to Me. But she did not return, and her unfaithful sister Judah saw it all. Judah also saw that I divorced Israel and sent her away because she had turned from Me, and had become a prostitute. But Judah, Israel's unfaithful sister, was not afraid. She too became a prostitute and was not at all ashamed. She defiled the land and she committed adultery with pillars and poles. (Jer. 3:2, 6-9, Good News Bible)

God may be heard to be weeping when He pleads:

> Turn, O backsliding children saith the Lord; for I am married unto you; . . . and I will bring you to Zion . . . . At that time they shall call Jerusalem the throne of the Lord, and all the nations shall be gathered unto it, to the name of the Lord, to Jerusalem; neither shall they walk anymore after the imagination of their evil heart. (Jer. 3:14-17, Good News Bible)

Jeremiah's voice contains some hope.

Isaiah speaks explicitly:

> You worship the fertility gods by having sex under those
> sacred trees of yours. You offer your children as sacrifices
> in the rocky caves near stream beds. You take smooth
> stones from there and worship them as gods. You pour out
> wine as offerings to them and bring them grain offerings.
> Do you think I am pleased with all this? You go to the high
> mountains and offer sacrifices and have sex. You set up
> your obscene idols just inside your front doors. You forsake
> Me; you take off your clothes and climb in your large beds
> with your lovers whom you pay to sleep with you. And
> there you satisfy your lust. You put on your perfumes and
> ointments and go to worship the god Molech. (Isa. 57:5-10,
> Good News Bible)

Ezekiel speaks for YHVH's bitterness:

> You used some of your clothes to decorate your places
> of worship, and just like a prostitute you gave yourself to
> everyone. You took the silver and gold jewellery that I had
> given you, used it to make male images, and committed
> adultery with them. (Ezek. 16:17-18, Good News Bible).

All the minor prophets of the Tanak were reformers, and they
tried hard to cleanse the Hebrews of idolatry. Idolatry was not a
simple bowing down to images of metal, wood, and stone. It
was a frenzied event in which the worshippers were involved in
sensuality and licentiousness. Unrestrained sexual expression was
the big attraction. Research into the idolatry of Egypt, Canaan, and
Mesopotamia has been extensive. Phallic and clitoral emblems
were the predominant theme. Male and female prostitutes were
kept in the heathen temples and were ready for sexual promiscuity
with the idol worshippers. They ate, drank, danced, and engaged
in lascivious sexuality. That is why the Hebrews were so prone to
idolatry. At some time or other, Israel indulged in all of it.[239]

The influence of Hellenism and the Roman period of domination that followed could be considered a further dalliance of Israel with idolatry. Many Jews admired the religion and culture of this civilization, and they changed their lifestyle and religion as they imitated the extravagances of this period and the worship of the Greco-Roman gods. Saul Lieberman, considered an expert in Talmudic literature, has written extensively of the influence not only of the Jewish culture of the period, but also the influence on the rabbinic sages who composed the Gemara.[240] The human body became an idolized version of estrangement from God. Thousands of Hellenised Jews took their eyes off their redemptive God.

Thankfully, at the same time there was a Jewish outreach to the pagan world, albeit a weak effort. The Sibylline Books had as "their avowed object to reform paganism . . . endeavoured to act as Jewish missionaries."[241] High points of Jewish devotion could be considered to have taken place during the years of the composition of the Bavli in Babylon and Yerushalmi in Canaan, and also during the European Yeshivas, during the 2,000-year diaspora. There was a period of reformation during the period of modern Zionism. Unfortunately the Judaism practiced at the time was Talmudic and did not sustain the wandering, diasporic Jew. The Enlightenment, which brought Zionism in its wake, created a longing for the redemptive Judaism of Abraham, Jacob, Moses, and King David, but it was not available. It had been replaced by the Talmudic minutiae, which were considered the husks of their lost redemptive Judaism. But their land has now been restored, and their Torah can be magnified and can show them their Messianic salvation. It is the Abrahamic Covenant, long since forgotten by the nearly seven million secular Israeli and Anglo-American diasporic Jews.

Israel is back as a nation in the Promised Land. Israel must not fall into any form of idolatry again.

CHAPTER 16

THE DESTRUCTION
OF THE FIRST TEMPLE

The First Temple, or Solomon's Temple (Beit HaMikdash), was built on the Temple Mount and replaced the Tent Tabernacle, which was built in the wilderness not long after the Mt. Sinai experience. Both structures had been patterned after the Heavenly Temple. Both catered to the same services, administered by the Aaronic priesthood. King David had installed the Tent Tabernacle on Mount Zion after the vicissitudes the Ark of the Covenant had been through in the time of King Saul, High Priest Eli, and the Prophet Samuel. David had danced his holy naked dance in having brought the Ark back to Jerusalem. David wanted to build the glorious permanent temple, but God felt his hands were too bloody and commissioned David's son Solomon to do the job. Solomon's Temple was built as the permanent structure and was opulent. It would take volumes to adequately describe the Temple and its significance, and as such it will be dealt with here only very briefly.

The historical aspects of the reigns of King David and King Solomon have been brilliantly placed in the Jewish perspective in the book *Jerusalem: The Biography*, by Simon Sebag Montefiore.[242] The information he provides is taken from the Tanak and is supplemented by the meagre archaeological findings available. Some of his conclusions lack the true spiritual insight that a devout Jew may have. Very often he portrays an event devoid of the true spiritual nature that clothes it. But then, he is not a theologian nor an avowed devotee. An occasional error creeps in—for example, King David wore the high priestly ephod, and not a loin cloth, when he did his naked dance before the Ark of the Covenant. Nonetheless, the serious student is well directed to Montefiore's work. He describes the cogent religio-political events of the kingdoms of these two glorious kings of Israel in whose reigns the zenith of Jewish national achievement occurred. The crowning event of their illustriousness after a territorial accomplishment has to be the erection of Solomon's Temple. Montefiore does not elaborate on the deeply religious, redemptive elements of the Judaism of Moses, but these are eminently present in the Tanak. The instructions of Moses to the Aaronic priesthood on these spiritual matters are detailed in the Tanak.

The Temple had a courtyard where interaction between the priests and the public occurred. The sacrifice was brought and the reason explained. The Altar of Sacrifice stood in the courtyard at the entrance to the Holy Place. The Holy Place housed the Table of Showbread, the Golden Lampshade, and the Altar of Incense. The Most Holy Place housed the Ark of the Covenant and the Mercy Seat. The Holy Place was separated from the Most Holy Place by a very grand curtain. The greatest motivation for building the Temple was God's command: "Let them make Me a sanctuary that I may dwell among them." The Shechinah, God's fiery presence, dwelt in the Most Holy Place in that First Temple, having transferred from the Tent Tabernacle with the placement of the Ark of the Covenant there. The site of the Most Holy Place was the exact site where Abraham sacrificed Isaac. Tradition has it that God created Adam on that very site. Over the history of the First and Second Temples, the blood shed on the Day of Atonement was sprinkled on that very site.

The contents of the Ark of the Covenant have been variously described. Principally, it contained the two stone tables of the Ten Commandments. At some time or other, before its disappearance, the Ark may have also contained the Pot of Manna and Aaron's Rod. The Talmud gives an account that states the pieces of the first two tables, which Moses broke in anger, were also in the Ark. It should be mentioned at this juncture that the Second Temple's Most Holy Place was empty, and there was no Shechinah there.

The main business of the Temple was the expiation of sin, but thanksgiving and praise to God also occupied very important functions. The maintenance of the work of the Temple was paid for by the Temple levee; everyone paid a half shekel every year. The following were the main sacrifices.

The Yearly Sacrifice for Sin

On the Day of Atonement, the chief priest sacrificed an animal without blemish for his own sins. He then sacrificed an animal without blemish for all the sins of all the people and took the blood into the Most Holy Place, where it was sprinkled on the Ark of the Covenant and the Mercy Seat.

The Daily Sacrifice for Sin

This was the regular burnt offering: "This is the offering made by fire which ye shall offer unto the Lord; two lambs of the first year Without Spot, day by day, for a continual burnt offering . . . one in the morning and the other at even" (Num. 28:3-4).

The Personal Sacrifice for Sin

This was called the trespass offering. The sinner came with repentance and his sacrificial animal, placed both his hands on the animal, and confessed his sins, and the blood was shed. Parts of the carcass were burned, and this brought him absolution.

These three sacrifices for sin were there to remind the transgressor of the law (the Torah), emphasizing that disobedience to the Torah causes death. The animal without blemish was symbolic of the Messianic atonement that God would make for Israel and all humanity. Without the shedding of blood, there was no remission in Israel. This occurred during the times of the Tent Tabernacle and the First and Second Temples. God would pay the price of disobedience to His law. It was the redemption, and He was the redeemer. He was the destroyer of eternal death. This was the whole thesis that had come with the Torah from the Garden of Eden, through the lives of all the Patriarchs from Adam to Abraham, and carefully installed under the auspices of the Aaronic priesthood. The most important initial aspect of the sacrificial system was that there had to be repentance, and this was the work of the Ruach Hakodesh. In Psalm 51 David, the malignant arch sinner, wrote:

> For Thou desirest not sacrifice, else would I give it; Thou delightest not in burnt offering. The sacrifices of God are a broken spirit; a broken and a contrite heart, O God, Thou wilt not despise . . . . Then shalt Thou be pleased with the sacrifices of righteousness, with burnt offerings and whole burnt offering; then shall they offer bullocks upon thine altar. (Ps. 51:16-19, KJV)

Without repentance, sacrifices count for nothing. With repentance, the sins were forgiven and the sinner stood righteous before the Torah. David states emphatically that "a broken spirit [and] a broken and a contrite heart" must precede the sacrifice. David was a grateful sinner.

> Bless the Lord, O my soul, all my being, His holy name.
> Bless the Lord, O my soul and do not forget all His bounties.
> He forgives all your sins, He heals all your diseases.
> He redeems your life from the Pit . . . .
> He has not dealt with us according to our sins,
> Nor has He requited us according to our iniquities.
> For as the heavens are high above the earth,
> So great is His steadfast love toward those who fear Him.
> As east is far from west,
> So far has He removed our sins from us.
> As a father has compassion for His children,

So the Lord has compassion for those who fear Him.
For He knows how we are formed;
He is mindful that we are dust.
(Ps. 103, *The Jewish Study Bible*)

Micah the great reformer emphasizes the Psalmist's gratitude.

Who is a God like you,
Forgiving iniquity and remitting transgression;
Who has not maintained His wrath forever
Against the remnant of His own people,
Because He loves graciousness!
He will take us back in love;
He will cover up our iniquities,
You will hurl all our sins into the depths of the sea.
(Mic. 7:18-19, *The Jewish Study Bible*)

Without doubt the main business of the Temple was the extolling of repentance and the forgiveness of sin. Judaism was a redemptive religion at its inception.

There were many other sacrificial offerings made in the Temple. The other regular ones were the Sabbath sacrifice, the new moon, Passover week, Feast of Pentecost, Feast of Trumpets, and Feast of Tabernacles. The personal Thanksgiving, peace and votive, dedicatory (e.g., at circumcision), and others were incidental to personal worship. Drink, flour, and oil offerings were accompaniments of many of these offerings.

Unfortunately, Solomon not only built a grand Temple to the God of Israel, but in his later years he slid into wholesale idolatry. This story is written under the chapter heading "The Idolatry of Israel." The division of the Israelites into the northern Kingdom of Israel and the southern Kingdom of Judah, and the devastations committed by their idolatrous kings, followed, which resulted in the Assyrian conquest of the Northern Kingdom in 722 BC and the Babylonian conquest of Judah in 586 BC.

After all the reforms instituted by good King Josiah, the idolatrous Jehoahaz, Jehoiakim, and Jehoiachin (who followed Josiah) undid all the reforms and filled the land and Temple with idolatry, injustice, and the criminal shedding of innocent blood (see 2 Kings 22-24). The idolatrous wickedness of the Kingdom of Judah was great.

Jeremiah was sent to warn them:

> Thus saith the Lord [to Jeremiah]: Stand in the court of the House of the Lord and speak to [the men of] all the towns of Judah, who are coming to worship in the House of the Lord, all the words which I command you to speak to them . . . . Thus saith the Lord: If you do not obey Me, abiding by the Teaching that I have set before you . . . I will make this city a curse for all the nations of the earth. The priests and the prophets and all the people heard Jeremiah speaking . . . and seized him, shouting "You shall die!" . . . When the officials of Judah heard about this, they went up from the king's palace to the House of the Lord. The priests and prophets said to the officials and to all the people, "This man deserves the death penalty, for he has prophesied against this city as you yourselves have heard." Jeremiah said to the officials and to all the people, "It was the Lord who sent me to prophesy against this House and this city all the words you heard. Therefore mend your ways and your acts, and heed the Lord your God, that the Lord may renounce the punishment He has decreed for you . . . ." And some of the elders of the land arose and said to the entire assemblage of the people, Micah the Morashtite, who prophesied in the days of King Hezekiah of Judah, said to all the people of Judah, Thus said the Lord God of Hosts: "Zion shall be ploughed as a field, Jerusalem shall become heaps of ruins and the Temple Mount a shrine in the woods." (Jer. 26:2-18 *The Jewish Study Bible*)

That is exactly what happened to the First Temple and Jerusalem. The idolatry of Israel was responsible for its destruction. Montefiore gives an account of it.

> Nebuchadnezzar ordered his general to obliterate the city. Nebuzaradan burned the House of the Lord, the king's palace and all the houses of Jerusalem and brake down the walls. The Temple was destroyed, its gold and silver vessels plundered, and the Ark of the Covenant vanished forever . . . . The destruction of the Temple must have seemed to be the death not just of a city, but of an entire nation.[243]

Seventy years later, the exiles were allowed to return and rebuild the Temple, the Second Temple. It was made more opulent and glorious by Herod the Great. It would also have a sad end.

CHAPTER 17

THE DESTRUCTION
OF THE SECOND TEMPLE

The Abrahamic Covenant is the major foundation landmark in the history of Israel and in the destiny of humanity. It constitutes Israel's legitimacy and reason for existence. No other nation has been entrusted with the vital role, which is the implementation of God's restoration of immortality and perfection in the human race. That is the message of the Tanak: God gave Torah. It was broken. Immortality was lost. God's Messianic intervention provided redemption and restoration, and the condition that follows redemption is glorification. Gershom Scholem labels it the utopia.

Israel was asked to build the Tent Tabernacle in the wilderness. "Let them make Me a Sanctuary, that I may dwell among them." The Almighty God, blessed be He, condescended to dwell on earth with a special people whom He loved intensely. He wanted them to be the vehicle of His salvation. In that Tent Tabernacle He installed the Aaronic priesthood, whose main purpose was to provide an atonement for their sins; the sacrificial animal without blemish prefigured the salvation to be provided by the Messiah. The Day of Atonement was the main and vital function of that Tent Tabernacle when once a year, having procured cleansing for himself from sin by an initial animal sacrifice, the high priest then took the blood of the animal he had sacrificed for all the sins of all Israel into the Most Holy Compartment, where God dwelt among them. The law was given formally at Sinai, and so was the Messianic sacrifice. The Day of Atonement was the most sacred service of the Tent Tabernacle and was the holiest day of the Jewish year. It still is.

In the chapter titled "The Destruction of the First Temple," there was a brief description of the Temple services carried out by the Aaronic priesthood. I pointed out that its main business was the forgiveness of sins. God knew that all humanity was composed of law breakers from Eden, and He instituted repentance, confession, forgiveness, and expiation of sin. After the vicissitudes that the Tent Tabernacle passed through during Israel's wanderings in the desert, and then in the battles that followed in the conquest and procurement of the Promised Land, Solomon was allowed to build the permanent Temple edifice on Mount Moriah, Israel's Temple Mount. Abraham had already enacted the sacrifice of his son Isaac there, prefiguring the Messianic function. Solomon's glorious Temple was built on that Temple Mount, and God resumed His dwelling place with Israel. The Shechinah manifested His awesome presence with them. In both the Tent Tabernacle and Solomon's Temple Israel saw the Day of Atonement continue as Israel's cleansing from sin. And what was their sin? It was the transgression of the Torah. No Jew or any human being has kept the law perfectly, and neither can they—hence the necessity of the cleansing by the blood of the sacrificial animal without blemish. That was the most important aspect of the redemptive religion, which was and is primitive Judaism.

When Nebuchadnezzar destroyed Solomon's Temple, Israel was devastated. The Aaronic priesthood and the Day of Atonement cleansing of Israel abruptly ended. It was not until the Second Temple was built that the daily sacrifice for sin and the yearly Day of Atonement services were reinstated, and Israel again rejoiced in the sacrificial system that defined it as a redemptive religion. Why did God allow the beautiful Temple that Solomon built, and where His Shechinah dwelt, to be destroyed, thus evicting Himself from His earthly abode? Solomon built the Temple, but he also initiated the slide into idolatry and wretchedness, which was the history of Israel that followed. Solomon had many foreign wives and concubines, and he built idols and holy places for them, surrounding the Temple.

> And Solomon loved many foreign women in addition to the
> daughter of Pharaoh, women of the Moabites, Ammonites,
> Edomites, Sidonians, and Hittites . . . . Solomon clung
> unto these in love . . . . For Solomon went after Ashtoreth,
> the goddess of the Sidonians, and after Milcom, the
> abomination of the Ammonites . . . and Chemosh the
> abomination of Moab . . . and Molech, the abomination of
> the children of Ammon. (1 Kings 11 selected verses, KJV).

He surrounded the Temple on Mount Moriah with the altars and
worship of these idols. Solomon was Israel's wisest man and also
Israel's most foolish. As punishment, God permitted the victorious,
glorious nation of Israel to be divided into two weak kingdoms. But
the idolatrous slide continued until the Assyrians carried away the
10 tribes, and the Babylonians destroyed the Temple and carried
Judah and Benjamin into slavery.

Solomon's Temple was rebuilt about 516 BC and became called
the Second Temple. The priesthood was restored, the sacrificial
system resumed, and Israel's redemptive religion received a
new beginning. But Israel could not stay out of trouble. The
deterioration of Israel is chronicled well by Malachi. Domination
by Medo-Persia, Greece, and Rome followed the rebuilding of
Solomon's Temple and Jerusalem. During Roman domination,
Herod the Great renovated the Second Temple into a very grand
structure.[244] What was the problem that led to the repeat destruction
of Jerusalem and the Second Temple? The religious atmosphere in
Israel prior to this eventuality needs to be described. The Temple
became increasingly desecrated and polluted by a new kind of
idolatry. It started with the corruption of the Aaronic priesthood,
described well by Malachi:

> Ye offered polluted bread upon Mine altar . . . And if ye
> offer the blind for sacrifice, is it not evil? And if ye offer
> the lame and the sick, is it not evil? Mal. 1:13, KJV)

Instead of requiring offerings that were without blemish, the priests
tolerated sacrificial offerings that the people no longer valued and

that were fit for the garbage heap. The priests were supposed to check the offering to ensure that it was without blemish, but they were accepting bribes and kickbacks to allow tainted offerings to be sacrificed. This represented a challenge to the deity of the Messianic sacrifice. They had lost the significance of the Messianic perfection, which was symbolised by the sacrifices without blemish. The Temple grounds became a huge marketplace where there was trade traffic in cheap, deformed animals, which were bought and sacrificed after bribing the priests. God would no longer accept them. "If only you would lock My doors, and not kindle fire on My altar to no purpose! I take no pleasure in you . . . and I will accept no offering from you" (Mal. 1:10). The people also robbed God in the tithes and offerings (Mal. 3).

Just as evil was the use of the sacrificial system as an indulgence to sin. There was no repentance in the heart, no restitution, no confession, and no redemption. The sin offering was more correctly labelled the willful sin offering. God uttered a loathing as He looked down on it. He had not graced Herod's Temple with the Shechinah; the Most Holy Place was empty. He had been evicted from His earthly abode. He punished idolatry by allowing the destruction of Solomon's Temple. He now would allow the Second Temple to be destroyed.

There were other factors. The Hellenistic Age was one of the greatest challenges to redemptive Judaism. *The Jewish Encyclopedia* writes very aptly about the inroads of Hellenism on Judaism. From about 400 BC, through the Greek domination and the Roman period, and to about AD 100, Hellenism made an onslaught on Judaism.

> Except in Egypt, Hellenic influence was nowhere stronger than on the eastern shore of the Mediterranean . . . . The Hellenistic influence pervaded everything, and even in the very strongholds of Judaism it modified the organization of the state, the laws, and public affairs, art, science, and industry, affecting even the ordinary things of life and the common associations of the people.[245]

The multiplicity of Greek gods, the worship of the human body, and stoicism dominated the thinking of highly educated and ordinary Jews by the thousands. Study of the Greek language and Greek philosophy became the preoccupation of the majority of the Jews, who neglected the study of the Torah. They embraced all the whims and fancies of Greek lifestyle.

The Jewish Hellenistic historians—Aristeas, Eusebius, Philo of Alexandria, and Jason of Cyrene—and the Roman Jew Josephus bear out the ubiquitous nature of this Hellenistic influence. The outcome was that in the great adoration of Hellenism the focus was taken away from Messianic redemptive Judaism.[246] It was therefore easy to corrupt primitive Judaism. The Hellenistic-Roman milieu that followed was a continuum of this degrading influence. Jerusalem became a brothel. In the Temple the priests made a daily animal sacrifice as homage to the Roman emperor.[247]

Into this corrupted age came the Pharisees, Sadducees, and the Essenes. These leaders that arose in Israel became champions of their own causes and further corrupted and devastated the redemptive religion of primitive Judaism. The Jewish Virtual Library correctly attributes their emergence under the influence of Hasmonean rule.

The Pharisees majored in the emerging Talmudic writings and lost sight of the redemptive aspect of Judaism, even though the sacrificial system was still continuing in the Temple. They embraced the self-centered Hellenistic influence. They were looking for a temporal Messianic ruler to give them national exaltation, not the redemptive salvation, as had been prescribed by Moses. In contrast to the Sadducees, their belief in the resurrection of the dead was prominent and was their only redeeming feature, but they showed no understanding of apocalypticism and would rather maintain their religious style at any cost. These Pharisaic leaders were referred to as "Grandees" and were interested in religion only for the monetary gain and the maintenance of their wealthy status. They had no yearning for a Messiah.

"The Sadducees were elitists who wanted to maintain the priestly caste, but they were also liberal in their willingness to incorporate Hellenism into their lives."[248] They rejected the emerging Talmudic writings, basing their belief on the Tanak, but they erroneously believed that the Tanak did not support the resurrection of the dead. They were focussed on the rituals of the Temple but did not see in the rituals the symbolism of redemptive Messianic salvation. They were also participants in the corruption and moneymaking of the Temple. Their Messianism was not prominent and non-Tanakian because they believed there was no resurrection of the dead.

The Essenes rose up as a sect who were disgusted with the religiosity of both the Pharisees and Sadducees. They moved into a monastic life in the desert, were strict in the observance of dietary laws, and committed themselves to celibacy. The reason for celibacy is not understood, except as part of their monastic lifestyle. They were very studious.

The Jewish Virtual Library carefully summarises the beliefs and religious differences of these three groups. The great shortcoming of these religious leaders in Israel was the loss of focus on the Abrahamic Covenant and the redemptive nature of Judaism. The longing for the Messiah was still in some hearts, but there was no discerning of the kind of Tanakian definition of that Messiah. Their Messianic focus was on a conquering human to take them to national glory and exaltation.

Simon Sebag Montefiore, whose very brilliant and credible historical biography of Jerusalem, brings into focus another group called the Samaritans, whom he correctly describes as semi-Jewish. They consisted of the poor Jews with mixed blood who survived the annihilation of the Assyrians and who had no national standing.

> The Samaritans were already developing their separate semi-Jewish cult, based on a Judaism formed before the introduction of the new Babylonian [Bavli] rules . . . Their exclusion from Jerusalem encouraged them to set up their

own Temple at Mount Gerizim and they embarked on a
feud with the Jews and Jerusalem.[249]

It is difficult to understand what Montefiore means by "a Judaism
formed before the introduction of the new Babylonian rules."
I surmise that he is referring to the Talmudic transformation that
had overtaken Judaism in favour of a law-focussed salvation,
made available to Jews by their Talmudic sages. The Samaritans
preferred a more sacrifice-oriented Judaism, a more redemptive
type of Judaism. It appears very likely that this view is correct,
because Montefiore goes on to say,

> The Samaritans became second-class citizens, despised by
> the Jews as heathens . . . . Around a thousand Samaritans
> still live in Israel: long after the destruction of the Jewish
> cult of sacrifice, the Samaritans in the 21st century still
> annually sacrifice the Passover Lamb on Mount Gerizim.[250]

Montefiore's observation is shockingly revealing. It is astounding
that he labels the Mosaic installation at Sinai as "the Jewish cult
of sacrifice." It seems that he has accepted unequivocally that
the destruction of the Second Temple signalled the end of the
sacrificial system installed by Moses and practiced by the long line
of the Aaronic priesthood. It appears to be an acceptable occurrence
because the practice of sacrifice is now obsolete. In this case, it is
the great Passover lamb that signified the Hebrew salvation from
slavery in Egypt as well as the Messianic salvation from sin that
it prefigured: "When I see the blood I will pass over you" (Exod.
12:13, *The Jewish Study Bible*). Under what authority does
Montefiore seek to set aside the great Passover festival installed by
Moses? Under what authority does he label the sacrificial system
established outside the Gates of Eden and reinstated by Moses
at Sinai as cultic? Does it matter to him that the "semi-Jews"
practice it? What do the "non-semi-Jews" eat on the evening of
Passover? Is it lamb slaughtered at the abattoir, where the blood
runs down the drain into the sewer? Does Montefiore similarly
view the sacrificial animal without blemish that was sacrificed by
"non-semi-Jews" and "semi-Jews" on the greatest Jewish festival,

the Day of Atonement? That blood was taken into the Most Holy Place of the destroyed Second Temple. Is he labelling as cultic the sprinkling of the blood of the animal without blemish on the Mercy Seat? Montefiore sets aside Sinai as cultic and irrelevant. What kind of service will be carried out when the Third Temple is built on the Temple Mount, where Abraham sacrificed Isaac? Does the blood of the animal without blemish, sprinkled on the Ark of the Covenant and the Mercy Seat—over which the Shechinah hovered, and where God dwelt among humanity—count for naught? Is the Most Holy Place cultic? Is he calling the Shechinah a cultic invasion? Does it not matter that the top of Mount Moriah, the very site of the Most Holy Place, is soaked with centuries of the spilling of symbolic, Messianic blood? It is a Jewish calamity that modern Judaism has strayed so far from primitive Tanakian Messianic Judaism. No wonder that some Christians think that God has written off the Jews.

In his book *Everyman's Talmud*, Abraham Cohen gives a very insightful but devastatingly disappointing description of the feeling in Jewry about the destruction of the Second Temple.

> The Temple and its ritual played a very prominent part in the life of the people, and much space is devoted in the Talmud to their description. *For the Rabbis the sacrifices were divinely enacted.* What, then, was their attitude when the Temple ceased to exist? The answer is best indicated in the story told of R. Jochanan b. Zakkai and his disciple R. Joshua. On one occasion, when they were leaving Jerusalem, the latter gazed upon the destroyed Temple and cried out, "Woe to us! The place where Israel obtained atonement for sins is in ruins!" Rabbi Jochanan said to him, "My son, be not distressed. We still have an atonement *equally efficacious*, and that is the practice of benevolence" (ARN iv).[251]

What a shame—the redemptive act of the Messiah substituted by benevolence! Gershom Scholem takes issue with such a stance, and he formulates his traditional, restorative, and utopian factors as he contemplates Messianic redemption in the cataclysmic apocalypticism he embraces.[252] What a tragedy that redemptive Judaism has been replaced by benevolence! Moses would not have approved of the dictum "Do a good deed and your sins will be forgiven." If such is the case, Israel has destroyed her Messianic redemption. If such is the case, why do they need a Messiah? Cancel the Day of Atonement! Just do good deeds all day, and God will forgive all your sins. Forget Abraham, Jacob, Moses, and the prophets. Israel does not need another Temple at all. Zerubbabel, Ezra, and Nehemiah wasted their time restoring the First Temple. Herod wasted money renovating it. Why prolong cultic Judaism? Why weep and pray at the Wailing Wall? Why fight over Jerusalem? Let the Moslems have it, and let all the aliya Jews return to the diaspora where cultism can be quietly avoided. Remove Messianic redemption, and you destroy the spiritual legitimacy of Israel. Remember the Abrahamic Covenant? Remember the offering of Isaac? What a dry, soul-less Judaism is being advocated by Cohen and Montefiore! No wonder the great majority of Israelis have never set foot in a synagogue.

Cohen goes on to describe the scenario where God decries the burned offerings being offered, preferring the practice of justice and righteousness. Cancel Messiah. He seems to want to say that God had cancelled redemptive Judaism. He quotes from the Talmud for support, and he is right in one sense. In the time of the Romans, Israel was using the sacrificial system for the hoped-for release from the guilt of wilful sinning, which was devoid of repentance and confession. There was no justice and righteousness in that kind of sacrifice; God called it an abomination. God could not tolerate that and reprimanded Israel for it on many occasions. In Psalm 51 David is seeking forgiveness for his dreadfully evil triple sin: coveting Bathsheba, his neighbour's wife; committing adultery with her; and then murdering her husband so that he could hide the coveting, the adultery, and Bathsheba's pregnancy, so that he could take her as a wife. He had transiently, and perhaps conveniently, forgotten his naked dance before God and what he had been enacting. He sought absolution by offering a burned animal sacrifice. But then he was struck with the realization that without repentance he would be destroying the intercession of Ruach Hakodesh and Ha-Mashiach. Thank God he found repentance and could subsequently lay his guilt on that sacrificial lamb without blemish, which symbolized a willing substitute victim and saviour, because that is what the animal represented. God would bear his guilt and punishment. David's broken and contrite spirit was acceptable to God. He then went to the Temple and offered the sacrifice (Ps. 51, KJV).

Benevolence and intense study of Torah are intrinsically good, and God delights in such activities, but He never commissioned these as instruments of absolution for sin. God desperately wants confirmation that His provision of redemptive salvation is what was in the eternal Torah in His mind. Remember Cain, who brought fruit, and Abel, who brought the lamb without blemish? Why does worldwide Jewry still crowd the synagogues on Passover and the Day of Atonement? Israel is still dependent on Messianic Judaism for absolution for breaking the Torah, although the act of animal sacrifice is missing.

In the days before the destruction of the Second Temple, it was full of the same corrupt sale of 'Papal' indulgences. Bribe the priests, use sacrifices with blemishes, and get absolution for your willful sins. There was no need for repentance under such a setup. No wonder God was in a state of depression and anger. No wonder the Second Temple was destroyed. But His mercy followed.

The loss of the Second Temple was a great tragedy. God still wants to dwell with Israel. The command is still there, Israel! Make Him a sanctuary that He might dwell among us. It is incumbent on every Jew to bring that to pass, especially now that Israel is back in the Holy Land. Israel is mature enough to see the symbolism of sacrificing the lamb without blemish without bringing back animal sacrifices. But Jewry is behaving again like a group of idolatrous slaves just released from Egypt, despite being at the foot of a more fiery Mount Moriah that is more cataclysmic than Sinai.

After AD 70, Israel was scattered throughout the world, and the Abrahamic Covenant was forgotten. The Jews sought absolution for sin in the study of Torah and Talmudic writings. The prevailing Judaism of today presumes to become acceptable to God by self-righteousness achieved by perfect keeping of the law, though they will admit that no Jew has ever kept the law perfectly—and never will. Redemptive Judaism was set aside with the loss of the sacrificial system; Messiah was relegated to mysticism. The Tanak became obscured, and the significance of the Passover festival and the Day of Atonement no longer pointed to redemptive Messianic salvation. Judaism has become a confused, multifaceted philosophy. The Tanak has been wilfully discarded and trampled underfoot. Israel is worshipping another golden calf, while the world awaits the Moriah mountaintop experience of Messianic redemption.

In a description of the commencement of this period after the destruction of the Second Temple, I refer again to Herbert Danby, the great theologian who translated into English the Mishnah as redacted by Rabbi Judah the Prince, the Lion.

> Although the Mishnah was compiled in its present form at the end of the second century [AD], it deals fully with phases of legislation and religious practice which for more than a hundred years had ceased to have any practical bearing on Jewish life. The destruction of Jerusalem [and the Second Temple] in AD 70 made an end of the last vestiges of national self-government, and it marked also the extinction of the [Aaronic] priesthood and the Temple worship . . . . When we turn to Mishnah's religious importance . . . within a generation of its compilation we find it described as "the iron pillar of the Law" . . . In the most exact sense the Mishnah is the final expression of the Jewish nation's unimpaired religious life: whatever modifications may have since arisen in the observances of Judaism, have arisen out of conditions in which the religion indeed persisted, but persisted as a thing incomplete, as a maimed survival. Approximately the half of the Mishnah

has no longer any practical bearing on the present religious practice of Judaism.[253]

Danby also cites Leviticus Rabba reporting Joshua ben Levi: "The study of the Mishnah was as meritorious as offering sacrifice."[254]

Again, this is a tragic and sad statement, totally negating Moses. By what authority has Joshua ben Levi set aside the entire sacrificial system symbolizing Messianic redemptive Judaism, first set up by God before the Creation of the universe, implemented at the Gates of Eden, inaugurated by Moses in the Aaronic Priesthood and the Day of Atonement service in the Tent Tabernacle at Sinai, and later transferred to Solomon's Temple? This was the sanctuary where God chose to dwell with humanity. Talmudic Judaism has strayed far away from primitive Messianic Judaism. There is no redemptive merit in the study of Torah, much as it is commendable and advisable to study the Tanak. To apply an equivalence of the study of the Talmud as being as meritorious as Messianic redemption borders on blasphemy. After David committed his heinous triple sin, would study of the Torah and benevolent acts have provided him with repentance and forgiveness of sin? What is the point of celebrating the Day of Atonement? Should not all Jews stay in their houses and study the Torah, and then go out and perform acts of benevolence in order to get absolution for their sins? That is not the religion of Abraham, Jacob, and Moses; they have been discarded to cultism and mysticism.

Today, primitive Judaism is being destroyed by secularism, extremism, and humanism. The big unanswered question is, What kind of Messiah is Israel expecting? If he is a human, national, political, and temporal leader, will he be the leader of the nation for a short lifetime? And what happens after that? Will we bury him in Jerusalem and create another holy shrine? To do Israel and all humanity any lasting good, the Messiah must be divine and eternal. Otherwise there will be no restoration of perfection and immortality, and life with all its miseries must go on forever. Some will continue to dream of Kabbalistic reincarnation like the Buddhists do, until they reach Nirvana. That is not Tanakian Judaism.

Rabbi Judah the Prince was more attune with redemptive Judaism.

> The Rabbis maintain that his [Messiah's] name is "the leprous one of the School of R. Judah the Prince," as it is said, "Surely he hath borne our griefs, and carried our sorrows; yet we did esteem him stricken, smitten of God and afflicted" (Isaiah 53:4). Rab declared, The Holy One, blessed be He, will hereafter raise up for Israel another David, as it is said, "They shall serve the Lord their God and David their king, whom I will raise up unto them" (Jeremiah 30:9). It is not stated "'has raised" but "will raise" (Sanh. 98b).[255]

The Psalmist—the same one who committed the heinous triple sin of covetousness, adultery, and murder; the same one whose sin was forgiven by the blood of the lamb without blemish—found forgiveness proffered by the "Leprous One" who bore his leprosy, who "carried his sorrow." But in the triumph of forgiveness, David saw another but different picture of the Messiah: He is not a leprous one on this occasion, but a conquering king.

> Lift up your heads, O ye gates, and be lifted up,
> Ye everlasting doors,
> And the King of Glory shall come in.
> Who is this king of Glory?
> The Lord strong and mighty in battle.
>
> Lift up your heads, O ye gates;
> Even lift them up, ye everlasting doors;
> And the King of Glory shall come in.
> Who is this King of Glory?
> The Lord of hosts, He is the King of Glory.
> (Ps. 24:7-10. KJV)

The Messiah is a leprous one, and the Messiah is a conquering king of glory. O Israel, look again into the Tanak and identify your Messiah; He is waiting at the door. Abraham's Covenant with God must be kept. You have land and Torah. Now identify and claim your Messiah.

The Second Temple was destroyed, and with it the focus on Messianic redemptive Judaism. Montefiore pens the saddest words in his book, describing the destroyed Temple and the city of Jerusalem, which lay waste: "Jerusalem was just the wilderness of a failed faith". [256] Weep and mourn, ye daughters of Jerusalem; there is no comfort for the disconsolate! Miseries, hopelessness, and tears are the substances of the future being offered to you.

Jerusalem, the symbol and function for the salvation of the world, now is depicted as a "failed faith." Montefiore says that Josephus, who witnessed the burning of the Temple and the Holy City, also mourned the loss with the words, "We've [the Jews] introduced the rest of the world to a very large number of beautiful ideas. What greater beauty than inviolable piety? What higher justice than obedience to the Laws?" In the hands of humans, there is no such thing as inviolable piety as their own achievement. Inviolable piety is not the property of human beings; these are hollow words. All are sinners in need of a redeemer. Josephus changed his mind later in his life. Alas, in the centuries of the diaspora that followed, Talmudic Judaism replaced Messianic Judaism; it supplanted the Judaism of Abraham, Jacob, Moses, and David. Israel needs to rebuild the Temple and restore redemptive Judaism. Nothing is more urgent.

The final few years occupied by the Great Revolt, which occurred from AD 66-70, were started by the rise of the Zealots. The Zealots had an ancient history and defined their motivation as being anti-idolatry and antimarriage with idolatrous heathens. They took the name of Kanna'im in the spirit of defenders of the law and the national life of the Jewish people. They drew their inspiration from "the revenge of Levi and Simeon for the rape of Dinah" (see Gen. 34) and that of Phineas "for sexual relations with idolatrous women" (see Num. 25). They were also inspired by the Maccabbean reforms. These contemporary Zealots organized as a political party that was intensely anti-Roman. They morphed into the Sicarii, with daggers (sicae) hidden underneath their cloaks, hoping to kill Herod, who discovered the plot and slaughtered many of them. Under the leadership of Judas Zelotes of Gamala and his sons, they organized into a political party. Strife came to a head when procurator Florus came to power. They resorted to extreme measures to force the Jewish leaders and the Jewish population to action against the Romans. The Sicarii pillaged and murdered anyone who opposed them; they assassinated numerous Jewish leaders who opposed them. Eventually they succeeded in annihilating Cestius's army. But reinforcements arrived from Rome with Vespasian, who massacred Zealots throughout the countryside. Finally the siege of Jerusalem commenced. The saddest chapter of Jerusalem began—it is too sad to enumerate here the horrors that occurred.[257]

This very sad chapter will be closed with the tragic description of the destruction of the Second Temple. The immediate lead-up to the destruction of Jerusalem and the Second Temple had its roots in the Great Revolt. Taxes, Roman control of the high priest, Jewish leaders who were 'soft' on the Romans, and the general bad treatment of the Jews by the Romans are cited as the causes of the revolt. The Zealots started the rebellion and slaughtered the Jewish leaders (mainly Pharisees and Sadducees) who opposed them. These leaders had stood for the status quo and had opposed the reform-minded rebels because they felt they would never succeed against the Romans. The revolt did fail, as after suffering some setbacks, the Romans surrounded the city.[258] Eventually the Romans entered and destroyed Jerusalem, and they built wooden platforms to reach the Temple. Here are the words of historian Josephus, who was an eyewitness in the friendly company of Titus, who wrought the destruction.

> These Romans put the Jews to flight, and proceeded
> as far as the Holy House itself. At which time one of the
> soldiers . . . set fire to a golden window. As the flames

went upward, the Jews made a great clamour, such as so mighty an infliction required, ran together to prevent it; and now they spared not their lives any longer, nor suffered anything to restrain their force, since that Holy House was perishing . . . thus it was the Holy House burned down . . . Nor can one imagine anything greater or more terrible . . . for there was at once a shout of the Roman legions, who were marching all together, and the sad clamour of the seditious, who were now surrounded by fire and sword . . . made sad moans at the calamity they were under . . . Yet was the misery itself more terrible than the disorder; . . . the hill itself on which the Temple stood, was seething hot, as full of fire on every part of it. [259]

But we may sum it up by saying that no other city has ever endured such horrors, and no generation in history has fathered such wickedness. In the end they [the seditious] brought the whole Hebrew race into contempt in order to make their own impiety seem less outrageous in foreign eyes, and confessed the painful truth that they were slaves, the dregs of humanity, bastards, and outcasts of their nation. [260]

The Zealots were mighty patriots 'gone wrong,' and their motivation was misguided religion, national aspiration, and political madness. Despite being anti-idolatry and paying doctrinal homage to circumcision, they had forgotten the Abrahamic Covenant and Messianic redemptive Judaism. The reforms they urged were for political, religious 'distortion', and national autonomy. They were misunderstood, and their methods were questionable.

What promise AD 1948 holds! Jerusalem rebuilt, modern, unified, looking eternal, and standing resplendent in the morning sun when I beheld your glory—but you are still empty!

Where is your Temple? Where is the Shechinah? Where is your Messiah?

CHAPTER 18

MODERN ISRAEL

Modern Israel is a democracy and is best discussed under its political, national, and religious entities. Its political structure is largely determined by its religious diversity, but a discussion of the religious make-up is best left for last. Israel has a large population of Palestinian Arabs living in its pre-1967 national boundaries, and a much larger Palestinian Arab population in its post-1967 boundaries, which include the Occupied Territories composed of Gaza and the West Bank (Judaea and Samaria). As a democracy practiced in the pre-1967 borders, which now include a United Jerusalem, the Golan Heights, and Jewish Settlements, it holds elections. Every citizen in this jurisdiction, Israeli and Palestinian Arab, gets to vote. The Knesset is Israel's Parliament and has 120 seats. The prime minister is the head of government. There is also an appointed president, who is a titular head of state and functions in a largely ceremonial capacity. There are currently 12 political parties represented in the Knesset.[261]

Party	Leader	Seats
Likud Yisrael Beitenu	Benjamin Netanyahu	31
Yesh Atid	Yar Lapid	19
Labour	Shelly Yachimovich	15
Habayit Hayehudi	Naphtali Bennett	12
Shas	Eli Yishai	11
United Torah Judaism	Yakov Litzman	7
Hatenua	Tzipi Livni	6
Meretz (Zionist Social Democratic)	Zahavah Gal-On	6
Hadash (Jewish-Arab Soc. Front)	Mohammad Barakeh	4

Ra'am Ta'al	Ahmad Tibi	4
National Democratic Assembly	Jamal Zahalka	3
Kadima	Shaul Mofaz	2
	Total	120

At last count there are 27 other parties active today without Knesset representation. Since 1948, 92 other parties have existed with sometime representation in the Knesset. Some of these parties have merged with current parties. Likud, Labour, Hatenua, and Kadima are considered to be secular parties, but they do have religious elements. Most of the other parties are religious parties. The religious penetration of politics is to be expected in Israel because they are a people who have descended from Abraham and have the Torah. However, the religious plethora works against them because of the lack of unity.

Benjamin Netanyahu is the current prime minister and leads a minority government. He is considered a strong prime minister and is reputed to be managing the economy very well. Despite an international economic depression, Israel's economy is prospering.[262] Israel is hampered with a minority coalition government, but I assess Netanyahu as Israel's strongest prime minister after Ben Gurion. His coalition following the last election in early 2013 has not been announced yet as of this writing. The current president is Shimon Peres.

Despite the strong religious penetration of politics, 50 percent of Israelis consider themselves secular. Notwithstanding, they celebrate the national holidays as if they were religious holidays. Political stability will only be achieved if greater religious unity is realised.

The nation of Israel has not been stronger as at the present since King David. In the numerous wars since its inception in 1948, Israel has soundly routed her enemies. Its courageous IDF with brilliant tactical leaders and the support from the United States of America in terms of money and arms have helped. But because

Israel has not been able to make peace with all its Arab neighbours, it is constantly in a state of preparedness for another war, which saps its morale, security, and prosperity. The aim of Islamic jihad to Judenrein Israel is the primary cause of this situation, as well as the nonrealization of a negotiated settlement with Palestinian Arabs who live in Gaza and the West Bank. To strengthen the nation's security and bring a release from the constant paranoia of impending conflict, there has to be a negotiated settlement with Palestinian Arabs without risking the security of Israel.

The religious disunity in Israel is seen by many as its greatest threat. This book has tried to point out that Judaism has evolved from a redemptive religion to a philosophy. Israel's religious definition is confused and lacking in direction and consummation. The development of the Talmud has taken the religious Jews down multiple paths of confusion and legalism. There is much majoring in the minutiae of the Talmud, which has replaced the Tanak as the sole canon in Judaism. There has been an eclipse of its focus on the redemptive primitive Judaism of the Tanak; its redemptive consummation has been relegated to incoherent mysticism.

I refer to Thomas Friedman's excellent book *From Beirut to Jerusalem.* He does not point to a departure from the redemptive aspects of primitive Judaism, and neither does he focus on the neglect of the Abrahamic Covenant. He does not define the changed "post-Second Temple destruction" emergence of a different Judaism ruled by the Talmud. But he sees a confusion and the great lack of religious fervour in Israel that has resulted. Friedman identifies the factions in Judaism and laments the situation.

> In fact, each of the four main schools in the great Israeli identity debate was so convinced that the others would wither away that as a group they were never willing, or able, to sit down and hammer out a consensus about the meaning of the State of Israel and the land of Israel for the Israeli people. As a result the different visions grew side by side. Israel became more secular and more orthodox, more mundane and messianic, all at the same time. Far

from having built a "new Jewish identity," or a "new Jew," Israel seems to have brought out of the basement of Jewish history every Jewish spiritual option from the past three thousand years; the country has become a living museum of Jewish history.[263]

The cause for this is the poor clarity of the comprehension of the identity of the true, God-given Torah, which should be exclusively the Tanak and not the Talmud. Friedman makes a further observation: "Jews in Israel are not differentiated by synagogue affiliations as much as how they relate to the land of Israel and to the state."[264]

Friedman outlines four broad divisions of Israelis.[265] The first four are his; I add some other small groups.

> *1. Secular and Nonobservant Jews* (about 50 percent of the population): "Being back in the land of Israel, erecting a modern society and army, and observing Jewish holidays as national holidays all became a substitute for religious observance and faith . . . . For them, coming to the land of Israel and becoming 'normal' meant giving up religious ritual as the defining feature of their religious identity. Science, technology, and turning the desert green were their new Torah."

> *2. Religious Zionists* (about 30 percent of the population): "These are the traditional or modern Orthodox Jews, who fully support the secular Zionist state but insist it is not a substitute for the synagogue . . . . They serve in the army, celebrate Israel's Independence Day as a new religious holiday, and send their children to state-run religious educational institutions."

> *3. Messianic Zionists* (about 5 percent of the population): "For them the rebirth of the state is not simply a religious event; it is the first stage in a process that will culminate

with the coming of the Messiah . . . . That means in particular, settling every inch of the land of Israel."

4. The Haredim (about 15 percent of the population): "Those filled with the awe of God . . . content to live in the land of Israel . . . because they can fulfil more of the Jewish commandments there, and in order to be on hand when the Messiah arrives."

5. Messianic Jews (about 50,000 living in Israel, and 1,000,000 diasporic worldwide): They believe that Yeshua of Nazareth, the son of Mary, was the fulfilment of the Messiah. They live as religious Jews, celebrate all the Jewish festivals, and keep the Jewish Sabbath. They look forward to the return of Yeshua and the resurrection; these are major future events in their eschatology. They differentiate themselves from Christians but accept the B'rit Hadasha (the New Testament) as part of their expanded Torah. They hold the Abrahamic Covenant as the basis for Jewish identity; whether they understand it correctly is difficult to know.[266]

6. Karaites Jews: They reject the Talmud as the infallible source of law and Halachah. They study the Tanak as their divine source of instruction and direction.

7. Reform and Conservative Jews: At the time of Friedman's publication in 1989, they had just arrived in Israel from America. According to Friedman, they were not really welcomed by the Israeli Orthodox Jews.

The majority of American Jews are reform and conservative. Together, they are the largest group of Jews, and nearly all still in diaspora. Reform and conservative Jews are not a united group and are in fact two separate organizations, however they are often placed together because of their "liberalism." Their doctrinal stances are greatly varied despite identification with synagogue organization. Many of the tenets advanced by different groups are at variance with the Tanak and sometimes with the Talmud, as well as with each other. There is hardly any recognizable semblance to the redemptive Judaism of Abraham, Moses, and King David, although these men are cited as their leaders in religion.

Thomas Friedman aptly places American Jews into the Jewish milieu.

> In America, Jewish life is organised around the synagogue, yet most American Jews in this day and age join a synagogue not for religious or ritual reasons but for communal solidarity. The synagogue is the island clung to by American Jews in order to avoid assimilation in a sea of Gentiles . . . the actual religious content of the synagogue's service is secondary for most people . . . .

In Israel, by contrast, the vast majority are nonobservant Jews. They don't need to join a synagogue in order to avoid assimilation or feel part of a community because there are other outlets for that which do not take synagogue or ritual forms. They avoid assimilation simply by paying taxes to a Jewish state, speaking Hebrew, and sending their children to state schools, which observe the Jewish holidays as national holidays. That is why a majority of Israelis neither belong to synagogues nor even know what to do once they get inside one.[267]

There are reportedly 6.5 million American Jews. Despite their not being Israelis, they are very important to Jewish existence. Israel's chances of survival include their support. Their current and future relationship with Israel is vital both in the political and national arenas, as well as in the Jewish religious turmoil. Thomas Friedman has further valuable insights. He laments his assessment of the relationship between Israel and American Jews, and he cites his attendance at Rosh Hashanah and Yom Kippur services in Washington. He found them:

> strikingly flat. At various luncheons and dinners, after the services, I asked different friends about their rabbis'

sermons. Everywhere I inquired, people seemed to be dissatisfied with what their rabbis had to say. My rabbi asked the question, Why be Jewish? Another talked about homosexual rights. Another spoke of the need for more community volunteerism. Nobody talked about Israel. As I thought about this, I realised that the American Jewish community, in my lifetime, had been held together and motivated to action by four vicarious experiences—all of which were fading away in the 1990s. The most important of these experiences was Israel.[268]

This is a staggering observation. When American Jews saw Israel making peace with Egypt, Jordan, and the Palestinian Arabs, and there were signs also of thawing of the relationship with Syria, the challenge to American Jews faded; the risk to Israel's security was disappearing. Begin, Peres, and Rabin had all scored Nobel Prizes. (There is now a rethink of the situation taking place, with Egypt, Jordan, and Syria being greatly destabilised in an Arab Spring). Friedman further cites:

(i)   The visitation of American Jews to Israel as tourists, going there simply to enjoy the Eilat beaches and the fish restaurants in Jaffa.

(ii) The disappearance of "*Fiddler on the Roof* Judaism" of the grandfathers who had died off.

(iii) Repatriation of the majority of the Russian Jews.

(iv) Secularisation of the Holocaust Museum in Washington DC, which had become a tourist attraction instead of a religious shrine.

(v)   Proliferation of Pizza Huts, Toys R Us, and Ace Hardware in Israel.

He found that these issues caused a weakening of the bonds between Israel and American Jewry. He sees American Jews increasingly assimilating into the Western world.[269] He sees American Jews thinking and behaving more like Americans than Jews; to him this was assimilation. I see the remedy to be in the adoption of the practice of a Jewish spirituality that is redemptive and not extreme or indifferent.

In this plethora of religious interpretation and belief, it is difficult to fit in the redemptive Judaism of primitive Tanakian origin. Variety of belief is a mark of religious liberty, but Jews need consensus and compromise to produce a united front to their enemies. It is desirable to achieve a middle ground between icy secular indifference and fiery fanatical fervour. Faithfulness to the conceptual and contextual interpretation of the Tanak should be the watchword. Primitive Judaism is a Tanakian redemptive Judaism and is basic to the most important days of the Jewish year, Passover and the Day of Atonement. Both these point to redemption; the Passover brought them freedom from slavery. It also included the shedding of blood, which was splashed on their doorposts and lintels, and which bestowed life instead of death. The Day of Atonement freed them from sin and guilt. Again, the blood of the animal without blemish was the symbol of Messianic propitiation.

Attention to the Abrahamic Covenant needs to be paid. Jews have a responsibility to the world. It is my belief that this is tantamount to the preservation and survival of the Jewish nation of Israel and the Jews still in the diaspora. It would solidly unify them all.

CHAPTER 19

THE FUTURE OF ISRAEL

Israel has an immediate future that does not look secure. Beset by enemies in a sea of extremist Arab rage, her vulnerability is obvious. Some of this rage is present within her post-1967 borders. Arab jihad has the publicly declared intention to Judenrein the whole planet. There is also a subtly prevalent simmering sentiment of anti-Semitism in the world, which could raise its ugly head and undermine Israel's existence in certain circumstances. This is unpredictable in some countries where Israel has a strong presence of diasporic Jews. It is predictable among declared Arab friends and committed allies of the Arabs. Israel lacks a essential unity in its own collective definition. Jewishness is a blur, and Israel is being assimilated within its own borders by secularism. Judaism, which should clarify and build Israel's secure foundation, is in a confused state of internal war. An internal betrayal of loyalties is a constant threat. Diasporic Jewry, which is still in the majority despite the availability of aliya, is not united in support of Israel. In fact there are influential elements abroad among diasporic Jews that undermine Israel's current government and security. Currently Israel does not have very secure borders. The perceived future with a Palestinian state west of the Jordan will be a constant threat. These are some of the minuses in Israel's perceived 'bleak' future.[270]

What are the pluses? Israel currently has an excellent economic status. But this economy has its drawbacks, mainly because of its dependence on Arab Palestinian labour and the restricted availability of friendly markets. The world economy also has a great influence on Israel's prosperity. No small country in the global community can be totally independent economically.

Israel has the excellent Israeli Defence Force (IDF), which has demonstrated time and again the ability to vanquish her enemies at war. But this ability is partially dependent on the lack of unity among her Arab enemies and on the supply of arms from her friends. This support from her friends is often grudgingly allowed. The United States is Israel's greatest ally, but any weakness of the United States is Israel's weakness. The idea of American troops on the ground in Israel in her defence is viewed in some quarters as World War III. The strength of the Jewish lobby is not independent of the economic strength of the United States. It may be secure in fair weather, but it cannot be relied upon in foul weather. Israel may have a nuclear arsenal, which could be a deterrent to being attacked, but nuclear arsenals in other countries have not prevented their economic decline. Nuclear bombs are not easily deployed, especially close to home. It is apparent that some of Israel's pluses are partial minuses.

So what is Israel's future? It is my deep conviction that her security is found in the unity of Israel. What is this unity, where does it lie, and how can it be achieved? What is Israel's legitimacy? Why try to preserve nation status for a minority of Jews on a miniscule piece of land in a sea of Arab belligerence? It is my conviction that the Jews are the only extant indigenous people with a legitimate 4,000-year claim to the Holy Land. But that is not enough to declare rights and defend the preservation of their nation status. Many other peoples have slid into national oblivion over the passage of time, and they have been absorbed into the global setting with the rise of modern countries. In fact, the majority of Jews today live comfortably and happily in diaspora, and they have no desire to aliya. So why is it so necessary to expend such great determination and energy to preserve a national status for them? Israel is only one lost war away from another annihilation and scattering. Even with current national status, they are very insecure and precariously situated. Would they not be more secure assimilated and hidden in other countries? There are many Jews who hold this to be their best destiny. Indeed, where are the answers to these questions?

Jews who do not practice Judaism cannot be labelled Jews, for Judaism is their mark of distinctness. Secular Jews in Israel are Jews only in situation, not in definitive qualification. Were they to yerida, they would not be identified or labelled as Jews unless they label themselves. So what is it about Judaism that is a mark or label of distinctness? Herein lies the problem of Jewish unity. Judaism is the indispensable ingredient in the future of Israel. In this book I have defined what I believe is true, primitive Judaism: it is the Judaism of Abraham, Jacob, and Moses. All three had a close and personal dialogue with God—which is the true definition of Judaism, and not the philosophical sophistries of the rabbinic dissertations in the Talmud. In the next chapter, I will extract the divine. existential future of Israel and all humanity as spelled in the eschatology of the Tanak.

CHAPTER 20

THE ESCHATOLOGY OF THE TANAK

The Tanak lays the foundation and declares the future of Israel and the whole world. It is the greatest document produced by mankind, and its mulling has provided the greatest pronouncements of civilization down through the ages. The Tanak spells out our collective conversation with God, and because it is the indelible history of the Jews, it is the indelible will of God through them for the future of the human race. Whatever has happened or will happen to the Jews as predicted in the Tanak will determine the future of all humanity and civilization. This may be a preposterous claim to make, but it does reside in the Tanak, and the Jews are God's chosen vehicle to provide Messianic fulfilment, which is the predicted channel to immortality. This book has stridently declared that the restoration of immortality is God's desired future for the planet, and it is to be accomplished through Messianic fulfilment. That is the foundation of the Tanak and the legitimacy of the Jewish race. That was the reason for God choosing Abraham and bringing the Jewish race into existence; there is no other reason. If this is not the future for all humanity, then we are most miserable and there is no hope beyond the grave.

Many nations have come into being because of the unravelling of the genetic laws of existence, but only the Jews have been chosen for the blessedness of all humanity through the provision of Messiah. The definition of Messiah and the eschatology of existence on this planet is in the Tanak and must be extracted from its pages. The Tanak is our past, present, and future.

A. Elohim: YHVH, Ruach Hakodesh, and Ha-Mashiach

YHVH is synonymous with Jehovah and Elohim, but Elohim describes God's functions in some detail. Human contemplation of Elohim is naturally voiced in human terms and concepts. Our understanding of the divine, celestial vocabulary is extremely limited even though we know God wrote the Ten Commandments with His finger in Hebrew. The Tanak clearly endorses Elohim as a complex deity who loves supremely and is actively reclaiming His lost Creation. As clearly stated elsewhere in this book, the plurality of Elohim has defined God's incorporation of Ha-Mashiach power and Ruach Hakodesh power within Himself. The function of Ha-Mashiach and Ruach Hakodesh are the best facets of Elohim open to us, because they are active towards us. It does not destroy the essential tenet of Monotheism but simply describes the multiple powers of a monotheistic God in redeeming humanity. He created, He redeems, and He glorifies.

(i) Ruach Hakodesh

God's Ruach Hakodesh manifestation is clearly spelled out in the Tanak and in the Talmud as the Shechinah expression of God (see the chapter on "The Shechinah: God with Us"). The Messianic manifestation of God is clearly expressed in the Tanak as the pre-existent, eternal property of the divine to be expressed in the restoration of immortality (Isa. 9:6). The Ruach Hakodesh provides the gift of repentance (Ps. 51), and God's Messianic manifestation provides propitiation and entrance into immortality (Isa. 53). Together, manifesting Himself as both Ruach Hakodesh and Ha-Mashiach, God accomplishes repentance, redemption, and immortality. The Lord our God is one Lord, blessed be He.

The original loss of immortality needs to be invoked here. It is necessary to resort to significant repetition. The presence of the Serpent or Satan as an influence in the Garden of Eden invokes a previous conflict, and *The Jewish Study Bible* translates the Satanic being in Genesis 3 as "the Serpent." That Satanic presence caused the loss of immortality when Eve and Adam disobeyed God. That Satanic being has a previous history; Moses wrote of it in the Book of Job. In Job 2, *The Jewish Study Bible* translates the Satanic being as "the Adversary." In the garb of the King of Babylon, this previous conflict is also described by Isaiah 14.

> How art thou fallen from Heaven, O Shining One, Son of Dawn!
> How are you felled to earth, O vanquisher of nations!
> Once you thought in your heart, "I will climb to the sky:
> Higher than the stars of God I will set my throne.
> I will sit in the mount of assembly, On the summit of Zaphon;
> I will mount the back of a cloud—
> I will match the Most High."
> Instead you are brought down to Sheol,
> To the bottom of the Pit.
> (Isa. 14:12-15, *The Jewish Study Bible*)

The Hebrew Masoretic Text for this passage is as follows:

> Verse 12: "eykh' nafal'Ta miSHamayim heylel Ben-shachar nig'DaTa laaretz cholesh al-Goyim
> Verse 13: w'aTah amar'Ta vilvavkha haSHamayim eeleh miMaal l'khokh'vey-el ariym Kis'iy w'eshev B'har-moed B'yar'K'tey tzafon
> Verse 14: eeleh al-Bamotey av eDaMeh l'el'yon
> Verse 15: akh' el-sh'ol Turad el-yar'K'tey-vor.

Invoking the apotelesmatic principle in the heavenly context, we see the Satanic being having an origin as a created heavenly being who had exalted himself with the challenging move to "match the Most High." Jealousy, pride, and the idolatry of himself had been his downfall; this is the origin of pollution in the universe. The Satanic being had therefore been cast down to the Pit. He lost his immortality and will eventually die. The questions may be asked: Did God love the Satanic being as He loved Adam and Eve and humanity? Did God plan to redeem him as He did plan redemption for humanity? Did God provide him with Messianic redemption? The answer to these questions is a resounding yes. Because there is to be an immortal New World, there will be no Satanic presence in that New World. All Creation will have learned the lesson of obedience to the Torah. The Satanic being and his evil host will either be saved or destroyed when the universe is cleansed of pollution. From the trend of eschatological, catastrophic, apocalyptic events in the Tanak, it appears that the probation period of Satan has ended.

The Tanak's definition of the work of Ruach Hakodesh and Messianic intervention embodies the Tanakian eschatology. The word "ruach" has been translated variously in Scripture, sometimes "perhaps inappropriately and nonapplicably." "The wind" is an appropriate description. But the word has so many applications. It is the life-sustaining "Breath of God," the quiet inhalation and exhalation of blood gases that keep our bodies working. Its loss results in death of the body and soul, which constitutes the human mechanism. Its loss can also constitute spiritual death. The Ruach Hakodesh can speak softly and convincingly to the hearts of humans, helping to overcome sin and cleanse life. It can part the Red Sea and the Jordan River. It can carry Elijah into the wilderness and save him from a murderous, idolatrous woman. It can carry him up to God in a chariot by a whirlwind. It causes lightning and thunder and rain to fall to nourish the earth. It can both trouble and calm the sea. It can sink a ship and also speed one to its destination. The Ruach Hakodesh brings special messages through inspiration to specially chosen, inspired messengers (see my chapter on inspiration and love). A great outpouring on all receptive flesh is predicted for end times: "I will pour out My Spirit upon all flesh" (Joel 2:28). Many are the metaphors that describe the work of God in Ruach Hakodesh nomenclature. But the most important function of Ruach Hakodesh is to convince of sin and provide the gift of repentance.

God's Ruach Hakodesh has been pervasive in Creation (Gen. 1:1-2) and has always been intimately involved with humanity.

The Ruach Hakodesh has always had a restricted access to human minds and has sometimes been described as the super ego. Despite being a somewhat wooing, pleading, intrusive influence, the Holy Spirit has a restricted access to humanity. A personal, individual restriction to limit the influence of the Spirit by reluctant humans can occur. The Holy Spirit works in accordance with free will. The Holy Spirit invites Himself into communication with the human mind, but the human mind has to be receptive and must grant entry. The Holy Spirit has to be listened to and accepted in order to be received. Genesis 6:3 says, "My Spirit shall not always strive with man," and in the Hebrew Masoretic Text it is rendered: "waYomer y'hwah lo-yadon ruchiy vaadam l'olam B'shaGam hu vasar w'hayu yamayw meah w'es'riym sahnah." The word here 'lo-yadon' translated as 'to strive' is greatly emphasized. It has the meanings 'to rule', 'to judge', 'to ensheathe'.

The Holy Spirit is prominent in devekut, the personal companionship with God as was described by King David: "Cast me not away from Thy presence and take not Thy Holy Spirit from me" (Ps. 51:10, KJV). It is emphasized as a "presence." Every human being should plead at all times, "Cast me not away from Thy presence and take not Thy Holy Spirit from me. Restore unto me the joy of Thy salvation, and uphold me [with Thy sweet] Spirit." It is by the Holy Spirit that God dwells with the individual human, just as the Shechinah dwelt in Israel's Tabernacle and Temple. Companionship with the Holy Spirit is the great and satisfying process of sanctification. It raises the standard of moral living and satisfies humanity with better living. Prayer and meditation are vehicles for the working of the Ruach Hakodesh in talking to and listening to God, and in loving Him with all our heart. It is devekut with the divine, Elohim Himself.

Apart from the wooing of and guidance of the human mind in personal contact, the Ruach Hakodesh has a very prominent function in inspiration. The seers and judges and prophets, and some of Israel's kings, were gifted by the Holy Spirit in the guidance of Israel and humanity, in the great proclamations of the Tanak. Divine communication in the conversation of the Holy One with Israel and humanity occurs through the ministry of the Ruach Hakodesh. Through the ages and after the closure of the Tanak, with the death of the prophets Haggai, Zechariah, and Malachi, the rabbinic sages imagined and mourned the loss of the prophetic voice that they clumsily stated as "the Holy Spirit ceased from Israel." They invented the idea of the Bath Kol (literally, a "daughter voice" of the Holy Spirit) as a substitute retention of the Holy Spirit, a sort of reaccessing their conversation with God.[271] But the Bath Kol is a Talmudic invention and is unnecessary, because according to the Tanak, at no point was the Ruach Hakodesh withdrawn from Israel. But the Ruach Hakodesh did withdraw, by having been excluded from the antediluvian world, sparing Noah and his family.

Isaiah describes the Messianic "bearing of the burdens of humanity" in close collusion with the Holy Spirit. Moses was a type of the Messiah in his sufferance of the rebelliousness of the wayward, idolatrous, and uncouth Israelite slaves he led out of Egypt. This is further discussed below under the heading of Ha-Mashiach. Isaiah presents it as "the major hurt," which God suffers because of the waywardness of all humanity (e.g., Hosea 4:17, "Ephraim is joined to his idols, let him alone," is an expression of God's utter despair).

> In all their affliction He was afflicted, and the angel of His presence saved them; In His love and His pity He redeemed them; and He bore them, and carried them all the days of old. But they rebelled, and *vexed his Holy Spirit;* therefore He was turned to be their enemy, and He fought against them. Then *He remembered* the days of old, Moses and his people, saying, Where is He who brought them up out of the sea with the shepherd of His flock? Where is He who put His Holy Spirit within him? . . . As a beast goeth down into the valley, the Spirit of the Lord caused him to rest. (Isa. 63:9-14, KJV; emphasis added).

The Holy Spirit will play a major part in the eschatological events of the last days, as described by the prophet Joel:

> After that,
> I will pour out My Spirit on all flesh;
> Your sons and daughters shall prophesy;
> Your old men shall dream dreams,
> And your young men shall see visions.
> I will even pour out My Spirit
> Upon male and female slaves.
> (Joel 3:1-2, *The Jewish Study Bible*)

The Talmud hugely endorses the deity, sustaining work, and influence of the Holy Spirit. Abraham Cohen, that great expositor of the Talmud, states:

> Another Rabbinic concept to indicate the nearness of God and His direct influence on man is that of the Ruach Hakodesh (the Holy Spirit). Sometimes it seems to be identical with the Shechinah as expressing the divine immanence in the world as affected by what transpires there. For instance, it is related that after the destruction of the [Second] Temple, the Emperor Vespasian dispatched three shiploads of young Jews and Jewesses to brothels in Rome, but during the voyage they all threw themselves into the sea and were drowned, rather than accept so degraded a fate. The story ends with the statement that on beholding the harrowing sight: "The Holy Spirit wept and said, 'For these do I weep.'"[272]

The tears of God are shed by the Holy Spirit more often than the rain falls on the earth. This divine sorrow is barely perceived by the human race. The idolatrous and selfish disposition of humanity is a major affront to the tenderness and love, which found its divine expression in the Abrahamic offering of Isaac on Mount Moriah. Can anyone spare an atom of sympathy for God? Can anyone offer the Almighty a morsel of love? Can anyone hear

His moaning in Isaiah 63:3-5: "I have trodden the winepress ALONE . . . I looked and there was none to help" (KJV)? Is there anyone who will weep with the Holy Spirit about the suicide of the glorious young men and women who cast themselves into a churning sea? The callousness of the human race is so far removed from the Edenic creation of God that the great likeness between God and His created beings in that love affair in Eden is almost effaced. And man's inhumanity to man daily spells much of the suffering experienced on the planet; it is the travail of God. But the expression of His great love on Mount Moriah surpasses all that and has bound humanity closer to Him than before the fall of the human race.

> It is because of the Lord's mercies that we are not consumed, because His compassions fail not. They are new every morning; *Great is Thy faithfulness.* (Lam. 3:22-23, KJV; emphasis added)

Abraham Cohen ends his dissertation on the work of the Holy Spirit as the embodiment of God with these words:

> Sufficient has been quoted to demonstrate how untenable is the view that the Talmudic conception of God is wholly transcendental. However reluctant the teachers of Israel were to identify God with His Universe and insisted on His being exalted high above the abode of men, yet they thought of the world as permeated through and through with the omnipresent Shechinah [His Holy Spirit]. God is at once above the Universe and the very soul of the Universe.[273]

This is a mighty concept and a great reality. The Holy Spirit is God. Indeed, the function of Elohim Himself, His plural salvific performance, is manifested by His Ruach Hakodesh, His own self. Hear, O Israel, the Lord our God is one, blessed be He. Monotheistic Jews are not reluctant to accept the Ruach Hakodesh as God Himself; it does not damage their monotheism one iota. But there is a reluctance to accept Ha-Mashiac's oneness with God. This will be discussed now.

(ii) Ha-Mashiach

Having established the Holy Spirit function of God, the Messianic function of the Elohim in the Tanak must be explored. Extracts from the Talmud will also be employed to illustrate the interaction and discussion of the rabbinic sages on this topic.

At the outset, it must be firmly accepted that Ha-Mashiach is a very important and prominent concept, as well as a huge part of the eschatology in Judaism. Without Ha-Mashiach, Judaism is dead. The origin of the Messianic concept will be discussed later in this section, with special reference to Tanakian and Talmudic ideas of definition, which are clearly in conflict. In the terrestrial setting, it is true that anyone anointed by God in the Tanak had a special job to perform, and the usual anointed ones were kings. The leaders or kings of Israel are sometimes referred to as shepherds. But Ha-Mashiach as an anointed one is always given special status and is clearly designated in the Tanak. The definition of Ha-Mashiach is a prominent part of the Tanak and the Talmud. All passages suggesting that a coming king will be from the House of David, a branch stemming from the root of Jesse, are indicative of Ha-Mashiach. The following prophetic passages from the Tanak are accepted by many past and current Jewish scholars as Messianic.[274] The core thoughts of these Scriptures are excerpted:

Psalms 1 and 2
"Thou art My Son; This day have I begotten Thee."

Isaiah 2:1-4; 9:6-7; 11:1-9; 26:2; 32:15-18; 52-53; 63:16
"For out of Zion shall go forth the Law and the WORD of the Lord from Jerusalem." "Unto us a Son is given, and His name shall be called The Mighty God, The Everlasting Father."

Jeremiah 23:5,6; 30:7-10; 31:33-34; 33:14-16
"I will raise unto David a righteous BRANCH and a KING."

Ezekiel 34:11-31; 37:21-28
"And David My servant shall be King . . . My servant David shall be their Prince FOREVER."

Daniel chapters 2, 7, and 12
"And at that time shall MICHAEL stand up, the great Prince who standeth for the children of thy people."

Hosea 2:20-22; 3:4-5
"Afterward shall the children of Israel return, and seek the Lord their God and DAVID their KING."

Amos 9:13-15
"And I will bring again the captivity of My people of Israel."

Micah 4:1-4
"The House of the Lord shall be established on the top of the mountains . . . and people shall flow unto it."

Zephaniah 3:8-20
"The King of Israel, even the Lord, is in the midst of thee, thou shalt not see evil anymore."

Zechariah 6:12; 8:23; 14:9
"Behold, the Man who is the BRANCH . . . and he shall build the Temple of the Lord."

Malachi 3:1-3
"The Lord whom ye seek shall suddenly come to His Temple, even the Messenger of the covenant."

There are numerous others not listed above. The Messiah has been discussed elsewhere in this book, but the subject bears a detailed repetition here.

Messianic descriptions and scenes in the Tanak are of two types:

1. *A Suffering human who makes His death with the wicked and with the rich in His death* (Isa. 52, 53)
2. *A mighty, eternal, divine king:*

(Ps. 2). Messiah's glory and power and majesty are equal with God.

Curiously, Isaiah and the Psalmist link up to connect the two descriptions, in the Messianic definition of sonship. There is a solid connection between the two.

Isaiah 9:6-7 declares:

> For a Child has been born to us,
> A *Son* has been given us.
> And authority has settled on His shoulders.
> He has been named
>
> The Mighty God is planning *grace*;
> The Eternal Father, a peaceable Ruler
> In token of abundant authority
> And of peace without limit
> Upon David's throne and kingdom,
> That it may be firmly established
> In justice and equity
> Now and evermore.
> (*The Jewish Study Bible*; emphasis added).

This is a mighty rendition by Isaiah, and no Jewish rabbi has successfully challenged the implication that this passage denotes the Messiah who will sit on the throne of David. The King James Version is pure literary art and is so triumphant that its reading is sheer pleasure.

> For unto us a *CHILD* is born, unto us a *SON* is given,
> And the government shall be upon His shoulder;
> And His name shall be called *wonderful, counselor,*
> *The Mighty GOD, the Everlasting Father,*
> *The Prince of Peace.*
> Of the increase of His government and peace
> There shall be no end.
> Upon the Throne of David, and upon his kingdom,
> To order it and establish it, with justice
> And with righteousness from henceforth even forever.
> (KJV; emphasis added).

In fantastic collusion, the Psalmist declares in the second psalm:

> Why do the nations assemble and people plot vain things;
> Kings of the earth take their stand, regents intrigue together
> against the Lord and against *His anointed?* Let us break the
> cords of their yoke, shake off Their ropes from us! He who
> is enthroned in heaven laughs; The Lord mocks at them
> in anger, terrifying them in His rage, "But I have installed
> *my King on* Zion, My Holy Mountain!" Let me tell of
> the decree: the Lord said to me, *"You are My Son, I have*
> *fathered You this day."* Ask it of Me, and I will make the
> nations your domain; your estate, the limits of the earth.
> You can smash them with an iron mace, shatter them Like
> a potter's ware. (Ps. 2, *The Jewish Study Bible*; emphasis
> added).

The King James Version uses the word "begotten" instead of "fathered," but they have the same meaning. The important two original Hebrew words are "beni" ("are My Son") and "'ye-lid-ti-ka" ("fathered" or "have begotten"). Some would insist that these words imply a sexual etiology, but wherever described in the Tanak, the "Fatherhood" of God, and humans as His "children," is totally devoid of sexuality. It is therefore empirically apparent that the use of the word "Father" for God is the best human invention or garb for the relationship. Similarly, the prophets had used the husband-wife relationship in describing Israel's

302

unfaithfulness to God; no one will insist that there is sexuality in that relationship. Therefore, why insist in a sexual mechanism for the existence of the divine "Father" and "Son." Again, it is a human way of expressing the containment and functional relationship between Ha-Mashiach and Elohim. It is so much more sensible to see Ha-Mashiach as a function of the great "Us" who is Elohim. This relationship simply implies the penetration of humanity by deity, which had to happen to have Ha-Mashiach come to earth, first to provide atonement, and then to live here forever and ever as eternal king.

The two passages quoted above are unmistakably and incontrovertibly references to Messiah. The anointed one, who is the son installed as king in Zion, and the son placed on the throne of David, are one and the same. The child born and the son who is "fathered by God" are one and the same. The humanity of Messiah is here predicted as a human birth, but the source from whence He comes is unmistakably divine. The Messiah is one and the same as God Himself, again unmistakably proclaimed by Isaiah as the mighty God and the everlasting Father, and proclaimed by the psalmist as the anointed one, who in human terms carries the Father's genes. Messiah is God with a human form, a son, to function for humanity's redemption. Messiah the son and Ruach Hakodesh are part and parcel of God, one with Elohim, one and the same, indivisible from eternity. There is no maleness nor femaleness or sexuality in the relationships of these functions of Elohim; it is simply a method of human expression and human understanding. The Lord our God is one, blessed be He. God created, God redeems, and God will glorify. The glorification is the restoration of immortality. The work of redemption is described in the passage from Isaiah by *The Jewish Study Bible* translation as a *work of grace.* The grace of God is the unmerited favour bestowed by God: Sins are wiped out and immortality is restored. The Messianic child is indeed "the mighty God who is planning grace."

In the Tanak the names of God are interchangeable and synonymous with Messiah. Isaiah 63:11-14 is interpreted by *The Jewish Study Bible* as an exposition of God's movement from wrath to grace in judgement(see p. 909). Grace is a Messianic provision. Isaiah pleads, "Surely You are our Father; . . . From of old, Your name is 'Our Redeemer'" (Isa. 63:16, *The Jewish Study Bible*).

Despite variant views expressed in the Talmud, the rabbinic sages stated that one of the big questions asked in the final judgement is, "Did you hope for the Salvation of the Messiah?"[275] Obviously redemption or salvation is the function of the Messiah. The different appellations of the Messiah in the Tanak are all synonymous with deity. If YHVH is redeemer, then that specific redeemer is YHVH. Here are the names of God with Messianic function:

1. YHVH is the divine Goel, redeeming His people (Isa. 63:16)
2. YHVH is El Shaddah, Adonai, saviour in the escape from Egypt (Exod, 6:2-3)
3. YHVH is the redeemer who delivers Israel from "the clans of Edom," who seek to destroy them (Exod. 15:13)
4. YHVH is the redeemer who gathers Israel from the ends of the earth in judgement (Ps. 107:2-3).
5. YHVH is majestic in the role of deliverer (Isa. 62:11; 63:1)
6. YHVH is vindicator, redeemer, and judge, conducting judgement at the latter day upon the earth (Job 19:25)
7. YHVH is Haggoel, the redeemer (Job 19:25; Ps. 19:14)
8. YHVH is Goel, kinsman redeemer (Num. 5:8)
9. YHVH is Goel Yisrael, the redeemer of Israel (Lev. 25; Ps. 39:7)
10. YHVH is Goel Haddam, the avenger of blood (1 Sam. 6:20)
11. YHVH is Adonai Tsuri v'go'ali, Lord my rock and my redeemer (Ps. 19:14)
12. YHVH is Tsidkenu (Sid-qe-nu), the Lord our righteousness (Jer. 23:5-6)

God and Ha-Mashiach are one and the same in the redemptive act.

As stated above, here are two pictures of Messiah in the Tanak.

1. The ***human form*** that is born as a son, a child, and who is elaborated further by Isaiah as a suffering Messiah. The child born in human form suffers and dies as the sacrificial lamb without blemish as the atonement for sin (Isa. 52; 53). Messianic propitiation comes heralded by the Elijah forerunner (Mal. 3:1-3).
2. The ***divine form*** comes as king and judge, whose estate will be the limits of the earth. He smashes the nations with an iron mace. The entire book of Joel the prophet is a declaration of this picture of king. After the pouring out of the Holy Spirit (Joel 2:28, KJV; Joel 3:1-2, *The Jewish Study Bible*), there is judgement (Joel 3:12, KJV; Joel 4:1-21, Ps. 2, *The Jewish Study Bible*). Malachi presents the king in final judgement (Mal. 3:16-18).

1. The human form arriving with divine credentials is elaborated in Isaiah 9, 52, and 53 as the suffering Messiah. Briefly:

> He was despised, shunned by men,
> A man of suffering, familiar with disease.
> As one who hid his face from us,
> He was despised, we held him of no account.
> Yet it was our sickness he was bearing,
> Our suffering that he endured.
> We accounted him plagued,
> Smitten and afflicted by God;
> But he was wounded because of our sins,
> Crushed because of our iniquities,
> He bore the chastisement that made us whole,
> And by his bruises we are healed.
> We all went astray like sheep,
> Each going his own way;
> And the Lord visited upon him
> The guilt of all of us . . . .
> But the Lord chose to crush him by disease,
> That, if he made himself an offering for guilt,
> He might see offspring and have long life,

And that through him the Lord's purpose
might prosper.
Out of his anguish he shall see it;
He shall enjoy it to the full through his devotion.
(*The Jewish Study Bible*)

This clearly is a propitiation for sin. The Messianic intonation here as a propitiation is clearly accepted and acknowledged by Rabbi Judah the Prince, the redactor of the Mishnah.[276]

2. The divine form arriving with human credentials as a king and judge of all the earth.

As I looked on, in the night vision,
One like a human being came with the clouds of heaven;
He reached the Ancient of Days and was presented to Him.
Dominion, glory, and kingship were given to Him;
All peoples and nations of every language must serve Him.
His dominion is an everlasting dominion that shall not pass
away,
And His kingship, one that shall not be destroyed. (Dan.
7:13-14, *The Jewish Study Bible*)

The Tanak mixes the two pictures, and they need to be deciphered through conceptual and contextual interpretation. The Talmud does recognise that there are two pictures, but it also looks for a Messiah to accomplish both functions in a foggy sort of manner. It is described as "foggy" because the chronology is important: one must precede the other. The atonement must precede the judgement, the resurrection, and the setting up of the New World. Gershom Scholem unmistakably sees his restorative factor as a prerequisite to his utopian factor. And between the two, Scholem clearly sees what he enthusiastically embraces as catastrophic apocalypticism. Both are Messianic functions. (See chapter 21 of this book, "The Ha-Mashiach of Israel.") To my knowledge, the Talmud is not clear on the chronology of Messianic functions. First and second comings are not discussed or argued in the rabbinic schools. But setting dates for the messianic coming are argued. Messianic atonement and kingly functions are not adequately deciphered and separated. Most rabbis seem to avoid a deep discussion of the Messianic atonement. It is clearer with hindsight, but when the Tanak and Talmud were composed (which occupied a period of about 1,000 years), matters did not have the clarity that scholars now have as they look back. But no chronology is expressed, and no sequence of two different Messianic acts are defined in the Talmud. The Talmud denies the eternal pre-existence of the Messiah as God Himself, and defines the Messiah only as a "created being" although it has 'divine' expectations from Messiah. Only a divine Messiah can atone. Abraham Cohen notes:

> The belief was general [in the Talmud] that the sending of the Messiah was part of the Creator's plan at the inception of the Universe. "Seven things were created before the world was created: Torah, Repentance, the Garden of Eden (ie Paradise), Gehinnom, the Throne of Glory, the Temple, and the name of the Messiah" (Pes. 54a). In a later work there is the observation: "From the beginning of the creation of the world King Messiah was born, for he entered the mind (of God) before even the world was created" (Pesikta Rab. 152b).[277]

This statement is conceptually and contextually compatible with the Tanak as long as it is interpreted as applying to the origin of the name of Messiah, and not to the origin of the Messiah Himself. The Tanak clearly and adamantly names Messiah as God Himself, functioning as such (see Isa. 9:6). But unfortunately the Talmud interprets Messiah as a separate being from God, a created being who is not divine and not deity. This is incompatible with both types of pictures of Messiah: the atonement for sin, and the judge and king of all the earth. Both are clearly defined in the Tanak as God Himself.

The Talmudic rabbis argued about the names and functions of the Messiah as portrayed in the Tanak:

> The School of R. Sheila said, "Shiloh, as it is written, Until Shiloh come" (Genesis 49:10). The School of R Jannai declared, "Jinnon, as it is said, His name shall be continued (Hebrew jinnon) as long as the sun" (Psalm 72:17). The School of R. Channina declared, "Chaninah, as it is said, I will show you no favour" (Hebrew chaninah) (Jeremiah 16:13). Others contend that His name is Menachem son of Hezekiah, as it is said, "The comforter (Hebrew menachem) that should refresh my soul is far from me" (Lamentations 1:16). The Rabbis maintain that his name is the "leprous one" of the School of R. Judah the Prince, as it is said, "Surely He hath borne our griefs, and carried our sorrows; yet we did esteem Him stricken, smitten of God, and afflicted" (Isaiah 53:4). Rab declared, the Holy One, blessed be He, will hereafter raise up for Israel another David, as it is said, "They will serve the Lord their God and David their King, whom I will raise up unto them" (Jeremiah 30:9). It is not stated "has raised" but "will raise" (Sanh. 98b).
>
> Other designations suggested for Him are given in these extracts: "R. Joshua b. Levi said, His name is Tzemach" ("the branch," cf. Zechariah 6:12). R. Judan said, It is Menachem. R. Aibu said, "The two are identical since the numerical value of the letters forming their names is the same" (p. Ber. 5a). R. Nachman asked R. Isaac, "Have you heard when Bar Naphle ("son of the fallen") will come?" He said to him, "Who is Bar Naphle?" He answered, "The Messiah." The other asked, "Do you call the Messiah Bar Naphle?" He replied, "I do, because it is written, In that day will I raise up the Tabernacle of David that is fallen" (Amos 9:11) (Sanh. 96b).[278]

Expectation of the Messiah was a major contemplation of the rabbinic schools. Cohen again describes it well:

> The hope for the coming of the Messiah naturally became more fervent in the time of severe national eclipse. When the oppression of the conqueror grew intolerable, the Jews instinctively turned to the Messianic predictions contained in the Scriptures . . . . To hearten the people in their misery and encourage them to persevere in the face of the severest hardships, the Rabbis preached the doctrine that there will be "the travail of the Messiah," i.e. his coming will be attended by pangs of suffering.[279]

The timing of the coming of the Messiah was of significant impact on Israel. The Book of Daniel has excited everyone's thinking about His coming kingdom. The image in Nebuchadnezzar's dream in chapter 2 has a thrilling finale attached to it. Babylon was the head of gold, Medo-Persia was the breast and arms of silver, Greece was the belly and thighs of bronze, Rome was the legs of iron, and its feet a mixture of iron and clay representing the weak and strong nations succeeding the Roman Empire. And then the stone cut out of the mountains without hands comes and strikes the image on its feet, and grinds it into powder. That stone then grows and fills the entire world. The stone represents the Messianic kingdom that is now imminent, and it has been imminent since the fall of Rome. Daniel 2:44 triumphantly declares, "And in the days of these kings shall the God of heaven set up a kingdom which shall never be destroyed . . . and it shall stand forever." In his book Daniel gives further details of events that are to take place during the period of the feet and toes of the image.

In Daniel 7, there are two heavenly visions seen by Daniel. The first is that of the "Ancient of Days" (7:9-10). The second vision is as follows:

> As I looked on, in the night vision,
> *One like a human being*
> Came with the clouds of heaven;
> He reached the Ancient of Days
> And was presented to Him.
> Dominion, glory, and kingship were given
> to Him;
> All peoples and nations of every language
> must serve Him.
> His dominion is an everlasting dominion
> that shall not pass away,
> And His kingship, one that shall not be destroyed. (Daniel
> 7:13-14, *The Jewish Study Bible*; emphasis added).

It is true that Daniel appears to describe "the Ancient of Days" and the "one like a human being" as two separate persons, but he combines them in the previous declaration: "in the days of these kings shall the *God of Heaven* set up His kingdom." Lo and behold, in this vision Daniel has already described the "one like a human being" as the God of Heaven, as He is the great ruler accepting the "Dominion, glory and kingship." These two visions describe the eventual fulfilment of Messianic redemption achieved by Elohim Himself. For want of better nomenclature, Elohim is defined as plural in power and function. The Lord our God is one, blessed be He. The description of the "one like a human being" is none other than the suffering Messiah (embraced by Judah the Prince), the Ha-Mashiach penetration of humanity by deity, the lamb without blemish who achieves the atonement for sin and guilt. Death is vanquished, and He has now finalized the atonement. His kingdom is declared, and His subjects are blameless. He has prepared them for eternal life. He will reign forever and ever, or as the great rabbinic schools preferred, "From Everlasting to Everlasting!"

In these two visions, Daniel describes both pictures of the Messiah, the "one like a human" and the "kingly" one. The divine penetrates as a human; the human penetrates as divine. The two pictures are presented as realities in heavenly places.

Then in the final chapter Daniel talks about the dramatic interference by Michael.

> Michael, the great Prince who standeth for the children of thy people, and there shall be a time of trouble, such as never was since there was a nation even to that same time; and at that time thy people shall be delivered, every one that shall be found written in the book. And many of those who sleep in the dust of the earth shall awake, some to everlasting life, and some to shame and everlasting contempt. And they that be wise shall shine like the brightness of the firmament; and they that turn many to righteousness as the stars forever and ever. (Dan. 12:1-3, KJV)

Michael the great prince is none other than the Ha-Mashiach penetration of humanity by deity, synonymous with the "one like a human being," the suffering Messiah, but now not suffering but rejoicing, because He has now claimed a kingdom that shall not pass away. Michael is Israel's special guardian, the Ha-Mashiach.

Summary

The eschatology of the Tanak is spelled in the Abrahamic Covenant. The blessedness of all nations is achieved by the Son of David, the Messiah. There is repentance, a gift effected by the Ruach Hakodesh. There is redemption, a gift of grace by the Ha-Mashiach penetration of humanity by divinity. The first picture of the Messiah is fulfilled as the offering of the lamb without blemish. The atonement is thus accomplished. The resurrection then takes place because judgement has declared for those who grasped the atonement. The atonement was accomplished for all humanity. But now, those who had accepted grace, those who availed of salvation by the atonement, have been invested in the righteousness of the righteous one. God sees their law keeping in the righteous one as perfect. Finally comes glorification by the establishment of the everlasting kingdom of the eternal king, one with the Ancient of Days and the Ruach Hakodesh. Immortality is restored to those who have embraced the gifts of repentance, grace and perfection of character.

David prophetically declared, "As for me, I will behold Thy face in righteousness; I shall be satisfied *when I awake with Thy likeness"* (Ps. 17:15, KJV).

When David arises out of the dust of the ground, he will bear the likeness of His Lord because David is clothed with his Lord's righteousness. David will be satisfied indeed with the way he looks. God has accepted the perfection seen in the once sinful, lawbreaking human, that coveter, adulterer, and murderer who found repentance and atonement, now perfect in His sight through the gift of grace and Messianic perfection. The Lord our God is one in our redemption, blessed be He.

It is obvious from the above statements that the two pictures of the advent of the Messiah are not one and the same. The "suffering Messiah" must first bear the sins of a guilty world. He must be offered as the lamb without blemish. When that offering is completed and His oneness in purpose with and as the Ancient of Days is portrayed, He will then appear as judge and king. Daniel 2, 7, and 12 eloquently establish the sequence.

In the unravelling of the eschatology of the Tanak, the suffering Messiah comes first and accomplishes the atonement. Then He subsequently becomes the judge and king of kings, and He establishes His eternal kingdom. At the resurrection the old world ends and the new world begins. Mortality is replaced by immortality, and Gan Eden is restored. Israel must find the Messiah in the Tanak in order to usher in the New World. The old ends with Gog and Magog. The new begins with the resurrection.

B. The Judgement and the Resurrection

The resurrection of the dead is a vital doctrine of the Tanak. The Tanak recognizes death as a sleep; it is a temporary silence. Enoch (Gen. 5:21-24) and Elijah (2 Kings 2:11) did not die but were taken up to glory. God promised and provided redemption, and so it has to be grasped. If the disobedience in Eden spelled death, and God made the promise to restore immortality through His Messianic atonement, then the dead must be raised. Why would God forgive people if that is the end of it? A resurrection must take place. *The resurrection is implicit in Judaism.* Without it Judaism is a dead, useless, and hopeless religion, and the Jews are the most deluded and illegitimate people on earth. But rejoice greatly, for primitive Judaism, with its Messianic and redemptive foundation, is the most exciting and positive religion on earth. The resurrection is essential to Messianic, redemptive Judaism; it is full of hope and joy and happiness that is unequalled in the history of the world. Abraham (Gen. 23), Jacob (Gen. 50), and Joseph (Josh. 24:32) went to great lengths to have their bones buried in the Promised Land, because that was where they wanted to be resurrected. Moses wrote in the words of Job of the resurrection:

> For I know that my Redeemer liveth, and that He shall stand at the latter day upon the earth; And though after my skin worms destroy this body, yet in my flesh shall I see God, Whom I shall see for myself, and mine eyes shall behold, and not another. (Job 19:25-27, KJV)

And again, Job is willing to die in his suffering. But he challenges God thus:

> Oh, that Thou wouldest hide me in Sheol, that Thou wouldest conceal me until Thy wrath be past; that Thou wouldest appoint me a set time, and remember me! If a man die, shall he live again? All the days of my appointed time will I wait, till my change come. Thou shalt call and I will answer Thee. (Job 14:13-15, KJV)

Job and Moses believed in the resurrection. King David also embraced the resurrection of the dead. In his fervent prayer to God he pleaded, "Keep me as the apple of the eye; hide me under the shadow of Thy wings" (Ps. 17:8, KJV). He makes the case for being redeemed despite being surrounded by the condemnation of his accusers who would destroy him. He was well aware of his bad record, which God had forgiven. With great confidence he grasped the reason for his being raised in the resurrection: "As for me, I will behold Thy face in righteousness; I will be satisfied, when I awake, with Thy likeness" (Ps. 17:15, KJV).

He was of course expecting to be gifted by God with the Messianic, perfect character appropriated to him. He believed in the Messianic atonement, and he obtained it by faith and reality. Again the Psalmist bears witness: "But God will redeem my soul from the power of Sheol; For He shall receive me" (Ps. 49:15, KJV).

It was with triumphant confidence that he exulted in his redeemer's assurance:

> Yea though I walk through the valley of the shadow of death I will fear no evil, For Thou art with me; Thy rod and Thy staff, they comfort me. Thou preparest a table before me in the presence of mine enemies; Thou anointest my head with oil; my cup runneth over. Surely goodness and mercy shall follow me all the days of my life; and I will dwell in the house of the Lord forever. (Ps. 23:4-6, KJV)

He was so triumphant that he counted death as so momentary that he skipped mentioning it again, when he entered eternal life forever. He credited it all to the goodness and mercy of his Lord.

The very crowded cemetery in Jerusalem skirting the Mount of Olives attests to the reason for the overcrowding there: everyone buried there wanted to be raised in the resurrection in the Holy City, to be close to the action when the Messiah appears as a mighty king.

Isaiah describes an apocalypse that is discouraging in chapters 24-27. But right in the middle of it, he firmly plants the triumphant resurrection.

> And He will destroy on this mount the shroud
> That is drawn over the faces of all the peoples
> And the covering that is spread
> Over all the nations:
> He will destroy death forever.
> My Lord God will wipe the tears away
> From all faces
> And will put an end to the reproach of His people
> Over all the earth—
> For it is the Lord who has spoken.
> "In that day they shall say:
> This is our God
> We trusted in Him, and He delivered us.
> This is the Lord, in whom we trusted;
> Let us rejoice and exult in His deliverance!
> (Isa. 25:7-9, *The Jewish Study Bible*)

Daniel spoke very explicitly about the resurrection:

> And many of those who sleep in the dust of the earth shall awake, some to everlasting life, and some to shame and everlasting contempt. (Dan. 12:2, KJV)

Again Daniel is in consternation about this vision, his last. It is the vision of the glory of God, the final judgement, and the resurrection. Its beginning is in Daniel 10:5. Daniel is on the banks of the Tigris River, and he sees a man who informs him of events of the latter days. The man was "dressed in linen, his loins girt in fine gold. His body was like beryl, his face had the appearance of lightning, his eyes were like flaming torches, his arms and legs had the colour of burnished bronze, and the sound of his speech was like the noise of a multitude" (Dan, 10:5-6, *The Jewish Study Bible*). Daniel faints and then revives with the man's aid. The man tells Daniel that Michael the Prince has aided him in bringing the vision to Daniel; a running account of the vision takes place. But Daniel protests that he does not understand the timeline outlined. A further explanation follows that is still difficult for Daniel. Finally the man tells him:

> Go, Daniel, for these words are secret and sealed to the time of the end. Many will be purified and purged and refined . . . the knowledgeable will understand [the timeline] . . . But you, go on to the end, you shall rest, and arise to your destiny at the end of days. (Dan. 12:9-13, *The Jewish Study Bible*)

Here is a further reference to the final judgement and the resurrection in which Daniel will arise after his "sleep." It will happen when Michael will stand up (Dan. 12:1).

Ezekiel was a contemporary of Daniel, and he is very elaborate in describing the resurrection in his vision of the Valley of the Dry Bones.

> The hand of the Lord came upon me. He took me out by the Spirit of the Lord and set me down in the valley. It was full of bones . . . There were many of them spread over the valley, and they were very dry. He said to me "O mortal, can these bones live again?" I replied "O Lord God, only You know." And He said to me "Prophesy over these bones and say to them: O dry bones, hear the word of the Lord! Thus said the Lord God to these bones: I will cause breath to enter you and you shall live again . . . ." And while I was prophesying, suddenly there was a sound of rattling and the bones came together . . . There were sinews on them . . . and flesh . . . and skin over them . . . [and] breath entered them, and they came to life and stood up on their feet, a vast multitude.
>
> And He said to me, "O mortal, these bones are the Whole House of Israel. They say 'Our bones are dried up, our hope is gone, we are doomed.' Prophesy therefore, and

say to them: Thus said the Lord God: I am going to open your graves, and lift you out of the graves, O My people, and bring you to the land of Israel. You shall know, O My people, that I am the Lord, when I have opened your graves and lifted you out of your graves. I will put My breath into you and you shall live again, and I will set you upon your own soil. Then you shall know that I the Lord have spoken and have acted." (Ezek. 37:1-14, *The Jewish Study Bible*)

Ezekiel has more to say about the New World. Talking about the righteous, God says:

Then I will appoint a single shepherd over them to tend them—My servant David. He shall tend them, he shall be a shepherd to them. I the Lord will be their God, and My servant David shall be a ruler among them . . . .

And I will cleanse them. Then they shall be My people and I will be their God. My servant David shall be king over them. They and their children . . . shall dwell there forever with My servant David their prince for all time . . . I will place My sanctuary among them forever. (Ezek. 34:23-24; 37:23-28, *The Jewish Study Bible*)

God will bring this "whole house of Israel" to the New World, the new land of Israel, an immortal one where Messiah is king forevermore. He is no ordinary human.

Abraham Cohen summarizes the doctrine of the resurrection of the dead and its place in Judaism.

No aspect of the subject of the Hereafter has so important a place in the religious teaching of the Rabbis as the doctrine of the Resurrection. It became with them an article of faith the denial of which was condemned as sinful; and they declared: "Since a person repudiated belief in the Resurrection of the dead, he will have no share in the Resurrection" (Sanhed. 90a).

The prominence which this dogma assumed was the effect of religious controversy. It was one of the differences between the Pharisees and Sadducees. The latter as we know from other sources (See Josephus, Antiq. xviii. i. 4) . . . taught that the soul became extinct when the body died and death was the final end of the human being. This denial of a Hereafter involved the doctrine of reward and punishment [following judgement] to which the Pharisees attached great importance, and for that reason they fought it strenuously. They made it the theme of one of the Eighteen Benedictions which formed part of the daily service of prayer: "Thou sustainest the living with lovingkindness, revivest the dead with great mercy, supportest the falling, healest the sick, loosest the bound, and keepest Thy faith to them that sleep in the dust. Who is like unto Thee, Lord of mighty acts, and who resembleth Thee, O King, Who killest and revivest, and causest salvation to spring forth? Yea, faithful art Thou to revive the dead. Blessed art Thou, O Lord, Who revivest the dead."[280]

Much discussion and argument occurred among the rabbinic sages, who took great pains to deduce the doctrine of the resurrection from the Tanak and elsewhere, sometimes making unnecessary and erroneous conclusions. The Tanak eminently supports the doctrine of the resurrection.[281]

Having dealt with the resurrection first, in reverse order, it is obvious that judgement must precede the resurrection to decide who is worthy to be saved and who will be damned. In Daniel's last vision, he is told that at the last days Michael, the great prince will appear. "At that time, your people will be *rescued* [if they are found worthy], all who are found inscribed in the book" (Dan. 12:1-2). So a judgement has already taken place in the lives of everyone sleeping in the dust of the earth, and a decision made; they are marked for resurrection, and their names are written in the special book.

When Sodom and Gomorrah were going to be destroyed by God for their full cup of iniquity, Lot was living there. Abraham was very upset that God was going to do it, and he pleaded with God. Abraham felt there were innocent, righteous people in those cities who would be destroyed. Not so, said God, and Abraham quoted the great doctrine of the Final Judgement to God's face, which determines the fate of every individual born on the planet: "Shall not the judge of all the earth do justly?" (Gen. 18:25, *The Jewish Study Bible*)

When and where and how is God's final judgement for each human to be made? And what is the standard?

1. The Standard: It is the primitive Torah, the law of God. The person will be found guilty by this standard if the law has not been kept perfectly. There will be no 50 percent plus one, or no 99.9 percent pass mark. It *must* be 100 percent. The Tanak does not support the Kabbalistic idea of reincarnation to facilitate eventual perfect obedience to the Torah. No one born on the planet can claim 100 percent obedience, and there is only one lifetime to achieve it.

2. When? Obviously, it has to be made sometime in the life of the individual. There is no evidence in the Tanak that there will be a last-minute line-up at the judgement bar of God. The evaluation must take place during the life because there is no Tanakian second chance after death.

3. Where? God is the judge, and so the place of judgement is in Heaven, God's home. But because God is ubiquitous, we cannot pin Him down to any spot. God knows every individual's personal standing with Him, and He promises the assurance of a just judgement for them.

4. How? Here is where the great provision of the Ha-Mashiach atonement is the only determinant factor. When the Jews celebrate Yom Kippur, they assemble before God with the gift of repentance in their hearts. The Ruach Hakodesh has gifted every one of them with repentance. Before they came, they made confession and restitution for their sins. The shed blood of the lamb without blemish is symbolically offered, symbolic of the Ha-Mashiach provision of absolution. God accepts the propitiation, the sacrifice. Then those assembled Jews stand perfect before God; there is no guilt or blame or shame attached to them anymore. How can God work such a miracle? It is because in the place of every Jew present there before God, there stands a substitute in their place. It is the Ha-Mashiach redemption. That is the mechanism by which God was able to snatch Enoch and Elijah to keep Him company upstairs, to remind Himself continually that He had a Messianic obligation to the human race. That is what Adam, Abel, Enoch, Elijah, Noah, Abraham, Jacob, and Moses believed. That is what the great Aaronic priesthood stood for, and what the Israelites were taught and by which they lived. Israel has forgotten that stupendous miracle since the loss of the Second Temple. The advertised religious system they now appear to believe is that they can pass the judgement bar of God through their own perfect keeping of the law, or through Kabbalah. The Tanak teaches no such alternate routes. There can be no substitution for Messianic redemption, as Cain the son of Adam and Eve discovered. No fruits and vegetables will avail. The blood of the lamb without blemish must be shed on their behalf.

King David understood the Final Judgement extremely well; he faced it every time he broke the law of God, the primitive Torah. After he had committed the most heinous triple sin of his life, for a moment he thought he could get away with it. But there was a knock at his covetous, adulterous, murderous bedroom door where he had sequestered Bathsheba. It was Nathan the Prophet with the accusation: "Thou art the man" who had stolen the sheep of the poor man and feasted with its flesh. Here is Nathan speaking the words of God:

> And Nathan said to David, That man is you! Thus said the
> Lord, the God of Israel: "It was I who anointed you king
> over Israel and it was I who rescued you from the hand of
> Saul . . . And I gave you the House of Israel and Judah; and
> if that were not enough, I would give you twice as much

more. Why have you flouted the command of the Lord, and done what displeases Him? You have put Uriah the Hittite to the sword; you took his wife . . . and [you] had him killed by the sword of the Ammonites" . . . [Then] David said to Nathan *"I stand guilty before the Lord!"* (2 Sam. 12:7-13, *The Jewish Study Bible*; emphasis added)

David stood there at his adulterous bedroom door, with Bathsheba tremblingly cowering behind him, before God, the great judge of all the earth, accused and convicted and sentenced to eternal death. So stands every human born on the planet. All humanity stands guilty of breaking the law of God. Psalm 51 records how the Ruach Hakodesh found David and gifted him with repentance, which he embraced with his whole heart. Messianic redemption was his only hope.

> Have mercy upon me, O God . . .
> Wash me thoroughly of my iniquity
> And purify me of my sin . . .
> Against You alone have I sinned . . .
> You are just in your sentence
> And right in your judgement . . .
> Hide Your face from my sins
> Blot out all my iniquities . . .
> Do not cast me out of Your presence
> Or take your Holy Spirit from me . . .
> Save me from bloodguilt,
> O God, God my deliverer . . .
> You do not want me to bring sacrifices . . .
> True sacrifice to God is a contrite spirit
> God, You will not despise
> A contrite and crushed heart . . .
> Then You will want sacrifices offered in Righteousness,
> Burnt and whole offerings;
> Then bulls will be offered on Your altar.
> (Ps. 51, selected verses. *The Jewish Study Bible*)

It is all there: the scene of the crime; the criminal who had broken the Torah; the judgement bar with the judge of all the earth seated on His throne; the repentance gifted by the Holy Spirit in David's frightened, frail, fallen, quivering human heart; the confession and restitution (the sentence that was passed which he had to bear); and finally the sacrificial animal without blemish, the Ha-Mashiach absolution. It was a private Day of Atonement for King David, one of the most heinous sinners of all time. But he stood perfect before God because God now saw only the Messiah, bleeding and dead on the altar, mightily protecting David, who is now perfect in his blamelessness. He is forgiven. The blood has been splashed on the Ark of the Covenant and the Mercy Seat. That is sheer grace. That is the Messianic miracle that is available to everyone born on the planet. Primitive Judaism is the most exciting and saving religion. *Where has it gone?*

David talks further about the Final Judgement. He understood that he was a sinner, but he exulted in the Ha-Mashiach shield that protected him, realising that it would cost blood—divine Ha-Mashiach blood. That is not antinomian! This teaching of the Lord was his delight:

> Happy is the man who has not followed the counsel of the wicked . . . rather, *the teaching of the Lord* is his delight. Therefore the wicked will not survive judgement, nor will sinners, in the assembly of the righteous. For the Lord cherishes the way of the righteous, but the way of the wicked is doomed . . . . But I have installed My King on Zion, My holy mountain! Let me tell of the decree: the Lord said to me, You are My Son, I have fathered You this day. (Ps. 1, 2, *The Jewish Study Bible*)

The translators of *The Jewish Study Bible* recognize that this is a reference to the Messiah.[282] David recognized that the Ha-Mashiach intervention was lacking in the wicked who were doomed. The Ha-Mashiach intervention is a gift that must be grasped. It is pure grace; it is not forced and not compulsory. It abides by free will, which was a quality bestowed in Eden. It must be claimed wholeheartedly.

The wisdom book of Koheleth (Ecclesiastes) concludes with these words.

> The sum of the matter (much study), when all is said and done: Revere God and observe His commandments! For this applies to all mankind: that God will call every creature to account for everything unknown, be it good or bad. (Eccles. 12:13, *The Jewish Study Bible*)

Destiny is the outcome of obedience to or disregard for Torah. Because all are disobedient at some time or other, it is those who grasp Ha-Mashiach intervention who are judged as righteous. That is the only Tanakian route to being deemed 100 percent righteous, required by God's law. Isaiah classifies all humanity as being on level ground.

> We have all become like an unclean thing, and all our virtues like a filthy rag. we are all withering like leaves, and our iniquities, like a wind, carry us off. (Isa. 64:5, *The Jewish Study Bible*)

The Talmud has definite views about the final judgement. The judge will award Gan Eden for the righteous and Gehinnom for the wicked. But if God is to deal justly, He must send all to Gehinnom, because all are as filthy rags, and all have broken the law. The rabbinic sages stated that one of the big questions asked in the Final Judgement is, "Did you hope for the salvation of the Messiah?" (Shab. 31a, cited in Cohen p. 375). If you did, you are counted righteous.

Humans die at different times, and so their final judgement is meted out at different times. The fate of the dead righteous is hidden in the salvation of the Messiah, and they are awarded Gan Eden at the resurrection. And what of the living righteous at the time of the resurrection? They are also trusting in Messianic salvation and will be awarded Gan Eden. The major standard of judgement is the salvation provided by the Messiah. The righteous are those who trust in the Messiah; that is the grace spoken of by the rabbinic sages.

C. The New World

The New World will be proclaimed after the Judgement and the Resurrection. The Messiah will be in charge. Much of what has been described above as the Tanakian portrayal of events encompassing the Ha-Mashiach and the Resurrection include the proclamation of the New World as a natural follow on. The scriptures quoted above smoothly slide into the realization of the New World.

Daniel 2, which was the dream of Nebuchadnezzar, pictured the stone cut out of the mountain that grinds the image to powder.

> And in the time of those kings, the God of Heaven will establish a kingdom that shall never be destroyed, a kingdom that shall not be transferred to another people. It will crush and wipe out all these kingdoms, but shall itself last forever. (Dan. 2:44, *The Jewish Study Bible*)

> I looked on . . . until the Ancient of Days came and Judgement was rendered in favour of the holy ones of the Most High, for the time had come, and the holy ones took possession of the kingdom. (Dan. 7:21-22, *The Jewish Study Bible*)

There are several pictures of the New World in the Tanak. Many are mixtures of the Messianic sacrifice and the release it brings, together with the triumphal arrival of the Messianic Judge and King who will reign from Jerusalem. Many of the Tanakian writers mix the two events. Isaiah is prolific in these pictures and mixes up the Messianic accomplishments of atonement and judgement and kingly reign. David also is prolific in Messianic utterances and mixes the same. Jeremiah saw the New World through Messianic realization. Here are some of their pictures:

> But a shoot shall grow out of the stump of Jesse
> A twig shall sprout from his stock . . . .
> Justice shall be the girdle of his loins,
> And faithfulness the girdle of his waist.
> The wolf shall dwell with the lamb,
> The leopard lie down with the kid,
> The calf, the beast of prey, and the fatling together,
> With a little boy to herd them.
> The cow and the bear shall graze,
> Their young shall lie down together;
> And the lion, like the ox, shall eat straw.
> A babe shall play over a viper's hole
> And an infant pass his hand
> Over an adder's den.
> In all My sacred mount
> Nothing evil or vile shall be done;
> For the land shall be filled with devotion to the Lord
> As water covers the sea.
> (Isa. 11:1, 5-9, *The Jewish Study Bible*)

> For Behold! I am creating a new heaven and a new earth;
> The former things shall not be remembered,
> They shall never come to mind.
> Be glad and rejoice forever in what I am creating.
> For I shall create Jerusalem as a joy,
> And her people as a delight;
> And I will rejoice in Jerusalem
> And delight in her people.
> Never again shall be heard there
> The sounds of weeping and wailing . . . .
> The wolf and the lamb shall graze together,
> And the lion shall eat straw like the ox,
> And the serpent's food shall be earth,

In all My sacred mount
Nothing evil or vile shall be done.
(Isa. 65:17-25, *The Jewish Study Bible*)

For as the new heavens and the new earth
Which I will make
Shall endure by My will—declares the Lord—
So shall your seed and name endure.
And new moon after new moon
And Sabbath after Sabbath,
All flesh shall come to worship Me—saith the Lord.
(Isa. 66:22-23, *The Jewish Study Bible*)

And your people, all of them righteous,
Shall possess the land for all time;
They are the shoot that I planted,
My handiwork in which I glory.
(Isa. 60:21, *The Jewish Study Bible*)

But I have installed My King on Zion,
My holy mountain . . .
Ask it of Me,
And I will make the nations your domain;
Your estate, the limits of the earth.
(Ps. 2:6-8, *The Jewish Study Bible*)

Shepherds [kings] who let the flock of My pasture stray and scatter . . . . And [now] I Myself will gather the remnant of My flock from all the lands to which I have banished them, and I will bring them back to their pasture . . . And none of them shall be missing—declares the Lord. See a time is coming . . . when I will raise up a true branch of David's line. He shall reign as King and shall prosper, and He shall do what is just and right in the land. In His days Judah shall be delivered and Israel shall dwell secure. And this is the name by which he shall be called: "The Lord is our Vindicator." (Jer. 23:1-6, *The Jewish Study Bible*)

This passage from Jeremiah is recognized by Jewish scholars as referring to Ha-Mashiach and the establishment of the New World.[283] The Hebrew word translated here by *The Jewish Study Bible* as "vindicator" is "sid-qe-nu," which appears in several places in the Tanak and is translated variously as "prosperity," "straight" (in business), "vindicator," and "righteousness." "YHVH sid-qe-nu" is one of God's Ha-Mashiach names, and it is very appropriate here as "righteousness." The righteous people who have gained entrance into the New World are there because of the Ha-Mashiach provision of His perfect righteousness.

> Ah, that day is awesome;
> There is none like it!
> It is a time of trouble for Jacob,
> But he shall be delivered from it.
> In that day . . . . I will break the yoke
> From off your neck
> And I will rip off your bonds.
> Strangers shall no longer
> Make slaves of them;
> Instead, they shall serve the Lord their God
> And David, the King
> Whom I will raise up for them.
> (Jer. 30:7-9 *The Jewish Study Bible*)

> See the days are coming—declares the Lord—when I will fulfil the promise that I made concerning the House of Israel and the House of Judah. In those days and at that time, I will raise up a true branch of David's line, and He shall do what is just and right in the land. In those days Judah shall be delivered and Israel shall dwell secure. And this is what she shall be called: "The Lord is our Vindicator."
> (Jer.:14-16, *The Jewish Study Bible*)

In this passage the word "sid-qe-nu," which is translated as "vindicator," can also be translated as "righteousness." The intent of the passage is to provide assurance that a New World is coming where the Messiah will restore Israel. All the foregoing prophetic utterances about Messiah, resurrection, and the New World are not restricted benefits for only Jews in current, literal Israel. The atonement and the restoration of immortality are not for Jews alone; it is not the plan laid out in the Tanak. However, current, literal Israel has a job to do: to carry out the Abrahamic Covenant and to herald the coming Messiah. There is a definite purpose in this plan for Israel to occupy its own homeland at this time. In the New World there will be no sin, no death, and no wrongdoing, and the Messiah will reign over immortal human subjects as king from everlasting to everlasting. Because the Abrahamic Covenant is the basis of primitive Judaism, literal Israel is not the sole beneficiary of the Torah, Messiah, resurrection, and the New World. The agreement between God and Abraham shows that all nations are to find blessedness through the influence of the Jews. This places a tremendous responsibility on the shoulders of every Jew on the planet. Salvation is of and through the Jews, and Jews have a responsibility to declare the Messianic advent. The central benefit is the role and accomplishment of the Ha-Mashiach atonement, a plan laid down at Creation according to the Tanak. Therefore literal Israel today must move back to primitive redemptive Judaism.

Talmudic Judaism broadly denies primitive redemptive Judaism, the Judaism of Abraham, Jacob, and Moses, since the loss of the Second Temple. A gradual substitution has been made to replace Messianic entrance to the New World with a pretended personal perfect keeping of the Torah. To keep God's law should be the avowed aim of sanctified living, but it can and will never be perfect in this mortal life. The original pathway inaugurated by God at Creation was Messianic atonement. Apart from assembling together on the Day of Atonement, Israel has not seized hold of the Tanakian Messiah who provides that atonement.

Speaking for the Talmudic scholars, Abraham Cohen says:

> The divinely appointed agent for the accomplishment of the Resurrection is Elijah. "The Resurrection of the dead will come through Elijah" (Sot. IX. 15), who will likewise act as the herald to announce the advent of the Messiah

(See Malachi 4:5). The reawakened life will be of endless duration. "The righteous whom the Holy One, blessed be He, will restore to life will never return to their dust" (Sanh. 92a).[284]

This is a marvellous statement by Cohen and agrees with the context of the Tanak. Unfortunately, the Talmud does not get the clear picture of Messianic redemption. The more the great rabbinic scholars magnified the Torah as a substitute salvation, the more they strayed from Ha-Mashiach redemption. And for their lack of deciphering the redemptive work of the Ha-Mashiach, redemptive Judaism was slowly relegated to mysticism, and many educated and prominent Jews disavowed it over the 2,000 years of the diaspora. The Jewish scholars became rather sensitive to claims of Messianic figures that arose, like Bar Kockba, Shimon Ben-Koshiba, Shabbetai Zevi, and Yeshua of Nazareth. They feared reprisals and slaughters by their conquering occupiers. They also were looking more for a political and military figure who could restore their homeland and secure their freedom from their occupiers and enemies.

Cohen goes on to make a very cogent further observation on analysis of the Talmud.

> In the eschatological doctrine of the Talmud a clear divergence of opinion may be traced. The earlier generations of the Rabbis identified the Messianic era with the World to Come. The promised Redeemer would bring the existing world-order to an end and inaugurate the timeless sphere in which the righteous would lead a purely spiritual existence freed from the trammels of the flesh. Subsequent teachers regarded the Messianic period as but a transitory stage between this world and the next.[285]

Cohen cites rabbinic reticence to explore the transition between this world and the next.

"This world is like a vestibule before the World to Come; prepare yourself in the vestibule that you may enter into "the hall" (Aboth IV. 21). But what is to be experienced by those who will be privileged to enter "the hall" has not been disclosed even to the seers of Israel.[286]

Apparently the Talmudic seers of Israel had a mental block and did not fathom the statement of Isaiah: "No eye hath seen what God, and nobody but Thee, will work for him that waiteth for Him (sic) Isaiah 64:4, Ber.34b."[287]

But the Tanak abounds in Messianic prophecies, which lead to the denouement of the world to come. Everything is disclosed in the Tanak. The Talmudic seers did not grasp the redemptive Messianic function. Obviously they saw that there was a sinful mortal state in the "vestibule" and a sinless, immortal state in "the hall." But they did not comprehend Messianic atonement to be the doorway between. They had forgotten the promise made outside the gates of Eden of Messianic atonement necessary for re-entry. They had forgotten the significance of the Temple service in the sacrifice of the animal without blemish before the high priest could take the blood into the Most Holy Place. Instead they came up with the following substitute mechanisms.

Sufferings which were innocently incurred and privations voluntarily assumed in this world must help to gain admittance into the World to Come.

Rabbi Judah the Prince said, Whoever accepts the delights of this world will be deprived of the delights of the World to Come.

Man best qualifies himself in the "vestibule" for the pure, spiritual atmosphere of "the hall" by devoting himself to the study and practice of the precepts revealed by God. "He who has acquired for himself words of Torah has acquired for himself life in the World to Come" (Aboth II. 8) . . . . In the hour of man's departure from the world neither silver nor gold nor precious stones nor pearls accompany him, but only Torah and good works.

When R. Eliezer was ill, his disciples went in to visit him. They said to him: "Master, teach us the ways of life whereby we may be worthy of the life of the World to Come." He said to them, "Be careful of the honour of your colleagues; restrain your children from recitation (parading of superficial knowledge), and seat them between the knees of the Sages; and when you pray, know before Whom you stand; and on that account will you be worthy of the life of the World to Come." (Ber. 28b)

Among those who will inherit the World to Come are: who resides in the land of Israel and who rears his son in the study of Torah. (Pes. 113a)

He who studies the Laws of Judaism is assured of being a son of the World to Come. (B.M. 59a)

He who is meek and humble, walks about with a lowly demeanor, studies the Torah constantly, and takes no credit to himself"(Sanh. 88b).

Who will inherit the World to Come? He who joins the benediction: "Blessed art Thou Who hast redeemed Israel" to the Eighteen Benedictions. (Ber. 8a)[288]

In these quoted passages above, the only statement with any Tanakian merit is the last one, because it recognizes the Messianic redeemer of Israel: "Blessed art Thou who hast redeemed Israel." He is the door between the vestibule and the hall. Good works must be perfect works to gain entry to heaven. But no human has perfect lawkeeping to offer as an entrance ticket. "All are filthy rags." The most righteous person must go through Ha-Mashiach.

To be fair to Abraham Cohen, his comment about the Talmudic reasons he lists, for and against entry into the World to Come, is very insightful.

> It must be obvious that in these utterances we cannot have a dogmatic verdict on the eternal fate of the persons concerned. They are nothing more than a hyperbolical expression of approval or disapproval. More importance must, however, be attached to this extract: "All Israel has a share in the World to Come, as it is said, 'Thy people shall be all righteous, they shall inherit the land for ever'—Isaiah 60:21.[289]

This is a marvellous realization by Cohen, and I am sure he understood that no one can keep the law 100 percent of the time and must rely on repentance, Messianic atonement, and Messianic righteousness to enter the World to Come. God allows no other mode of entry; that is the gist of Tanakian Judaism.

Another contentious issue in the Talmud was whether Gentiles would be permitted to enter the World to Come.

> R. Eliezer declared, "No Gentiles will have a share in the World to Come; as it is said: The wicked shall return to the nether world, even all the nations that forget God" (Psalm 9:17)—the "wicked" refers to the evil among Israel. R. Joshua said to him, "If the verse had stated, The wicked shall return to the nether world and all the nations," and had stopped there, I should have agreed with you. Since, however, the text adds, "that forget God," behold there must be righteous men among the nations who will have a share in the World to Come (Tosifta Sanh. XIII. 2). Maimonides . . . declared, "the pious of the Gentiles will have a share in the World to Come" (Hil. Teshubah III. 5).[290]

A further contentious issue in the Talmud is the age of accountability in children. Some of the answers listed in the Talmud are: "From the hour of birth . . . From the time it can Speak . . .

From the time of conception . . . From the time of circumcision . . . From the time that it utters Amen."[291]

To close this chapter dealing with judgement and entrance to the New World, or the World to Come, the Tanakian operative condition for qualification is righteousness (Isa. 60:21). The outcome of the judgement is the declaration that those found to be righteous are saved, and the wicked are damned. Entrance to the World to Come is given only to the righteous. Righteousness is perfect obedience to Torah. Because all humanity before God since Eden have no lifetime record of perfect obedience to Torah, then all should be assigned to Gehinnom. Therefore in order to declare some righteous and deserving of immortality, there has to be Messianic intervention. That is why YHVH has assumed the name 'Sid-qe-nu," which means "Righteousness." That is the achievement of Ha-Mashiach, who provides atonement and righteousness. God Himself provides. The Lord our God is one in Creation and redemption and glorification. Blessed be He forevermore. Amen.

CHAPTER 21

THE HA-MASHIACH OF ISRAEL

God is a complex being. His existence is complex, and not in the sense that He is infinite or omnipotent or omniscient, or in any of His other attributes. *God is complex in His emotional personality.* God has emotions eminently demonstrable in all His dealings with humanity. The Tanak is His conversation with humanity, and this document is signed, sealed, and delivered as a sacred document because it contains God's thoughts, emotions, opinions, and plans. It is an extraordinarily emotional document making real His intrigues. There is none other that has evolved in the history of Israel claiming to be sacred until the arrival of the B'rit Hadashah, which also claims to be a conversation with God; that claim will be dealt with in a work I plan to publish in the future. It deserves attention because it is also a completely Jewish document, written by Jews and about a Jew. The B'rit Hadashah claims to be a fulfilment of the Tanak and claims a solid connection with the Tanak. However, this present work is about the Tanak, closed by the Sanhedrin, Israel's most authoritative body.

In human terms an emotion may be defined primarily as a state of mind that is expressed or suppressed by the body. God's emotions of love, anger, patience, sympathy, forgiveness, forbearance, desire, satisfaction, disappointment, sorrow, remorse, and pleasure are expressed or suppressed in the context of creating, redeeming, and glorifying His lost treasure, the human race. His motivation is to restore the face-to-face communion with humanity that He had in Gan Eden. This is His greatest pleasure known to us, and the reason for the Creation of the world. All His plans and methods to enable this restoration are expressed in Ruach Hakodesh and

334

Ha-Mashiach manifestations of Himself. These powers of His majesty are directed to the human race to redeem, sanctify, and glorify humanity. Humanity is His greatest treasure, and He wants us back in His bosom. To be perfectly and adamantly clear, there is only one God who manifests as Elohim. His final goal is accomplished by Himself. Ruach Hakodesh and Ha-Mashiach are the media of His emotions, and they are one in Elohim. They are not separate from Himself but are part and parcel of the emotional mechanisms of Elohim, blessed be He, the Lord our God is one. Ruach Hakodesh and Ha-Mashiach are God's creative, redemptive, and glorifying actions in handling humanity, to bring them back to Eden and immortality.

In my contemplation of primitive Tanakian Judaism, I see the history and future of planet earth summarised in the three words: creation, redemption, glorification. All three concepts have been part of Torah from eternity, and they are embodied as central and emphatic Tanakian concepts. They are the effective operative thoughts of Elohim, blessed be He. All God's emotions familiar to us are expressed through Ruach Hakodesh and Ha-Mashiach. In my search of Jewish writings, I find much in the Talmud that authenticates these three Tanakian concepts. The endorsement of the Ruach Hakodesh and the Ha-Mashiach as effective in the desires and aspirations of the Hebrews is massively supported in the Tanak and the Talmud. They are the essential parts of the Jewish fabric, and they are the lifeblood of Israel. They are the Jewish past, present, and glorious future.

In this chapter I want to analyse and discuss the structure and function of Ha-Mashiach. There is already an extensive preamble in the previous chapter. Gershom Scholem, whom I regard as a modern giant in Judaism, has made an intensive and inspiring study of the above concepts, and I will lean heavily on his keen insights and sensibilities. In his essay "The Crisis of Tradition in Jewish Messianism," he makes Isaiah 2:3 pivotal in his definition of Torah. In this chapter Isaiah is describing the apocalyptic "End-Time." Isaiah 2:3 states, "From Zion goes forth the Torah and the word of the Lord from Jerusalem." Scholem interprets this verse to be referring to Messianic Torah. He qualifies it as follows.

> It is simply Torah, not old Torah and not new Torah. It is *untouched* Torah, which has not known any crisis and which in the prophetic vision is seen in its full development. Related to this is the notion, widely found in Rabbinic literature, that the Torah of the Messianic Age will solve the contradictions and difficulties which now exist in regard to several points. On this issue the sources of Jewish tradition are nearly all clear. There is progress in the understanding of the Torah which in the Messianic age reaches its height. But the idea of a radical change or a questioning of the *traditional* element was eliminated and was not even perceived as a real possibility.[292]

Scholem quotes from W. D. Davies's *Torah in the Messianic Age.*

> Since the Days of Messiah represent the religious and political consummation of the national history and, however idealized, still belong to the world in which we live, it is only natural that in the Messianic Age the Torah not only retain its validity but be better understood and better fulfilled than ever before.[293]

In his discussion, Scholem is protective of "traditional Judaism" and wants to see Messianic Torah in tune with it. It is not clear why Scholem finds it necessary to envisage a 'Messianic Torah' that is neither 'old' nor 'new'. Currently, Torah in Jewry is generally viewed as the combined written Torah (the Tanak) and oral Torah (the Talmud). Why Scholem needs reassurance that these will not be cast aside by Messianic Torah is unclear, unless he had the feeling that traditional (Talmudic) Judaism was being threatened by the B'rit Hadashah, which is also a "concentrate" of Messianism. Certainly the Christian Church had conducted a kind of vendetta against the Jews by saying that the Jewish dispensation had been replaced by the Christian dispensation, and that the Tanak had been superseded by the B'rit Hadashah. Several religio-political Christian powers in medieval Europe destroyed synagogues as well as banned and burned Jewish books and Torah scrolls; this was irrational and misguided. But there are several Jewish thinkers and organized bodies (e.g., the Karaites Jews and the Messianic Jews) who reject the Talmud as Torah, whereas the Tanak has virtual universal acclaim as Torah among both Jews and Christians. In fact, Scholem himself has already recognized and described the entire Messianic scene from the Tanak, as I will show shortly. I believe that there is only one earthly Jewish Torah and that is the Tanak. The Torah of Messianism is the central and dominant part of it. I am not certain exactly why Scholem uses the word "untouched" Torah. Perhaps he means "unfulfilled" Torah.

The dream, the beauty, and the completeness of the Messianic description in the Tanak clearly needs to be carefully deciphered. More than any other modern Jewish writer to my knowledge, Scholem has carefully deciphered the Messianic revelation in the Tanak. It must be acknowledged that there is a kind of unintentional fudging or mixing of the various portrayals of the Messiah by the writers of the Tanak. They appear to have been so overawed and overwhelmed by the coming of the Messianic Age that they let separate 'suffering' and 'majestic' events of Messianic action run together so that they were not functionally and clearly comprehended by the general Jewish rabbinic readership of the Tanak. Perhaps the Tanakian writers expected everything Messianic to be accomplished in one swoop. There is absolutely no doubt that two roles for Messiah are described in the Tanak. These separate roles appear to have been planned by God from eternity, are basic to the Judaism of Moses, and are supported by parts of the Talmud. They also conveniently and perfectly fit into the plan of Scholem's scheme, described below. The Ha-Mashiach is depicted both as 'a suffering redeemer' and 'a glorious conquering king', both being well described in the apocalyptic writings of the Tanak. They both are the definitive, directional, and dominant Messianic themes of the Tanak. These Ha-Mashiach themes of the Tanak are inexorably driven by the will of YHVH. Rabbi Judah the Prince recognized the two roles of Ha-Mashiach. So does Scholem:

> Revelation in Judaism is considered the voice which resounds from Sinai throughout the world, a voice which, although it can be heard, is not immediately meaningful . . . .

> In juxtaposition to all of this in the history of Judaism stands *Messianism in its manifold facets*. It expresses the intrusion of a new dimension of the present—redemption—into history which enters into a problematic relation with tradition. The Messianic idea required a long period of time until it could emerge in post-biblical Jewish literature as the product of very diverse impulses, which in the Hebrew Bible still exist side by side without connection or unity. Only after the Bible did such varying conceptions as that of an ideal state of the world, of a catastrophic collapse of history, of the restoration of the Davidic Kingdom, and of the "Suffering Servant" [of Isaiah] merge with the prophetic view of "The Day of the Lord" and "A Last Judgment." . . .

> *Two elements* are combined in the Messianic idea and they determine the historical configurations which Messianism has assumed in Judaism. These two elements are the *restorative and the utopian*.[294]

The description of "manifold facets" and "two elements" allows for the different roles of the Messiah in Scholem's mind. These restorative and utopian roles are initiated as temporal roles of the Ha-Mashiach, and therefore the redemption must come before the catastrophic apocalyptic events, which are superbly triumphal. Atonement must precede triumph; it is the preparation for triumph. The atonement is the restorative role. The triumphal catastrophic event ushers in the utopian role.

In two earlier chapters of this book, I have twice produced the Messianic names, culled from the Tanak, with qualities eminently taught in the Tanak and upheld in the Talmud. They must be emphasized again here. They come garbed in the emotional expressions of YHVH as Elohim, blessed be He. The Lord our God is one. It becomes clear that God's names in the Tanak are interchangeable and synonymous with the Ha-Mashiach. Isaiah 63:11-14 is interpreted by *The Jewish Study Bible* as an exposition of God's movement from wrath to grace in judgement. The provision of grace is a Messianic function according to the Tanak, and it is upheld as such in the Talmud as well.[295]

Isaiah pleads, "Surely You are our Father . . . From of old Your name is 'Our Redeemer'" (Isa. 63:16, *The Jewish Study Bible*). Here the Father and redeemer are unmistakably merged into one.

Despite variant and confusing views in the Talmud, the rabbinic sages clearly agreed that the dominant question asked in the Final Judgement is, "Did you hope for the Salvation of the Messiah?"[296] It is therefore quite poignant to conclude that the redemption or salvation is the work of the Messiah. The different appellations of the Messiah in the Tanak are all solidly synonymous with deity. If YHVH is redeemer, then that specific redeemer is YHVH. Here are the names of God with Messianic function, unmistakably written in Hebrew and allowed within God as Elohim.

1. YHVH is the *divine Goel,* redeeming His people (Isa. 63:16)
2. YHVH is *El Shaddah, Adonai,* saviour in the escape from Egypt (Exod. 6:2-3)
3. YHVH is *Ga'a-leta,* the redeemer who delivers Israel from the "Clans of Edom" who seek to destroy them (Exod. 15:13)
4. YHVH is *yom'ru G'uley y'hvah asher G'alam miYad-tzar,* the redeemer who gathers Israel from the ends of the earth in judgement (Ps. 107:2-3)
5. YHVH is *ha-dur,* majestic in the role of deliverer (Isa. 62:11; 63:1)
6. YHVH is *goali,* vindicator, redeemer, and judge, conducting judgement at the latter day upon the earth (Job 19:25)

7. YHVH is *we-goali, Haggoel,* the redeemer (Job 19:25; Ps. 19:14)
8. YHVH is *Goel,* kinsman and redeemer (Num. 5:8)
9. YHVH is *Goel Yisrael,* the redeemer of Israel (Lev. 25; Ps. 39:7)
10. YHVH is *Goel Haddam*, the avenger of blood (1 Sam. 6:20)
11. YHVH is *Goel Adonai Tsuri v'go'ali,* the Lord, my rock and my redeemer (Ps. 19:14)
12. YHVH is *Tsidkenu (Sid-qe-nu)* the Lord our righteousness (Jer. 23:5-6).

The Tanak further presents the Messiah in two emergent forms:

- *The Human Form—A son that is born and becomes a "suffering servant" Messiah* (Isa. 9; 52; 53; Ps. 1 and 2). These passages strongly support the human manifestation of Messiah. He is "fathered" by God and is therefore a divine penetration of humanity.
- *The Divine Form—An eternal, majestic, and powerful king and judge* (Joel 2:28; 3:1-2; 3:12; 4:1-21; Ps. 2). The Books of Isaiah and Daniel attest to Messianic power, majesty, and divinity.

Messiah is one with deity and has two roles, and these roles are manifested in human and divine forms or expressions. Earthly Messianic portrayal begins in Gan Eden, and I am exhilarated by Scholem's understanding and deciphering of it. Scholem strongly and clearly recognizes the great concepts active in the history of the world in terms of Creation, redemption, and glorification. He describes but does not subscribe to the variant Lurianic reinvention of Creation, redemption, and glorification. He identifies and rejects the Lurianic perversion of Messiah as he enthusiastically endorses the Tanakian Edenic story. He sees the fall of Adam into sin and the need for redemption. Scholem's association of the Tree of Life in Gan Eden with Messiah, and the Tree of Knowledge of Good and Evil as leading to eternal death, is masterful: it reveals his commitment to Messianic restoration of immortality and a perfect world. In his essay 'Toward an Understanding of the Messianic Idea' (*The Messianic Ideea in Judaism*, p. 23) he is absolutely clear.

> The power of evil, of destruction and death, has become real in the free will of man. The purpose of the law, which as it were constitutes the Torah as it can be read in the light—or shadow!—of the Tree of Knowledge, is to confine this power if not to overcome it entirely. But in the Messianic redemption the full glory of the utopian again breaks forth, although characteristically and in keeping with the idea of the Tree of Life it is conceived as a restoration of the state of things in Paradise.

Scholem sees the entire Jewish dispensation as being active in the three spheres he labels as conservative, restorative, and utopian factors. He does not see the Jewish dispensation as a final failure. These factors are quite appropriate and Tanakian.

Scholem's Factors:

1. CONSERVATIVE FACTOR: Here he cites the Jewish Body of Halachah, which came into prominence post-Second Temple destruction, the Mishnah, which was redacted by Rabbi Judah the Prince. It is Talmudic, and its formation can be argued to have commenced soon after the Babylonian conquest centuries before, evolving into Mishnah and Gemara. It filled the hiatus after the prophetic utterances of the Tanak 'ceased'. In this hiatus, the Tanakian conversation with God was followed by a Talmudic conversation of the Jews with each other. Scholem sees the Body of Halachah that resulted as a cleansing agent, a necessary factor—which indeed it is, if one is describing cleansing as sanctification. He describes tension between Halachah and Messianism.

> The opposition between restorative and purely utopian, radical elements in the conception of the Messianic Torah

brings an element of uncertainty into the Halachah's attitude to Messianism. The battle lines are by no means clearly drawn.

Unfortunately, a penetrating and serious study of this relationship of the medieval Halachah to Messianism is one of the most important yet unfulfilled desiderata of the scientific study of Judaism....

As long as Messianism appears as an abstract hope, as an element totally deferred to the future which had no living significance to the life of the Jew in the present, the opposition between the essentially conservative rabbinic and the never completely defined Messianic authority, which was to be established from entirely new dimensions of the utopian, could remain without real tension; indeed, there could be attempts to create a certain harmony between such authorities.

But whenever there was an actual eruption of such [Messianic] Hope . . . the tension which exists between these two forms of religious authority immediately became noticeable.[297]

Scholem sees Messianism as superior to Halachah and labels the relationship between the two as tension. This is pure Tanakian theology as described by all its writers. Nowhere does the Tanak teach that a redemptive Messiah is not necessary or is superseded by Halachah. Scholem's significant lament is that the relationship between Halachah and Messianism has not been given "scientific study."

If Scholem places the inability of humanity to keep Halachah perfectly (a fallen and sinful state)—which he certainly admits—between Halachah (as Torah) and Messianism, then he will see the relationship between the two. Ha-Mashiach provides redemption from sin, which is disobedience to the Torah. But Scholem errs in sometimes confusing Halachah with the Messianic redemption in his writings. Halachah is a sanctifying agent but is not a redemptive one, because *atonement is by Messiah, not by Halachah.* Scholem is reluctant to abandon Halachah as a quasi redemptive agent, which is why he includes it here. Halachah need not be abandoned, but it needs better definition for the modern age as "sanctifying guidelines by which to live." Mosaic halachah was the educative and refining agent for a mob of unruly slaves from Egypt, and it also serves as a discipline for all wayward sinners. But Scholem knew that sin came into the world because humanity was disobedient to Edenic primitive Torah, which was an 'Edenic Halachah'. All humanity is weak in Halachah, and there is no perfect human record. A redeemer is needed.

2. THE RESTORATIVE FACTOR: Another great concept in Judaism that has lamentably not received "scientific study" is that of Isaiah's 'suffering servant'. Both Judah the Prince and Scholem consider this title a Messianic figure. In the redemption described in Isaiah 53, the suffering servant is "crushed" and dies. The suffering servant later achieves the reward of a conquering King.

> For He was cut off from the land of the living,
> Through the sin of my people, who deserved the punishment.
> And his grave was set among the wicked,
> "And with the rich in his death.
> (Isa. 53:8-9, *The Jewish Study Bible*)

But Isaiah does not leave Him dead in the grave:

> *My righteous servant makes many righteous,*
> *It is their punishment that he bears;*
> Assuredly, I will give him the many as his portion,
> He shall receive the multitude as his spoil.
> For he exposed himself to death
> And was numbered among the sinners,
> Whereas he bore the guilt of the many
> And made intercession for them"
> (Isa. 53:12, *The Jewish Study Bible*)

King David's Naked Dance

How can this be the fate of an eternal Messiah for whom death is not an expected end? This idea is repelled by Jews because they want a powerful political Messiah to usher in the Messianic Age where they will be dominant.

Years before Isaiah described the 'suffering servant', King David, as a Messianic figure, grappled with this redemptive Messianic idea in Psalm 4 and 6 where he is fighting the death of his body. He achieves denouement in Psalm 16 where he names his body parts and pleads for their preservation. We all know that King David died and was buried, and his body turned to dust, but in this triumphant, Messianic psalm he proclaims:

> So my heart rejoices, my whole being exults,
> And my body rests secure.
> For you will not abandon me to Sheol,
> Or let your faithful One see the Pit"
> (Ps. 16:9-10, *The Jewish Study Bible*)

The King James Version is more dramatic:

> Therefore my heart is glad, and my glory rejoiceth;
> My flesh also shall rest in hope.
> *For Thou wilt not leave my soul in Sheol,*
> *Neither wilt Thou permit Thy HOLY ONE to see corruption.*
> (Ps. 16:9-10, KJV)

In the Masoretic text, the Hebrew words "cha-si-yd-kha" must be translated as "Your Holy One," instead of "Faithful One." The Messianic intent here is very secure, he is the Holy One.

The Tanak insists that death must be conquered to regain immortality, and Messiah is the redeemer and the one to do it. The 'suffering servant' does indeed taste of death, to vanquish it, but he does not stay in Sheol. In his power all Israel—indeed, all humanity—can leave the Pit. Isaiah is perfectly clear about this, and so is David, who saw atonement in it.

Scholem cites the Messianic intervention, giving the Messiah the job of redemption. This thrills my soul. And just as Moses and the prophets saw two pictures of the Messiah, so does Scholem. Just as they described the Messiah as redeemer and king, so does Scholem. But he lets the two functions or roles of the Messiah run into each other, and he does not appear to be able to assign the two roles a temporal chronological sequence. He must do this because he is very enthusiastic and excited about the apocalyptic events that are involved, which he strongly espouses.

3. UTOPIAN FACTOR: Here Scholem clearly sees the success of the restorative or redemptive factor, because he endorses it and sees its fruition in the apocalyptic events. He sees this as a Messianic intervention that portends catastrophe. He calls this utopian because he sees that the old, sinful order is catastrophically and totally wiped away. He subscribes to a new, perfect world order, a utopia ushered in by the Messiah. He does not subscribe to the Kabbalistic distortion of the Messiah as not being a personal intervention by God; Scholem terms Kabbalah as "anarchic" in this respect. He labels all forms of Messianic denial or dilution or liquidation as 'anarchic'. He sees Messiah as a king and the final ruler of a redeemed Israel and the whole world. In its many approaches, Kabbalah does not see it that way. Instead, Kabbalah sees the future in a "continuous but changed" present existence. Kabbalah does not embrace catastrophic apocalypticism, which is basic to the Tanakian concept.

Scholem believes in the resurrection of the dead, the restoration of immortality, and a perfect new world, all of which are apocalyptic, triumphal, and Tanakian. Most of the great rabbinic sages believed in the resurrection of the dead; they castigated those who did not. Scholem is quite challenged by the apocalypticism in the Tanak, and despite his immersion in Kabbalah, he will not let go of apocalypticism. The way I read him, he sees it as the most exciting part of Judaism.[298] And so it is!

Scholem does not discuss the origin, deity, or eternity of Messiah in his essay. But he does not see the Messiah as a transient human figure that is a flash in the pan, or that is restricted to one human lifetime. It seems to me that the Messiah's eternity and deity must be accepted if one is to embrace the apocalypticism of Isaiah and Daniel. In the Messianic function of Elohim, Ha-Mashiach is the architect and enabler of the resurrection. If the Messiah is to be king of the universe, He cannot be that for a day or a human lifetime. So if He comes as a human, He must also embody divinity and eternity. If He is king of the cleansed and immortal New Earth (utopia), He must stay on the throne forever and ever. In traditional (conservative) Judaism there is an enthusiastic embrace of Ruach Hakodesh as God, without surrendering the principle of monotheism. But there is a reluctance to accept Ha-Mashiacch as God. And if Messiah is accepted as deity, then He must be one with God. Blessed be He, the Lord our God is one. In the Talmud there is a specific picture to which I have already drawn attention, where Shechinah is owned by Messiah (or Michael, who is Israel's special guardian) in the Heavenly Temple (see the chapter on Shechinah).

In the progression of Scholem's commitment to conservative, restorative, and utopian factors, he describes these factors as the working elements of God's reclamation of human immortality and a perfect Gan Eden. Tanakian Halachah (if defined as God's initial instruction to Adam and Eve and His continued conversation in the Tanak) is not to be discarded—it is a vital part of primitive Judaism that sanctifies and ennobles, but because it does not achieve absolute human perfection, it cannot be regarded as redemptive. The Tanak specifically identifies the Messiah as the redeemer and the implementer of the atoning redemption. Messiah redeems, and so He is able to bring about the apocalyptic resurrection and Scholem's utopia. Scholem firmly believes in the Tanakian Messiah and the resurrection.

Scholem railed against the nineteenth-century idea of Messianism in Judaism.

> The Nineteenth Century and nineteenth century Judaism, have bequeathed to the modern mind a complex of ideas about Messianism that have led to distortions and

counterfeits from which it is by no means easy to free ourselves. We have been taught that the Messianic idea is part and parcel of the idea of the progress of the human race in the universe, is achieved by man's unassisted and continuous progress, leading to the ultimate liberation of all the goodness and nobility within him. This, in essence, is . . . the result of an attempt to adapt the Messianic conceptions of the prophets and of Jewish religious tradition to the ideals of the French Revolution.

Traditionally, however, the Messianic idea in Judaism was not so cheerful; the coming of the Messiah shakes the foundations of the world. In the view of the prophets and Aggadists, redemption would only follow upon a universal revolutionary disturbance, unparalleled disasters in which history would be dislodged and destroyed. The nineteenth-century view is blind to this catastrophic aspect. It looks only to progress toward infinite perfection. In probing into the roots of this new conception of the Messianic ideal as man's infinite progress and perfectability, we find, surprisingly, that they stem from the Kabbalah . . . .

History was not a development toward any goal. History would reach its terminus, and the new state that ensued would be the result of a totally new manifestation of the divine. In the prophets this stage is called "The Day of the Lord" . . . Accordingly, upon the advent of the "Day of the Lord" all that man has built up in history will be destroyed.

Classical Jewish tradition is fond of emphasizing the catastrophic strain in redemption. If we look at the tenth chapter of the Sanhedrin, where the Talmudists discuss the question of redemption at length, we see that to them it means a colossal uprooting, destruction, revolution, disaster, with nothing of development of progress about it. "The Son of David [Messiah] will come only in a generation wholly guilty or wholly innocent"—a condition beyond the

> realm of human possibility . . . . *Liberation of Israel is the essence, but it will march in step with the liberation of the whole world.*[299]

Scholem truthfully and realistically sees the human condition of being "wholly innocent" as "a condition beyond the realm of human possibility." Scholem thus approves and espouses the Tanakian concepts of Creation, redemption, and glorification of the whole world through Israel, which is the essence of the Abrahamic Covenant. As a modern spiritual giant in Judaism, he accepts the Tanakian concept without reservation, despite being deeply involved with Kabbalah. He adroitly and tenaciously clings to the Tanakian blueprint written by God's servants, the prophets. These plans are laid down by the eternal Elohim, blessed be He. This is the solution to the whole Jewish problem as well as the whole human problem. But Scholem wavered in his adjustment to the rabbinic claims of Halachah as a redeemer. However, he clearly preferred the personal Messianic redeemer, with God being involved in the accomplishment of redemption. He speaks quite plainly about Kabbalah: "For the Kabbalists had no special need of a personal Messiah."[300]

Scholem also clearly perceived that Halachah (the law) could not be kept perfectly throughout a human lifetime. He saw that repentance, confession, and absolution were essential elements of a heavenly redemption by a Messiah in his elaboration of the restorative factor. Scholem desperately embraced the redemptive expiation as a prerequisite to the apocalyptic ushering in of a utopia, a perfect New World where sin was totally eradicated and history was totally destroyed. He discarded the Lurianic inventions of Kabbalah. The cataclysmic apocalypticism of Daniel and Isaiah excited him immensely, and he resisted the Kabbalian attempt to ignore or explain it away with its substitution of reincarnation and Lurianic interpretation. I salute him for being a giant in Israel by his magnification of the Tanak.

What, then, is Israel and all diasporic Jewry looking for when they longingly desire Messiah?

The history of Israel provides a cogent account of her longing for the Messiah. Even before the loss of the Second Temple, the great rabbinic sages in Babylon lost sight of the Aaronic priesthood, the sacrificial system, and the true meaning of the Day of Atonement. After its destruction, with no Temple to remind them, they veered away from redemptive Messianic Judaism. Isolated in Babylon and in a "foreign" Jerusalem, with no Jewish national status to bolster them, the two schools majored in Halachah to fight domination and assimilation. In doing this Jewry was attempting to analyze its soul but was losing sight of its saviour. Subsequently, Greek civilization veered Judaism into its idolatrous lifestyle and philosophical sophistry. Rome reinforced the Hellenistic trend and crushed all national hopes of the Jews. With no Temple and no national pride, they wrapped themselves in Halachah and forgot their redeemer. They wanted political freedom and nationhood, and they wanted a Messiah to be their deliverer and to free them from bondage. They made that desire more important than their redemption from sin. Moses the Patriarch and the Aaronic priesthood were left for dead. The lamb without blemish lost its redemptive meaning. The redeemer from sin was forgotten as they looked for a Messiah to provide only political and national freedom.

The criteria being used in post-Second Temple destruction, medieval, post-Enlightenment, and modern Judaism to identify a Messiah are a shambles. And there is no Tanakian guideline being used. The desire for strong nationhood and release from the diaspora overwhelmed the desire for redemption from sin.

Rabbinic attention to Halachah, and the confusion of Kabbalah with loss of personal Messianic redemption, have led to the problem causing the current religious nightmare. Gershom Scholem is a refreshing fountain of excitement and hope in modern Jewry. Unfortunately he appears to be ignored by the established orthodoxy.

Scholem rejects outright the Enlightenment that followed the French Revolution as a Messianic invention in Judaism. He then describes two historical Messiahs in his writings that did not fit his bill, that did not fit his idea of qualifications for Messiah. They were Yeshua of Nazareth and Sabbatai Zevi. He describes a great gulf between these two Messiahs he rejects.

> One cannot overlook the abyss which yawns between the figure of the Messiah who died for his cause upon the Cross and this figure [Sabbatai Zevi] who became an apostate and played his role in this diguise.[301]

But he gives Yeshua of Nazaraeth very little space and defines his Messiahship as equivalent with "Pauline antinomianism."

> Whereby Christ could be proclaimed "The End of the Law" (Romans 10:4).[302]

Scholem here does not dig deep into the Pauline neurones. He should have remembered his discussion of Abraham Miguel Cardozo's ideas of the written law and the oral law.[303] He also misses the point that the original Greek language of Romans 10 emphasizes the idea that Yeshua is the accomplishment of the law for the sinner who cannot keep it perfectly and stands condemned. According to Paul, Yeshua protects the sinner who repents by providing His perfect lawkeeping. This recalls the messianic intent of Jeremiah 23:5-6, Sid-qe-nu, "the Lord *our* righteousness," in the work of the Messiah's redemptive (substitutionary and mediatorial) capacity.

But Scholem writes reams about Sabbatai Zevi, whom he perceives as having brought great distress and shame to Judaism. He differentiates the two Messiahs qualitatively, although he calls them both antinomian.

Scholem disregards Yeshua of Nazareth's words: "Think not that I came to set aside the Law or the Prophets. I came not to destroy but to fulfil. Till Heaven and Earth pass, one jot or one tittle shall in no wise pass from the Law, till all be fulfilled" (Matt. 5:17-18). And again: "I came not to call the righteous but sinners to repentance" (Luke 5:32). Sinners are transgressors of the law. These words of the Nazarene are not antinomian. Scholem will have to make a better case against the Nazarene.

Scholem also disregards the Pauline dissertation in Romans 3:

> Now do you see it? No one can ever be made right in God's sight by doing what the Law commands. For the more we know of God's laws, the clearer it becomes that we are not obeying them. These laws are meant to show that we are sinners. But now He has shown us a new way, though not new for the prophets spoke about it long ago. (The Living Bible)

Here Paul is recognizing the weakness of the human frame to keep Torah perfectly and pointing to a Messianic alternative of forensic justification and redemption. Perfect keeping of the law has to be forensic because no human can achieve it. That is the meaning of Jeremiah's "Sid-qe-nu," the Lord our righteousness.

Scholem finds Sabbatianism reprehensible because of the abrogation of the law that he had advocated. He titles an entire essay on Sabbatianism as "Redemption Through Sin," which speaks volumes. He goes into a lengthy discussion, full of invective, of the deceptive movement. Scholem goes through intense scrutiny of the reasons why the Jews were led astray by it. In doing this, he illustrates that there is much confusion in Jewry about what the Jews are looking for in a Messiah. They were led astray because they ignored the Messiah promised in the Tanak, first a suffering redeemer and then an apocalyptic and catastrophic arrival of an eternal king.

But in his endeavours to destroy the authenticity of both Sabbatai Zevi and the Nazarene, Scholem does not lay down a set of criteria or have a yardstick from the Tanak to measure the redemptive work of the Messiah. To be fair, in my opinion Scholem has not proved that Yeshua of Nazareth abrogated the Torah. But he quite adequately demonstrates the Sabbatian abrogation of the Torah and the horrible disgrace it caused Judaism.

So we are still looking for what the Jews are wanting in a Messiah, and whether they have a Tanakian blueprint in recognizing Him when He appears. There is no unity in their aspirations or desires, even taking into account all that the Talmud has to say. Scholem comes close to espousing a blueprint, but he has not mastered the chronology of the redemptive function (restorative) and the kingly function (utopian). He vaguely identifies the latter with the resurrection, in which he firmly believes, but he has not fathomed how the preparation for the resurrection is accomplished. Perhaps it was in his comprehension of Isaiah's 'suffering servant'. But he seemed to avoid the exploration of that enormous, redemptive Messianic description as a 'suffering servant'. Scholem is jaundiced by his half-hearted assumption that Halachah had redemptive power, although he conceded that perfect obedience to the law is humanly impossible. But Scholem must be lauded for rejecting outright the Messiahs of the Enlightenment and Kabbalah; instead, he wholeheartedly embraced the Messiah he saw in the Tanak.

There are fixed expressions of Messiah among the different Jewish sects today, from the secular to the ultra-Orthodox. But there have also been evolutionary changes of the ideas of Messianism over the centuries, away from and contrary to Tanakian theological concepts.

The Messiah of Kabbalah and Hasidism

The neutralizing of Messianism in Kabbalah and Hasidism are two related examples of wandering away from Tanakian theology. Gershom Scholem's essay "Neutralization of Messianism in Early Hasidism" tells the whole story. The fact that he uses the word "neutralization" indicates the evolution that took place in basic Kabbalah and early determinant Hasidism, as shaped by Israel Baal Shem. Both in Hasidism and Kabbalistic writings, there is a dedication to tikkun (the re-establishment of the harmonious condition of the world) being achieved by devekut (communion with God). Scholem is clear about his opinion and points out the errors of Kabbalism, the Sabbatian heresy, and Hasidism in dealing with the doctrines of devekut and tikkun.

> What these changes have in common is precisely that element which concerns us here, namely the elimination of the acute Messianic tension or Messianic reference which it had in the primary sources [Tanakian] and its transference onto another plane where the sting of Messianism has been neutralized.[304]

I see a great significance in Scholem's defining Messianic interference or realization as a "sting." It is consistent with his belief that the Messianic apocalypticism of the Tanak brings catastrophe to the existing order of things on the planet. Lurianic Kabbalists believed that there was "catastrophe" when sin entered the world, which they describe as a "scattering of the sparks," but Kabbalism shrinks away from the catastrophic Tanakian apocalypticism of Messianic intervention, as a latter-day "Day of the Lord."

The first Scholem dictum concerns Lurianic Kabbalah and its sparks. He describes this erroneous doctrine as follows.

> This non-Messianic meaning of devekut is brought out with utmost clarity by the highly significant qualification which is given to the Lurianic doctrine of "lifting up of the sparks." In its original conception there is no connection between this notion and devekut . . . . To lift up the scattered sparks of light [God] and to restore them to the place they were intended to occupy had not catastrophe intervened—this is the essential task of man in the process of tikkun. To fulfill this task is the preparation for Messianic Redemption in which each of us plays his part . . . . The soul of all mankind was originally contained within Adam. Now, its sparks were scattered throughout the terrestrial universe, and the continued existence of sin has evermore increased their dispersion. They are in exile and must be led home and restored to their primordial spiritual

structure, which is at the same time the structure of Adam and the structure of the Messiah. Everybody must work on this task . . . of collecting the sparks . . . from the husks in which they are held captive by the dark power of the "other, or demonic, side."[305]

Strangely, in this evolutionary process described above, there is a defining emphasis of the extraneous evil power described as "the husks," in which they are held captive by the dark power of the "other, or demonic, side." Kabbalah describes this power as the Sitra Achra (the other side), which it professedly mythologizes as demons and devils. This assertion appears to contradict the idea that God built in the tendency to evil as in the Jetser tov and Jetser hara theory of the origin of evil. Kabbalah preposterously claims that the Other Side, at its root, is not separate from the divine and is a part of God.[306]

The second Scholem dictum concerns Hasidism.

> Of course, the Hasidim speak of tikkun too but its meaning has been qualified . . . into the strictly personal sphere of man, where tikkun is achieved by devekut . . . . Luria is primarily interested in . . . sparks . . . whereas Baal Shem and his followers emphasize the mystic connection between man and his immediate environment . . . . Only the Zaddik [he who attains the state of devekut] is granted the privilege of meeting the sparks of his own soul.[307]

Isaiah Tishby wrote much on Hasidism; see his numerous writings easily referenced on the Internet, but notably "Messianic Mysticism: Moses Hayim Luzzatto and the Padua School." Tishby denies that there is weakening of the Messianic concept in Hasidism. Scholem criticizes Tishby's observations on an essay written by Rivka Shatz, which Scholem himself endorses as qualifying Hasidism. Scholem states:

> Rivka Shatz who quite correctly had underlined this process [in Hasidism] of replacing acute Messianism by a personal

and mystical concept of salvation . . . . He [Tishby] quotes several passages stating that the Zaddik is empowered to bring about the coming of the Messiah, ie., there is in him a potential to bring on redemption. Tishby goes so far as to argue that "the bringing on of the national redemption is considered here as the principal function of the outstanding Zaddik." The truth of the matter is quite different. The stressing of this *potential* capacity of the Zaddik is by no means accidental—for he is expressly forbidden to use it! But this decisive point is not even mentioned by Tishby. The Zaddik has the power to annihilate the forces of severity and rigour by getting *down* to their root and "sweetening" them at their original place . . . .

This "restoration" or "sweetening" of the unclean powers, the husks, is the reverse of the usual doctrine that the powers of evil or rigour are annihilated by the lifting up the sparks that are in them and giving them life . . . . if all the dinim, these powers of rigour, are sweetened, then redemption would come. But the Rabbi of Lizensk warns the Zaddik . . . that he should not exert himself to annihilate the unclean power altogether, *because by this he would cause the immediate coming of the Messiah* (No'am Elimelekh, Lvov, 1786, f. 54b, section vayikra). In other words: Messianic exertion is forbidden. Even when there is a Messianic potentiality in an outstanding personality, it must be held back and not be actualised. To see in such an idea proof of acute Messianic tension seems strange to me. It is precisely what I call neutralization of the Messianic element . . . .

But redemption of the soul without redemption of the social body, i.e., of the nation from its historical exile, of the outward world from its broken state, has never had a Messianic meaning in Judaism.[308]

Scholem clearly sees that the redemption of the soul comes with a new world order. Scholem is not in favour of the Messianic concepts in Kabbalah and in Hasidism. There is no doubt that Gershom Scholem will not let go of what he calls "acute Messianism," which is basic to Tanakian Judaism. He also sees in it the mission of the Abrahamic Covenant that enables the blessedness of all humanity. He loves the catastrophic apocalypticism of Daniel and Isaiah of the Tanak and virtually rebukes Kabbalah and Hasidism for neutralizing it. In keeping with this belief in acute Messianism, Scholem takes particular exception to the interpretation of Genesis 28:16 by Ephraim of Sedylkov. This text, which says, "And Jacob awoke from his sleep, and he said, surely the Lord is in this place, and I knew it not," is interpreted by Ephraim of Sedylkov as:

> It is known that the exile is designated by the word sleep and this refers to the state where God removes Himself and hides His face. And redemption means that God reveals Himself through the light of the Torah through which He is awakened from sleep . . . . And this is what the verse "And Jacob awoke from his sleep" hints at, namely the awakening from exile which is likened to the state of sleeping, as it is said we would be like dreamers.[309]

In criticizing this specific interpretation, Scholem scathingly states:

> The central position which anti-eschatological exegeses of this type occupy in the classics of Hasidic literature points to the degree to which Messianic terms were transformed and neutralized.[310]

Gershom Scholem spends a lot of time showing how Lurianic Kabbalism and Hasidism reacted to Sabbatianism, and perhaps unwittingly, he blames Sabbatianism for their spiritualization and neutralization of the Messiah. But he nonetheless castigates all three movements for damaging Tanakian Messianism in Judaism.

> The School of Lurianism made every Jew a protagonist in the great Messianic struggle; it did not allegorize

Messianism into a state of personal life. Hasidism in its most vigorous stages took precisely this step. The one and unique great act of final redemption, "the real thing", if I may say so, was thrown out, i.e., was removed from the sphere of Messiah in man's immediate responsibility and thrown back into God's inscrutable councils. But let us face the fact: once this has been done, all the mystical talk of a sphere of Messiah in one's own life, wonderful as it may sound, becomes but an allegorical figure of speech. If, as has been remarked by Hillel Zeitlin, every individual is a Redeemer, the Messiah of his own little world—and I would agree that this is the essence of early Hasidism—then Messianism as an actual historical force [the Tanakian doctrine] is liquidated, it has lost its apocalyptic fire, its sense of imminent catastrophe . . . . The creative power of Hasidism was centred on the mystical life, on the revival of the Jew in exile. This may have been a very great thing to achieve. But let us not forget that while Hasidism brought about an unheard-of intensity and intimacy of religious life, it had to pay dearly for its success. It conquered in the realm of inwardness, but it abdicated in the realm of Messianism.[311]

Scholem does not approve of the neutralization of acute Messianism by Kabbalah and Hasidism, And he is right. The great patriarchs Abraham, Jacob, and Moses cannot be set aside. The Tanak must stay supreme in Judaism. Messianism is indeed a personal intervention by deity to redeem and create a resumption of perfect obedience to the law in our restored immortal state. This is amply declared in the books of Isaiah and Daniel.

A consideration of other ideas of Messianism in Israel is worthwhile in pointing out the varied and un-Tanakian views of most Jewish sects.

The Karaites' Messiah

In my reading of the literature in Karaism, the most prominent feature is that their sole accepted Torah is the Tanak. I applaud this greatly; they are willing to discuss the Talmud, but they subordinate all their belief systems to the Tanak only. It is alleged that there are two Messiahs in Karaism, and there is some evidence for this in their multiple "centrally unedited" writings. The basis for this two Messiah assertion appears to be the scripture.

> And he shall build the Temple of the Lord, and he shall bear glory. And he shall sit and rule on his throne, and the priest shall be on his throne. And a counsel of peace shall be between them. (Zech. 6:13)[312]

There is Messiah the Aaronic priest, interpreted sometimes as Elijah the forerunner, and Messiah the Son of David. Basic to this is the liturgical prayer in Karaism: "for the restoration of the priesthood and the Davidic Kingdom." They deduce these ideas strictly from the Tanak and start at the Malachi prediction of Elijah being the forerunner of the Messiah. Some of their writers assign some of the Messianic actions to Elijah, giving the impression that he is also a Messiah.[313]

I do not profess an exhaustive knowledge of Karaism, but I am inclined to believe that there is a wide range of interpretation by a wide range of writers in Karaism, with some conceptually unclear statements, and with fringes of confused statements. Considering the Tanakian scriptures from which they draw, all references are conceptually and contextually Messianic in the single Messianic sense. I mean that the Tanakian texts they use do not indicate two Messiahs, and therefore the idea that two different Messiahs exist in core Karaism is unjustified. The desire to have the Aaronic priesthood and Temple service restored, which reflects the Messianic sacrifice, expands the Messianic functions of Karaism into two roles. Therefore the conclusion is that the "first Aaronic priesthood Messiah" written about is parallel to the role of the suffering servant Messianic function, the sacrifice without blemish crushed for the sins of all humanity, according to Isaiah. And the "second Messianic function of the conquering king ben David" role belongs to the apocalyptic era, both implicit in Daniel and Isaiah. These roles are parallel to Scholem's restorative factor and utopian factor, respectively. If this is the ideation in the core essence of Karaism, it is Tanakian, and they have only one Messiah who functions in two chronological temporal roles.

The Messiah of the Messianic Zionists

Rabbi Abraham Isaac Kook (HaRav) and his followers form the bulwark of the Messianic Zionists and have a nationalist ideology encapsulating their Messiah.

> The great ingathering of the exiles is a revelation of the light of the Messiah, which does not depend on our teshuvah [deliverance, salvation] but on the decree that "this people I formed for Myself" (Isaiah 43:21).[314]

Aviezer Ravitsky, Chairman of Jewish Thought at Hebrew University, has made a remarkable study of the Messianic Zionists titled "The Revealed End: Messianic Religious Zionism." I quote from him.

> Unlike the traditional Kabbalistic sages, who saw redemption as hinging on spiritual rectification and the fulfilment of a mystical, cosmic mission, this activist school gives precedence to perfecting this world and achieving historical, political fulfilment. For them it is a Zionist undertaking, in all its concreteness, that embodies the needed collective rectification and truly reflects the Jewish people's response to the divine call. And it is Zionism that, in the last analysis, prepares the way for universal personal redemption as well. Thus Kook wrote, "The End is being revealed before our very eyes, and there can be no doubt or question that would detract from our joy and gratitude to the Redeemer of Israel . . . The End is here!"[315] (See Shlomo

Aviner, "Am ke-lavi," Jerusalem 1983, 2:192-194;
Uriel Tal, "Mithos u-tevunah be-yahadut yamenu,"
Tel Aviv, 1987, p. 102).

In the two generations since Rabbi Abraham Isaac Kook's
death, his Messianic hopes have come much closer to
realization in the material than in the spiritual realm.
Independence, the enormous growth of the Yishuv [the
Jewish community in the land of Israel], the recovery of
the dominion over the land of Israel, success in making
the land productive, military power and victory, all these
material achievements have given encouragement to the
belief in the revealed End. But the spiritual picture is rather
different: a nonreligious majority that stubbornly refuses to
heed the Call and ground its national identity in faith . . . .
In sum, the visible elements of salvation have become more
visible, while the invisible ones have become more deeply
hidden . . . . Why has faith not yet surfaced on the level of
personal conscious affirmation, as expected? . . .

But what he [Rabbi Abraham Kook] hoped for was a
gradual convergence of the outward and the inward, an
imminent merging of outward historical salvation with
inward religious awakening. He firmly believed that when
the secularists achieved their worldly goals—legitimate
goals, in his view—they would quickly realize that what
they had really wanted all along was something more,
something higher, a return to the Jewish soul and the
commandments. He thus foresaw a process of perfection
taking place in both realms, matter and spirit, land and
Torah.[316]

There is no doubt that the Messianic Zionists are expecting to create
the Messianic advent themselves, by achieving material national
possession of the land and hoping for Torah to be kept perfectly.
But the latter is not happening because the gap between the
religious minority and the secular majority is widening. Ravitsky
sees this and creates a lamentation on behalf of the Messianic

Zionists. Their Messiah is not going to be realized anytime soon. Although Zionism is to be highly lauded, these Messianic Zionists' hopes of turning it into a Messianic reality is lamentable. What they do not realize is that they are not looking for the Tanakian Messiah, but one of their own concoction. As Gershom Scholem sees it, in his acute Messianism, they must embrace the Ha-Mashiach of the Tanak, who is the fulfilment of Isaiah's and Daniel's descriptions. They must embrace the 'suffering servant' being "crushed" for the atonement, and the conquering king of the apocalypticism of Isaiah and Daniel who at the resurrection catastrophically creates a new world.

The Messiah of the Religious Zionists (Modern Orthodox Jews)

It is extremely difficult to describe Jewish Orthodoxy because there are so many branches or subsets, as well as American and modern brands of it. It is generally defined as Jews who traditionally believe in Torah, which is defined as Tanak and Talmud. The Talmud has come to be its main ideological base, but with the prolific variant rabbinic leadership and their divergent opinions of the last three centuries, there is no unity of Messianic belief that can be circumscribed as orthodox. They constitute at least 30 percent of the population of Israel in addition to the American Orthodox Jews, who are difficult to enumerate but must be of significant number. The description of orthodoxy encountered online under "My Jewish Learning" indicates there is no unified definition of Messiah that can be found as being the Orthodox Jewish Messiah. Concerning Orthodox Messianism, "My Jewish Learning" declares:

> Can we hope for a better, more perfect existence—either after we die, or in some future era? Judaism is famously ambiguous on this matter. The immortality of the soul, the World to Come, the resurrection of the dead, and the Messianic age all feature prominently in Jewish tradition, but their details are fuzzy.

The belief in a Messiah, a person who will redeem the people Israel and usher in a better, more perfect era—the messianic age—is often thought of as one of Judaism's defining characteristics.[317]

The above excerpt is acceptable. But the next sentence is grossly erroneous, confusing, and misleading.

Interestingly, however, the Bible [Tanak] does not use the word Messiah to refer to an eschatological redeemer.[318]

Some clarity is forthcoming.

The word Messiah is derived from the Hebrew mashah, to Anoint.[319]

I have amply shown elsewhere in this book where there is a Ha-Mashiach in the Tanak as the anointed one, and the Talmud agrees. The Ha-Mashiach has been in the mind of God from eternity, and the rabbinic sages of the Talmud agree. There is no question about this, as is further admitted by "My Jewish Learning."

Though messianism is rarely discussed in the Mishnah, it is very much present in the Gemara and Midrash. Here the Redeemer is called "Messiah" and he is described . . . [as] a military, political figure . . . a being with supernatural abilities . . . . Dressed like a blighted beggar, sitting at the gates of Rome, awaiting Jewish repentance.[320]

The Jewish Virtual Library gives another definition of modern Orthodox Judaism, where the Messiah is mentioned.

An excellent summary of the core beliefs of Orthodox Judaism may be found in the Rambam's 13 Principles of Faith. Number 12 is about the coming of the Messiah.[321]

In tandem with this, Chabad.org provides a discussion titled "Who is Moshiach?"

> The Messianic Redemption will be ushered in by a person, a human leader, a descendant of Kings David and Solomon, who will reinstate the Davidic royal dynasty . . . . If at any moment the Jews are worthy of redemption, this person would be directed from Above to assume the role of the redeemer".
>
> During the Messianic Era, the Moshiach . . . will be a monarch, ruling over all of humanity with kindness and justice, and upholding the law of the Torah . . . .
>
> The following are the criteria for identifying Moshiach, AS WRITTEN BY MAIMONIDES: If we see a Jewish Leader who
>
> (a) Toils in the study of Torah and is meticulous about the observance of the mitzvoth [fulfilment of the Commandments of the Jewish Law],
> (b) influences the Jews to follow the ways of the Torah and
> (c) wages the "battles of God"—such a person is the presumptive Moshiach.
>
> If the person succeeded in all these endeavours, and then rebuilds the Holy Temple in Jerusalem and facilitates the ingathering of the Jews to the Land of Israel—then we are certain that he is the Moshiach.[322]

This set of criteria is reflective of the longings of the Jews, but it is not a blueprint from the Tanak. It is dependent on Jews keeping the law perfectly, which will never happen. It appears that the Messiah will be chosen by a committee by observation of his behaviour and lifestyle. The Tanakian plan for the expiation of sin by the Messiah and then his apocalyptic catastrophic ushering in of the judgement and the resurrection have been abandoned. There is no new earth and no restoration of immortality. The picture is restricted to a temporal and transient setting only, which appears to be the lifetime of that Messiah. The presumption is that Messiah will be a created being. This concept is not Tanakian.

The Messiah of the Messianic Jews

The Messianic Jews believe that Yeshua of Nazareth, the son of Mary, is the Ha-Mashiach of Israel. They are estimated at 30,000 in number living in Israel, 250,000 living in the United States, and 1 million worldwide. They live as religious Jews, celebrate all the Jewish festivals, practice circumcision as a sign of the Abrahamic Covenant, and keep the Jewish Sabbath. They see the two roles of Messiah in the Tanak. The role of the 'suffering servant' of Isaiah as the expiatory death of Yeshua on the Cross as the atonement for the sins of the whole world. They look forward to the return of Yeshua in his second role as judge and king at his second coming. This fulfils the apocalyptic predictions of Isaiah and Daniel, ushering in the resurrection and the making of a new earth and a restoration of immortality. They do not identify as Christians, but they accept the B'rit Hadasha as their expanded Torah.[323]

The Messiah of Reform Judaism

Originating in Germany, reform Judaism sought to adapt the prevailing Jewish beliefs to modern times in the 1800s. As a movement, it grew in America and has over 1.5 million adherents. Rabbi Joseph Meszler gave a lecture in 2006 at the Temple Sharon in Massachusetts on Rosh Hashanah. It is as follows, in a very abbreviated form.

> One of the first things that the early Reform rabbis did was cut out any reference to the theological belief in the Messiah . . . . Resurrection . . . [and] rebuilding of the Temple in Jerusalem. In the 19th century, these early Reform Rabbis found these beliefs in the supernatural to

be too fantastic to be true. A point of distinction . . . is the complete rejection of a personal Messiah, resurrection, and the restoring of the sacrificial rite of a Third Temple . . . . [However] the Reform Jewish belief is that humanity must and can save itself . . . . Reform Judaism believes in a partnership with God, where each person has a role to play in making the world a better place, and not waiting for divine intervention . . . . The first thing we can do is start the process of Teshuvah, of repentance . . . the next thing to do is act and give Tzedakah [the practical support of benevolent causes] . . . . And finally . . . We must also become advocates . . . to be "a light to the nations" . . . There is a potential piece of the Messiah in each of us, and the Messianic Age can be had, if we all do our part.[324]

Here again, there is no guidance from the Tanak for deciphering and realizing a Messiah. Redemption and the restoration of immortality have been abandoned.

The Messiah of Conservative Judaism

The conservative camp of Judaism constitutes the vast majority of worldwide Jewry, enumerated at 4.5 million adherents and constituted mainly by American Jews. Arising in Europe around 1886 as Masorti Judaism under the inspiration of Zecharias Frankel, with a belief system professedly based on the Tanak and Talmud, their headquarters are now in New York City. Conservative Jews see themselves occupying the space between the ultra liberal reform Jews and the traditional Orthodox Jews. But as such a large group, it is not truly unified under a specific body of doctrine. There are now branches of conservative Jews with variations in beliefs. It is therefore difficult to arrive at a definition of Messianism in conservative Judaism. One view that might be representative is available from Wikipedia, under the heading of "Jewish Messianism" and the subheading of "Conservative Judaism." I quote from the cited Emet Ve-Emunah, the conservative movement's statement of principles.

Since no one can say for certain what will happen in the Messianic Era each of us is free to fashion personal speculation. Some of us accept these speculations as literally true, while others understand them as elaborate metaphors . . . For the world community we dream of an age when warfare will be abolished, when justice and compassion will be axioms of all, as it is said in Isaiah 11: " . . . the land shall be filled with the knowledge of the Lord as waters cover the sea." For our people, we dream of the ingathering of all Jews to Zion where we can again be masters of our own destiny and express our distinctive genius in every area of our national life. We affirm Isaiah's prophecy (2:3) that " . . . Torah shall come forth from Zion, the word of the Lord from Jerusalem."

We do not know when Messiah will come, nor whether he will be a charismatic human figure or is a symbol of the redemption of humankind from the evils of the world. Through the doctrine of a Messianic figure, Judaism teaches us that every individual human being must live as if he or she, individually, has the responsibility to bring about the messianic age. Beyond that we echo the words of Maimonides based on the prophet Habakkuk (2:3) that though he may tarry, yet do we wait for him each day. [See beliefs of Orthodox Jews mentioning Maimonides, listed above.][325]

The Messiah of the Secular Jews of Israel

This group constitutes the majority of Israeli Jews, exceeding 50 percent. Thomas Friedman sums them up very well.

Being back in the Land of Israel, erecting a modern society and army, and observing Jewish holidays as national holidays all became a substitute for religious observance and faith . . . . For them, coming to the Land of Israel and becoming "normal" meant giving up religious ritual

366

as the defining feature of their Jewish identity. Science, technology, and turning the desert green were their new Torah.[326]

There is no discernible Messianic idea expressed, but I feel that they believe in a distant Messiah, although they do not define one.

The identification of the Messiah has been amply displayed generously and loudly by the Tanak, and it has existed from eternity, before the creation of the world. The great Talmudic rabbinic sages saw it in the eternal plans of God. The necessity and function of the Messiah was pivotally proclaimed as the rectifying power outside the Gates of Gan Eden. Abel's sacrifice of the symbolic lamb whose blood he shed for the expiation of his sins was the great initiation of the nature and function of the Messiah; it was highlighted by Abel's murder by the attempt of a rival system of fruits and vegetables to replace it, which God immediately rejected. God rejects all rival concoctions. All the Patriarchs shed the blood of the animal without blemish, symbolic of Messianic redemption to be free from the guilt of their disobedience to Torah. The Abrahamic Covenant was made for a vehicle and venue for the propagation of Messianic redemption to the whole world through the Jews. Moses crafted a people to fulfil the covenant and gave them the Aaronic priesthood to daily enact the shedding of blood for the propitiation. The greatest and most important Day of Atonement was instituted by Moses for the blood of the animal without blemish to be sprinkled on the Ark of the Covenant and Mercy Seat, where Elohim had taken up His abode in the Most Holy Place. He was there to witness it and remind Israel that Messiah was coming. Whenever Israel polluted the Temple with idolatry of any kind, God allowed the Temple to be destroyed, allowing His eviction from His earthly abode. There is no doubt that God has kept trying desperately to bring His Messianic redemption to fruition; that is why Israel has been brought back to the Holy Land after 2,000 years. The Ha-Mashiach is waiting at the door to be recognized and to enter.

Why did God choose Israel to be the vehicle of the propagation of the Messiah? I do not know. He needed someone; you can ask God when you see Him. My answer is that He greatly loved Jacob, who understood His plan more than any other at that time, even Abraham. Jacob had clung to Him so tenaciously. Would to God that modern Israel and all diasporic Jews would do the same.

I close this chapter with the recognition that current Judaism is not united in its concept of the Messiah for whom Israel is looking so eagerly. But I am elated that Rabbi Judah the Prince and the highly esteemed Gershom Scholem have Tanakian concepts of the expected Ha-Mashiach. They saw Him as a redeemer and king who would bring the atonement and the catastrophic apocalyptic Messianic kingdom, where there will be a new earth and immortality. This Tanakian Judaism is an exciting redemptive religion, the patriarchal religion of Abraham, Jacob, and Moses.

Here is the Tanakian blueprint. God is one and expresses His plurality as Elohim in Creation, redemption, and glorification. This plurality is simply a functional one and does not indicate a division within the Infinite One. His functionality is expressed in human understanding as Ruach Hakodesh and Ha-Mashiach, both highly active in Creation, redemption, and glorification. Elohim exists from eternity, and His plurality will be manifest within eternity. Elohim's conversation with His Creation is understood within that plurality, which Moses expressed as "Us," but He is one God, blessed be He. Through the functionality of Ruach Hakodesh and Ha-Mashiach, Elohim provides the restoration of immortality. This will be through the medium of this human understanding expressed in the Tanak. Ruach Hakodesh is the Shechinah, ever present with humanity to provide repentance. Atonement is also accomplished by God Himself, by His power to vanquish death; this is accomplished by His Ha-Mashiach power. The atonement is eminently described in the Tanak, notably by Isaiah, who sees the 'suffering servant' and the anointed son in a penetrance of humanity. This modality was embraced by Judah the Prince and Gershom Scholem, both giants in Judaism. In the vision of Ha-Mashiach as king, Scholem saw the vanquishment of history and the tarnished world as we know it. He coined this Tanakian vision as 'acute' Messianism. Judgement, the resurrection, and the restoration of immortality were part of that acute Messianism. Scholem saw it in the catastrophic apocalypticism of the prophetic utterances in the Tanak, notably by Isaiah and Daniel.

Both Ruach Hakodesh and Ha-Mashiach manifestations are within Elohim and are existent from eternity. They are part of the mind of God, part of infinite Torah. Blessed be He, the Lord our God is one.

Israel *must* embrace this vision and look for the Messiah of the Tanak.

CHAPTER 22

THE DREAM OF JACOB

Jacob was the son of Isaac, a twin born to Rebekkah; he came out of her womb after Esau. The whole story of Jacob's deception and "stealing" of the birthright from his slightly older brother seems almost unnecessary, because Esau had already disqualified himself for several reasons. There is a similarity of the brothers Esau and Jacob with Cain and Abel. Jacob was religious; Esau was not. Jacob was a shepherd, and Esau was a hunter. Esau spent very little time at home, whereas Jacob was a home bird. Esau fell in love with idolatrous Canaanite women. Isaac and Rebecca went to great lengths to send Jacob to find a wife from among her religious clan, those who worshipped YHVH. Esau had his own agenda and timetable; Jacob's allegiance was to the Abrahamic Covenant. Esau was gullible, but Jacob was shrewd. Esau was governed by appetite, whereas Jacob was abstemious. Jacob prayed and sacrificed to God, but Esau was preoccupied with idolatry and sex. Esau absolutely was not the candidate to whom the preservation and practice of Torah and the Covenant were to be entrusted. He had not even memorized it. But Jacob was a dreamer who dreamed of the future of Israel, and he saw a ladder by which all humanity could climb up to God. He saw the Messiah's deliverance through the Abrahamic Covenant, the ladder to Heaven.

In Malachi is recorded an attitude of God that some have found difficult to understand and accept. Some even allege that Malachi misspoke the words, which were in God's mouth:

> I have loved you, saith the Lord. Yet ye say, In what way
> hast Thou loved us? Was not Esau Jacob's brother? Saith

the Lord; yet I loved Jacob, And I hated Esau. (Mal. 1:2-3, KJV)

Malachi's message is hinged to Israel's offering of "tainted bread" and "lame and sick animals," which were not the animal sacrifices without blemish that God required. These emblems were symbolic of the Messiah, perfect deity, God Himself, who is instrumental in their redemption. And yet Israel brought what they knew was inappropriate and what they were about to discard as garbage. How dared Israel do this! It was a form of illogical and irreligious thinking, a form of saving money. After all, the animal was to be slaughtered and burned, so who cared if it was blemished? Esau was totally engrossed with sex, and this had led him into idolatry to please the women he loved. He did not bother finding repentance; he could not bother with symbolic animal sacrifices. He was the "fool who said in his heart, No God" (Ps. 14:1). *The Jewish Study Bible* translates this more succinctly: "The benighted man thinks, God does not care." Esau did not even care enough to bring a hypocritical sacrifice devoid of repentance. This is a gross form of pride, and God abhors pride. The parallel is there with Cain and Abel. God's requirement of an animal without blemish *has no substitute*. After all, it was the symbol He had chosen to represent Himself. Fruits and vegetables, the produce of our own works, our meticulous observation of rituals, our good deeds of benevolence—these were not required by God as salvific measures, and they will not save us. As redemptive agents, they are an affront to Him. It is the blood of the sacrificial animal without blemish that does, for it is symbolic of Messianic redemption. Jacob believed that with all his heart and soul, and that is why God loved him.

The great imponderable here is not why God "hates" Esau, but why He loves Jacob. The reason God loves Jacob so much is because despite all his unworthiness, Jacob earnestly desired and strenuously grasped the fact that he would be the ancestor of the Messiah. He wholeheartedly embraced the Abrahamic Covenant, and that was his whole life. Esau and Jacob both knew that their grandfather, Abraham, had raised the knife to kill their father, Isaac, on Mount Moriah. Jacob saw in that act the supreme sacrifice, which God Himself would offer to save all humanity, and that was the overwhelming factor in Jacob's life. Isaac had told his twins that story over and over. Jacob had thrilled to recall that story: how Isaac had been so excited to make that trip with his father; how he had carried the wood for the sacrifice; how he questioned their grandfather about the need for a sacrificial animal; how he suddenly realised that he was to be the sacrifice; how he was bound with the rope so he could not run away; how his father had pulled out the knife and raised it to cut his throat. The twins had shuddered at hearing the story. They had trembled on hearing about their father being bound. They had screamed in terror when they heard that the knife was raised to cut his throat. They nevertheless wanted to hear the story over and over again. Isaac always ended the story the same way: His father had spared him because God interfered to stop him. But one day the Messiah, one of their children's sons, would come down from Heaven. He would be God Himself, to be their sacrifice for sin and to eradicate sin from the universe. And that knife that symbolizes sin would be permitted to cut His throat, and He would die for all humanity so that they could live eternally. He could do it because He was God, and He had the power to take up His human life again.

When the nights were too hot to sleep in the tent, they loved sleeping under the stars. They would ask where Heaven was up there, and from where would the Messiah come down to be the sacrificial lamb. Jacob did not have to lie and deceive to get the birthright. It was his because he understood the longing in God's heart to reclaim lost humanity. Humanity was and is God's great love object, His preferred love object in the entire universe. Jacob shed tears with the sadness that came over his deepest emotions when he recounted the near-death experience of his father. Isaac kept that knife that had nearly cut his throat as a keepsake of that epochal moment, and the children were allowed to view it. It reminded them that sin meant death. It reminded them that one day the Messiah would be crushed for the remission of the sin of the whole world. God's great love could not have been greater in their minds. And wherever he went, Jacob thrilled when thinking about the near-death experience of his father.

Jacob's religion was indeed a redemptive one. At the Brook Jabbok, when he thought Esau was about to kill him, he quaked with the fear that the Abrahamic Covenant was in danger, that the coming of the Ha-Mashiach was in danger were he to die. He clung to God so tenaciously for salvation that God had to dislocate Jacob's hip to release Himself from his grasp. God changed his name to Israel on that spot: "And He said, Thy name shall be called no more Jacob, but Israel; for as a prince hast thou power with God and with men and hast prevailed" (Gen. 32:28, KJV). His awesome position in the plan of God to restore the lost Eden overwhelmed him, and he carried that conviction to his deathbed. There was no one in Israel that had the vision and foresight of the Messianic role as clearly as Jacob did—not even Moses, who was eloquent about the Torah and punishment for disobedience. Moses felt the quake of Sinai as he instituted the symbol of the Messianic sacrifice, but Jacob saw his redemptive God as the ladder to heaven and immortality. How marvellously privileged were Abraham, Jacob, and Moses! How sacred is the Abrahamic Covenant! They were pivotal in the powerful plans of the almighty Elohim from the days of eternity in the mind of God.

Jacob lived in the experience of the sacrifice of his father. He had the richness of the hugs of his grandfather, who had faced the killing of his own son before he had understood what exactly was involved in his calling by God. It was not just to have a homeland and a place to live in the world, although that was very vital. It was not just to repeat the Torah and make his children memorize it, although that was important to the propagation of God's law. They all realised they could not keep that law perfectly because of the weakness of the flesh. They grasped that their sins would be forgiven and that they would be reconciled to God through the Messianic gift. It was necessary so that Eden would be restored. That was the plan that existed already, at the foundation of the world. Jacob knew more than anyone else that he was pivotal in those powerful plans of the eternal God. He dreamed about it at Bethel. He grasped it with all his tenacity at Jabbok. He faced his murderous brother with the assurance that God would not allow him to be killed. Oh, that Israeli today may be like Jacob and realise that they are princes with God because of Jacob. But they need to be as dedicated to the Abrahamic Covenant as he was.

Jacob had been a conniving liar and thief. He did not have to be, because Esau was not interested in the Abrahamic Covenant. Esau had comprehended the Messianic mission; he also had screamed in terror as a child when Isaac told them the story. But he turned a blind eye to it. He said no to God. The upshot was that Esau traded in his birthright for a mess of pottage. Jacob was running ahead of God, adopting measures that were unnecessary, to fulfil God's plans. His grandmother Sarah had set a bad example trying to get a son for Abraham from Hagar. She assessed herself as old and barren, and her humility saw her status as an impediment to God's great covenant with her husband. She was desperately trying to facilitate God's plan. Like Sarah, his mother, Rebekkah, aided and abetted Jacob's deception. There was now trouble between the twins, and the peaceful home life was shattered because he had "stolen" the birthright. Esau was ready to kill Jacob as soon as their father was dead; Esau planned it and leaked his intention. He merely wanted to inherit his father's possessions. He felt he needed no repentance for his idolatry. Isaac and Rebekkah were exceedingly worried that Jacob might find an idolatrous wife. They did the right thing by sending Jacob to live with and work for her brother Laban in Padan-Aram, and to find a wife there. But listen to the farewell blessing that poured out of Isaac's mouth as he said good-bye to the son he would not see again. Jacob practiced no deception for this blessing.

> And God Almighty bless thee, and make thee fruitful, and multiply thee, that thou mayest be a multitude of people; And give thee the blessing of Abraham, to thee and to thy seed with thee, that thou mayest inherit the land wherein thou art a sojourner, which God gave unto Abraham. And Isaac sent Jacob away. (Gen 28:3-5, KJV)

Jacob was well aware that he was interposed in the succession to the fulfilment of the Abrahamic Covenant. Now he realised that his father was no longer deceived and knew to whom he was bestowing the birthright and blessing of the Abrahamic Covenant. He fled his home in the fear of being murdered by his brother. He went on his way to Padan-Aram, now a part of modern-day Syria.

> And he came to a certain place and tarried there all night, because the sun was set; and he took of the stones of that place, and put them for his pillows, and lay down in that place to sleep. And he dreamed, and behold a ladder set up on the earth, and the top of it reached to heaven: and behold the angels of God ascending and descending on it. And, behold the Lord stood above it, and said, I am the Lord God of Abraham, thy father, and the God of Isaac: the land whereon thou liest, to thee will I give it, and thy seed; and thy seed shall be as the dust of the earth . . . and *in thy seed* shall all the families of the earth be blessed . . . . And Jacob awaked out of his sleep, and he said, Surely the Lord is in this place! This is none other than the house of God, and this is the *gate of Heaven* . . . . And he called the name of that place Bethel . . . And this stone that I have set for a pillar, shall be God's house. (Gen. 28:1-22, KJV; emphasis added).

Here is the Abrahamic Covenant now being reinforced by God with Jacob; here is land, Torah, and Messiah. Jacob's dream is that there is a ladder to Heaven. God stands at the top and wants all humanity back in Paradise. Jacob is officially given the task of the Abrahamic Covenant. The dream of connecting earth and heaven through the Messiah by the Abrahamic Covenant would energize him for his whole life. The Messiah was the ladder, the way to immortality, the way to Heaven. Messiah was the greatest expression of God's love for Israel and all humanity. Oh, that Israel today might understand the Abrahamic Covenant and the Messianic mission.

Jacob had first to stabilize and prosper himself before that Abrahamic mission could be tackled; he was still a lone bachelor. He continued his inspired journey to Padan-Aram. He entered the household of Laban and worked hard for his uncle for 14 years, accumulating two wives, two concubines, several children, and much livestock. He was the father of 11 sons, and another was born later. Then he had another dream while still in Padan-Aram.

> And the angel of God spoke unto him in a dream . . . . I am the God of Bethel, where thou anointedst the pillar, and where thou vowest a vow unto Me: now arise, get thee out from this land, and return unto the land of thy kindred. (Gen. 31:11-13, KJV)

Jacob was reminded of his vision of the ladder to Heaven. He had initialled the Abrahamic Covenant that night at Bethel. God reminded him that he had "vowed a vow." He returned to the Promised Land to possess it. On his journey back, he built altars along the way and sacrificed. He built a special altar at Bethel, where he had dreamed his dream. He also built an altar at Shalem. He bought a piece of land in Shalem and settled down. He called the altar Elelohe-Israel, "the mighty God of Israel" (Gen. 33:17-20, KJV). His parents were now dead. There was no homecoming, and he still feared he would be murdered by his brother Esau.

There is not the slightest shadow of a doubt that Jacob's religion was a redemptive religion. He built altars and sacrificed animals without blemish, because this was a symbol of what the Messianic redeemer was all about. Messiah was that ladder to Heaven. Repentance came when people were sorry for disobeying the Torah. Repentance was a gift from Ruach Hakodesh, God Himself. Repentance led to confession and restitution. Confession led to forgiveness after the guilt had been removed by the spilling of the blood of the sacrificial animal without blemish. Jacob understood that the Messiah would atone. The Abrahamic Covenant was exceedingly fresh and important in his mind because he was Abraham's grandson and was the one in the family who insisted on worshipping the only true God. His life of belief and trust in his redemptive God gave him the leadership of the family. He realised that now he had the full responsibility of carrying out the Abrahamic Covenant, of being the ancestor of Ha-Mashiach. Abraham was dead, and his father Isaac had been blind and had been getting ready to die when he had left his home. Now Isaac was also dead. There was nothing more important to him than land, Torah and Messiah.

Jacob sent messengers to Esau with a peace offering, and he was now confronted with the reality that Esau was coming to meet him with an army of 400 men. Jacob was greatly afraid and distressed. He planned a strategy and sent the whole family and all his possessions ahead with a present and a peace offering to Esau. He stayed in the background by himself, quaking with fear by the Brook Jabbok. Let us relive the Jabbok experience.

> Jacob was left alone; And a Man wrestled with him until the break of dawn. When He saw that he had prevailed against Him, He wrenched Jacob's hip at its socket . . . . Then He said, Let me go for dawn is breaking. But he said I will not let you go, unless you bless me. Said the other: What is your name? He replied "Jacob." Said He, Your name shall no longer be Jacob, but Israel, for you have striven with beings *divine and human*, and have prevailed. Jacob asked, Pray tell me your name. But He said, You must not ask My name! And He took leave of him there. So Jacob named that place Peniel, meaning, I have seen a divine being face to face, yet my life has been preserved. (Gen. 32:24-30, *The Jewish Study Bible*; emphasis added)

The KJV renders this last sentence: "For I have seen God face to face, and my life is preserved."

The Hebrew word translated "God" here is Elohim (the majestic God) and not YHVH. This is an intended plurality. Moses was denied seeing God's face: "Thou canst not see My face; for there shall no man see My face and live" (Exod. 33:20). *The Jewish Study Bible* therefore translates it in keeping with the ideation of Moses not being allowed to see God's face, because no human mortal survives. This is acceptable and has the meaning of a close encounter. But the Hebrew word is "Elohim" in both verses 28 and 30 in the Masoretic Text, and it *must* be translated as "Elohim" (God). The other factor here is that the being with whom he wrestled was referred to as a "divine and human" being. The translators of *The Jewish Study Bible* used God's plural name correctly, translating it as two natures in functionality, divine and human. Using Talmudic application, this is the correct terminology for the coming Messiah: He would be "divine and human." It signified the condescension of Ha-Mashiach to humanity. This is highly compatible with Daniel, Isaiah, and Psalms 1 and 2. The Tanak is conceptually congruent here.

Jacob had placed himself at the back of the pack that was his retinue. Now he limped up the bank of the Brook Jabbok in complete dependence on God to save him from death at his brother's hand. Jacob had the courage to go to the head of the pack behind the gift he had prepared for Esau, hoping to appease his anger and prevent him from killing him. He had won the wrestling match with God, and now he knew that he had divine protection against Esau. Jacob had dealt with all his doubts and had vanquished them. He had his sins forgiven by the Messianic sacrifice. He had great strength and determination to take the Promised Land, and he had divine propitiation to appease his brother's anger. Protected by his Messiah, he was now invincible.

> Looking up Jacob saw Esau coming, accompanied by four hundred men . . . He himself went on ahead and bowed low to the ground seven times until he was near his brother. Esau ran to greet him. He embraced him and, falling on his neck, he kissed him, and they wept. (Gen. 33:3-4, *The Jewish Study Bible*)

Abraham was the great advocate of monotheism and gave the Jews their ethnicity and special place and destiny. But Jacob was the inspired, pivotal person who gave birth to an inspired nation with the mission to show the world the redeeming Messiah. The vision of Jacob at Bethel and the tenacity of his embrace of God at Jabbok would typify the entire history of the Jewish people. He was no longer Jacob; he was now Israel. He was a prince, the son of the eternal king. That mission is not yet complete. Jacob's dream has still to come alive and be realised nationally and globally. After 2,000 years, will the dream come true and embrace reality?

On his death bed, Jacob pronounced the future of his sons. Surprisingly, some of his predictions were curses. His best future was reserved for Judah.

> You, O Judah, your brothers shall praise;
> Your hand shall be on the nape of your foes;
> Your father's sons shall bow low to you.
> Judah is a lion's whelp;
> On prey, my son, have you grown.
> He crouches, lies down like a lion,
> Like the king of beasts—who dares rouse him?
> The sceptre shall not depart from Judah,
> Nor the ruler's staff from between his feet;
> So that tribute shall come to him,
> And the homage of peoples be his.
>
> He tethers his ass to a vine,
> His ass's foal to a choice vine,
> He washes his garments in wine,
> His robe in blood of grapes.
> His eyes are darker than wine,
> His teeth are whiter than milk.
> (Gen. 49:8-12, *The Jewish Study Bible*)

Jacob made assessments, cursings, and blessings on all his 12 sons on his deathbed. The blessing of Jacob on his son Judah is by far the best and greatest. It is enormous and was predictive of the future of the Jewish nation and the Messiah, the redeemer of the world. Its analysis is extremely important.

The translation above by *The Jewish Study Bible* renders Genesis 49:10 differently than the King James Version, which translates it, "The sceptre shall not depart from Judah, nor a lawgiver from between his feet, *until Shiloh come*; and unto him shall the gathering of the people be."

379

In the original Hebrew:

> Lo yasur shevet (The sceptre shall not depart)
> M'Y'huda oomkhokek meeveyn (From Judah nor a
>   lawgiver from between)
> Raglav ad kee yavo Sheelo (His feet until Shiloh comes)
> V'lo yeekatameem (And to him the people will gather)

The Aramaic translation known as Targum Onkelos renders this:

> God shall uphold His promise to Judah even till the royal
> figure comes to claim the dominion that is His due.[327]

Most Jewish scholars see in the Judah blessing the glorious King David, and they look past David to the Messiah.[328] Having only the oral Torah and the Abrahamic Covenant, which was now the covenant made by God with him at Bethel, in his blessing of Judah, Jacob was clearly pointing forward to the coming of the Ha-Mashiach.

The Messianic import of this prediction by Jacob is accepted universally among rabbinic scholars.[329] Also, in the Tanak there is no doubt that these verses allude to the Messiah: Genesis 49:8, Psalm 72:8-11, Daniel 2:35; 7:14.

Although the identity and mission of the Messiah are topics of significant dissension among the rabbis, they agree this verse definitely alludes to Messiah. Rabbi Zlotowitz stated, "The overwhelming consensus of Rabbinic commentary interprets this verse [Genesis 49:10] to allude to the Messiah."[330]

The following two verses expand the Messianic description. Rabbi Ovadiah Sforno, an Italian commentator of the 16th century AD, states:

> The Messianic King rides an ass rather than a horse because
> it is God who wages the wars by which he comes to rule,
> "and He will be the King of Peace."[331]

Horses were portents of war, but donkeys were symbols of peace. Another universally accepted Messianic reference among the rabbinic sages was Zechariah 9:9, "Rejoice greatly, O daughter of Zion; shout, O daughter of Jerusalem; behold, thy King cometh unto thee; He is just and having salvation; lowly, and riding upon an ass, and upon a colt, the foal of an ass."

Jacob's vision did not get stymied in the intricacies of establishing a nation; Moses was to do that in God's timetable. Jacob was overwhelmed with what he saw through the centuries of time to the Messianic arrival. Did he see the sacrificial nature of the Messiah? All Hebrew commentators I have read seem to avoid a deep explanation of Gen. 49:11-12, or they attach these verses to a "time of prosperity" in the Messiah's reign. But I see the Messiah's blood being shed in the verse:

> He washes His garments in wine; His robes in the blood of
> grapes.

I see the bloodshot eyes in the agony of the sacrifice in the words:

> His eyes are darker than wine.

The whiteness of His teeth is accentuated against the rest of His body because of the drainage of His blood, shed for the sins of the whole world and soaked into his garments. It is a gory sight to behold the sacrifice of the Messiah as Jacob saw it, but that is what it will take to cleanse the whole world in that final day of Messianic atonement. Isaiah saw a similar sight but of the shedding of the blood of the enemy in a great victory (Isa. 63:1-3). That reference points to the fact that Messiah earned the victory by Himself: "I have trodden the winepress alone . . . .".

Ah! That bloody spot—stained with centuries of the Day of Atonement splashing by the high priest in the Most Holy Place on the Temple Mount—is the very spot on which Abraham raised the knife to kill his son.

The dual description of the Messiah by Jacob in his blessing of Judah must be noted here. He is described as a sacrificial lamb without blemish, soaked in His own blood that atones for the whole world, but He is also Judah's young lion who has preyed upon the forces of sin and death; He has also shed the blood of his enemies in a mortal blow. He is a conquering king. Nobody will dare to rouse Him. Jacob reveals the salvific redemptive power and the rulership of the universe by Elohim. Hear, O Israel, the Lord our God is one Lord. His name is Elohim. Blessed be He.

Ah, Jacob, dreamer of dreams, if only all Israel would dream your dreams, which would let them embrace the reality of their high calling for their God-ordained destiny.

> Rejoice greatly, O daughter of Zion, shout, O daughter of Jerusalem; behold, thy king cometh unto thee . . . . He is the righteous saviour . . . . and He shall speak peace unto the nations. (Zech.9:9-10, KJV)

The End

ENDNOTES

Chapter 1

[1]   See Cohen, *Everyman's Talmud,* The Major Teachings of the Rabbinic Sages, Schocken Books, New York, 1995, pp. 364-367. (Hereafter cited as 'Cohen')

[2]   See "Biblical Hebrew Lessons," Bible Online.

[3]   Leeland Dayton Mooring, "Carried to the Table."

[4]   Psalms 18:50; Lament. R. 1.51.Rabbinic literature calls the Messiah the Son of David.

[5]   See Cohen, pp. 346-356.

[6]   Quoted from Cohen, pp. 347-348.

Chapter 2

[7]   See the work of Nobel Prize Winner Ada Yonath, who has opened up the complex machinery of the ribosomes.

[8]   See Catherine Brady, *Elizabeth Blackburn and the Story of the Telomeres—Deciphering the Ends of DNA.* Available online. Elizabeth Blackburn was awarded the Nobel Prize for her work.

[9]   See Gen. R. 1. 3; Deut. R. 11. 31 (Citations from the Talmud).

[10] Cohen, pp. 16-18.

[11] Ber. 7a, ibid., p. 19; emphasis added. (Citations from the Talmud).

[12] Aboth 111. 19, ibid., p. 20.

[13] Michael Berg, *The Way,* pp. 58-59.

[14] See "Sheba, Queen of," Jewish Encyclopedia.com.

Chapter 3

[15] Cited in Cohen, p. 30.
[16] Ibid., pp. 30-31.
[17] Ibid., p. 4.
[18] See Gen. TR. 1. 3, cited in Cohen, p. 4.
[19] See p. Ber. 13a, cited in Cohen, p. 50.
[20] See Ber. 4b, Exod. R. 5, Cohen, p.50.
[21] B.M. 86b.
[22] Deut. R. XI. 10, ibid.
[23] Exod. R. XVIII. 5, ibid., p. 51
[24] Esth. R. VII.12, ibid.
[25] B.M. 86b, ibid., p. 52.
[26] Ber. 61a, cited in Cohen, pp. 90-92.
[27] Gen. R. xx11. 6, cited in Cohen, pp. 93-95.
[28] Cohen, p. 54.
[29] Deut. R. 111. 11
[30] Deut. R. x1. 10
[31] B.B. 16a; see Cohen, p. 54.
[32] Cohen, pp. 54-55.
[33] See Jefferson Vance, "Sheol: The Old Testament Consensus." Available online
[34] See the Book of Job, part 6: Satan, as discussed by Alexander Goldberg, guardian.com.uk, Monday 2 August 2010. See also Cohen, "The Two Impulses," in *Everyman's Talmud*, pp. 89-93.
[35] Desmond Ford, *Daniel 8:14, The Day of Atonement and the Investigative Judgement,* Glasier View Manuscript, 1980, p. 345.
[36] See Cohen, "Angelology," in *Everyman's Talmud*, pp. 45-58.
[37] Cohen, pp. 54-58, 88.

Chapter 4

[38] Sanh. 11a, cited in Cohen, p. 124.
[39] Ber. 34b., Cohen, p. 124.
[40] p. Meg. 70d, Cohen, p. 124.
[41] Cohen, p. 124.

42 Based on Numbers 6:22-27; the Talmud: Num. R. xi. 5, and p. Ber. 13a, ibid., pp. 43-44.

43 Pes. 54a; Cohen, p. 347. See also Pesikta Rab. 152b; Cohen, p. 347.

44 See also Lament. R. 1. 51, ibid., pp. 346-347.

45 Pes. 54a, ibid., Cohen p. 104.

46 Joma 86a et seq; Ber. 34b; Deut, R. II. 24; Cohen p. 104.

47 B.B. 10a, Cohen, p. 223.

48 Shab. 31a, Cohen, p. 375.

Chapter 5

49 See Bible Study Charts, www.biblestudycharts.com. See also Cohen p 388 where he cites Sopherim xvi. 8 and Sanh. 68a as sources.

50 See Allan Russell Juriansz, *The Fair Dinkum Jew—The Survival of Israel and the Abrahamic Covenant.*

51 Cohen, p. ix; emphasis added.

52 A. J. Jacobs, *The Year of Living Biblically.*

53 See John MacArthur, NKJV, Nelson Bibles.

54 Charles Freeman, *A New History of Early Christianity*, p. 13.

Chapter 6

55 Cohen, p. 346.

56 Ibid., pp. 346-356.

57 See Simon Sebag Montefiore, p. 15.

58 See references: (p. Jeb. 14d; Ber. 40a; Midrash to Ps. xxxvii. I;, 126b). Also see the Jerusalem Targum on Genesis 14:18, quoted in Cohen, p. 236.

59 For a discussion of the significance of Melchizedek, see also Montefiore, pp. 21 and 184n.

60 Ibid.

61 See *The Jewish Study Bible*, p. 1,078; comments in margin.

62 Jewish Encyclopedia.com on Molech, "Nature of Worship—Critical View."

63 See Jewish Encyclopedia.com on Molech, "Motive of Sacrifices."

[64] Quoted in Cohen, pp. 56-57.
[65] See Cohen, pp. 346-347.
[66] Cohen uses the KJV here; see pp. 346-348.
[67] See Cohen, pp. 346-349.
[68] Suk. 52a, quoted in Cohen, p. 348.

Chapter 7

[69] Genesis 12:4.
[70] Genesis 23:1-19; 25:7-11.

Chapter 8

[71] See The Year of Living Biblically by A. J. Jacobs.
[72] Ibid., p. 316.
[73] Ibid., pp. 200-201.
[74] See *The Stanford Encyclopedia of Philosophy* on "Existentialism," accessible online.
[75] See Collins, *English Dictionary*, Google online.
[76] See Cohen, p. xiii.
[77] Ibid., p. 1.
[78] Ber. 6a, R.H. 17b, A.Z. 3b, and Chag. 5b, quoted in Cohen, p. 7.
[79] Mech. To xii. I, 2a, B.B. 25a, quoted in Cohen, p. 9.
[80] Ber. IX. 2, quoted in Cohen, p. 11.
[81] Gen. R.II. 5, quoted in Cohen, p. 14.
[82] See Cohen, p. 14.
[83] Ibid., p. 16; emphasis added.
[84] Joma 69b.
[85] See Cohen, pp. 18-20; emphasis added.
[86] Aboth III. 18, cited in Cohen, p. 22.
[87] Kid. 36a, cited in Cohen, pp. 20-22.
[88] Lev. R. XXIV. 9; see Cohen, p. 23.
[89] The Collins Dictionary, available online.
[90] Joma VI. 2, cited in Cohen, pp. 25-26.
[91] See Dictionary.com on Immanence.net.
[92] Chag. 13a, quoted in Cohen, p. 40.
[93] See p. Ber. 13a, cited in Cohen, p. 41.
[94] See chapter 14, "Kabbalah."

95   See chapter 3, "The Population of Heaven and the Origin of Evil."
96   Sifre Deut. S 306; 132a.
97   Genesis 9:6, Aboth III. 18, cited in Cohen, p. 67.
98   Leviticus 19:18, KJV, cited in Cohen, p. 67.
99   Aboth III. 19.
100   Mak.10b; see Cohen, p. 94.
101   Shab. 104a; see Cohen, p. 94.
102   Joma 39a, cited in Cohen, p. 94.
103   Cohen, p. 95.
104   Cohen, p. 72.
105   Ibid., p. 95.
106   Lev. R. XXVII. 4, cited in Cohen, p. 73.
107   Ber. 61a, cited in Cohen, pp. 88-89.
108   Aboth II. I f, cited in Cohen, p. 103.
109   See Goodreads Online, "Charles Dickens Quotes."
110   See Cohen, pp. 72-76.
111   Shab. 55a, cited in Cohen, p. 73.
112   (Rambam) Psalm 2 in Hebrew: Mizmor Bet, Google online.
113   See Wikipedia: "The Names of God in Judaism."
114   *The Jewish Study Bible,* p. 909; emphasis added.
115   Shab.31a, cited in Cohen, p. 375; emphasis added.
116   See 'Hebrew name for God' Google online
117   Pes. 54a, cited in Cohen, p. 104.
118   Joma. 86a et seq., cited in Cohen, p. 104.
119   Pes. 119a, cited in Cohen, p. 104.
120   Deut. R. 11.12, Talmud reference.
121   Tosifta Joma v9.
122   Psalm 51:17, Lev. R. vii 2, quoted in Cohen, p. 105.
123   Sanh. 90a, quoted in Cohen, p. 357.
124   Cohen, pp. 347-348.
125   See Suk. 52a, cited in Cohen, pp. 347-348.
126   See *The Jewish Study Bible* comments in margins of pp. 891-892, citing the Talmud b. Sot. 14a.
127   Excerpted from Cohen.
128   See Irving M. Zeitlin, The *Jews—The Making of a Diasporic People,* pp. 56-63.

[129] See Banks and Wiggins, *101 Things Everyone Should Know about Judaism.*

[130] See *Israel Record—Yearning for Zion*: "The Dream," excerpted from Theodor Herzl, *Der Judenstadt*, published in February 1896.

Chapter 9

[131] See *The MacArthur Study Bible: The New KJV*, for all dates used in this chapter.

[132] See Simon Sebag Montefiore.

[133] Ibid., p. xxviii.

[134] Ibid., pp. xxviii-xxix.

[135] Adin Steinsaltz, *The Essential Talmud*, p. 175.

Chapter 10

[136] See Gershom Scholem, *The Messianic Idea in Judaism*, pp. 203-227.

[137] See Jewish Encyclopedia on "tefilin."

[138] Quoted from Cohen, pp. 40-44.

[139] Lament. R. 1. 45 etc., quoted from Cohen, p. 45.

Chapter 11

[140] See Cohen, p. 347.

[141] See Meir ben Gabbai, *Avodat Ha-Kodesh*, cited in Scholem, pp. 298-300.

[142] See Hagigah 15b, cited in Scholem, "Revelation and Tradition as Religious Categories in Judaism," *The Messianic Idea in Judaism*, p. 301.

[143] See Steinsaltz's chapter on "Sacrifices."

[144] See Stephen A. Geller, "The Religion of the Bible," *The Jewish Study Bible*, pp. 2,021-2,040.

[145] See "Jewish Interpretation of the Bible," *The Jewish Study Bible*, pp. 1,829-1,908.

[146] See Cohen in his references to these schools.

[147] See Jacobs.

[148] See Ber. 28b, The Talmud
[149] Cohen, pp. 346-347.
[150] Ibid., p. 346.
[151] See chapter 5, "Inspiration and Love." Also see Jacobs.
[152] Cohen, pp. 133, 142-143.
[153] B.B 14b et seq, cited in Cohen, p. 143.
[154] See *The MacArthur Study Bible*, for suggested sequence and chronology.
[155] Cohen, pp. 143-146.
[156] Num. R 14, 4, quoted in Cohen, p. 145.
[157] See Cohen, pp. 128-132.
[158] Sanh. 34a, cited in Cohen, p. 147.
[159] See Cohen, pp. 146-149.
[160] Ibid., p. 148.
[161] Ibid., p. 133.
[162] See chapter 14, "Kabbalah."
[163] Chaim Rabin, *A Short History of the Hebrew Language*.
[164] See Enrico and Bazzi, "The History of the Aramaic Language" in *Journal of Eastern Studies*.
[165] Steinsaltz, chapters 1-3.
[166] See Clare Goldfarb, *Judaism and Hellenism: The Encounter*.
[167] Ibid.
[168] See Wikipedia.
[169] Steinsaltz, p. 143.
[170] See The Sanhedrin.org.
[171] Joel 2:28 Num. xv. 25, cited in Cohen, p. 125; emphasis added.
[172] See Scholem, p. 284.
[173] See essay on "Revelation and Tradition as Religious Categories" in Scholem, pp. 284-286.
[174] Ibid., p. 297; emphasis added.
[175] Scholem, pp. 176-202.
[176] Ibid., pp. 203-227.
[177] Ibid., pp. 300-303.
[178] Ibid., p. 286.
[179] Ibid., p. 286.
[180] Ibid., pp. 287-289; emphasis added.

Chapter 12

[181] See Jewish Encyclopedia and Encyclopedia Britannica; also see Herbert Danby, *The Mishnah.*

[181] The Jewish Virtual Library, Google online.

[182] See My Jewish Learning: "Mishnah."

[183] Steinsaltz, pp. 33-34.

[184] Ibid., p. 34.

[185] Ibid., p. 35.

[186] See Wikipedia, "Usha."

[187] Stensaltz, p. 38.

[188] Ibid., pp. 38-39.

[189] See preface to Danby.

[190] See introduction to Steinsaltz.

[191] See preface to Danby.

[192] Introduction to Danby.

[193] Ibid.

[194] See Walter Laqueur, *A History of Zionism*, pp. 17-18.

[195] See Steinsaltz.

[196] Ibid.

[197] Cohen, p. ix.

[198] See Juriansz.

[199] Cohen, preface.

[200] Ibid.

[201] Ibid., pp. 346-347.

[202] Pes. 54a, Pesikta Rab. 152b.

Chapter 13

[203] Steinsaltz, pp. 3-4.

[204] See Encyclopedia Britannica Online.

[205] Steinsaltz, pp. 279-283.

[206] Encyclopedia Britannica Online.

[207] See the introduction in Solomon Schechter, *Studies in Judaism*; emphasis added.

[208] Ibid.

[209] Cited in Ismar Schorsch, Wordtrade.com, "Judaism."

210 Thomas Friedman, *Beirut to Jerusalem,* p. 288,
211 Steinsaltz, p. 266; emphasis added.
212 Ibid.
213 Ibid., p. 269.

Chapter 14

214 See Wikipedia, "Safed."
215 Berg, pp. 26-29.
216 Ibid., p. 1.
217 See My Jewish Learning: "Tikkun in Lurianic Kabbalah."
218 See "Mishnah mip nei Tikkun ha-olam and Gittin 4:2." See also 'The Messianic Idea in Judaism' by Gershom Scholem pp 43-48.
219 See Scholem's essay "The Neutralization of Messianism in Early Hasidism" in *The Messianic Idea in Judaism,* pp. 185-186.
220 See Wikipedia, "Immanence."
221 See "Tikkun olam" in Wikipedia, and the Hebrew Wikipedia of March 2012.
222 Scholem's *The Hessianic Idea in Judaism,* pp. 37-48.
223 Arthur Hertzberg's foreword to Scholem's *The Messianic Idea in Judaism,* p. xvi.
224 Ibid.
225 Ibid., pp. ix-x, 1-36.
226 Berg, p. 56.
227 Ibid.
228 Ibid., pp. 14-15; emphasis added.
229 Ibid., pp. 77-79.
230 Ibid., pp. 53-58.
231 Ibid., p. 58; emphasis added.
232 Ibid., pp. 58-59.
233 *The Jewish Study Bible,* comments in margin of Genesis chapter 3.
234 See b. B. Bat. 16a.

Chapter 15

235 Quoted in Robert Silverberg, *If I Forget Thee O Jerusalem*, pp. 344-345.
236 See Vexen Crabtree, *The Human Condition: Single-god Religions*.
237 See Simon Sebag Montefiore, pp. 35-36.
238 Ibid., pp. 49-50.
239 See online: "Idolatry and Sex Worship in Ancient Israel" Part 1, written by Administrator. The following sources are quoted: "Unger's Bible Dictionary" p. 413; "Encyclopedic Dictionary of Religion" Volumes F-N, p. 1,343; "The Interpreter's Dictionary of the Bible" Volume 2, p. 256; "Jewish Encyclopedia" Volume 3 p. 430 "Collier's Encyclopedia" on idolatry; and "Encyclopedia Judaica" Volume 11, p. 144.
240 *Greek in Jewish Palestine/Hellenism in Jewish Palestine*, By Saul Lieberman, JTS Press, 1994.
241 See Jewish Encyclopedia Online, "Hellenism."

Chapter 16

242 See the bibliography and biographical sketches of this book.
243 Simon Sebag Montefiore, pp. 53-54.

Chapter 17

244 Ibid., pp. 102-118.
245 See Jewish Encyclopedia.com, "Hellenic influence on the Jews."
246 Ibid.
247 Simon Sebag Montefiore, pp. 148-150.
248 Jewish Virtual Library.
249 Simon Sebag Montefiore, p. 64.
250 Ibid., p. 64.
251 See Cohen, p. 157; emphasis added.
252 See chapter 21, "The Ha-Mashiach of Israel."
253 See introduction to Danby.

254 See Leviticus Rabba, 21,4 reporting ben Levi, early 3rd Century AD.
255 Cohen, pp. 347-348.
256 Simon Sebag Montefiore, p. 159.
257 See Jewish Encyclopedia.com, "Zealots."
258 About Judaism.com, available online.
259 Josephus, *Antiquities* xi. 1.2.
260 Josephus, *The Jewish War*, p. 292.

Chapter 18

261 See current Knesset member list of the nineteenth Knesset, Knesset Website.
262 See my assessment in my book *The Fair Dinkum Jew*, pp. 177-184.
263 Friedman, p. 288.
264 Ibid.
265 Ibid., pp. 284-321, 470-490.
266 See Rabbi Mottel Boleston, "Beliefs of Messianic Congregations," *The Abrahamic Covenant—The Basis for Jewish Identity*. See also P. E. Globe, trans., *The Jewish Orthodox B'rit Hadasha,* AFI International.
267 Friedman, pp. 474-475.
268 Ibid., pp. 235-236.
269 Ibid., pp.567-568.

Chapter 19

270 See my book *The Fair Dinkum Jew* for an interesting assessment of Israel and the diaspora.

Chapter 20

271 Cohen, pp. 45-46.
272 Ibid., p. 45; Lament. i. 16; Lament. R. 1. 45; emphasis added.
273 Cohen, p. 47.

[274] See Cohen, chapter 7, and "Jews for Judaism" online, October 2012.

[275] Shab. 31a, quoted in Cohen, p. 385.

[276] Cohen, pp. 348-350.

[277] Ibid., p. 347.

[278] Ibid., p. 347-348.

[279] Cohen, pp. 348-349.

[280] Ibid., p. 357.

[281] Ibid., pp. 358-364.

[282] *The Jewish Study Bible.* See comments in the margin, p. 1,285.

[283] See "Jews for Judaism" online, October 29, 2012.

[284] See Cohen, p. 364.

[285] Ibid.

[286] Ibid.

[287] Ibid.

[288] Ibid., pp. 365-368.

[289] Ibid., p. 368.

[290] Ibid., p. 369.

[291] Ibid.

Chapter 21

[292] Scholem, p. 53; emphasis added.

[293] Ibid., p. 53.

[294] Ibid., pp. 50-51; emphasis added.

[295] *The Jewish Study Bible,* p. 909.

[296] Shab. 31a, Cohen, p. 385.

[297] Scholem, pp. 21-22. emphasis added.

[298] Ibid., pp. 1-36. See also 'Religious Anarchism' in pp. 18,21,26, 63,77,109,131,134,144,152,161,245,256, and 323

[299] Ibid., pp. 37-38; emphasis added.

[300] Ibid., p. 48.

[301] Ibid., p. 62.

[302] Ibid., p. 58.

[303] Ibid., pp. 64-70, 71-77.

[304] Ibid., pp. 184-185.

[305] Ibid., pp. 186-187.

³⁰⁶ See online on Kabbalah on "Evil: Kabbalistic views."
³⁰⁷ Scholem, pp. 191-192.
³⁰⁸ Ibid., pp. 189-192.
³⁰⁹ Degel Mahane Ephrayim, koretz, 1810, f. 17a.
³¹⁰ Scholem, pp. 200-201.
³¹¹ Ibid., pp. 200-202.
³¹² See online, "What do Karaite Jews believe about the Messiah?" Also see "As It is Written: A Brief Case for Karaism" by Shawn Lichaa, Nehemiah Gordon and Meir Rekhavi, newsletter, available online.
³¹³ See online, "The Doctrine of the Two Messiahs Among the Karaites." See also N. Wieder, "The Damascus Fragments" and "The Manual of Discipline" in the *Journal of Jewish Studies*, 1953, p. 168. See also J. T. Milik, *Revue Biblique*, 1953, pp. 280-291.
³¹⁴ Zvi Yehudah Kook, Le-netivot Yisrael.
³¹⁵ See Shlomo Aviner, "Am ke-lavi," *Jerusalem* 1983, 2:192-194; Also see Uriel Tal, "Mithos u-tevunah be-yahadut yamenu," *Tel Aviv*, 1987, p. 102.
³¹⁶ Aviezer Ravitsky, "The Revealed End: Messianic Religious Zionism."
³¹⁷ See "My Jewish Learning."
³¹⁸ Ibid.
³¹⁹ Ibid.
³²⁰ Ibid.
³²¹ The Jewish Virtual Library.
³²² Chabad.org; emphasis added.
³²³ See Boleston. See also "B'rit Hadasha Messianic Jewish Synagogue"; "Torah and Messiah," Nazarene.net: B'rit Hadasha. See also P. E. Goble, trans., *The Orthodox B'rit Hadasha*. See also *Union of Messianic Jewish Synagogues/ Union of Messianic Judaism.*
³²⁴ "Do Reform Jews Believe in the Messiah?" an address by Rabbi Joseph Meszler on Rosh Hashanah, 5767/2006.
³²⁵ Emet Ve-emunah; the statement of principles of Orthodox Jews.
³²⁶ Friedman, p. 288.

King David's Naked Dance

Chapter 22

³²⁷ *The Jewish Study Bible* margin commentary, p. 97.
³²⁸ Ibid.
³²⁹ See for an example Midrash Rabah, commenting on Genesis 49:8-10; Psalm 72:8-11, Daniel 2:35; 7:14,
³³⁰ Rabbi Zlotowitz stated, "The overwhelming consensus of Rabbinic commentary interprets this verse [Genesis 49:10] to allude to the Messiah."
³³¹ Ibid.

GLOSSARY

Aggadah (Haggadah)—The text that guides the performance of ritual acts and prayers at the Seder dinner celebrating Passover. It retells the story of the Exodus. The term can also refer to the part of rabbinical literature not concerned with the law.

Aliya—Immigrating to Israel

Araboth—The "Seventh Heaven" home of God

Asmakhta—Support, reliance, a legal obligation that is one-sided

Bavli—Babylonian Gemara (Talmud)

Chayyoth—The name of the "living creatures" of Ezekiel 1:5-25

Derek Eretz—Tractates of the Talmud

Devekut—Communion with God

Din—Judgement

Eduyot—A collection of testimonies

Ein Sof—God's hidden essence

Esh—Fire

Gemara—The Babylonian and Jerusalem commentaries on the Mishnah

Goel—Kinsman, redeemer

Ha-Mashiach—Messiah

Haskala—The Enlightenment

Jetzer Hara—Proclivity to evil; explaining the origin of evil

Jetzer Tov—Tendency to good

Kethubhim—The "Writings" that follow the law and the prophets in the Tanak

Kodashim—Holy things

Machon—Where the treasuries of snow, hail, and dew originate

Moed—Festivals

Maon—Where the angels live

Mayim—Water

Midot (Middot)—The principles used to explicate the meanings of biblical words and passages

Midrashim—Ancient rabbinic expositions of holy writ

Mishnah—Commentary on the Tanak

Mitzvoth—Fulfillment of the Commandments

Nashim—The third order of the Mishnah concerning women and wives

Nethinim—The Temple servants

Nevi'im—The Prophets

Nezikin—Damages

Nidah—A woman in menstruation

Pentateuch—The five books of Moses: Genesis, Exodus, Leviticus, Numbers, Deuteronomy

Peshaim—The Babylonian Talmud

Rakia—The layer of Heaven containing the sun, moon, stars, and planets; the firmament

Reshimu—Residue

Ruach Hakodesh—The Holy Spirit

Sabbatianism—The teachings of Shabbatai Zevi, a false Messiah

Sefira, Sefirot—any of the 10 Emanations from God in Jewish (Kabbalah) Mysticism

Shamayim—The place where there is water; synonymous with Heaven

Shechinah—Dwelling, God's presence as His dwelling with us

Shekakim—Where manna is ground

Shekalim—Pertaining to the offering (levy) for Temple maintenance

Shevirot Haqelim—The breaking of the vessels

Sitra Achra—The other side

Sofia—Divine attribute of wisdom

Talmud—The combined Mishnah and Gemara

Tamid—Treatise in the Talmud regarding the morning and evening burned offering

Tanak—The Hebrew Bible or Old Testament

Tannaim—Those who study

Tefilin—Phylacteries

Teshuah—Salvation, deliverance

Tikkun Olam—Re-establishment of the harmonious condition of the world

Toharot—Purities

Torah—Conversation with God, at first oral and then written

Tsidkenu (Sid-Qe-Nu)—"The Lord our Righteousness" (Jer. 23:5-6)

Tzedakah—Support of benevolent causes

Tzimzum—literally, "contraction of God's essence"

Vilon—The work of the renewal of Creation; "issues forth in the evening and retires in the morning"

Yeridah—Emigrating from Israel

Yerushalmi—Jerusalem Gemara (Talmud)

Yomah—Talmudic tract pertaining to the Day of Atonement

Zaddik—He who attains the full state of devekut

Zaphon—A city on the east of the Jordan

Zebul—The heavenly habitation of God where are located God's throne, and the "Heavenly Jerusalem and Temple"

Zeraim—Seeds

Zevahim—A message from our heritage

BIBLIOGRAPHY

Banks, Richard D., and James B. Wiggins. *101 Things Everyone Should Know about Judaism.* Adams Media.

Berg, Michael. *The Way.* Safed: John Wiley and Sons.

Cohen, Abraham. *Everyman's Talmud.* New York: Schocken Books, 1975.

Danby, Herbert, trans. *The Mishnah.*

Encyclopaedia Britannica, available online.

Ford, Desmond. *Daniel 8:14—The Day of Atonement and the Investigative Judgement.* 1980, available online.

Freeman, Charles. *A New History of Early Christianity.* New Haven and London: Yale University Press.

Friedman, Thomas. *Beirut to Jerusalem.* Harper Collins, 1998.

Jacobs, A. J. *The Year Of Living Biblically.* Simon and Schuster, 2008.

The Jewish Study Bible—Tanakh Translation. Featuring the Jewish Publication Society, Oxford University Press, 2004.

Juriansz, Allan Russell. *The Fair Dinkum Jew—The Survival of Israel and the Abrahamic Covenant.* Bloomington, IN: iUniverse, 2012.

Laqueur, Walter. *A History of Zionism.* New York: Schocken Books.

Montefiore, Claude G. *The Old Testament and After.* London: Macmillan & Company, 1923.

Montefiore, Simon Sebag. *Jerusalem—The Biography.* Weidenfield and Nicolson, Orion House, London, 2011.

Neusner, Jacob. *The Talmud of Babylonia: A Complete Outline.* Scholars' Press, 1995.

Neusner, Jacob. *The Talmud: An Academic Commentary.* Atlanta: Scholars' Press, 1994-1996.

Schechter, Solomon. *Studies in Judaism,* 3 volumes. Gorgias Press.

Scholem, Gershom. *The Messianic Idea in Judaism and Other Essays on Jewish Spirituality.* Reprint with foreword by Arthur Hertzberg, New York: Schocken Books, 1995.

Silverberg, Robert. *If I Forget Thee O Jerusalem.* Morrow, 1970.

Steinsaltz, Adin. *The Essential Talmud.* Translated from the Hebrew by Chaya Galai, Basic Books, Harper Collins, USA, 1976.

The Tanak:
- King James Version
- New King James Version
- Good News Bible
- The Living Bible

Vermes, Geza. *The Complete Dead Sea Scrolls in English.* Penguin Books, 1962.

Zeitlin, Irving M. *The Jews as a Diaspora People.* Cambridge: Polity Press.

BIOGRAPHICAL NOTES ON CONTRIBUTORS TO MY BIBLIOGRAPHY

Michael Berg

(b. 1973) Born in America of Orthodox Jewish parents. He is codirector of the Kabbalah Centre in Safed, Israel; his mother, Karen Berg, and his brother Yehudah Berg are the other codirectors. He is the son of Philip Berg, the founder of the modern Kabbalah Centre. Michael edited an unabridged English translation of the Zohar. He is also the author of several books, including *Secrets of the Zohar, Becoming Like God, The Way, The Secret, Well of Life, What God Meant,* and *Days of Connection.* He also has a website called Ukabbalah, offering interactive lectures and live events. Many of his views are opposed by other scholars. I am indebted to Michael Berg in my understanding of basic Kabbalah, and I quote him extensively.

Abraham Cohen

(1887-1957) British Jewish scholar, educated at the London University and University of Cambridge. He was appointed rabbi at the Birmingham Hebrew Congregation in 1933. He participated in the World Jewish Congress and the Zionist Movement. His major works are *Everyman's Talmud, The Major Teachings of the Rabbinic Sages,* and *The Parting of the Ways: Judaism and the Rise of Christianity. Everyman's Talmud* was published first in 1949 and reprinted in 1975 and 1995. Jacob Neusner, who wrote the foreword for the 1995 printing, spoke highly of him: "Cohen's *Everyman's Talmud* is the right place to begin not only to learn about Judaism in general but to meet the substance of the Talmud in particular." This spectrum encompasses both primitive Judaism and the esoteric nature of Talmudic philosophy. He eerily relies on the Tanak in what may be deciphered to be his personal beliefs. This book I have written takes every advantage Cohen has afforded me in understanding the Talmud.

Herbert Danby

(1889-1953) Danby was an Anglican priest and a writer who is credited with playing an important role in the change of attitudes toward Judaism in the first half of the 20th century. He was educated at Leeds and at Keble College, Oxford, where he won several prizes. He obtained an MA in oriental languages and was outstanding in Hebrew. He achieved a doctor of divinity in 1923. He translated the Jewish documents of Tractate Sanhedrin, the Mishnah, and the Tosefta. In addition, he translated the remarkable work *Jesus of Nazareth* by Joseph Klausner. He also assisted in the Yale translation of *Mishnah Torah of Maimonides*. He wrote five other books on related Hebrew topics, including the outstanding work *The Jew and Christianity*. He translated two other Hebrew books into English. He lived in Jerusalem from 1919 to 1936, when he moved back to Oxford as Professor of Hebrew.

Desmond Ford

(b. 1929) An Australian, Ford started his theological tertiary education at Avondale College. He was ordained a minister in the Seventh-day Adventist Church. He obtained a PhD from Michigan State University for his dissertation "The Rhetorical Analysis of Paul's Letters", in 1961. His second doctorate was for his dissertation "The Abomination of Desolation" from the University of Manchester in Britain, in 1972. This was a study of the apocalypticism of the Tanak. He spent 14 years as chairman of the Theology Department at the prestigious Avondale College, SDA's university in Australia. He became a reformer in the SDA Church, from which he was ejected in 1980 for refuting the "Biblical basis" of the SDA doctrine of the "Investigative Judgement." He has numerous publications, notably commentaries on the books of Daniel and Revelation, which deal with the apocalypticism of the Tanak and the B'rit Hadashah. His biography by Milton Hook is available online. It details the illustrious nature of his studies, the doctrinal controversies within the SDA Church and the injustice of Ford's treatment by the powerful hierarchy of administrative leaders of the SDA Church, whose doctrinal knowledge took a backseat to Ellen White's supremacy. Ellen White is the SDA prophetess. As my friend since I met Ford in 1957, he had a great influence on me. I have acknowledged him as the motivation for the writing of this book.

Charles Freeman

(b. 1943) Freeman is a British writer and historian who did archeological digs in collaboration with Ipswich Museum. He studied at Trinity College, Cambridge, London University, and the University of East Anglia before being appointed head of history at St. Clare's, Oxford. I have counted 10 publications to his name. The most renowned is *The Closing of the Western Mind: The Rise of Faith and the Fall of Reason*, published in 2003. He is widely considered a specialist on the ancient world and its legacy. The one book I have read with intense curiosity is *A New History of Early Christianity*, which gives special attention to the tensions in the Judaism of the time of Yeshua of Nazareth. This book presents an exciting perspective and fresh insights into the development of the Christian Church, highlighting the contributions the early Christian leaders who pioneered the pronouncements of Christian belief and doctrines. In many of his considerations he brilliantly ties in the basic Judaism on which many of these beliefs were based. He also exposes the departures from Tanakian principles that many of these evolving doctrines made. The book is intensely riveting.

Thomas L. Friedman

(b. 1953) Friedman is a American Jew educated at the University of Minnesota, Brandeis University, and St. Anthony's College, Oxford. His outstanding book *From Beirut to Jerusalem* was written after his experiences of five years in the Middle East as bureau chief, first in Beirut and then in Jerusalem, for the *New York Times*. This is one of six bestselling books he has written from his experience as a reporter and columnist for the *New York Times*. He has won three Pulitzer Prizes, and he is very knowledgeable about Israel and the diasporic Jews. I have paid tribute to him in my book *The Fair Dinkum Jew—The Survival of Israel and the Abrahamic Covenant*. His brilliant mind has made him an expert on many topics, and he sways opinion through his op-eds in the *New York Times*. His regular columns for this newspaper educates people who want to stay in touch with what is going on in the world at a level deeper than ordinary news. His background knowledge is enormous. It is rumoured that he has been an adviser of the Obama Administration.

A. J. Jacobs

(b. 1968) Jacobs is a Jewish American educated at Brown University, and he is editor at large at *Esquire Magazine*. He is the author of three *New York Times* bestsellers, the most important one in my opinion being *The Year of Living Biblically*. Not professing any expertise in theology, he pretends to have written this book as a light-hearted view of Judaism. But in his very down-to-earth style, his consideration of some aspects of Judaism has demonstrated remarkable insight into the Tanak and its significance for modern times. His book is essential reading for any student or devotee of Judaism.

Walter Laqueur

(b. 1921) Laqueur was born to Jewish parents in Germany. He was educated at the Breslau Johannes Gymnasium. He left Germany in 1938 for Palestine, where he lived on a Kibbutz as a labourer for a year; then he moved to Jerusalem and worked as a journalist. He moved to London as editor of *Survey* from 1955-1964. He was appointed director of the Wiener Library from 1964-1993, and he became the founder and editor of *The Journal of Contemporary History*. He was a visiting professor to four universities: Chicago, Johns Hopkins, Harvard, and Tel Aviv. He became a professor of history of ideas at Brandeis University (1967-1971), and then a professor at Georgetown University (1980-1991). He is the author of several books, the most important considered to be *The History of Zionism*, which is instructive for any student of Judaism and is not only a history of modern Zionism but also covers centuries of the torrid experiences of the Jews.

Claude Goldsmid Montefiore

(1858-1938) Claude Montefiore was the great nephew of Sir Moses Montefiore, and he was from the famous Montefiore family of Britain but had roots in Lithuania. He was educated in the classics at Baliol College, Oxford, and he studied theology in Berlin. It was hoped that he might join the ministry of the Reform Jewish Congregation in England, but instead he became a scholar and writer. He is well-known for giving the Hibbert Lectures in London in 1892 on the subject "The Origin of Religion as Illustrated by the Ancient Hebrews," which subsequently was published in book form. He authored at least 12 other books, the most significant of which appears to be *The Old Testament and After*. He is considered a controversial figure in that he studied Christianity extensively and wrote books about Jesus, St. Paul, and the Synoptic Gospels. His views on liberal Judaism have also created some controversy.

Simon Sebag Montefiore

(b. 1965) Simon Montefiore comes from the same famous Lithuanian Jewish family pioneered by Sir Moses Montefiore, banking partner of N. M. Rothschild and Sons. Simon was born in Britain, where he became a popular historian and writer and a fellow of the Royal Society of Literature. He was educated in Caius College, Cambridge, where he read history but then went on to work as a banker and foreign affairs journalist. He wrote many books such as *Catherine the Great and Potemkin*, *Stalin*, and *The Young Stalin*. His most recent book is the outstanding *Jerusalem—The Biography*. This one has made the great survey of the holy city, from its beginning to beyond history! He is perhaps unaware of the deep spiritual events his story has uncovered and described.

Jacob Neusner

(b. 1932) Neusner is a Jewish American who is a recognized academic scholar in Judaism. He was educated at Harvard, the Jewish Theological Seminary of America, Yale, and Oxford. He taught at several American Universities but is now known for his attachment to the University of South Florida. His books, articles, and reviews are too numerous to count, but he appears to be most well-known for his commentaries on the Talmud. He has many critics in Jewish circles; I see him go overboard in some of his statements and conclusions. Among his multiple critics is the late Saul Lieberman, also a scholar of the Talmud. It appears they criticized each other over the analysis of the Yerushalmi.

Solomon Schechter

(1847-1915) Schechter was a Moldavian-born Jew who studied at the Rabbinic College in Vienna with Meir Friedmann, a renowned European Talmudic teacher. Schechter then studied at the University of Berlin and the Berlin Hochschule before settling in Britain, where he started writing his well-known works *Studies in Judaism* and *Aspects of Rabbinic Theology*. He was appointed professor of Hebrew at University College, London. In this position he was instrumental in bringing from Egypt the Cairo Jewish Manuscript fragments found in the attic of the Ben Ezra Synagogue in Cairo. He then moved to New York as president of the Jewish Theological Seminary, where he placed an accent on "positive historical Judaism." This was more or less a mediation between the conservative and reform brands of Judaism in America. Although he ameliorated the relationship between the two factions, the problem of their differences has not yet been solved.

Robert Silverberg

(b. 1935) Silverberg was born to American Jewish parents in the United States, and he was educated in Columbia University, majoring in comparative literature. He produced numerous works of science fiction. His main religio-political work was the book *If I Forget Thee O Jerusalem*, in which he recounts the formation of the modern nation of Israel. It is written as a dramatic story of how American Jews and the United States helped create Israel. For those who believe in the sacred destiny of the Jews, it is a most exciting and fulfilling adventure. His other works of fiction and nonfiction are assessed as quite enterprising.

Gershom Scholem

(1897-1982) Scholem was born in Berlin as Gerhardt to an "assimilated" Jewish couple. His father had become a German nationalist. At the age of 14 he rejected his father's politics and espoused Zionism. It is told that this departure from his father's influence was hailed by his mother, who bought him a portrait of Theodor Herzl. Having no Jewish education prior, he started learning Hebrew and studied the Talmud and Kabbalah. Judaism became the centre of his life, and he tried some religious observation, which by his own estimation was unsuccessful. In his biography of his early life, *From Berlin to Jerusalem*, he appears committed to secularism. It is alleged he looked at Jewish history and Kabbalah "from the outside." He was turned out of home by his father, changed his first name from Gerhardt to Gershom, and began a friendship with Zalman Shazar, who later was to become the third president of Israel. He loudly expressed disapproval for the start of World War I but was drafted into the German army. He was discharged from the army a mere two months later, labelled as a "psychopath temporarily unfit for duty." He then entered the University of Berlin and began the study of pure mathematics. During this time he met Martin Buber and Walter Benjamin, who influenced him considerably. He transferred to the University of Munich, where he translated and annotated the Sefer ha-Bahir (the Kabbalistic Book of Illumination) as his dissertation, graduating summa cum laude.

He soon after immigrated to Palestine, where he obtained the position of librarian of the Hebrew section of the newly opened National Library. While there, he produced highly critical reviews and essays of Kabbalistic authors, which were published in the German-Jewish journal *Der Jude* and in the Hebrew journal in Jerusalem, *Keriat Sefer*. His dissertation "Das Buch Bahir" was published in Leipzig in 1923. He then began publishing arduous and prolific books and articles on Kabbalah and Judaism. He dissected and criticised Kabbalistic theory and history, and he wrote succinctly in topics in Judaism, notably Messianism. In the latter he chose to stick close to the Tanakian theology rather than the opalescent Talmudic portrayal, though he did not spurn the Talmud. I find his Tanakian "acute Messianism" and espousal of the apocalypticism of Isaiah and Daniel enthralling, to say the least. His highly critical view of Sabbatianism is extraordinary in the analysis of the disastrous effect that heretical movement had on Jews and Judaism. He felt very keenly the desire of the Hebrews for the Messiah, and his opinions reveal his own commitment and yearning for Messiah. He wrote 32 books. He is the primary subject of 18 books, besides 44 articles published about him in the religious literature. The admiration other scholars had for him is enormous, and I consider him a giant in Judaism. More than a lifetime is needed to study his works. He occupied the chair of the first professorship in Mysticism at the Hebrew University in Jerusalem. His many awards included the Israel Prize, Yakir Yerushalayim, and the Bialik Prize for Jewish Thought. His greatest accomplishment, in my view, is the intended preservation of the redemptive aspects of Tanakian Judaism, so neatly packaged in his "restorative" and "utopian" terminology. His love for the apocalypticism of Isaiah and Daniel is very palpable, and he has correctly defined Jewish mysticism and its place, making some severe criticism of Kabbalah and Hasidism. The Ha-Mashiach expected by him is real and will determine Israel's future. He believed wholeheartedly in the apocalypticism of the Tanak.

Adin Steinsaltz

(b. 1937) Steinsaltz was born in Jerusalem to secular Jewish parents. He studied mathematics, physics, chemistry, and rabbinical studies at the Hebrew University. He dedicated his life to the Talmud, completing the translation from the Aramaic to Hebrew in 2010 and into English in 2012; these are published with commentaries. He has stated his aim is to educate Jews in the Talmud. He is an accomplished writer of books and articles and is duly recognized as such. But he has also attracted controversies in several areas, particularly on the question, "Who is a Jew?" His book *The Essential Talmud* is a splendid work, especially in the consideration of its so-called controversies. His view is that it is a continuing discussion among Jews, and he defines the Talmud as an open document and a continuing discussion. In my opinion, he has a very healthy relationship with it and does not place it on the same canonical level of the Tanak.

Geza Vermes

(b. 1924) Vermes was born in Hungary to Jewish parents. When he was 7 years, he and his parents were baptized into the Roman Catholic Church. However, his parents perished in the Holocaust.

He studied oriental history and languages in Budapest and then in the Catholic University in Louvain, Belgium. He became a Roman Catholic priest. He obtained a doctorate in theology for his dissertation on the historical framework of the Dead Sea Scrolls. He left the Catholic Church in 1957, reasserted his Jewish identity, and moved to Britain, where he joined the Liberal Jewish Synagogue of London. He taught at the University of Newcastle-upon-Tyne and then at Oxford University. He is currently professor emeritus of Jewish Studies in Oxford, and he continues to edit the *Journal of Jewish Studies*, which he has done since 1971. More recently he has been a travelling professor to University of North Carolina, Duke University, Johns Hopkins University, and University of Louisiana.

His most important work appears to be *The Complete Dead Sea Scrolls in English* (1962), and he has written several commentaries on the Dead Sea Scrolls. He has published several other books and has developed a reputation as a Jesus scholar. Some of his well-known books are *Scripture and Tradition in Judaism* (1961), *Jesus the Jew* (1973), *Jesus and the World of Judaism* (1983), and *The History of the Jewish People in the Age of Jesus Christ* (1987).

Irving M. Zeitlin

(birth date unknown) Zeitlin is the professor emeritus at the University of Toronto in Canada. He has written widely concerning Judaism, Christianity, and Islam. His book *Jesus and the Judaism of His Time* makes excellent observations in Judaism. *The Making of a Diasporic People* is a meticulous piece of research. I have not read his work *The Historical Muhammad*, which has received a five-star review.

INDEX

Z